THE CANON LAW COLLECTION
OF THE
LIBRARY OF CONGRESS

CORPVS IVRIS CANONICI

Title page from a 1615 edition of the *Corpus iuris canonici*. Canon Law Collection, Law Library.

THE CANON LAW COLLECTION

OF THE

LIBRARY OF CONGRESS

A General Bibliography with Selective Annotations

Compiled by

Darío C. Ferreira-Ibarra

Hispanic Law Division, Law Library

Library of Congress   Washington   1981

Library of Congress Cataloging in Publication Data

Library of Congress.
   The canon law collection of the Library of Congress.

   Includes indexes.
   Supt. of Docs. no.: LC 10.2:C16/3
   1. Canon law—Bibliography—Catalogs.
2. Library of Congress—Catalogs. I. Ferreira-
Ibarra, Darío C. II. Library of Congress.
Hispanic Law Division. III. Title.
Law   [Z663.5.C35]   016.2629   81-607964
ISBN 0-8444-0367-9   AACR2

For sale by the Superintendent of Documents, U.S. Government Printing Office, Washington, D.C. 20402

CONTENTS

FOREWORD

SINCE 1832, when an act of Congress directed the Librarian of Congress to remove law books from the main collection, install them in a separate "apartment," and maintain a law library, legal materials from the United States and abroad have found a repository in the Law Library of the Library of Congress. The law collections now housed in the Law Library are unequalled in breadth or depth by those of any other institution. Approaching two million volumes, the holdings of the Law Library encompass all geographic areas and historical periods. These legal publications and the specialized staff who service them combine to give the Law Library its unique standing as a center for scholars pursuing research in American, foreign, and comparative law.

While the bulk of the law collections represent modern national legal systems, there are several special collections which are distinguished by their historical value, rarity, or topicality. One such special collection contains approximately twenty-eight hundred volumes of canon law, constituting a magnificent assemblage of treatises written by the most renowned canonists over the last seven centuries and other documents of invaluable worth and historical significance. The strongest elements of the collection are the works of important Church figures of the seventeenth and eighteenth centuries and manuscripts and early editions of the sources of ecclesiastical law of the Roman Catholic Church. Approximately half of the collection is in Latin, with the remainder written in eleven other languages, including English.

The present bibliography renders an important service to the scholarly community by revealing the presence in the Library of Congress of this extraordinary but little known treasure. This bibliography, which lists the rich canon law holdings in the Library of Congress and classifies them according to subject, has a dual purpose: to provide researchers of canon law with a simple, comprehensive, and functional reference book; and to assist legal historians, writers, and students interested in following the course of canon law research.

The importance of law is multifaceted. It contains the regulations and standards which support the work of the Church (in this case, the Roman Catholic Church, since almost 98 percent of the collection belongs to this Church's legislation), a worldwide and international society. In addition to the historical significance and the international scope of its legislation, the importance of the Roman Catholic law also derives from practical considerations. In the United States almost one-quarter of the population are members of the Catholic Church and therefore subject to canon law. Furthermore, current controversies surrounding the indissolubility of the bond of marriage, divorce, contraceptive practices, abortion, and the many changes in the life of the religious person, just to name a few, are directly related to this discipline. It is consequently apparent that a comprehensive bibliography will be both useful and necessary.

But the contribution of canon law goes beyond the immediate and the practical; it is present in the very heart of the western legal tradition. In fact, it was Gratian's work, *Concordance of Discordant Canons,* the first systematic legal treatise written in the West (ca. 1140), together with the ideal concept of *corpus juris* (body of law), which initiated the great change from customary law to legal systems in the western world. As the relationship between Church and state experienced profound changes, a considerable portion of the medieval canon law become secularized and was accepted into the provisions of civil law.

The development, maintenance, and circulation of the canon law collection has been entrusted to Darío C. Ferreira-Ibarra, compiler of this index and legal researcher with the Hispanic Law Division since 1975. Dr. Ferreira-Ibarra, who is also responsible for the development and servicing of the Roman law collection, received his education in Argentina, Italy, and the United States. In addition to advanced degrees in philosophy, education, and canon law, he holds a Ph.D. in theology and ethics. His teaching credentials include professorships at the School of Philosophy and Education of the Catholic University of Asunción, Paraguay, the School of Accounting and Administrative Sciences of the National University of Paraguay, and the School of Philosophy and Education of the Catholic University of Puerto Rico.

CARLETON V. KENYON,
Law Librarian

PREFACE

THE ORGANIZATIONAL SCHEME of this bibliography was selected for practical reasons and to elucidate the overall subject because canon law is generally not as well known as other legal systems. The first three sections of the bibliography cover: three early editions of the Code of Canon Law, valuable holdings in the Law Library; the code's historical foundations, which list many important editions of the code, and other basic documents of the early Roman Catholic Church; and the *Decisiones* of the Roman Rota, or the Church's jurisprudence. The remaining sections of this bibliography correspond exactly to the divisions of the Code of Canon Law and cover such subjects as persons, things, procedural law, and crimes and penalties.

Some annotations have been provided to highlight work considered historically significant or relevant to current social problems. The entries are arranged alphabetically according to the author within the various topical divisions and subdivisions. When necessary, a title or collective term is used as a main heading. Books in foreign languages are also entered in the same manner.

An appendix has been included to accommodate publications recently acquired by the Library of Congress and to update the bibliography through mid-1979. The appendix also contains entries which complete the collection of writings by famous canonists who already appear in the body of the work. Specifically, the prolific contributions of Agostinho Barbosa (1590–1649), the Portuguese canonist, and Giovanni B. de Luca (1614–1683), an Italian who became a lawyer at the age of twenty-one and later a cardinal under Innocent XI, are emphasized.

Comprehensive author and subject indexes appear at the end of the bibliography. In the subject index, many topics are enumerated which were not specifically classified in the body of the work.

INTRODUCTION

FEW PEOPLE are familiar with the legislation of the Roman Catholic Church. To gain a good understanding of its law today would require a journey back in time to consider the successive turning points in the centuries long history of the Church's legislation. The law as a living reality would then become clear. This work cannot cover such an extensive program, nor is it intended to do so. Nevertheless, to be able to comprehend the bibliography's arrangement and the importance of the works by the most influential canonists, the reader may find the following brief description of the Church and its legislation very appropriate.

The first significant factor to consider is that all power in the Church comes from above; this society, organized as an institution and universal in extent, is therefore not a democracy. Its constitution rests on the monarchical pattern. This fact gives canon law a special character: it is, at the same time, a sacred science and a juristic science.

The questions that naturally arise are then: who is the authority behind the law, and what are the instrumental sources of the law? The answer to the first question is that the *fontes essendi* or *existendi*, the productive sources of the law for the universal Church, are the pope, the ecumenical councils (if the deliberations are confirmed and promulgated by the pope), and the Roman congregations. The answer to the second question is that the *fontes cognoscendi* include divine-positive law and human-positive law, i.e., the Bible and tradition, and the collection of documents containing the legal provisions enacted by the legislative authority of the Church. The pope enacts all universal laws in person (in his apostolic constitutions, or in his *motu proprio*, depending on the importance of the documents), or through the Roman congregations (acting in his name), or the ecumenical councils (when he ratifies the provisions). Since the beginning of this century, the promulgation of laws has been effected in the manner introduced by Pius X on September 29, 1908, and later confirmed by the Code of Canon Law in 1917, i.e., by their publication in the official *Acta Apostolicae Sedis*.

In considering the written documents of the law, modern canonists divide canon law into three main periods. The first begins in the time of the apostles and ends with the Council of Trent (1545–1563), the second ends with Vatican II (1962–1965), and the third is the present time, i.e., since this council. Traditionally, however, the periods were divided into *jus antiquum, jus novum,* and *jus novissimum.* The first extends from the early years of the Church until Gratian (mid-twelfth century) whose monumental work is a landmark in the history of canon law; the second, from Gratian until the Council of Trent; and the third, from Trent to the codification of 1917.

Until the time of Gratian, canon law was considered a part of theology (*theologia practica externa*) and not a separate discipline. Gratian, a Camaldolese monk who died in A.D. 1160, committed himself to the task of reducing to some sort of order the mass of laws through coordination and synthesis. The title he chose for his work was *Concordia Discordantium Canonum (Concordance of Discordant Canons).* This meritorious work eliminated, whenever possible, the contradictions existing between the various texts and coordinated them into one complete system. Later his compilation became known as *Decretum Magistri Gratiani,* or more simply *Decretum Gratiani.* While enjoying great prestige, the *Decretum* did not have official character; nevertheless, the popes of the sixteenth century promoted a revision and the publication of an official edition. This task was approved by Gregory XIII in two constitutions (1580 and 1582), and since then subsequent editions have been made in accordance with the official revised text.

After the publication of the *Decretum,* many collections followed, some of which were approved and authenticated. The most important during this period, because of their authority and completeness, were the *Quinque Compilationes Antiquae,* the third and the fifth of which were considered official because they were compiled at the request of two popes. New needs for a collection that would include all the laws enacted until that time were satisfied by Gregory IX; this collection became known as *Sexta,* to distinguish it from the *Quinque Compilationes,* or *Liber Extra* because it contained the decretals *Extra Decretum Vagantes.* A more complete work was approved and published by Boniface VIII, then added to the five books of Gregory IX. It became known as *Liber Sextus* (March 3, 1298).

Following the tradition set by his predecessors, Clement V ordered a new collection to complete the previous compilations; although it was approved and published in 1314, it was not sent to the universities during his lifetime. Only after his death did John XXII, his successor, dispatch it and call it *Liber Septimus.* Later it became known as the *Clementinae Constitutiones.* With the collection of Clement V, the *Corpus Juris Canonici,* as it was called in 1437 by the Council of Basilea, was considered closed. This *Corpus* was made up of the *Decretum Gratiani,* the *Liber Extra,* the *Liber Sextus,* and the *Liber Septimus.*

The *Corpus* was expanded by two collections published in 1500 by John Chappuis, a canonist from Paris. The *Extravagantes,* as his work is known, contain the *Extravagantes Joannis XXII* and the *Extravagantes Communes,* i.e., constitutions and decretals of John XXII and of several popes, from Boniface VIII (d. 1303) to Sixtus IV (d. 1484). Any person interested in the study of canon law must consider the *Corpus Juris Canonici* as the most fundamental and essential source. The Library of Congress holds many editions of the *Corpus,* separate editions of the *Decretum Gratiani,* as well as two editions of the *Extravagantes.*

Equally important in the development of canon law is the Council of Trent (1545–1563). Pius IV promulgated on January 26, 1564, by the Constitution *Benedictus Deus,* the disciplinary laws enacted by this Council; this compilation became the most important source of canonical legislation until the promulgation of the code.

The profusion of canonical legislation as well as the difficulty in consulting and enforcing it led to a necessary revision and reorganization of the existing materials. After twelve years of work, Benedict XV solemnly promulgated on May 27, 1917, in his Constitution *Providentissima Mater Ecclesia,* the *Codex Juris Canonici* to become effective for the universal Church on May 19, 1918, the Pentecost of the following year. The code contains 2,414 canons and is divided into five books related to general provisions, persons, things, trials and hearings, and offenses and their punishments. This codex is placed above any previous collection for it is an authentic, public, and legal collection of laws having all the force of exclusive, unitary, and universal law, in that it has been approved and promulgated by the supreme authority of the Church.

With the *motu proprio, Cum Juris,* of September 15, 1917, Benedict XV created a Pontifical Commission (*consilium*) for the authentic interpretation of the code. The *responsa* (answers) of this commission were published in the official gazette *Acta Apostolicae Sedis* because, like the provisions of the code, they have legislative authority and value.

In recent years the Church experienced a monumental turning point, the Second Vatican Council. Immediately after it ended, Paul VI created, among other things, a special commission to interpret the decrees of the Church. This commission is known as the *Commissio Centralis coordinandis post Concilium laboribus et Concilii Decretis interpretandis.* Until this commission publishes a new revised edition of the code, the most important and current canonical laws are to be found in the *Acta Apostolicae Sedis.*

The compiler is grateful to Kathryn J. Dahlberg and Sandra A. Sawicki, of the Hispanic Law Division, who spent many hours transforming thousands of index cards into a readable manuscript, and to Miss Sawicki, in particular, for refining the manuscript and offering many suggestions regarding bibliographic format which were adopted. Their assistance was invaluable to this publication's development.

BIBLIOGRAPHY

CODE OF CANON LAW

1

Catholic Church. Codex juris canonici. Codex juris canonici Pii X pontificis maximi iussu digestus Benedicti papae XV auctoritate promulgatus. Praefatione, fontium annotatione et indice analytico-alphabetico ab emo Petro card. Gasparri auctus. Romae, Typis polyglottis vaticanis, 1918. 2 v.

Pius X in his *motu proprio* of March 19, 1904, entitled *Arduum sane,* expressed his desire to collect in a code the laws of the Church which "had so increased in number and were so separated and scattered, that many of them were unknown not only to the people, but to the most learned scholars as well." A commission of cardinals, led by Pietro Gasparri who later became a cardinal himself, prepared the code which was promulgated on May 27, 1917, by the constitution *Providentissima Mater Ecclesia* of Benedict XV (1914–1922) and became effective a year later.

The code contains 2,414 canons, or standard units of subdivision, and is divided into five books: general provisions, persons, things, trials and hearings, and offenses and their punishments. The code is preceded by several writings and documents: an illuminating preface, written by Pietro Cardinal Gasparri, which synthesizes the history of the Church's law; the above mentioned constitution of Benedict XV; *Cum iuris canonici,* a *motu proprio* of the same pontiff providing for the creation of a commission for the authentic interpretation of the canons; and the profession of faith. The code ends with eight documents or constitutions by different popes, from Gregory XIII (January 25, 1585) to Pius X (December 25, 1904), and a very useful analytico-alphabetical index as a final section.

2

Catholic Church. Codex juris canonici. Codex juris canonici Pii X pontificis maximi iussu digestus Benedicti papae XV auctoritate promulgatus praefatione fontium annotatione et indice analytico-alphabetico ab Petro card. Gasparri auctus. Romae, Typis polyglottis vaticanis, 1919. 928 p.

3

Catholic Church. Codex juris canonici. Ad Codicem jvris canonici Benedicti XV pont. max. avctoritate promvlgatvm commentario minora comparativa methodo digesta, concinnavit doct. Albertvs Toso. Romae, Marietti [1921].

HISTORICAL FOUNDATIONS

4

Catholic Church. Pope, 1305–1314 (Clemens V). Clementinae Clementis Quinti Constitutiones, quas Clementinas vocant, ab Aegidio Perrino officiali de Iosayo, diligenter recognitae, cum Summarijs, Casibus notabilibus, Iuris patronatus Arbore, ac Additionibus tam ex Ioannis Imolae, quam Petri Ancharani Zabarellae, Barbatiae, Panormitani, doctoris Vankel, aliorumqz doctorum collectis. Lvgdvni, a Porta, 1550. 184, [11] p.

5

Catholic Church. Pope, 1316–1334 (Joannes XXII). Extravagantes. Extrauagantes XX. Joannis vigesimisecundi innumeris pene mendis recens purgatae, vt ex aliorum codicum collatione facile constabit. Et praeter ea, que prior editio continebat, addidit Iacobus Fontanus, utriusqz iuris mystes, nunc Scholia quedam breviter annotantia, que vix longis commentarijs videbantur posse explicari. Remota est etiam historia, que priori impressione falso Iannis vigesimisecundi vita inscribebatur, a apposita noua & verrissima ex clarissimis scriptoribus Sabellico, Nauclero, Platina, Volaterrano, Aemilio, Ritio, Egnatio compilata, sententijs Iurisperitorum rerumqz memorabilium varietate plena. Lvgdvni, a Porta, 1550. 207, [7] p.

6

Catholic Church. Corpus juris canonici. Corpvs ivris canonici emendatvm et notis illvstratvm: Gregorii XIII pont. max. iussu editum. Indicibvs variis, et novis, et appendices Pavli Lanceloti. Accesserunt nouissime loci commvnes vberrimi, summa diligentia ex ipsis canonibus collecti. Lvgdvni, 1605. 2 v. in 1.

The *Corpus* is one of the most essential canon law sources before May 27, 1917, when Pope Benedict XV solemnly promulgated the Code of Canon Law. In 1437 the Council of Basilea considered completed what is now known as the *Corpus Juris Canonici* which includes the Decree of Gratian, the Decretals of Gregory IX (also called the *Liber Extra*), the Decretals of Boniface VIII (or *Liber Sextus*), and the *Clementinae Constitutiones* (or *Liber Septimus*), approved by Pope John XXII in October 25, 1317.

7

Catholic Church. Corpus juris canonici. Corpus juris canonici. [Venetiis, 1615] 3 v.

8

Catholic Church. Corpus juris canonici. Corpus ivris canonici emendatvm et notis illvstratvm: Gregorii XIII pont. max. iussu editum. Nunc indicibus nouis, & appendice Pavli Lanceloti, Perusini, adauctum. Parisiis, 1618. 26 p., 454 p., [12], 459–727, [7], 732–885, 72, [159] p.

9

Catholic Church. Corpus juris canonici. Corpus ivris canonici emendatvm et notis illvstratvm: Gregorii XIII pont. max. iussu editum. Nunc indicibus nouis, & appendice Pavli Lanceloti, Perusini, adauctum. Parisiis [Compagnie de Lagrande navire de l'année 1618] 1618. 454 p., 459–727, [7], 732–885, 72, [159] p.

10

Catholic Church. Corpus juris canonici. Corpvs ivris canonici emendatvm et notis illvstratvm. Gre-

gorii XIII pont. max. jussu editum: indicibvs variis et novis, et appendice Pauli Lancellotti Perusini adauctum. ... His postrema hac editione accesservnt constitutiones nouae pp. ss. quae VII Decretalium loco iure meritò esse possint: illustrati notis doctissimorum jctorum. Vna cvm locis commvnibvs vberrimis, opvs certe nunc perfectissimum. Lvgdvni, 1622. 5 v. in 1.

11

Catholic Church. Corpus juris canonici. Corpvs ivris canonici emendatvm et notis illustratum. Gregorii XIII pont. max. ivssv editvm. Indicibvs variis, et novis, & appendice Pavli Lancellotti Perusini adauctum. ... Accesservnt novissime loci commvnes vberrimi. [Romae], 1650. 1272 p., 752 p., 406 p., 158 p.

12

Catholic Church. Corpus juris canonici. Corpus juris canonici Gregorii XIII pont. max. jussu editum a Petro Pithoeo, et Francisco fratre. Parisiis, Sumptibus Jo. Friderici Gleditschii, Bibliopol, 1695. 2 v. in 1.

13

Catholic Church. Corpus juris canonici. Corpus juris canonici academicum, emendatum et notis P. Lancellotti illustratum, in suos tomos distributum, usuique moderno ad modum Christoph. Henr. Freiesleben, alias Ferromontani ita accommodatum, ut nunc studiosorum quivis, etiam tyro, uno quasi intuitu, omnes canones, causas et capitula invenire possit. Accesserunt loci communes uberrimi et indices titulorum canonumque omnium summa diligentia ac nova methodo concinnati. Coloniae Munatianae, Thurnisiorum, 1728.

13a

Catholic Church. Corpus juris canonici. Corpus juris canonici academicum, emendatum et notis P. Lancellotti illustratum, in suos tomos distributum, usuique moderno ad modum Christoph. Henr. Freiesleben, alias Ferromontani ita accommodatum, ut nunc studiosorum quivis, etiam tyro, uno quasi intuitu, omnes canones, causas et capitula invenire possit. Accesserunt loci communes uberrimi et indices titulorum canonumque omnium diligentia ac nova methodo concinnati. Coloniae Munatianae, Thurnisiorum, 1730–35 [v. 1, 1735]. 2 v.

14

Catholic Church. Corpus juris canonici. Corpus juris canonici emendatum, et notis illustratum, Gregorii XIII pont. max. jussu editum, libro VII Decretalium, et Jo. Pauli Lancelotti Institutionibus adauctum. Accesserunt loci communes uberrimi, et indices titulorum, canonumque omnium summa diligentia, ac nova methodo concinnati. . . . Editio magna fide a mendis purgata. Augustae Taurinorum, Typographia Regia, 1745. 2 v.

15

Catholic Church. Corpus juris canonici. Corpus juris canonici Gregorii XIII pont. max. jussu editum a Petro Pithoeo, et Francisco fratre, jurisconsultis, ad veteres codices manuscriptos restitutum, et notis illustratum, libro VII, decretalium, et Johannis Pauli Lancelotti institutionibus adauctum, accesserunt loci communes uberrimi, & indices titulorum, canonumque omnium summa diligentia, ac nova methodo concinnati. Augustae Taurinorum, Typographia Regia, 1746. 2 v.

16

Catholic Church. Corpus juris canonici. Corpus iuris canonici Gregorii XIII Pontif. Max. Auctoritate post emendationem absolutam editum in duos tomos divisum et appendice novo auctum cum necessariis indicibus Justus Henningius Boehmer IC. Halae Magdeburgicae, Impensis Orphanotrophei, 1747. 2 v.

17

Catholic Church. Corpus juris canonici. Corpvs ivris canonici post emendationem absolvtam editvm et appendice nova avctvm. Ivstvs Henningivs Boehmer recensvit cvm codicibvs veteribvs manvscriptis aliisqve ed. contvlit, variantes lectiones adiecit notis illvstravit atqve necessariis indicibvs instrvxit praemissa praefatione dvplici. Halae Magdebvrgicae, Impensis Orphanotrophei, 1747. 2 v.

18

Catholic Church. Corpus juris canonici. Corpvs ivris canonici Gregorii XIII post emendationem absolvtam editvm in dvos tomos divisvm et appendice novo avctvm cvm necessariis indicibvs Ivstvs Henningivs Boehmer . . . illvd recensvit cvm codicibvs veteribvs manvscriptis aliisqve editionibvs contvlit variantes lectiones adiecit et notis illvstravit praemissa praefatione dvplici. Cvm privilegiis Sacr.

Caes. Maiest. nec non regis Polon. ac Borvss. Halae Magdebvrgicae, Impensis Orphanotrophei, 1747. 2 v.

19

Catholic Church. Corpus juris canonici. Corpus iuris canonici emendatum et notis illustratum Gregorii XIII pont. max. iussu editum libro VII decretalium et Jo. Pauli Lancelotti institutionibus adauctum. Accesserunt loci communes uberrimi indices titulorum canonumque omnia summa diligentia ac nova methodo concinnati. Augustae Taurinorum, Typographia Regia, 1776. 2 v.

20

Catholic Church. Corpus juris canonici. Corpus juris canonici academicum, emendatum et notis P. Lancellotti illustratum, in duos tomos distributum, usuique moderno ad modum Christoph Henr. Freiesleben, alias Ferromontani ita accomodatum, ut nunc studiosorum quivis, etiam tyro, uno quasi intuiti, omnes canones, causas et capitula invenire possit. Accesserunt loci communes uberrimi et indices titulorum canonumque omnium summa diligentia ac novo methodo concinnati. Coloniae Munatianae, Impensis Emanuelis Turneysen, Bibliopol & Typogr., 1783. 2 v. in 1.

21

Catholic Church. Corpus juris canonici. Post justi Henningii Boehmeri curas brevi adnotatione critica instructum ad exemplar Romanum. Denuo edidit Aemilius Ludovicus Richter. Opus uno volumine absolutum. Lipsiae, Tauchnitz, 1839. 2 pts. (1271, 1239 p.)

22

Catholic Church. Corpus juris canonici. Corpus iuris canonici. Editio lipsiensis secunda; post Aemilii Ludouici Richteri curas ad librorum manu scriptorum et editionis romanae fidem recognouit et adnotatione critica instruxit Aemilius Friedberg. Lipsiae, Tauchnitz, 1879–81. 2 v.

23

Trent, Council of. Canones et decreta sacrosancti oecvmenici et generale concilii Tridentini, svb Pavlo III, Ivlio III, et Pio IIII. Index dogmatum, & reformationis. Antverpiae, Philippum Nutium, 1565. 110, [14] p.

24

Trent; Council of. Sacrosancti et oecvmenici Concilii tridentini. Pavlo III, Ivlio III et Pio IIII pontific. maximis celebrati, canones et decreta. His nunc recens accesserunt duorum eruditissimorum virorum d. Iohannis Sotealli, theologi, & Horatii Lvtii, iuriscosulti, vtilissimae ad marginem annotationes. . . . Additae praetera sunt ad finem, Pii IIII pontificis maximi Bullae, vna cum triplici utilissimo indice. Antverpiae, Christophori Plantini, Prototypographi Regij, 1571. 302, [133] p.

25

Trent, Council of. Sacros. concilium Tridentinum additis declarationibus cardinalium, ex ultima recognitione Ioannis Gallemart: Et citationibus Ioan. Sotealli theologi, & Horatii Lucii . . . necnon . . . P. Augustini Barbosae. Lugduni, Boissat, 1640. 479, [60], 47 p.

26

Trent, Council of. Sacrosancti et oecumenici concilii Tridentini Pavlo III, Ivlio III, et Pio IV . . . celebrati canones et decreta quid in hac editione praestitum sit sequens Philippi Chiffletii. Coloniae Agrippinae, Balth. ab Egmond, 1688. 196, [58] p.

27

Trent, Council of. Sacrosanctum, oecumenicum Concilium rideninum, additis declarationibus cardinalium ejusdem Concilii interpretum, ex ultima recognitione Joannis Gallemart, nec non remissionibus Augustini Barbosae, et annotationibus practicis cardinalis de Luca, cum variis Rotae romanae decisionibus. Editio novissima exactiore correctione (quam umquam alias) castigata; & mendis . . . diligentissimè expurgata. Matriti, Escribano, 1779. 677 p.

28

Catholic Church. Codex juris canonici Orientalis. De personis. Code of Oriental canon law, the law on persons: rites, persons in general, clergy and hierarchy, monks and religious laity. English translation and differential commentary by Victor J. Pospishil. Ford City, Pa., St. Mary's Ukrainian Catholic Church, 1960. 342 p.
Bibliography: p. xv–xvi.

29

Catholic Church. Codex juris canonici Orientalis.

De sacramento matrimonii. Code of Oriental canon law, the law on marriage; interritual marriage law problems. English translation and differential commentary by Victor J. Pospishil. Chicago, Universe Editions, 1962. 221 p.
Bibliography: p. 13–16.

30

Church of England. Codex juris ecclesiastici anglicani: or, The statutes, constitutions, canons, rubrics and articles, of the Church of England, methodically digested under their proper heads. With a commentary, historical and juridical. Before it, is an introductory discourse, concerning the present state of the power, discipline and laws, of the Church of England: and after it, an appendix of instruments, ancient and modern. By Edmund Gibson. London, Baskett [etc.] 1713. 2 v.

This work, in two volumes divided into fifty-two titles, contains the statutes, constitutions, canons, rubrics, and articles of the Church of England, with historical and legal commentary. The state of the power, discipline, and laws of the Church at the time of the publication is discussed in the introduction. At the end of the digest an appendix is provided on ancient and modern instruments. This work is intended for use by the clergy to differentiate clearly the laws of the Church from the statutes and other pieces of legislation. The work clarifies that the Church of England, as a national church, has the same common head as the State, but as a spiritual society, it is of a different nature and governed by other laws.

31

Church of England. Codex juris ecclesiastici anglicani: or, The statues, constitutions, canons, rubrics and articles, of the Church of England, methodically digested under their proper heads. With a commentary, historical and juridical. Before it, is an introductory discourse, concerning the present state of the power, discipline and laws of the Church of England: and after it, an Appendix of instruments, ancient and modern. By Edmund Gibson. 2d ed., rev. and improved with large additions, by the author. Oxford, Clarendon Press, 1761. 2 v.

"Supplement, containing certain acts of Parliament relative to ecclesiastical matters; which have either been omitted in their places by the author, or been enacted since he prepared the present edition for the press": p. [1237]–1321.

32

Church of England. The English church canons of
1604: with historical introduction; and notes, critical and explanatory, showing the modifications of
each canon by subsequent acts of Parliament, etc.
And Appendices: on the new canons of 1865; the
vestment question; etc., etc. By the Rev. C. H.
Davis. London, Sweet, 1869. 138 p.

33

Church of Scotland. General Assembly. An abridg-
ment of the acts of the General Assemblies of the
Church of Scotland, from the year 1638 to 1820
inclusive, to which is subjoined an Appendix containing an abridged view of the civil law relating
to the Church. 2d ed., greatly enl. and improved.
By Robert Gillan. Edinburgh, Skelly, 1821. 373, 62
p.

34

Feghali, Joseph. Histoire du droit de l'Église ma-
ronite. Préf. de Jean Dauvillier. Paris, Letouzey et
Ané, 1962–   . (Bibliothèque de la Faculté de
droit canonique de Paris)
   Bibliography: v. 1, p. [347]–352.

35

Eastern Orthodox Church. Canons, novocanons,
decrees, etc. Nomocanon XIV titulorum. p.
433–655.

36

Gratianus, the canonist. Decretum. [Strassburg]
Eggestein, 1471. [460] 1.

   In the *Concordia Discordantium Canonum*, known
more simply as *Decretum Gratiani*, Gratian, the
Camaldolese monk, brought together some thirty-
eight hundred texts of prior sources of canon law,
and attempted to harmonize them through the use
of an analytical method drawing from the juristic
and scholastic approaches of the time. With this
work, which he completed around 1140, he earned
lasting recognition as the father of the study of
canon law; it became the basic text for the teaching
of this discipline for centuries thereafter. The
Decretum, including about four thousand chapters,
is divided into three parts: the first part comprises
101 *distinctiones* dealing with sources or topics of
canon law; the second part is devoted to thirty-six
causae, which in turn are subdivided into many
quaestiones. Although the *causae* number consider-
ably less than the *distinctiones*, they are more extensive when coupled with their corresponding *quaestiones* and constitute nearly 70 percent of the total
Decretum. This division concerned the various problems of the Church jurisdiction, offenses, and legal
proceedings; the third part, *De Consecratione*, deals
exclusively with the sacraments of the Church and
is divided into five *distinctiones*. Gratian particularly
emphasized consecration of churches, the Holy
Eucharist, feast days, Baptism, and Confirmation.

37

Gratianus, the canonist. Decretum. [Strassburg]
Eggestein, 1472. [460] 1.

38

Gratianus, the canonist. Decretum. Mainz, Schoeffer, 1472. [413] 1.

39

Gratianus, the canonist. Decretum. Venetiis, de
Colonia et Manthen, 1479. 418 1.

40

Gratianus, the canonist. Decretum. Basel (Basilea),
Wenssler, 5 Sept. 1482. [381] 1.
   Incipit concordia discordantium. With the com-
mentary of Bartolomeo da Brescia.

41

Gratianus, the canonist. Decretum. Nuremberg,
Koberger, 28 Feb. 1483. [416] 1.
   With the commentary of Bartolomeo da Brescia.

42

Gratianus, the canonist. Decretum. Strassburg
(Argētine), Grüninger, 4 Sept. 1484. [452] 1.
   With the commentary of Bartolomeo da Brescia.

43

Gratianus, the canonist. Decretum. Venice, de
Blavis, de Alexandria, 6 Feb. 1489. [520] 1.
   With the commentary of Bartolomeo da Brescia.

44

Gratianus, the canonist. Decretum. Venice, de Tortis, 30 Mar. 1496. 335 1.
   With the commentary of Bartolomeo da Brescia.

45

Gratianus, the canonist. Decretum. Venice, [Tor-
resanus, de Asula] 26 June 1498. [636] 1.
   With the commentary of Bartolomeo da Brescia.

46

Gratianus, the canonist. Decretum aureum Domini Gratiäni cu₃ suo apparatu. [Lugduni, Per Nicolaum de Benedictis, 1511] 582, [46] 1.

47

Gratianus, the canonist. Decretum Gratiani cum glossis dñi Johānis theutonici . . . annotationibus Bertholomei brixiensis. Diuisionibus Archidiaconi. Casibus a Bene. cōpositis per Bar. brixi. correctis & pro clariore intellectu plurib⁹ in locis extensis. Concordis ad bibliam. Tabula marginalium glossularum, omnium canonum & consiliorum. Margarita decreti. Additione in margine litterarū: quo minusculi characteres lineis intercepti: citius legenti appareāt. Basiliea, 1511 [i.e. 1512] 424 1.

48

Gratianus, the canonist. Decretum Gratiani. Glossis dñi Ioannis Theutonici prepositi alberstatensis: et annotationibus Bartholomei Brixiensis. Diuisionibus Archidiaconi. Casibus a Bene. cōpositis per Bart. Brixi. Correctis et pro clariore intelectu pluribus in locis extensis. Concordia ad biblia. Tabula marginalium glossularum. Omniū canonū et conciliōrum. Margarita decreti. Flodculus totius decreti a Joanne Diacono compositis. Additione in margine litterarum. [Venetijs, 1514] 652 p.

49

Gratianus, the canonist. Decretum aureum, cum suo apparatu. [Parisiis, Petit et Keruer] 1518. 582, [42] 1.

50

Gratianus, the canonist. Decretum Gratiani, nouissime post ceteras oēs impressiones: summa adhibita cura impressum: vna cu₃ glossis Joā. Theutonici & Bartho. Brixie. Additis etiā diuisionibus archidiaconi, casibusq₃ Benedicti, concordantijs item ad Bibliam, tabula insuper marginalium glossularu₃: tam canonum q̄₃ conciliorum. Margarita quoq₃ Decreti: longe diligētius emendata, flosculis preterea totius Decreti. Additione insuper apposita in margine litera₄ quo paruiusculi characteres lineis interiecti: citius oculis legentiū sese offerent. Tabulam etiā Ludouici Bolognini opposuimus: que in alijs perpera₃ fuerat tabulis decretalium inserta. [Venetijs, Scoti, 1528] [49], 939, [67] 1.

51

Gratianus, the canonist. Decretvm Gratiani iam recens innumeris pene mendis, ijsq; foedissimis quibus passim scatebat: non sine labore grauissimo repurgatum. Parisiis, Cheuallonij, 1538. 552 1.

52

Gratianus, the canonist. Decretorum collectanea ex varia copiosaque scriptorum ecclesiasticorum, tum vetustate, cum eruditione vitae sanctimonia maxime insignium, receptorum videlicet. Pontificum item romanorū, conciliorū oecumenicorū deniq₃ supellectile Gratianum in gratiam rei ecclesiasticae cōcihnata, ac suis classibus distincta. Praefixa sunt ab Antonio Demochare singulis fere quaestionibus distinctionibusque . . . Accesserūt postremo indices rerum. [Paris] Guillard et Gulielmum des bois, 1547.

53

Gratianus, the canonist. Decretvm divi Gratiani, totivs propemodvm ivris canonici compendivm, svmmorvmqve pontificvm decreta atqve praeivdicia. Vnà cum variis scribentium glossis & expositionibus: quae omnia pristino suo nitori restituta fuerunt ad fidem veterum codicûm. Lvgdvni, à Porta, 1560. 2004 columns, 96 p.

54

Gratianus, the canonist. Decretum d. Gratiani vniversi ivris canonici pontificias constitutiones, et cnaonicas [i.e., canonicas] brevi compendio complectens. Vna cum glossis, epitomis & thematibus, ac multorum iurisprudentum tam ad textum quam ad glossas adnotionibus illustratum, Venetiis, 1572. 52 p. 1., 1352, [26] p.

55

Gratianus, the canonist. Decretvm Gratiani: sev verivs, Decretorum canonicorum collectanea, ab ipso auctore Gratiano primum inscripta Concordia discordantivm cannvm . . . eiusdem Gratiani labore concinnata, & in suas classes digesta. Praefixa sunt ab Antonio Demochare . . . singulis fere distinctionibus et causarum quaestionibus ozáptla quaedam, summam totius rei succinte complectentia. Antverpiae, Apud Plantanum, 1573. 3044, 198 columns.

56

Gratianus, the canonist. Decretvm Gratiani emendatvm et notationibvs illvstratvm vna cvm glossis. Venetiis, Apud Magnam Socie:atem, Ferrario & Franzino, 1584. 2704 columns.

57

Gratianus, the canonist. Decretvm Gratiani, emendatvm, et notationibvs dilucidatum, vna cum glossis, Gregorii XIII pont. max. ivssv editvm, nec non cvm vtilissimo tripartito indice Marcelli Francolini, in calce operis adiecto. Et nunc recens perutilibus additionibus praeclarissimi iurisconsulti d. Andreae Alciati illvstratvm. Venetiis, apud socios Renouantis, 1605. 44 p. l., 1020 p.

58

Gratianus, the canonist. Decretvm Gratiani, Emendatvm, et Notationibvs Illvstratvm Vnà cum glossis, Gregorii XIII. Editio Vltima. Lvgdvni, Landry, 1613. 2071 columns, 76 p.

59

Gratianus, the canonist. Decretum Gratiani, emendatum et notationibus illustratum. Una cum glossis Gregorii XIII pont. max. jussu editum. Ad exemplar romanum diligenter recognitum. Editio ultima. Lugduni, Landry, 1613. 52 p., 2072 columns, 78 p.

60

Gratianus, the canonist. Decretum d. Gratiani, vniversi ivris canonici pontificias constitvtiones, et canonicas brevi compendio complectens. Vna cum glossis & thematibus prudentum, & doctorum suffragiis comprobatis: resectis uerò nothis, absurdis, difficilibus, ijus demq́; inutilibus hypotheseon ad rem minimè pertinentium ineptaumq́; summarum, & annotationum pseudographij. Textu deniq; suae integritati reddito, & glossis receptis à uitiis repurgatis. Opera & censura doctissimorum hominum & precio & precio conducta. Venetiis, [Bevilacqua] 1617. 52 p. l., 1352, [18] p.

61

Gratianus, the canonist. Gratiani canones genuini ab apocryphis discreti, corrupti ad emendatiorum codicum fidem exacti, difficiliores commoda interpretatione illustrati opera et studio Caroli Sebastiani Berardi. Taurini, Typographia Regia, 1752–57. 3 v. in 4.

62

Gratianus, the canonist. Gratiani canones genuini ab apocryphis discreti, corrupti ad emendatiorum codicum fidem exacti, difficiliores commoda interpretatione illustrati opera et studio Caroli Sebastiani Berardi. Venetiis, Petri Valvasensis, 1777. 4 v.

63

Gratianus, the canonist. Gratiani canones genuini ab apocryphis discreti, corrupti ad emendatiorum codicum fidem exacti, difficiliores commoda interpretatione illustrati opera et studio Caroli Sebastiani Berardi. Madrid, Escribano, 1783. 4 v.

64

Archaimbaud, Benoît. Abbrege historique du droit canon contenant des remarqves svr les Decrets de Gratien, avec des dissertations sur les plus importantes matieres de la discipline de l'eglise, & de la morale chrêtienne. Lyon, Certe, 1689. 11 p. l., 512, [39] p.

65

Baumgarten, Paul M. Spanische beiträge zur reformatio Decreti Gratiani unter Gregor XIII. Krumbach (Bayern) Schwaben, Aker, 1927. 76 p.

66

Berardi, Carlo S. Gratiani canones genuini ab apocryphis discreti, corrupti ad emendatiorum codicum fidem exacti, difficiliores commoda interpretatione illustrati. Taurini, Typographia Regia, 1752–57. 3 v. in 4.

67

Bernard, Antione. La sépulture en droit canonique du décret de Gratien a Concile de Trente. Paris, Domat-Montchrestien, 1933. 219 p.
"Bibliographie": p. [201]–215.

68

Chifflet, Jean. Apologetica dissertatio de ivris vtrivsqve architectis, Ivstiniano, Triboniano, Gratiano et S. Raymvndo. Antverpiae, Moreti, 1651. [2], 70 p.

69

Dauvillier, Jean. Le mariage dans le droit classique de l'église, depuis le Décret de Gratien (1140) jusqu'à la mort de Clément v (1314). Paris, Recueil Sirey, 1933. 517 p.
"Bibliographie": p. [491]–510.

70

Fornasari, M. Initia canonum. A primaevis collectionibus usque ad Decretum Gratiani. Roma, Multigrafica, 1972–   . (Monumenta Italiae ecclesiastica. Subsidia, 1)
"Elenco delle collezioni": v. 1, p. xxxiii–xlii. "Elenco delle edizioni": v.1, p. xliii–li.

71

Fournier, Paul E. L. Histoire des collections canoniques en Occident depuis les Fausses décrétales jusqu'au Décret de Gratien. Paris, Recueil Sirey, 1931–32. 2 v. (Bibliothèqve d'histoire dv droit)

"Bibliographie des travaux de m. Paul Fournier sur les collections canoniques antérieures au Décret de Gratien": t. 1, p. [xi]–xiii.

"Bibliographie des travaux de m. Grabriel Le Bras sur les collections canoniques antérieures au Décret de Gratien": t. 1, p. [xiv]–xv.

72

Fournier, Paul E. L. Histoire des collections canoniques en occident: dépuis les fausses décrétales jusqu'au Décret de Gratien. Aalen, Scientia-Verlag, 1972. 2 v.

[Réimpression de l'éd. Paris, 1931–32.]

73

Gillmann, Franz. Die abfassungszeit der dekretglosse des C[odex] l[atinum] m[onacensis] 10244. Mainz, Kirchheim, 1912. 34 p.

"Erweiterter separat-abdruck aus 'Archiv für kathol. kirchenrecht' XCII, 2."

Bibliographical footnotes.

74

Horoy, César A. Cours de droit canonique dans ses rapports avec le droit civil professé a la Faculté de droit de Douai, durant l'année scolaire 1884–85 (1er et 2er trimestres). Droit international et droit des gens public d'après le Decretum de Gratien. Paris, Chevalier-Marescq, 1887. [11]–367 p.

75

Horoy, César A. Gratien, auteur du Decretum et fondateur de l'enseignement du droit canonique; étude suivie d'un plan et projet d'encyclopédie du droit canon, sous forme de répertoire, comprenant le droit canonique des différentes communions chrétiennes. Paris, Marescq, Chevalier-Marescq, successeur, 1891. 240 p.

76

Lerouge, Joseph. Une des survivances de la doctrine de Gratien sur la formation du lien matrimonial; la dispensatio super matrimonium ratum et non consummatum. Paris, Letouzey et Ané, 1939. 118 p.

"Bibliographie": p. [115].

77

Maassen, Friedrich B. C. Paucapalea. Ein beitrag zur literargeschichte des canonischen rechts im mittelalter. Wien, Aus der k. k. Hof- und staatsdr.: in commission bei K. Gerold's sohn, 1859. 70 p.

78

Móra, Mihály. Magister Gratianus mint perjogász. Budapest, 1938. 43 p.

79

Omrčanin, Ivo. Graziano e la Croazia. Chicago, 1958. 53 p. (Istituto storico croato. Edizioni in lingua italiana, v. 1)

Bibliography: p. 49–53.

80

Paucapalea. Die Summa des Paucapalea über das decretum Gratiani. Hrsg. von dr. Joh. Friedrich von Schulte. Giessen, Roth, 1890. 146 p.

81

Plöchl, Willibald M. Das eherecht des magisters Gratianus. Leipzig und Wien, Deuticke, 1935. 113 p.

"Verzeichnis der hauptsächlich verwendeten literatur": p. [7]–[10].

82

Rufinus, bp. of Assisi. Die Summa magistri Rufini zum Decretum Gratiani. Mit einer erörterung über die bearbeitungen derselben hrsg. von dr. Joh. Friedrich von Schulte. Giessen, Roth, 1892. 496 p.

83

Rufinus, bp. of Assisi. Die Summa decretorum des magister Rufinus. Herausgegeben von dr. Heinrich Singer . . . Mit unterstützung der Gesellschaft zur förderung deutscher wissenschaft, kunst und litteratur in Böhmen. Paderborn, Schöningh, 1902. 570 p.

84

Rufinus, bp. of Assisi. Summa decretorum. Hrsg. von Heinrich Singer. Aalen, Scientia-Verlag, 1963. 570 p.

Includes bibliographical references.

85

Sangiorgio, Gianantonio da, Cardinal. Ardua & quotidiana Lectura iuriũ monarche dñi Joãnis Antonij de Sancto Georgio dicti de Placētia Mediolani p̄positi & cardinalis Alexādrini super causis Decretorum cum additionibus summarijs & numeris ac indice alphabetico. [Lugduni, Sachon; Opera & Impēsis V. de Portonarijs, 1519] 292, 27 1.

86

Schulte, Johann Friedrich, ritter von. Die geschichte der literatur über das Dekret Gratians. 1[–2]. Wien, In commission bei K. Gerold's sohn, 1870. 2 v.

87

Sohm, Rudolf. Das altkatholische Kirchenrecht und das Dekret Gratians. Im Anhang: Rezension von Ulrich Stutz. (Unveränderter reprografischer Nachdruck München und Leipzig 1918.) Darmstadt, Wissenschaftliche Buchgesellschaft, 1967. 685 p.
Bibliographical footnotes.

88

Stephanus Tornacensis, bp. Die Summa des Stephanus Tornacensis über das Decretum Gratiani. Hrsg. von dr. Joh. Friedrich von Schulte. Giessen, Roth, 1891. 280 p.

89

Studia Gratiana, post octava Decreti saecularia. [Bononiae] Institutum Iuridicum Universitatis Studiorum Bononiensis, 1953– . v. illus. (part col.)
Latin, English, Italian, German, etc.

90

Summa Coloniensis. Summa "Elegantius in iure diuino" seu Coloniensis. Edidit Gerardus Fransen, adlaborante Stephano Kuttner. New York, Fordham University Press, 1969– . (Monumenta iuris canonici. Series A: Corpus glossatorum, v. 1, t. 1–)

91

Torquemada, Juan de, Cardinal. Ioannis à Tvrrecremata In primvm[-secundum] volvmen cavsarvm commentarii. Nicolai Boërij additionibus & summariis illustrati. Lvgdvni, 1555. 2 v. in 1.
Commentaries on part 2 of the Decretum.

92

Torreblanca Villalpando, Francisco. Lectvra in lib. II decretalium, titulo I de iudiciis ad rubricam. [Granatae, 1609] 18 1.

93

Two essays on the Decretum of Gratian, by Hellmut Lehmann-Haupt and Charles McCurry. Together with an original leaf printed on vellum by Peter Schoeffer at Mainz in 1472. Los Angeles, Zeitlin & Ver Brugge, 1971. [17] p.

94

Vetulani, Adam. Dekret Gracjana i pierwsi dekretyści w świetle nowego źródła. [Wyd. 1.] Wrocław, Zakład im. Ossolińskich, 1955. 168 p.
Includes bibliography.

95

Weitzel, Joseph. Begriff und Erscheinungsformen der Simonie bei Gratian und den Dekretisten. München, Hueber, 1967. 155 p. (Münchener theologische Studien. 3. Kanonistische Abteilung, Bd. 25)
Bibliography: p. x–xvi.

ROMAN ROTA

96

Cerchiari, Emmanuele. Capellani papae et Apostolicae Sedis auditores causarum Sacri Palatii Apostolici, seu Sacra Romana Rota ab origine ad diem usque 20 Septembris 1870. Romae, Typis Polyglottis Vaticanis, 1921. 4 v. in 2.

97

Catholic Church. Rota Romana. Decisiones do. de rota noue antique cum additionibus marginalibus summarijsq cuilibet decisioni prefixis. Postposite sunt item quedam causarum cum suis questionibus decisiones; cum regulis cancellarie apostolice. Propositum etiam habes generale totius operis repertorium sententias speciales remissiue continens. Que omnia castigatissima legetib apparebunt. 1536.

98

Catholic Church. Rota Romana. Decisionum novissimarum diuersorum Sacri Palatij Apostolici auditorum. Opvs sane per qvam vtile, et in foro versantibus summe necessarium. His accessit practica qvaedam notabilivm quaorundam eiusdem Rotae perpetuo quidem memoriae comendanda, cvm svmmariis et indice locupletissimis. Omnia nunc recens in lucem edita. Ad Seraphinvm Oliuarium Razzalium Venetiis, Apud Zenarium & Francinum, 1590. 3 v. in 2.

99

Catholic Church. Rota Romana. Decisiones Rotae Romanae a Marcello Crescentio collectae. Novis argvmentis, svmmariis, additionibvs, indicibus, & aliquot decisionibus auctae, & fideliter correctae à Acharisio. Romae, Ex Typographia Reu. Cam. Apostolicae, 1617. 218 p.

100

Catholic Church. Rota Romana. Decisiones Rotae Romanae Francisci card. Mantica, a Germanico Mantica . . . in lucem. . . . Annexo elencho omnium causarum, & indice rerum, verborumque memorabilium locupletissimo. Venetiis, Apud Iuntas, 1618. 504 p.

101

Catholic Church. Rota Romana. Sacrae Rotae Romanae Decisiones coram R.P.D. Alexandro Lvdovisio Nvnc S.mo D.N. Gregorio XV. Ex originalibus summo studio, & diligentia depromptae adiectis summarijs, ac indice locupletissimo. Ingenio ac opera Olivieri Beltramini Tarvisini de Asilo . . . cum annotationibus eiusdem ad singulas fere decisiones. Romae, Ex Typographia Reuerendae Camerae Apostolicae, 1622. 666, 131 p.

102

Catholic Church. Rota Romana. Decisiones Sacrae Rotae Romanae Coram Iacobo Cavalerio S.R.E. Presbytero Card. Sancti Evsebii Dum esset eiusdem Rotae Auditor ad Sanctissimum Dominum Nostrum Vrbanvm Octavvm Pontificem Maximvm. Cum summarijs, & indice Marci Antonii de Benedictis I.V.D. Romani. Romae, Ex Typographia Reuer. Cam. Apostolicae, 1629. 617, 59 p.

103

Catholic Church. Rota Romana. Ludovici Cencii Additiones ad eius Tractatum de Censibus, una cum CXLII Sacrae Rotae Romanae Decisionibus ad materiam spectantibvs hactenous non impressis.

Cum duplici indici copiosissimo, capitum, & materiam ad . . . D. Bartholomaevm Vecchivm. Venetiis, Apud Thomasinum, 1629. 24, 243, 25 p.

104

Mantica, Francesco M., cardinal. Vaticanae lvcvbrationes de tacitis et ambigvis conuentionibus, in libros XXVII dispertitae. . . . Editio postrema, magno studio à mendis repurgata, & allegationibus characterum diuersitate distinctis ornatiùs edita: cum indice vberrimo. Coloniae Allobrogvm, Crispini, 1631. 2 v.

105

Merlini, Mercuriale. De legitima tractatus absolutissimus, Mercvriali Merlino . . . authore, vna cvm decisionibvs magistralibvs sacrae Rotae Romanae, hactenus non impressis, in eodem relatis, nec non combinationibus ad locos d. tractatus in calce earundem decisionum. . . . Cum locupletissimus indicibvs quaestionum, decisionum, & rerum. Coloniae, excudebat Aubertus, 1634. 676, [16] p.

106

Catholic Church. Rota Romana. Decisiones Sacrae Rotae Romanae Coram Pavlo Dvran nouissime ex originalibus authoris summo studio, ac diligentia depromptae; adiectis argumentis, summarijs & indice locupletissimo Ferdinandi Sciamannae. Interamnae, Apud Guerrerium, 1637–

107

Catholic Church. Rota Romana. Sacrae Rotae Romanae decisiones coram Reuer. P.D. bon. mem. Matthaeo Bvratto Bononiensi, ex originalibus summo studio, & diligentia depromptae. Adiectis argumentis, summarijs, ac indice locupletissimo. Ingenio, ac opera Io. Francisci Ferentillii Interamnatis. Cum annotationibus eiusdem ad singulas fere decisiones. Nunc primo communi omnium voto in lucem editae. Romae, Ex Typ. Rever. Camerae Apostolicae, 1637. 3 v. in 2.

108

Catholic Church. Rota Romana. Theodosii Rvbei . . . singvlaria ex sacrae Rotae Romanae decisionibvs selecta. Romae, Ex Typographia Vaticana, 1637. 2 v.

109

Catholic Church. Rota Romana. Decisiones Rotae

et fori ordinarij senensis cvm precedentibvs examinationibvs conclusionum ad alias pertinentium, D. Christophori Marii Medices. . . . Cvm summariis earvndem decisionvm, et examinationvm, ac duplici indice, argumentorum scilet, ac rerum notabilium locupletissimo. Venetiis, Apud Fontanam, 1638. 694, 73 p.

110

Catholic Church. Rota Romana. Decisiones Sacrae Rotae Romanae, coram . . . Pavlo Dvran . . . nouissimè ex originalibus authoris summo studio, ac diligentia de promptae adiectis argumentis, summariis, & indice locupletissimo. Ferdinandi Sciamannae. Lvgdvni, Caffin & Plaignard, 1638. 306 p., 258 p.

111

Catholic Church. Rota Romana. Sacrae Rotae Romanae Decisiones a Lvdovico Censio V.I.D. Collectae, et ad Tractatvm de ensibvs accommodatae. Non solvm, qvae hactenvs impressae verum etiam alia plurima in lucem nundum editae. Vna cvm Bvllis Pii V et Clementis VIII. In materiam censum alem promulgatis, Augustae Tavrinorvm, Apud Tarini, 1638. 349–868, 20 p,

112

Catholic Church. Rota Romana. Selectanea rerum notabilium ad usum decisionum sacrae Rotae Romanae in libris impressis per dioceses extensarum . . . Studio Io. Baptistae Cantalmai Eugubini. Romae, Phaei, 1639. 439 p.

113

Catholic Church. Rota Romana. Decisiones Sacrae Rotae Romanae, coram Pavlo Dvran Episcopo Vrgellensi nouissime ex originalibus authoris summo studio, ac diligentia depromptae; adiectis argumentis, summariis, & indice locupletissimo. Ferdinandi Sciamannae I.V.D. Interamnatis. Lvgdvni, Caffin & Paignard, 1639. 2 v. in 1.

114

Catholic Church. Rota Romana. Decisiones Sacrae Rotae Romanae coram eminentissimo Io. Garzia Cardinali Millino, eivsdem Rotae olim avditore. Venetiis, Apud Guerilios, 1649. 245 p.

115

Merlini, Mercuriale. De legitima tractatus absolu-

tissimus; vnà cvm decisionibvs magistralibvs Sacrae Rotae Romanae, hactenus non impressis, in eodem relatis, necnon combinationibus ad locos dicti tractatus in calce earumdem decisionum. . . . Additis etiam in hac vltima editione ad singulas ferè quaestiones eiusdem authoris additionibus . . . nec non alijs centum Sacrae Rotae Romanae decisionibus nullibi hucusque impressis. Cvm locvpletissimis indicibvs qvaestionvm, decisionvm, et rervm. Venetiis, Apud Baba, 1651. 584, 274, [37] p.

116

Catholic Church. Rota Romana. Decisiones Sacrae Rotae Romanae coram Petro Otthobono. Romae, Typis Reuerendae Camerae Apostolicae, 1657. 563 p.

117

Catholic Church. Rota Romana. Decisiones Sacrae Rotae Romanae a R.P.D.Joanne Mohedano & Marcello Crescentio Romano collectae, hac novissima editione ab erroribus, quibus ea, qvae circumferuntur, manuscripta exemplaria & priores editiones carebant emendatae, novis argumentis, summariis, additionibus indicibus & aliquot decisionibus aucte ab Acharisio Sqvarcionio. Marpurgi Cattorum Expresae, Prostant Francofurti, Apud Schureri & Götzii, 1662. 164, 28, 119, 16 p.

118

Catholic Church. Rota Romana. Excellmi et ill. mi d. d. Petri Carrillo de Acvña Decisiones Sacrae Rotae Romanae. Cvm svis argvmentis et svmmariis nec non indicibus necessariis summa cura & labore exornatae. Nvnc primvm in lvcem prodevnt. Lvgdvni, Borde, Arnavd, Borde et Barbier, 1665. 396 p.

119

Catholic Church. Rota Romana. Decisiones Sacrae Rotae Romanae coram R.P.D. Angelo Celso Romano, nvnc S.R.E. Cardinali. Romae, Ex Typographia Reuerendae Camerae Apost., 1668. 44, 500, 123 p.

120

Catholic Church. Rota Romana. Decisionvm coram Francisco Vbaldo & Benedicto card. Monaldo. de Vbaldis nvncvpato. Adiectis argumentis, summarijs, annotationibus, & indice. Avgvstae Pervsiae, Ex typographia camerali & episcopali, Apud Bartolos & Laurentium, 1668. 547 p.

121

Catholic Church. Rota Romana. Decisiones Bichius Coelius. Romae, Typographia Reverendae Camerae Apostolicae, 1671.

122

Catholic Church. Rota Romana. Decisiones S.rae Rotae Romanae coram R.P.D. bon.mem. Coelio Bichio cum argumentis, summarijs, ac indice locupletissimo in dvos tomos distinctae. Romae, Ex Typographia Reuerendae Camerae Apostolicae, 1671. 2 v.

123

Catholic Church. Rota Romana. Decisiones Sacrae Rotae Romanae coram Gvttierez Argvelles, Francisco Zarate & Ioseph Ninot. Ex propriis depromptae originalibvs. Cvm argvmentis, svmmariis et indice. Romae, Ex Typographia Reuerendae Camerae Apostolicae, 1673. 739 p.

124

Catholic Church. Rota Romana. Decisiones coram Io. Baptista Remboldo, eiusdem Sacr. Rotae auditore. . . . Addita . . . collectanea votorum, & responsorum diuersorum celebrium iure consultorum . . . Opera, et stvdio Iosephi Domitii. Romae, Corui & Lupardi, 1676. 604 p.

125

Catholic Church. Rota Romana. D. D. Francisci de Roxas Archiepiscopi Tarraconensis, decisiones Sacrae Rotae Romanae, ex originalibus depromptae stvdio et diligentia Iosephi Vileta, I.V.D., ac in Vniversitate Barchinonensi decretalium Cathedrae Moderatoris publici. Adiectis argvmentis, svmmariis, ac indice locupletissimo. Nunc demum in hac secunda impressione diligentiùs à quamplurimis mendis expurgatae. Romae, Ex Typ. B. Lupardi impressoris Cameralis & Vaticani, 1679. 651 p.

126

Catholic Church. Rota Romana. Decisiones Sacrae Rotae Romanae coram R.P.D. Io. Baptista Pamphilio Postea S.M. Innocentio X Pont. Max. Ex originalibus desvmptae cum earum argumentis, summarijs, adnotationibus, & indice. Romae, Ex Typographia Reu. Cam. Apost., 1681. 732, 284 p.

127

Catholic Church. Rota Romana. Decisiones Sacrae Rotae Romanae coram bo: me. r.p.d. Hieronymo Priolo . . . ex originalibus depromptae, ac argumentis, summarijs, & indice locupletissimo ornatae a Iosepho Sacripante. Romae, Typis Reuerendae Camerae Apostilicae, 1681. 732 p.

128

Catholic Church. Rota Romana. Decisiones Sacrae Rotae Romanae coram Carolo Cerro. Cum suis argumentis, summariis ac indice locupletissimo materiarum. Romae, Sumptibus Iosephi Corvi bibliopolae, 1682. 3 v.

129

Catholic Church. Rota Romana. Decisiones Sac. Rotae Romanane coram . . . Faelice Vbago et Rio . . . Ex svis propriis originalibvs depromptae argumentis summarijs, & indice locupletissimo ornatae. Romae, Ex Typographia P. Monetae, 1682. 224 p.

130

Catholic Church. Rota Romana. Iosephi Ramonij Pars Secunda in qua subduntur Sacrae Rotae Romanae, aliorumq; tribunalium decisiones nullibi adhuc impressae ad materiam prima partis conferentes, ac indices dou undique locupletissimi omnium conclusionum, rerum, & verborum, que in decisionibus, consilijs, & observationibus annexis continentur. Opera et stvdio Iacobi Balducii. Bononiae, Recaldini & Borzaghi, 1689. 241, [256] p.

131

Catholic Church. Rota Romana. Decisiones et reliqua insuper responsa . . . a Ramonij Josephi. Parmae, Apud Franciscum Mariam de Rosatis, 1695.

132

Catholic Church. Rota Romana. Sacrae Rotae Romanae Decisiones coram Petro Otthobono, postea sanctae mem. Alexandro VIII. Cum argumentis, summariis ac indice materiarum locupletissimo. Venetiis, Apud Balleonium, 1696. 340 p.

133

Catholic Church. Rota Romana. S. Rotae Romanae Decisiones et sum pontificum constitutiones recentissime et selectissime, theatrum veritatis et justitiae Cardinalis de Luca de Officiis Venal, et stat. successionibus, amplectantes, confirmantes, laudantes, etc. Studio & opera Clariss. J.U.D. Argumentis, summariis, & indicibus necessariis exornatae, &

juxta tituliorum seriem & discursuum ordinem dispositae. Coloniae Allobrogorum, Cramer & Perachom, 1700. 2 v.

134

Catholic Church. Rota Romana. S. Rotae Romanae Decisiones et sum. pontificum constitutiones recentissimae et selectissime, theatrum veritatis et justitiae eminentissimi D. Cardinalis de Luca eivsqve tractatus de officiis venal. Et stat. successionibus, amplectentes, confirmantes, laudantes, etc. Studio & opera Clariss. J.U.D. Argumentis, summariis & indicibus necessariis exornata & juxta tituliorum seriem & discursum ordinem dispositae. Coloniae Allobrogorum, Cramer & Perachon, 1700. 9 v. in 1.

135

Catholic Church. Rota Romana. Sacrae Rotae Romanae Decisiones, et summorum pontificum constitutiones recentissimae, theatrum veritatis & justitiae cardinalis de Luca, ejvsqve tractatvs de officiis venal. et stat. successionibus amplectentes, confirmantes, & laudantes. Argvmentis, svmmariis, et indicibvs necessariis exornatae, ac juxta tituliorum seriem & discursuum ordinem dispositae. Venetiis, Apud Balleonium, 1707–08. 4 v.

136

Paolucci, Marco Antonio. Dissertationum legalium materias utriusque juris in foro ad normam recentissimarum Rotae Romanae decisionum judicatas complectentium. Liber primus[-tertius] recollectus adjectis argumentis, summariis, et conclusionum indice locupletissimo per Thomam Torellum. Lucae, Venturini, 1707–33. 3 v.

137

Catholic Church. Rota Romana. Decisiones diversorum auditorum Sacrae Rotae Romanae alibi non impressae, et ad interpretationem Statutorum Almae Urbis in doubus tomis commentatorum selectae a Francisco Maria Constantino. Cum triplici indice. Appositis nonnullis observationibus ad aliquas decisiones. Venetiis, Apud Balleonium, 1711. 355 p.

138

Catholic Church. Rota Romana. Decisiones Sacrae Rotae Romanae coram R.P.D. Ansaldo de Ansaldis ... rursus in lucem editae, à veteribus mendis expurgatae; avctae numero earumdem deci-

sionum, nouisque additionibus ejusdem auctoris: demvm locupletiori indice refertae ab Andrea Lvpardo. Romae, Typis Reu. Camerae Apostolicae, 1711–43. 7 v.

139

Catholic Church. Rota Romana. Sacrae Rotae Romanae Decisiones coram P.D. Jacobo Emerix de Matthys Germano, ejusdem Sacrae Rotae olim Decano, ac Sacrae Poenitentiariae Regente. In tres tomos distinctae, cum argumentiis, summariis, ac indicibus locupletissimis. Venetiis, Apud Balleonium, 1712. 3 v.

140

Catholic Church. Rota Romana. Decisiones Sacrae Rota Romanae coram R.P.D. Alexandro Benincasa Patricio Perusino cum argumentis, summarijs, & indice. Romae, Ex Typographia Reverendae Camerae Apostolicae, 1714. 36, 442, 94 p.

141

Catholic Church. Rota Romana. Decisiones coram Alexandro Caprara in duas partes distinctae; argumentis, summariis, ac indice ornatae à Josepho Petto. Lucae, Venturini, 1725. 2 v.

142

Catholic Church. Rota Romana. Sacrae Rotae Romanae Decisiones coram R.P.D. Alexandro Falconerio in tres tomos distinctae cum argumentis, & summariis dispositae per titulos materiarum, adiecto conclusionum indice locupletissimo. Romae, Mainardi, 1726–28. 4 v.

143

Catholic Church. Rota Romana. S. Rotae Romanae Decisiones recentissimae nunquam antea in lucem editae, D. Joan. del Castillo Sotomayor, Opera omnia amplectentes, confirmantes, aludantes &c. super materias tam civiles quàm ecclesiasticas. Studio & operâ clariss. j. u. d. argumentis, summariis & indicibus necessariis exornatae, juxta tituliorum seriem & materiarum ordinem dispositae. Coloniae Allobrogum, Perachon & Cramer, 1728. [546] p.

144

Catholic Church. Rota Romana. Sacrae Rotae Romanae Decisiones coram Josepho Molines in quinque tomos distinctae juxtà temporis seriem dispositae, cum argumentis & summariis, nec non indice locupletissimo conclusionum ad sextum tomum adjecto. Studio, et diligentia Francisci Corazza. Romae, Zinghi & Monaldi, 1728.

145
Catholic Church. Rota Romana. Sacrae Rotae Romanae Decisiones recentiores in compendium redactae. Ad modum indicis per materias, & tractatus in quinque tomos a'nonnullis Mec. nensis Athenaei sociis distributae. Mediolani, Apud Gallum, 1730–31. 6 v. in 5.

146
Catholic Church. Rota Romana. S. Rotae Romanae Decisiones . . . D. Joannis Gutierres Hispani. Opera Omnia. . . . Coloniae Allobragum, Perachon & Cramer, 1731.

147
Catholic Church. Rota Romana. Decisiones Sacrae Rotae Romanae coram bon. mem. R.P.D. Joanne de Herrera eiusdem Sacrae Rotae auditore ex originalibus depromptae, ac argumentis, summariis, & indice ornatae A' Hieronymo Taja Senense. Romae, Maynardi in platea Montis Citatori, 1731. 598 p.

148
Catholic Church. Rota Romana. Decisiones diversorum Sacrae Rotae Romanae auditorum ad materiam boni regiminis, universitatum, & communitatum, signanter Status Ecclesiastici, spectantes editae zelo, & cura Josephi Renati Imperialis, ac quadruplici indice exornatae a Petro Andrea de Vecchis. De bono regimine. Romae, Mainardi, 17—. 3 v.

149
Catholic Church. Rota Romana. Sacrae Rotae Romanae Decisiones coram bon. mem. R.P.D. Francisco Carolo Kavnitz eiusdem Sacrae Rotae auditore Posrea Episcopo Labacensi in dvas partes distinctae cum argumentis, summarijs, & indice ornatae. Studio & diligentia Francisci Pandolphi de Montefalisco. Romae, Leoni & Mainardi Typographorum Cameralium, 1734. 2 v.

150
Catholic Church. Rota Romana. Mantissa Decisionum Sacrae Rotae Romanae ad Fratrum Veritatis & Justitiae Cardinalis de Luca . . . v. 3. Venetiis, Balleonium, 1734.

151
Catholic Church. Rota Romana. Decisiones diversorum auditorum Sacrae Rotae Romanae alibi non impressae, & ad interpretationem Statutorum Almae Urbis, in duobus tomis commentatorum selectae a Francisco Maria Constantino. Cum triplici indice. Appositis nonnullis observationibus ad aliquas decisiones. Venetiis, Balleonium, 1737.

152
Catholic Church. Rota Romana. Decisiones Sacrae Rotae Romanae coram Alexandro Tannario. Romae, Barbiellini, Salomonii, 1747–48. 2 v.

153
Catholic Church. Rota Romana. Sacrae Rotae Romanae Decisiones nuperrimae nunc primum collectae, argumentis, summariis, et accuratissimis indicibus instructae. Romae, prostant Venetiis apud Simonem Occhi, 1751–63. 9 v. in 10.

154
Catholic Church. Rota Romana. Decisiones Sac. Rotae Romanae coram bonae memoriae R.P.D. Thoma Ratto juxta temporis seriem dispositae cum argumentis, & summariis. Romae, Mainardi, 1749–52. 3 v.

155
Catholic Church. Rota Romana. Sacrae Rotae Romanae Decisiones recentiores in compendium redactae ad modum indicis per materias, & tractatus sex in tomos a nonnullis Mediolanensis Athenaei sociis distributae. . . . Editio primo a Veneta sedulo recognita, & emendata. Venetiis, Poletti, 1754.

156
Catholic Church. Rota Romana. Decisiones Sacrae Rotae Romanae coram R.P.D. Marcello Crescentio argumentis, summariis, & indice locupletissimo a Josepho Mapelli Mediolanensi S.T. & J.U.D. adornatae. Romae, Ex Typographia Joannis Zempel Prope Montem Jordanum, 1758–63. 5 v.

157
Bonetus de Sanbonetis, Josephus F. Tractatus de animalibus, curribus, et plaustris. . . . Cum Sac. Rotae Romanae novissimis decisionibus ad materiam spectantibus, & usque nunc non impressis. Quibus accedunt argumenta, summaria materiarum, & index generalis. In duos tomos divisus. Avenione, Fex, 1761. 2 v. in 1.

158
Trent, Council of. Sacrosanctum, oecumenicum Concilium tridentinum, additis declarationibus cardinalium ejusdem Concilii interpretum, ex ultima recognitione Joannis Gallemart; nec non remissionibus Augustini Barbosae, & annotationibus practicis cardinalis de Luca, cum variis Rotae Romanae decisionibus. Editio novissima exactiore correctione (quam umquam alias) castigata; & mendis . . . expurgata. Matriti, ex typographia regia, vulgo, de la Gazeta, 1769. 677 p.

159
Catholic Church. Rota Romana. Decisiones diversorum Sacrae Rotae Romanae selectae ad interpretationem diversorum statutorum almae urbis in duobus tomis commentatorum a Francisco Maria Constantino . . . Cum indice triplici; primo decisionum per dioceses altero argumentorum; ac tertio conclusionum, verborumque locupletissimo. Parmae, Carmignani, 1774. 2 v. in 1.

160
Catholic Church. Rota Romana. Decisio Sac. Rotae Romanae coram R.P.D. Mannelli in causa Ferentina, seu Anagnina Confinium Quoad Sententiam Anni 1730. Lun. lo. Junni 1782. Romae, Ex Typographia Rev. Camerae Apostolicae, 1783.

161
Catholic Church. Rota Romana. Index Decisionum Sacrae Rotae Romanae que anno 1751–(1760, and 1777) prodierunt alphabetico conclusionum ordine digestus opus tam advocatis, tum causae patronis, tum ipsis judicibus utilissimum. Romae, Retilii Thypographi in Aedibus Maximorum, 1753–84. 12 v.

162
Catholic Church. Rota Romana. Decisiones Sacrae Rotae Romanae coram Reverendissimo P.D. Bartholomaeo Olivatio . . . adjectis argumentis, et summariis nec non conclusionum indice copioso feorsim impresso. Romae, Apud Antonium Fulgonium, 1784–   . 8 v.

163
Catholic Church. Rota Romana. Decisiones Sacrae Rotae Romanae coram Josepho Alphonso de Veri in duos tomos distinctae argumentis, summariis, ac indice locupletissimo ornatae studio et diligentia Roberti Hondedei Pisaurensis. Romae, Apud Antonium Fulgonium, 1787. [Tomus primus]

164
Catholic Church. Rota Romana. Decisiones Sacrae Rotae Romanae coram Joseph Alphonso de Veri in duos tomos distinctae argumentis, summarijs, ac indice locupletissimo. Studio et diligentia Roberti Hondodei Pisaurensis. Tomos Secundus. Romae, Apud Antonium Fulgonium, 1787.

165
Catholic Church. Rota Romana. Decisiones coram Aurelio Roverella . . . ejusdem Sac. Rotae XIIviro, nvnc . . . Pii Papae Sexti auditore. Romae, Prostant apud M. Nicolj, 1790. 351 p.

166
Catholic Church. Rota Romana. Decisiones Sacrae Romanae Rotae coram R.P.D. Herculi Consalvi eiusdem Sacrae Rotae auditore nunc S.R.E. Diacone Cardinali Tituli S. Mariae ad Martyres SSMI D.N. Papae Pii VII. Status, breviumque a secretis quas Alexander ex comitibus specia Meviniensis J.C. praepositis argumentis, atque summariis, addito locorum, et conclusionum indice curiae comodo, utilitatique in unum collegit. Romae, Typis Bernardini Olivieri Typographi Archigymnasii Romani, 1822. 318 p.

167
Catholic Church. Rota Romana. [Decisiones Sacrae Rotae Romanae], 1828.

168
Nuvoli, Ioannis Balthassar, Index generalis conclusionum rerumque notabilium quae continentur in decisionibus a S. Romana Rota editis ab anno 1814 ad annum 1819. Cura et studio Ioannis Balthaxari Nuvoli I.U.D., et causarum S. Palatii Apostolici Procuratoris Collectus. Romae, Typis Mugnoz, 1840–53. 2 v.
[V. II ab anno 1819 ad annum 1824]

169
Catholic Church. Rota Romana. [Decisiones Sacrae Rotae Romanae], 1830. 3 v.

170
Catholic Church. Rota Romana. [Decisiones Sacrae Rotae Romanae], 1839.

171
Catholic Church. Rota Romana. [Decisiones Sacrae Rotae Romanae], 1840. 2 v.

172

Catholic Church. Rota Romana. Decisiones Sac. Rotae Romanae in re commerciali post legem diei 1 Junii 1821 ad annum 1842 chronologico ordine dispositae, additis argumentis, summariis, et indice locupletissiomo. Volumen unicum. Romae, Typis Mugnoz, 1842. 530 p.

173

Catholic Church. Rota Romana. Decisiones Sacrae Rotae Romanae coram Theodulpho Mertel quas additis nondum editis, argumentis praepositis atque summariis, nec non omnium conclusionum indice generali in finem adjecto, in unum collegit Casimirus Guglielmotti. Romae, Pallotta, 1853. 188 p.

174

Catholic Church. Rota Romana. Coram Petro Marini decisiones quas additis nundum editis in unum collegit; argumentis, summariis, syllabo auxit Camillus Baccelli. Romae, Pallotta, 1853. 3 v.

175

Catholic Church. Rota Romana. Decisiones S. Rotae Romanae coram R.P.D. Cosma de Cursiis Florentino. Argumentis, summariis et indice locupletissimo exornatae cura et studio Alexandri Advocate Cavallini. Romae, Ex Typographia Cajetani Chiassi, 1855. 5 v. in 3.

176

Avignon. Rota. Decisiones Rotae Avenionis, a Hieronymo Lavrentio collectae. Cum indice. Venetiis, Apud Polum, 1591. 180 1.

177

Gratianus, Stephanus. Disceptationvm forensivm ivdiciorvm. . . . Tomus primus[-quintus] in qvibvs, qvae in controversiam quotidie veniunt secundum doctorum receptas sententias, et veram praxim praecipue Sacrae Rotae Romanae definiuntur. Omnia nuper Venetiis correctius, & ornatius in lucem prodeunt, duplici indice tam rerum, quam argumentorum decorata. Venetiis, Apud Iuntas, 1629. 5 v.

178

Gutiérrez, Juan. Opera omnia civilia, canonica, et criminalia, decisionibus S. Rot. Roman. recentissimis. Coloniae Allobrogum, 1731. 16 v. in 6.

179

Mariotti, Annibale. De'perugini auditori della Sacra Rota Romana; memorie istoriche. Perugia, Baduel, 1787. 235 p.

180

Merlini, Mercuriale. De legitima tractatus absolutissimus Mercvriali Merlino . . . authore, vnà cvm decisionibvs magistralibvs sacrae Rotae Romanae, hactenus non impressis, in eodem relatis. . . . Cum locupletissimis indicibvs. Venetiis, Apud Zenarij, 1626. 722, [18] p.

181

Nachtman, Władysław. Trybunał Roty Rzymskiej; historia, organizacja, postępowanie. [Wyd. 1.] Lublin, Tow. Naukowe Katolickiego Uniwersytetu Lubelskiego, 1957. 149 p. (Katolicki Uniwersytet Lubelski. Wydział Prawa Kanonicznego. Rozprawy doktorskie, magisterskie i seminaryjne, 9)
Bibliography: p. 141–[147].

182

Novario, Giovanni A. Svmmae bvlarvm sive apostolicarum constitutionum vsu frequentiorum commentaria. In quibus celeriores iuris ecclesiastici, & pontificij explanantur. Addita in hac postrema editione semicenturia nouissimarum Sac. Rot. Rom. decisionum. . . . Opera, et stvdio Iosephi Domitii & postremo nonnulis additionibus. Romae, Caesaretti, 1679. 600, [196] p.

183

Schneider, Franz E. Die römische Rota; nach geltendem recht auf geschichtlicher grundlage dargestellt von F. Egon Schneider. Paderborn, Schöningh, 1914– . 1 v.

184

Tanaglius, Ioannes. Vrbis et orbis Svpremi tribvnalis Monvmenta, sive de Sacro Rotae Romanae avditorio, eivsqve decisionibvs. Opvscvlvm Ioannis Tanaglii i. c. volaterrani. . . . Vna cvm decisionibvs hactenvs non impraessis, et triplici indice. Liborni, ex typographia Io. Vincentij Bonfiglij, Apud Minaschi, 1654. 355, [54] p.

GENERAL

185
Abbo, John A. and Jerome D. Hannan. The sacred canons; a concise presentation of the current disciplinary norms of the church. St. Louis, Herder, 1952. 2 v.
Bibliography: v. 2, p. 873–89.

186
Abbo, John A. and Jerome D. Hannan. The sacred canons; a concise presentation of the current disciplinary norms of the church. Rev. ed. St. Louis, Herder [1957, 1952]. 2 v.
Bibliography: v. 2, p. 873–90.

187
Abbo, John A. and Jerome D. Hannan. The sacred canons; a concise presentation of the current disciplinary norms of the church. 2d rev. ed. St. Louis, Herder [1960]. 2 v.
Bibliography: v. 2, p. 873–90.

188
Acta ex iis decrepta quas apud sanctam sedem geruntur in compendium opportune redacta et illustrata. Romae, typis Polyglottae Officinae, S.C. de Propaganda Fide, etc., 1865–74. 8 v.

189
Catholic Church. Pope, 1775–99 (Pius VI). Acta consistorii secreti habiti die XXV iunii 1781. Romae, ex typographia sac. Congr, de prop. fide [1781]. 26 p.

190
Catholic Church. Pope. Acta Urbani P.P. VI (1378–89), Bonifacii P.P. IX (1389–1404), Innocentii P.P. VII (1404–06) et Gregorii P.P. XII (1406–15). E registris Vaticanis et Lateranenzibus aliisque fontibus collegit notisque adornavit Aloysius L. Tautu. Romae, Typis Pontificiae univercitatis Gregorianae, 1970. 356 p.

191
Congresso internazionale di diritto canonico, Rome, 1970. Atti del Congresso internazionale di diritto canonico. La Chiesa dopo il Concilio. Roma, 14–19 gennaio 1970. Milano, Giuffrè, 1972. 3 v.
Includes bibliographies.

192
Agustin, Antonio, abp. of Tarragona. Antonii Augustini. ... De emendatione Gratiani dialogorum libri duo, cum Stephani Baluzii et Gerh. Mastrichtii notis. Curante m. Jos. Ant. de Riegger. Venetiis, Pezzana, 1777. 2 v.

193
Akinian, Nersēs. [K'nnowt'iwn Sowrb Sahaki veragrowats kanonnerow] 1950– . 1 v.
Includes bibliographical references.

194
Alagon, Pedro de, abp. Totivs ivris canonici compendium. Romae, Zannetti, 1622–23. 2 v. in 1.

195
Alarius, Theophilus. Canones conscientiae ex vtroque iure et probatis d. d. cum antiquorum, tùm recentium sententijs collecti p. d. Olim corrupto titulo, & auctore fictitio Enchiridon casuum conscientiae Io. Francisci Svarez; hac verò noua & germana impressione ab infinitis mendis repurgati, nouisq; doctrinis longè plurimum aucti & locupletati, quibus adiecte sunt in calce, ac declarate clau e apponi solitae in dispensationibus tum in poenitentiaria pro foro interno, tum in dataria pro externo; omnia ad exemplar auctoris posthumum. Stvdio Ioannis Bapt. Mancini Cortonensis. Libvrni, Minaschi, 1651. 815 p.

196
Aldobrandini, Silvestro. Silvestri Aldobrandini Consiliorvm liber primus[-secundus]. Romae, ex typographia Vaticana, 1594–1617. 2 v.

197
Alexander III, pope. Die Summa magistri Rolandi, nachmals papstes Alexander III, nebst einem anhange: Incerti auctoris quaestiones. Hrsg. von dr. Friedrich Thaner. Innsbruck, Wagner, 1874. 303, [1] p.

198
Alier y Cassi, Lorenzo M. Manual jurídico-canónico, político-administrativo, civil y penal para uso del clero español. Barcelona, Horta, 1908. 399 p.

199

Alvarez, Carlos J. Elementos de derecho canónico. V. 1:El derecho público. Buenos Aires, Imprenta y librería de Mayo, 1872–73. 2 v. in 1.

200

Analecta Juris Pontificii recueil de dissertations sur différents sujets de droit canonique, liturgie et théologie. Rome, Marietti, Paris, Palmé, 1855–89. 1–28 Series (1853–89) [v. 1–28].

201

Ancarano, Pietro d'. Super tertio[-quinto] Decretalium facundissima commentaria. A plerisq; erratis nunc liberata. Cum suis summarijs, adnotationibus ac indice. Bononiae, Apud Societatem Typographiae Bononiensis, 1580–81 [v. 2, 1580]. 3 v.

202

André, Valère. Synopsis juris canonici per erotemata digesti et enucleati, juxta ordinem librorum & titulorum, in Decretalibus epistolis Gregorii IX p. m. Editio ultima emendatior & pluribus locis aucta. . . . Cui accessit methodus quaerendi textus juris canonici. Lovanii, typis Guilielmi Stryckwant sub aurea lampade, 1695. 308, [8] p.

203

André, Valère. Valerii Andreae Desselii Erotemata juris canonici, digesta et enucleata . . . Noviter edita cum quibusdam notis et animadversionibus. Praemissum est Georgi Struvi Programma, quo ad publicam hujus autoris explicationem auscultandam juris utriusque cultores invitantur. Jenae, Nisi, 1675. 636 p.

204

Andrea, Valerio. Synopsis juris canonici per erotemata digesti et enucleati. Lovanii, Stryckwant, 1695. 308 p.

205

Andreae, Joannes. Novella in sextum. Graz, Austria, Akademische Druck-u. Verlagsanstalt, 1963. 319 p.

206

Andreae, Joannes. Ioannis Andreae . . . In titulum de regulis iuris nouella commentaria ab exemplaribvs antiqvis, mendis, quibus referta erant, dili-

genter expurgatis, nunc impressa. Summis, ac rerum omnium memorabilium indice locupletissimo. Venetiis, apud haeredem Hieronymi Scoti, 1612. 98 l.

207

Andreae, Joannes. Ioannis Andreae . . . In sextum decretalium librum nouella commentaria ab exemplaribvs variis per Petrum Vendramenum in pontificio venetiarum foro aduocatum, mendis, quibus referta erant, diligenter expurgatis, nunc impressa. His accesserunt doctissimorum virorum annotationes, summis, ac rerum omnium memorabilium indice locupletissimo. Venetiis, apud haeredem Hieronymi Scoti, 1612. 173 l.

208

Andreae, Joannes. Nouella Ioannis Andree super Decretalibus cum apostillis nouiter editis. [Venetijs, Per Baptistam de Tortis, 1504–05 (v. 1–3, 1505)] 5 v. in 4.

209

Andrieu-Guitrancourt, Pierre. Introduction sommaire à l'étude du droit en général et du droit canonique contemporain en particulier. [Paris] Sirey, 1963. 1403 p. (Traités Sirey)
Bibliographical footnotes.

210

Angelis, Filippo de. Praelectiones juris canonici ad methodum Decretalium Gregorii IX exactae quas in scholis Pontificii seminarii romani tradebat Philippus canonicus de Angelis. Romae, ex typographia Della pace; Parisiis, apud Lethielleux, 1877–91 (v. 4, '91). 5 v. in 4.

211

Anselmo, Saint, bp. of Lucca. Anselmi episcopi lucensis Collectio canonum, una cum collectione minore iussu Instituti Savigniani recensuit Fridericus Thaner. Fasciculus I–[II] Oeniponte, librariae academicae Wagnerianae, 1906–15. 2 v. in 1.

212

Arbour, Guy. Le droit canonique particulier au Canada. Ottawa, Éditions de l'Université d'Ottawa, 1957. 167 p. (Universitas Catholica Ottaviensis. Dissertationes ad gradum laureae in facultatibus ecclesiasticis consequendum conscriptae. Series canonica nova, t. 3)
Bibliography: p. 145–53.

213

Argiro, Giovanni B. Joannis Baptistae Argiro Disceptationes ecclesiasticae selectiores, utilioresque juris canonici titulos ad forum magis accomodatos complectentes, quamplurimis sacrarum congregationum novissimus decretis ornatae. Romae, Komarek, 1739. 2 v.

214

Arias de Mesa, Ferdinandus. Variarvm resolvtionvm & interpretationum iuris libri tres. [Genevae] Chouet, 1658. 474 p.
Includes bibliographical references.

215

Assemani, Giuseppe S. Bibliotheca iuris orientalis canonici et civilis. Aalen, Scientia Verlag, 1969. 5 v.
"Neudruck der Ausgabe Rom 1762–[66]"

This work, in five volumes, offers published and unpublished collections of canons in Greek of the councils and the Fathers. The whole *corpus* of oriental canonical and civil law is distributed in four books: the first contains the code of canons, of the synods, and of the Fathers; the second, the constitutions of the Emperors or the Code of Civil Law; the third, synodal judgments and sanctions of the patriarchs and bishops; and the fourth, the *responsa* (answers) and treatises of the experts. A fifth book is devoted to the Sixth Ecumenical Council and to the Oriental Church, and more particularly to the Council of Constantinople, at the time of Emperor Constantine.

216

Audisio, Guillaume. Droit public de l'église et des nations chrétiennes . . . traduit de l'italien . . . par M. le Chanoine Labis. Louvain, Peeters, 1864–65. 3 v.

217

Avack, Pietro Agostino d'. Corso di diritto canonico. Milano, Giuffrè, 1956–   .

218

Aymans, Winfried. Das synodale Element in der Kirchenverfassung. München, Hueber, 1970. 389 p. (Münchener theologische Studien. 3. Kanonistische Abteilung, Bd. 30) (Münchener Universitäts Schriften. Katholisch theologische Fakultät)
Bibliography: p. xvii–xxxv.

219

Azuela-Güitrón, Mariano. Los grandes temas del derecho y del Estado a la luz de la doctrina pontificia contemporánea. México, 1960. 246 p.
Bibliography: p. 235–41.

220

Baccari, Renato. Elementi di diritto canonico. Nuova edizione rielaborata e aggiornata. Bari, Cacucci, 1972. 118 p.
Includes bibliographical references.

221

Baccari, Renato. Introduzione allo studio del diritto ecclesiastico. Bari, Cacucci, 1974. 106 p.
Includes bibliographical references.

222

Baiardi, Giovanni B. Additiones et annotationes insignes, ac solemnes ad Ivlii Clari lib. V. Receptarvm sentent, sive Practicam criminalem. Hac 3. ed. . . . Plurima quidem ad criminum materiam spectantia . . . complectentes. Parmae, Viothi, 1607. [100], 256 p.

223

Baiardi, Giovanni B. Ioannis Baptistae Baiardi, nobilis parmensis ivreconsvlti . . . Additiones, et annotationes insignes, ac pervitles ad Ivlii Clari Receptarvm sentent. librvm quintvm sive Practicam criminalem. Plurima quidem ad criminum materiam spectantia, nedum in communi tradita, sed etiam per motus proprios, bullas, & apost. sanctiones in Statu ecclesiast. et per constitutiones, capitula, ritus et pragmaticas in Regno neapolitano declarata, sanctita & abrogata, miro ordine, ac exactissimè complectentes. Lvgdvni, apvd Antonivm de Harsy, 1600. 340, [74] p. [*With* Claro, Giulio. Ivlii Clari . . . Receptarvm sententiarvm opera. Lvgdvni, 1600]

224

Balbus, Bernardus, Bp. of Pavia. Summa decretalium. Ad librorum manuscriptorum fidem cum aliis eiusdem scriptoris anecdotis edidit Ern. Ad. Theod. Laspeyres. Graz, Akademische Druck- U. Verlagsanstalt, 1956. 366 p.

225

Baldassini, Girolamo. Clementis V. Constitutiones in concilio Viennensi in Gallia editae anno 1312. Romae, Ripa, 1769. 304 p.

226

Baldo degli Ubaldi. Ad tres priores libros decretalium commentaria. Collatione vetustissimorum exemplarium nunc recens summo labore suae integritati restituta et ab innumeris mendis vindicata; quibus accesserunt Francisci a Perona et Petri Crassi adnotamenta. Neudr. d. Ausg. Lyon 1585. Aalen, Scientia-Verl., 1970. 285, 32 1.

This 1970 reprint of the 1585 Lyon edition contains an impressive commentary on the first three books of the Decretals; a list of the titles in the commentary appears on p. 286. In addition to having valuable remarks, the book is also commendable for its perfect organization which guides the reader through the diversity of topics examined, and for the completeness of the term and subject indexes offered at the end of the work.

227

Bánk, József. A káptalani dignitas fogalma. Irta . . . Külvonlenyomat a "Theologia" XI kötetének (1944) 4. számából. Budapest, Stephaneus Nyomda, 1944. 24 p.

228

Barbosa, Agostinho, bp. De canonicis et dignitatibvs, aliisqve inferioribvs beneficiariis cathedralium . . . tractatvs. Vltima ed., ab ipsomet auctore multis in locis locupletata. Lvgdvni, Dvrand, 1634. 407 p.

229

Barbosa, Agostinho, bp. Collectanea bvllarii, aliarvmve svmmorvm pontificvm constitvtionvm, necnon praecipuarum decisionum, qvae ab apostolica sede, et sacris congregationibus S.R.E. cardinalium Romae celebratis usque ad annum 1633 emanarunt. Lvgdvni, Dvrand, 1634. 688 p.

230

Barbosa, Agostinho, bp. Svmma apostolicarvm decisionvm, extra ivs commvne vagantivm, qvae ex variis approbatissimorvm doctorvm libris hucusque impressis, & ad calcem vniuscuiusque allegatis eorum sub fide collectae. Ad maiorem studiosorum omnium commoditatem alphabetico ordine disponuntur. Venetiis, apud Balleonium, 1646. 448 p.

231

Barbosa, Agostinho, bp. Augustini Barbosae, I.V.D. lusitani . . . Collectanea in Codicem Iustiniani, ex doctoribus tum priscis, tum neotericis. . . . Opus tam in scholis, quàm in foro versantibus apprimè necessarium, ac vtile. Editio ultima prioribus emendatior. Lugduni, Arnaud, Borde, & Arnaud, 1679. 2 v.

232

Barbosa, Agostinho, bp. Augustini Barbosae Collectanea doctorum, tam veterum quam recentiorum, in jvs pontificivm vniversvm . . . Praefixi sunt indices . . . Ultima editio ab ipsomet auctore aucta, recognita & à mendis expurgata. Lugduni, Borde & Arnaud, 1688. 5 v.

This work in five volumes contains a complete collection of the Decretals with commentaries. Volume one is devoted to what was called by Justinian *ta prota,* or the origins (book one of the Decretals), and to trials (book two of the Decretals). The second and third volumes contain the causes that originate trials, some of which are exclusively for clergymen of religious orders (book three of the Decretals), and others are exclusively for laymen, such as marriage (book four of the Decretals). Some causes are common to both clergymen and laymen, for example, crime (book five of the Decretals). Volume four includes the *Sextus Decretalium,* the *Clementinae Constitutiones,* and the *Extravagantes* of John XXII as well as the *Extravagantes Comunes.* The last volume is devoted to the Decree of Gratian.

233

Barbosa, Agostinho, bp. Pastoralis solicitudinis, sive De officio, et potestate parochi, tripartita descriptio . . . Ultima editio prioribvs emendatior. Cum summariis, & indicibus locupletissimis. Lugduni, Borde & Arnaud, 1688. 293 p.

234

Barbosa, Agostinho, bp. Pastoralis solicitudinis, sive De officio et potestate episcopi, tripartita descriptio. Nunc ultimum ab ipso auctore recognita, variis resolutionibus exornata, & multis doctorum citationibus, aliisque accessionibus illustrata. Lugduni, Borde & Arnaud, 1698. 2 v.

This is a comprehensive treatise, divided into three parts or books, on the functions and authority of the bishop. The first book deals with the appointment, election, consecration, and duties of the bishop, the creation of patriarchal Sees, and archiepiscopal superiority. The second book is devoted to the authority of the bishop in relation to the sacraments, ordination, and his faculty to grant dispensation. The third examines a variety of subjects, including reservation of cases, residence of the bishop, granting of benefices, visiting the parishes, and appointment of vicars. It also offers a *formularium episcopale* (episcopal formulary) in which many methods are suggested for the proper and useful exercise of episcopal jurisdiction, as well as apostolic constitutions and decrees, bulls and letters *in forma brevis*.

235

Barbosa, Agostinho, bp. Juris ecclesiastici universi libri tres, in quorum I. De personis, II. De locis, III. De rebus ecclesiasticis plenissime agitur . . . Cum triplici indice . . . Editio novissima, ab authore recognita, & erroribus ablatis, utiliter locupletata. Lugduni, Borde & Arnaud, 1699. 2 v.

This treatise on universal ecclesiastical law deals with persons, places, and things, in three books comprised in two volumes. Book one is devoted to ecclesiastical persons, beginning with the Pope, his authority and jurisdiction, and ending with clergymen receiving minor orders. Book two analyzes principles related to churches and ecclesiastical places; it studies church buildings, consecration, immunity, destruction, and violations, as well as privileges granted to churches and pious places. Book three analyzes general principles of ecclesiastical things and a diversity of themes, for example, ecclesiastical benefices, pensions, patronage, real estate, and alienation. The work provides indexes of chapters, terms and subjects, and of laws quoted.

236

Barbosa, Agostinho, bp. Tractatus de canonicis, et dignitatibus, aliisque inferioribus beneficiariis cathedralium, & collegiatarum ecclesiarum, eorumque officiis, tam in choro, quam in capitulo. Hac ultima editione ab ipso authore recognitu & quamplurimorum additamentorum accessione locupletatus. Cum summariis, et indicibus copiosis. Lugduni, Borde & Arnaud, 1700. 263 p. [*With his* Pastoralis solicitudinis, sive De officio, et potestate parochi, tripartita descriptio. Lugduni, 1688]

237

Barbosa, Agostinho, bp. Summa apostolicarum decisionum, extra jus commune vagantivm, quae ex variis approbatissimorum doctorum libris hucusque impressis, & ad calcem uniuscujusque allegatis, eorum sub fide collectae, ad majorem studiosorum omnium commoditatem alphabetico ordine disponuntur. Editio ultima aucta, et recognita. Lugduni, Borde & Arnaud, 1703. 506 p.

238

Bardus, Marcus A. Tractatvs ivris protomiseos, sive congrvi. Ad interpretationem bullarum, constitutionum, aliarumquè literarum apostol. super aedificiis construendis, ad decorem almae vrbis. In quo aliqua, stilum magistratus aedilium curulium, curatorumquè viarum, & aedificiorum publicorum, & priuatorum vrbis, respicientia, in eodem protomis iure; cum eiusdem magistratus facultatum insertione, cosbuntur. Cum aliquibus quaestionibus, & ipsarum tabula, ac indice generali. Romae, apud Ant. Bladum impr. cam. 1565.

239

Bareille, Louis G. Code du droit canonique; modifications introduites dans la précédente législation de l'église. Nouvelle éd. Montréjeau, Cardeilhac-Soubiron, 1922, 647, [1] p.

240

Barilis, Bernardus. De potestate legis mvnicipalis in advenas, et indigenas, tractatvs gemina disqvistione bipertitvs . . . Nvnc primvm prodit . . . Cvm indicibvs necessariis. Lvgdvni, Dv-Fovr, 1641. 124 p.

241

Barraza Meléndez, Martín. La masonería y su situación canónica. Bogotá, Edit. Voto Nacional, 1960. 115 p.

242

Bart(olomei?), Johannes B. Glos. super bulla Pii Quinti de Censibus. Perusise, Petrutÿ, 1592, 30 p.

243

Barth, Franz X. Hildebert von Lavardin (1056–1133) und das recht der kirchlichen stellenbesetzung. Stuttgart, Druck der Union deutsche verlagsgesellschaft, 1905. 81 p.

"Literatur": p. [x]–xv.

244

Battaglini, Marco. Istoria vniversale di tvtti i consilii generali, e particolari celebrati nella Chiesa. 2. ed. accresciuta di quattrocentotrè concilij, e di alcune risposte à gli argomenti, che da' medesimi concilij hà tratti contro la sede apostolica Luigi Memburgh. Venezia, Poletti, 1689. 2 v.

245

Bégin, Raymond F. Natural law and positive law. Washington, Catholic University of America Press, 1959. 177 p. (Catholic University of America. Canon law studies, no. 393)
Bibliography: p. 167–72.

246

Begnudelli Basso, Francesco A. Bibliotheca juris canonico-civilis practica, seu Repertorium quaestionum magis practicarum in utroque jure . . . studio ac opera concinnatum Francisci Antonii Begnudelli Bassi . . . post plures colonienses editio prima italica caeteris omnibus ornatior, in qua novissima praebentur additamenta, ex operibus Benedicti XIV summi pontificis feliciter regnantis deprompta. Mutinae, expensis Modesti Fentii veneti, 1757–58. 4 v.

247

Begnudelli Basso, Francesco A. Bibliotheca juris canonico-civilis practica, seu Repertorium quaestionum magis practicarum in utroque jure . . . concinnatum . . . Addito elencho quaestionum pro quolibet tomo, & indice generali totius operis copiosissimo in fine. Frisingae, sumptibus Joannis Caspari Bencard, Immel, 1712. 4 v.

248

Beidtel, Ignaz. Das canonische recht betrachtet aus dem standpunkte des staatsrechts, der politik, des allgemeinen gesellschaftsrechts und der seit dem jahre 1848 entstandenen staatsverhältnisse. Regensburg, Manz, 1849. 676 p.

249

Bellarmino, Roberto F., Saint. De officio principis christiani libri tres. Romae, Zannetti, 1619. 491 p.

250

Bellemère, Gilles de, bp. In secundam[-tertiam] secundi Decret. lib. partem praelectiones non minùs doctae, quàm elegantes: in quibus non an-

tiquitatem modò, uerùm totius antiquitatis autores facilè principes agnoscere licet: iamdiu desyderatae, nunc uerò tandem summa diligentia, ac fide doctissimorum virorum opera emendatae, & typis pulcherrimis excusae. Lvgdvni, ad salamandrae; apud Sennetonios fratres, 1549. 2 v.

251

Bellemère, Gilles de, bp. Remissorius ad commentaria in Gratiani decreta nunc primum typis excusus. Lvgdvni, apud Sennetonios fratres, 1550. 3 v.

252

Bellemère, Gilles de, bp. Sacrosanctae decisiones canonicae ab excellentissimis viris, i. c. clarissimis, iisdémque sacri palatij auditoribus collectae. Aegidio Bellamera, Gvlielme Cassiodoro, Capella Tholosana. Nunc demùm hac postrema editione diligentiùs recognitae, ac summarijs auctae, ab innumerísque quibus scatebant erroribus emendatae. Cum indice rerum & verborum locupletissimo. Lvgdvni, Beraud, 1579. 596 p.

253

Bender, Ludovicus. Legum ecclesiasticarum interpretatio et suppletio; commentarius in canones 17, 18, 19 et 20. Roma, New York, Desclée, 1961. 322 p.
Bibliographical footnotes.

254

Bender, Ludovicus. Ius publicum ecclesiasticum. Bussum, Brand, 1948. 232 p.

255

Bendix, Ludwig. Kirche und kirchenrecht. Eine kritik moderner theologischer und juristischer ansichten. Mainz, Kirchheim, 1895. 190 p.

256

Benedictus XIII, pope. Synodicon s. beneventanensis ecclesiae continens concilia XIX. Summorum pontificum sex, archiepiscoporum tredecim collecta summariis, notisque adaucta, claro, distinctoque indice locupletata cura, labore, et studio fr. Vincentii Mariae. Beneventi, ex typographia archiepiscopali, 1695. 718 p.

257

Benedictus XIV, pope. De synodo dioecesana libri

tredecim in dvos tomos distribvti. Ed. novissima ad postremam romanam ab ipso auctore curatam, & plurimis additamentis auctam diligenter exacta. [Venetiis] in typographia Bassanensi, sumptibus Remondinianis, 1767. 2 v. in 1.

258
Beneshevich, Vladimir N. Kanoničeskij sbornik : XIV titulov so vtoroj četverti VII věka do 883 g. : k drevnějšej istorii istočnikov prava greko-vostočnoj cerkvi; Vorwort von Jürgen Dummer. Leipzig, Zentralantiquariat der Deutschen Demokratischen Republik, 1974. 334, 101 p. (Subsidia Byzantina, v. 2a)
Bibliography: p. x–xiii.

259
Benincasa, Cornelia. De constitvtionibvs tractatus. In qvo omnia ibi disceptari solita erudite diffe-runtur, elegantique methodo explicantur. Eivsdem de allvvione compendiolvm vniuersum eius argu-mentum paucis clarissime complectens. Cum suo quoquo indice concinne disposito. Pervsiae, Excu-debat Andraeas Brixianus, 1572. 103 p.

260
Berardi, Carlo S. Commentaria in jus ecclesiasticum universum. Taurini, ex typographia Regia, 1766–67. 4 v.

In his extensive commentaries on universal ec-clesiastical law filling four volumes, the author studies the five books of the Decretals by Gregory IX. As explained in the general preface, the author adheres to the sacred canons' rules in his studies, but he appeals also to philosophical principles to expose the cause and origins of the arguments. There are instances in which Berardi contents himself with indicating the elements accepted by laws or customs. The seemingly divergent and mixed styles of the commentaries can be attributed to the author's desire to present faithfully his own creation, the opinion of other experts, the formulae of canons, and the pontifical constitutions. Each volume begins with a *tractatio,* or a brief and useful explanation of the parts of the Decretals under study.

261
Berardi, Carlo S. Commentaria in jus ecclesiasticum universum. Mexici, Gregor, 1851. v. 2 only.

262
Berardi, Carlo S. Institutions juris ecclesiastici. Opus posthumum in duas partes tributum. Mexici, ex typographia Ludovici Abadiano et Valdes, 1853. 2 v. in 1.

263
Berardi, Carlo S. De rebus ad canonum scientiam pertinentibus commentaria in jus ecclesiasticum universum. Mediolani, Rossi, 1846–47. 2 v.

264
Bernárdez Cantón, Alberto, et al. El Fenómeno religioso en España; aspectos jurídico políticos. Madrid, Instituto de Estudios Políticos, 1972. 402 p. (Estudios de derecho eclesiástico español y com-parado, 1) (Colección Serie jurídica)
Includes bibliographical references.

265
Bernhardt, Erich. Die normae generales des Codex juris canonici. Marburg [Kirchhain, Rindt] 1927. 78, [2] p.
"Quellen und schrifttum": p. [77]–78.

266
Bernstein, Georg H. De initiis et originibus reli-gionum in orienta dispersarum quae differunt a religione Christiana liber. Berolini, Maurer, 1817. 71 p.

267
Bertola, Arnaldo. Corso di diritto canonico: le costituzione della Chiesa. 3. ed. rifatta e ampliata. Torino, Giappichelli [1958]. 426 p.
"Nota bibliografica": p. [373]–401.

268
Bertola, Arnaldo. Lezioni di diritto canonico. To-rino, Giappichelli [1953]. 358 p.
"Bibliografia": p. 25–29.

269
Bertrams, Wilhelm. Quaestiones fundamentales iuris canonici. Roma, Libreria editrice Università gregoriana, 1969. 686 p.
Includes bibliographical references.

270
Besse-Fleureau, Suzanne. Les trois derniers livres inédits du recueil canonique de Saint Anselme de

Lucques. Genève, Mercure, [1954?]c1951. (Monumenta fontium juris, 77)

271
Beste, Ulric, father. Introductio in Codicem, quam in usum et utilitatem scholae et cleri ad promptam expeditamque canonum interpretationem, paravit et edidit. Collegeville, Minn., St. John's Abbey Press [1938]. 1000 p.
"Bibliographia": p. 4–5.

272
Beste, Ulric, father. Introductio in Codicem; quam in usum et utilitatem scholae et cleri ad promptam expeditamque canonum interpretationem paravit et edidit. Ed. 4. Neapoli, D'Auria, 1956. 1097 p.

273
Blanco Nájera, Francisco. El Código de derecho canónico, traducido y comentado. V. 1, Normas generales y personas. Cadiz, Establecimientos Cerón y librería Cervantes, s. 1.; 1942–[45]. 2 v.

274
Boccacci, Virginio. Tractatvs . . . De censibus super constitutionibus Pij quinti . . . De societatibus officiorum . . . De pactis & promissionibus . . . Denuo typis impressi & a plurimis erroribus expurgati, adiecto duplici indice. Romae, ex bibliotheca Io. Angeli Ruffinelli, Facciotti, 1610. 157 p.

275
Böcken, Placidus. Commentarius in jus canonicum universum sive in quinque libros ac titulos Decretalium Gregorii IX Pontif. Max. et concordantes alios tam ejusdem juris canonici quam civilis. Salisburgi, Mayr, 1735–39. 3 v.

276
Böcken, Placidus. Tractatus ad librum I Decretalium Gregorii IX. . . . In alma Archi-episcopali universitate salisburgensi praeside & authore p. Placido Böckn . . . disputationi academicae subjectus, et cum Parergis ex jure universo pro suprema laurea defensus ab admodum reverendo domino Antonio Josepho Dreser. Salisburgi, Mayr [1724]. 321, [15] p.

277
Boehmer, Georg L. Principia ivris canonici speciatim ivris ecclesiastici pvblici et privati qvod per

Germaniam obtinet. Editionem septimam cvravit d. Car. Travg. Gottlob Schoenemann. Gottingae, apvd Vandenhoek et Rvprecht, 1802. 702 p.

278
Boggiano-Pico, Antonio. Manuale di diritto canonico, con riferimento alla legislazione civile. Milano, CETIM, 1942. 420, [2] p. (Manuali CETIM [n. 20])

279
Böhmer, Georg L. Principia ivris canonici, speciatim ivris ecclesiastici pvblici et privati qvod per Germaniam obtinet. Editio 3. emendatior. Gottingae, apvd Vandenhoeck, 1774. 590 p.

280
Böhmer, Georg L. Principia ivris canonici speciatim ivris ecclesiastici pvblici et privati qvod per Germaniam obtinet. Editio sexta emendatior. Gottingae, apvd Vandenhoek et Rvprecht, 1791. 616, [32] p.

281
Böhmer, Justus H. Jus ecclesiasticum protestantium usum modernum iuris canonici. Halae, Litteris et Impensis Orphanõtrophei, 1731–36. v. 4 and 5; 2d. ed. 1723–27. v. 2 and 3; 3d. ed. 1730–63. v. 1 and 5; 4th. ed. 1754. v. 4; 5th. ed. 1756–74. v. 1–3.

282
Böhmer, Just[us] H. Tractatus juris ecclesiastici de jure parochiali quod a sua genuina fundamenta revocatum et falsis principiis aliquisque abusibus variis vindicatum. Halae Magdeburgicae, sumptibus Orphanotrophii Glauch [1701?]. 335, [3] p.

283
Boileau, Jacques. De antiquis et majoribus episcoporum causis, liber; in quo ss. patrum, pontificum, & conciliorum ecclesiae catholicae sententiae summà fide proferuntur, ad confutationem errorum Dauidij, in libro gallicè scripto, De iudiciis canonicis episcoporum. Autore Theologo parisiensi [pseud.]. Leodij, ex officina typogr. Joan. Mathiae Hovij, 1678. 394 p.

284
Bonacina, Martino. Martini Bonacinae Opera omnia. Ed. novissima. Lugduni, sumptibus Amisson

& Posuel, 1700–05 [v. 1, 1705; v. 3, 1700]. 3 v. in 2.

Includes bibliographical references.

285

Bonfini, Silvestro. Notabilia in bannimentis generalibus ditionis ecclesiasticae ... Quibus in hac tertia editione accesserunt suppletiones uberrimmae in singula capita ad norman juris communis romanorum, statutorum, legum, & consuetudinem particularium, rerumque in supremis tribunalibus judicatarum, opera, ac studio Francisci Antonii Bonfinii. Lucae, Venturini, 1714, 2 v.

286

Bonicelli, Silvio C. I concili particolari da Graziano al Concilo di Trento. Studio sulla evoluzione del diritto della Chiesa latina. Brescia, Morcelliana, 1971. 216 p. (Pubblicazioni del Pontificio seminario lombardo in Roma. Ricerche di scienze teologiche, 8)

Bibliography: p. [9]–13.

287

Bonizo, bp. of Sutri. Liber de vita christiana, herausgegeben von Ernst Perels. Berlin, Weidmann, 1930. 402 p. (Added t.-p.: Texte zur geschichte des römischen und kanonischen rechts in mittelalter, vorbereitet von Emil Seckel, hrsg. von der Preussischen akademie der wissenschaften. I. bd.)

288

Bonnefoi, Ennemond. Iuris orientalis libri III. Cum latina interpretatione. [Parisiis] Stephanus, 1573. 127, 304, [13], 312 p.

289

Bönninghausen, F. E. de. Dissertatio iuridico-canonica inauguralis. Monasterii, Frid. Regenberg, 1852. 62 p.

290

De bono regimine rervm ad vniversitates spectantivm in bullam X Clementis papae VIII commentaria a Iacobo Cohellio ... earundem vniuersitatum ditionis ecclesiasticae agente generali lucubrata multiplici doctrina, & eruditione repleta, ac diu exoptata Caroli Carthariii ... studio nunquam intermisso ab interitu vindicata. Romae, sumptibus Ioannis Casonij sub signo S. Pauli, 1656. 539 p.

291

Bouscaren, Timothy L. The canon law digest; officially published documents affecting the Code of canon law. Milwaukee, Bruce Pub. Co. [1934–] Includes vols. of various editions.

Includes bibliographies.

292

Bouscaren, Timothy L., and Adam C. Ellis. Canon law; a text and commentary. Milwaukee, Bruce Pub. Co. [1946]. 942 p.

Bibliographical footnotes.

293

Bouscaren, Timothy L., and Adam C. Ellis. Canon law; a text and commentary. 2d rev. ed. Milwaukee, Bruce [1951]. 1009 p.

Includes bibliographies.

294

Bouscaren, Timothy L., and Adam C. Ellis. Canon law; a text and commentary. 3d. rev. ed. Milwaukee, Bruce Pub. Co. [1957]. 980 p.

Includes bibliographies.

295

Bouscaren, Timothy L., Adam C. Ellis, and Francis N. Korth. Canon law; a text and commentary. 4th ed. Milwaukee, Bruce Pub. Co. [1963]. 1004 p.

Includes bibliographies.

296

Bouscaren, Timothy L., Adam C. Ellis, and Francis N. Korth. Canon law; a text and commentary. 4th rev. ed. Milwaukee, Bruce Pub. Co. [1966]. 1011 p.

Includes bibliographies.

This work offers a commentary on the basic elements of canon law and, more precisely, on the Code of Canon Law promulgated in 1917 and still in force. The authors make it clear that their commentary is intended to be used in coordination with the text of the code, since the exposition follows the code's order. Most of the canonical texts analyzed are mentioned but not provided. The book offers cases and questions to illustrate concretely the principles, with the intention of helping the student or pastor in the practical application of the provisions. It includes a number of corrections and additions which became necessary after the Second Vatican Council.

297

Bouscaren, Timothy L., and James I. O'Connor. The canon law digest for religious; officially published documents affecting the Code of canon law as pertinent to religious. Milwaukee, Bruce Pub. Co. [1965–   ] c1964–   1 v.

298

Box, Hubert S. The principles of canon law. With a foreword by R. C. Mortimer. London, New York, Oxford Univ. Press, 1949. 76 p.

299

Boyd, William K. The ecclesiastical edicts of the Theodosian Code. [1st AMS ed.] New York, AMS Press [1969]. 123 p. (Columbia University studies in social sciences, 63)
  Bibliography: p. 121–22.

300

Brabandère, Pierre de, bp. Juris canonici et juris canonico-civilis compendium praelectionibus accommodatum quas in Seminario brug. habuit illustrissimus ac reverendissimus dominus Petrus de Brabandere, episcopus brugensis. . . . Editio septima denuo recognita, expolitior et auctior, curante C. van Coillie. Brugis, sumptibus et typis Societatis sancti Augustini, Desclée, De Brouwer, 1903. 2 v.

301

Braun, Philippus. Principia juris canonici, quae ad capessendam ss. canonum notitiam sacrae themidos alumnis. Norimbergae, sumptibus Johannis Christophori Lochneri, 1698.

302

Brockhaus, Friedrich. Ueber das canonische recht. Kiel, Universitäts-buchhandlung (P. Toeche) 1888. 22 p.

303

Brunemann, Johann. De jure ecclesiastico tractatus posthumus in usum ecclesiarum evangel. et consistoriorum & concinnatus, et necessariis supplementis adauctus a Samuele Strikio, j. c. accesserunt praelectiones ad regulas juris canonici ejusdem autoris ut et tractatus de dissensu sponsalitio. Wittenbergae, apud Zimmermannum, 1721.

304

Brunemann, Johann. De jure ecclesiastico; tractatus posthumus, in usum ecclesiarum evangel. & consistoriorum concinnatus, post mortem autoris revisus & necessariis supplementis adauctus a Samuele Strykio. Accesserunt Praelectiones ad regulas juris canonici ejusdem autoris, ed. 2. revisa & emendata. Francofurti, Schret, Günther, 1686, 896 p.

305

Brydon, George M. Shall we accept the ancient canons as canon law? A reply to the pamphlet "The ancient canons, and an interpretation of the word 'discipline,' in the Book of common prayer" which was published by the Joint Commission on Discipline of the American Church Union and the Clerical Union. Richmond, Virginia Diocesan Library [1955]. 58 p.

306

Brys, Joseph. Juris canonici compendium, olim ab exc^{mo} De Brabandere et R^{dis} adm. Van Coillie et De Meester editum. Ed. 10., post Codicem 2. Brugis, Cesclée de Brouwer, 1947–49. 2 v.

307

Bubnn, Johan N. S., graf von. Institutiones juris canonici ad ordinem decretalium Gregorii IX P. M. Pragae Bohemorum, Gerzabeck, 1769. 535, [12] p.

308

Burchardus, bp. of Worms. Decretorum libri XX ex consiliis, & orthodoxorū patrū decretis, tum etiam diuersarū nationum synodis, ceu loci communes congesti, in quibus totum ecclesiasticū munus, luculenta breuitate, & veteres ecclesiarum obseruationes, complectitur. Opus denuò excusum. Parisiis, apud Foucherium, 1549. 339 l.

309

Burmester, Oswald H. E. The canons of Cyril II, LXVII patriarch of Alexandria. Louvain, Impr. orientaliste et scientifique, 1936. 246–288 p.

310

Bušek, Vratislav. Církev, stát a jinověrci v Codexu iuris canonici. Studie z veřejného práva církevního. V Praze, Nákl. "Všehrdu," 1922. 109, [3] p.
  Bibliography: p. [110]–[111].

311

Butrio, Antonius de. In sextum Decretalium volumen commentaria, nunc primum excussa; opus juris studiosis utilissimum et pernecessarium; nec pretio nummario aestimandum, appositis summarijs, atque indice copiosissimo: & quod supremum est, diligenti examine purgatum. Venetiis, apud Zilettum, 1575. Torino, Bottega d'Erasmo, 1967. 166 (n. e. 332) p.

312

Butrio, Antonius de. Super prima primi [-secunda secundi] Decretalium commentarij, summariis et indice rerum ac verborum memorabilium locupletissimis, universas Decretalium materias complectentibus, in studiosorum gratiam exornati, hac in editione summo studio, atque diligentia, a multis & varijs erroribus repurgati. Venetiis, apud Juntas, 1578. Torino, Bottega d'Erasmo, 1967. 7 v. in 4.

313

Cabassut, Jean. Juris canonici theoria et praxis, ad forum tam sacramentale quám contentiosum, tum ecclesiasticum, tum seculare. Opus exactum, non solum ad normam juris communis & romani, sed etiam juris francici. . . . Editio postrema ab ipso authore recognita & aucta. Lugduni, Borde & Arnaud, 1709. 600, [70] p.

314

Cabassut, Jean. Juris canonici theoria et praxis ad forum tam sacramentale quàm contentiosum, tum ecclesiasticum, tum saeculare, opus exactum non solum ad normam juris communis & Romani, sed etiam juris Francici. Ed. 1. Veneta juxta Lugdunensem ab ipso authore recognitam et auctam. Venetiis, Zane, 1728. 279 p.

315

Cabassut, Jean. Juris canonici theoria et praxis, ad forum tam sacramentale quam contentiosum, tum ecclesiasticum, tum saeculare. Opus exactum non solum ad norman juris communis et romani, sed etiam juris francici. Editio secunda veneta juxta lugdunensem ab ipso authore recognitam et auctam. Venetiis, Bettinelli, 1756. 263 p.

316

Cabassut, Jean. Juris canonici theoria et praxis, ad forum tam sacramentale, quam contentiosum, tum ecclesiasticum, tum seculare. Opus exactum non solum ad norman juris communis et romani, sed etiam juris francici. Dublin, Coyne, 1824. 2 v.

317

Cabassut, Jean. Notitia conciliorvm sanctae ecclesiae; in qva elvcidantvr exactissimè tùm praecipuae partes ecclesiasticae historiae . . . Editio altera, ab authore diligenter recognita, & aucta. Lvgdvni, Arnavd & Borde, 1670. 720, [60] p.

318

Cabreros de Anta, Marcelino. Estudios canónicos. Madrid, Editorial Coculsa, 1956. 747 p.

319

Cabreros de Anta, Marcelino. Iglesia y derecho, hoy: estudios canónicos postconciliares. Pamplona, Ediciones Universidad de Navarra, 1975. 388 p. (Colección canónica)

In this essay on the theological, social, and personal value of Church law, the author explains that canon law is not only a part of theology and other human sciences or realities within the church, but an essential element of the church of Christ. Canon law is also a necessary instrument for social order, including the spiritual life of the Church and of each person; without the ordinate internal and external communion with the mystical body, this life cannot subsist, much less develop. Several topics covered by Vatican II are also raised and discussed here.

320

Cabreros de Anta, Marcelino. Nuevos estudios canónicos. Vitoria, Editorial Eset, 1966. 809 p. (Victoriensia. Publicaciones del Seminario de Vitoria, v. 22)

321

Cabreros de Anta, Marcelino. Vigencia y estado actual de la legislación canónica. Pamplona, Ediciones Universidad de Navarra, 1974. 73 p. (Colección canónica de la Universidad de Navarra)

322

Cairns, Huntington. Legal philosophy from Plato to Hegel. Baltimore, Johns Hopkins Press, 1949. 583 p.

Bibliographical footnotes.

323

Calgagnini, Carlo de. Observationes practico-legales in duas partes distinctae Pars prima de Avocatione, et remissione causarum tam ad terminos juris communis, quam particularium constitutionum Apostolicarum De Causis Non Avocandis una cum praxi tribunalis signaturae gratiae, et justitiae. Pars secuda De Emphiteusi, et Feudo, tam ad terminos juris communis, quam particularium Constitutionum Apostolicarum De Bonis Emphiteuvticis, una cum Decionibus Sac. Rotae Romanae ad materiam alibi non impressis. Romae, Bernabo, 1715. 446, [53] p.

324

Calisse, Carlo. Diritto ecclesiastico. Nuova ed. corr. ed ampliata. Firenze, Barbèra [191–]. 367 p. (On cover: Manuali Barbèra di scienze giuridiche, sociali e politiche [Serie teorica] XX)

325

Campos y Pulido, José M. Derecho canónico (obra ajustada al programa de oposiciones al cuerpo de aspirantes a la judicatura y al ministerio fiscal, de 31 de enero de 1920). Madrid, Editorial Reus, 1920. 218 p.

326

Campos y Pulido, José M. Derecho canónico. Obra adaptada al programa de oposiciones a la carrera fiscal publicado el 16 de noviembre de 1926. Madrid, Editorial Reus, 1927 [cover 1928]. 232 p. (Biblioteca de oposiciones. Contestaciones Reus)

327

Campos y Pulido, José M. Legislación y jurisprudencia canónica novísima y disciplina particular de España; exposición y comentario de las maś recientes disposiciones dictadas en el pontificado de su santidad Pío papa X. Madrid, Hijos de Reus, 1914–25. 3– v.

328

Cance, Adrien, ed. Le Code de droit canonique; commentaire succinct et pratique. Paris, Gabalda et cᵢₑ, 1933–34. 3 v.

329

Cance, Adrien. Le Code de droit canonique; commentaire succinct et pratique. 7. éd. rev. et corr. Paris, Gabalda, 1946–49. 4 v.

330

Canisius, Heinrich. Svmma jvris canonici in qvatvor institvtionvm libros contracta. Qvarto recognita, restituta et notationibvs illvstrata. Accessit commentarivs in regvlas ivris lib. IV decret. item appendix de differentijs vtriusque iuris. Ingolstadii, ex typographeo Ederiano, apud Elisabetham Angermariam, 1620. 672, [60] p.

331

Canisius, Henricus. Opera qvae de jure canonico reliqvit: In libb. V Decretalium. In tit. de regulis juris lib. VI. De differentiis j. u. Summa juris canonici. Insertus est, auctarii vice, Commentarius brevis in librum V. Decretal. exceptus Lovanii sub. D. Ioan. VViringo. . . . Omnia studio & industriâ ValerI Andreae, DesselI . . . quà nunc primùm edita, quà suppleta & recensita, summariisǵue & indicibus aucta. Lovanii, typis ac sumptibus Andreae BouvetI, 1649. 1071, [25] p.

332

Canisius, Henricus. Summa iuris canonici in quatuor institutionum libros contracta. . . . Accessit commentarius de regulas iuris, Lib. VI Decret. Item appendix de differentiis utriusque iuris. Antverpiae, apud Hieronynum Verdussium, 1628. [22], 666, [46] p.

333

Capano, Andrea. De iure relevii totius ferè christiani orbis regnorum tractatus . . . Sive Commentarii ad constitutionem regni Neap. post mortem, sub. tit. De morte baronis nuncianda imperatori . . . Accesserunt catalogus feudistarum ad haec usque tempora, index argumentorum, & materiarum. Neapoli, ex typographia Secundini Roncalioli, expensis Dominici Vecchi, 1630. 428 p.

334

Caparros, Juan J. Disciplina eclesiástica general del oriente y occidente particular de España y última del Santo Concilio de Trento. Segunda edición. Madrid, Llorenci, 1847. 2 v.

335

Cappelli, Marcantonio. De appellationibus ecclesiae africanae ad romanam sedem dissertatio. Editio tertia. Ad bibliothecae albanae exemplar, ab authore ipso majori ex parte immutatum, correctum, auctum. Praefigitur Johannis Bortonii de ejusdem

Cappelli vitâ, & scriptis diatriba. Romae, typis sac. Congreg. de propagandâ fide, 1722. 210 p.

336

Cappello, Felice M. Summa iuris canonici in usum scholarum concinnata. Editio altera emendata et aucta. Romae, apud aedes Universitatis gregorianae, 1932–

337

Cappello, Felice M. Summa iuris publici ecclesiastici ad normam Codicis iuris canonici et recentiorum S. sedis documentorum concinnata. Editio quarta emendata. Romae, apud aedes Universitatis gregorianae, 1936. 632 p.

338

Cappello, Felice M. Summa juris publici ecclesiastici ad normam codicis juris canonici et recentiorum S. sedis documentorum concinnata. Editio 6. accurate recognita. Romae, apud aedes Universitatis gregorianae, 1954. 391 p.

339

Carè, Benedetto. Diritto ecclesiastico. [Napoli] Humus [195–?]. 14 p. (Parva favilla, collana di sintesi di preparazione agli esami universitari e al concorsi, 5)

340

Carpzov, Benedict. Jurisprudentia ecclesiastica seu consistorialis rerum et quaestionum in serenissimi ac potentissimi principis electoris saxon . . . Libr. III. Lipsiae, sumptibus praelo Timothei Ritzschii, 1665. 884 p.

341

Casali, Giovanni B. Annotationes in vniversvm ivs, tvm canonicvm, tvm civile attingentes etiam Extrauagantes, & Feuda. Omnia collecta passim ex labore longo . . . Domini Ioannis Baptistae Casalis . . . qui haec omnia disposuit pro faciliori studiosorum inuentione, iuxta antiquum ordinem titulorum, capituloru, legum & glossarum. Bononiae, ex typis Benatij, 1590. 100, 392 p.

342

Cassola, Ovidio. La recezione del diritto civile nel diritto canonico. 2. ed. Roma, Pontifica Università Lateranense, 1969. 163 p. (Utrumque ius, 1)
    Bibliography: p. [11]–15.

343

Castillo Sotomayor, Joannes del. Quotidianarum controversiarum juris tomus primus[-octavus]. . . . Opus revera pragmaticis forensibus utilissimum, cum summariis, & indicibus, ad sublevandum lectoris laborem, opportunis. Nova editio, ab innumeris veteris praeli mendis expurgata, & characterum varietate distinctis allegationibus non mediocri labore adornata. Coloniae Allobrogum, Perachon & Cramer, 1727, (v. 2–8) 1726. 8 v. in 7.

344

Castillo Sotomayor, Joannes del. Joannis Pauli Melii . . . Additiones et observationes ad Castillum De alimentis, cum S. Rotae romanae decisionibus ad materiam facientibus, hactenus non impressis, in quibus materiae ecclesiasticae non paucae tractantur. Nova editio, cum S. Rotae romanae decisionibus recentissimis super-additis, nunc primum in lucem editis, materiam de alimentis confirmantibus, laudantibus, approbantibus &c. Accesserunt quoque indices argumentorum & materiarum locupletissimi. Coloniae Allobrogum, Perachon & Cramer, 1727. 144, [16], 232, [27], 72, [10] p.

345

Castillo Sotomayor, Joannes del. Repertorium generale rerum notabiliorum seu materiarum omnium, quae in libris seu tomis octo Quotidianarum controversiarum juris D. Joannis del Castillo Sotomayor J. C. celeberrimi continentur. . . . Opera & singulari studio Nicolai Antonii. Coloniae Allobrogum, Perachon & Cramer, 1726. [784] p.

346

Catholic Church. Pope, 1513–21 (Leo X) Inter multiplices (4 May 1515). Bulla concilii in decima sessio//ne super materia montis pietatis: lecta per r. p. dñm Bertrandum episcopū Adrieñ. oratorē ducis Ferrarie in Romañ. curia. [Rome?, 1515?] [4] l.

347

Catholic Church. Pope. Bvllarivm sive Collectio diuersarum constitutionum multorum pontif. a Gregorio septimo, vsqve ad s. d. n. Sixtvm qvintvm pontificem opt. max. Cum rubricis, summariis, lucubrationibus & quadruplici indice. D. Laertij Cherubini . . . Editvm opera & industria haeredum Antonij Bladij impressorum cameralium. Romae, apud eosdem haeredes Antonij Bladij typographos R. Camerae Apost., 1586. 640 p.

348

Catholic Church. Pope, 1700–21 (Clemens XI). Bullarium. Romae, ex typographia Reverendae Camerae Apostolicae, 1723. 616, [15] p.

349

Catholic Church. Cancellaria Apostolica. Regulae ordinationes, et constitutiones Cancellariae Apostolicae . . . Clementis . . . papae XIV. Romae, typis Camerae Apostolicae, 1769. 90, [6] p.

350

Catholic Church. Codex juris canonici. Zakonik cerkvenega prava. Sestavljen po ukazu papeža Pija X in razglašen z oblastjo papeža Benedikta XV. Prevedel in z novimi odloki priredil Alojzij Odar. V Ljubljani, 1944. 1054 p.

351

Catholic Church. Codex juris canonici. Código de derecho canónico, texto latino y versión castellana, con jurisprudencia y comentarios, por los catedráticos de texto del Código en la Pontificia Universidad Eclesiástica de Salamanca, Doctor Lorenzo Miguélez Domínguez, Doctor Sabino Alonso Morán, y Doctor Marcelino Cabreros de Anta . . . prólogo del excmo. y rvdmo. Sr. Dr. Fr. José López Ortiz. Madrid [Editorial Católica, S. A.] 1945. 857 p. (Added t.-p.: Biblioteca de autores cristianos. [Sección II: Teología y cánones])

352

Catholic Church. Codex juris canonici. Código de derecho canónico y legislación complementaria, texto latino y versión castellana, con jurisprudencia y comentarios, por Lorenzo Miguélez Domínguez, Sabino Alonso Morán y Marcelino Cabreros de Anta. Prólogo del Excmo. y Revdmo. Sr. Dr. Fr. José López Ortiz. [4. ed. rev., ampliada y mejorada] Madrid [Editorial Católica], 1951. 1068 p. (Biblioteca de autores cristianos. Sección 2: Teología y cánones, v. 7)

353

Catholic Church. Codex juris canonici. Código de derecho canónico y legislación complementaria, texto latino y versión castellana, con jurisprudencia y comentarios, por Lorenzo Miguélez Domínguez, Sabino Alonso Morán, y Marcelino Cabreros de Anta. Prólogo del Excmo. y Revdmo. Sr. Dr. Fr. José López Ortiz. [5. ed. rev., ampliada y mejorada] Madrid [Editorial Católica], 1954. 1092 p. (Biblioteca de autores cristianos, 7. Sección 2: Teología y cánones)

354

Catholic Church. Codex juris canonici. Comentarios al Código de derecho canónico, con el texto legal latino y castellano, por Marcelino Cabreros de Anta, Arturo Alonso Lobo, Sabino Alonso Morán. Prólogo del Excmo. y Revdmo. Sr. Dr. Fr. Francisco Barbado Viejo. Madrid, Biblioteca de Autores Cristianos, 1963–64. 4 v. (Biblioteca de autores cristianos, 223, 225, 234, 240. Sección 2: Teología cánones)

355

Catholic Church. Collectio canonum in V libris. Cura et studio M. Fornasari. Turnholti, Typographi Brepols, 1970– . (Corpus Christianorum. Continuatio mediaevalis, 6)

Includes bibliographical references.

356

Catholic Church. Pope. Collectio constitutionum chirographorum et brevium diversorum romanorum pontificum pro bono regimine universitatum ac communitatum status ecclesiastici, & pro ejusdem status felici gubernio promulgatorum, ac specialiter disponentium . . . Ac zelo, & cura . . . Josephi Renati . . . Per materias, marginalibus, annotationibus, & alphabetico ordine disposita, ac multiplici indice exornata a Petro Andrea de Vecchis Romano. Romae, ex typographia Hieronymi Mainardi, 1731. 4 v.

357

Catholic Church. Pope. Collectio constitutionum, chirographorum et brevium diversorum Romanorum Pontificum, pro bono regimine universitatum, ac communitatum Status Ecclesiastici, & pro ejusdem status felici gubernio promulgatorum . . . Edita sub clementissimis auspiciis Clementis XII ac zelo & cura Josephi Renati Imperialis per materias, marginalibus annotationibus, & alphabetico ordine disposita, ac multiplici indice exornata a Petro Andrea de Vecchis. Romae, ex typographia H. Mainardi, 1732. 411 p. (Petrus Andreas de Vecchis. De bono regimine, 1 v.)

358

Catholic Church. Pope, 1724–30 (Benedictus XIII).

Concilium romanum in sacrosancta Basilica lateranensi celebratum anno universalis jubilaei MDCCXXV a Benedicto papa XIII nunc denuo recusum ragnante sanctissimo d. n. Benedicto XIV pont. max. Romae, typis Joannis Generosi Salomoni, sumptibus haeredum Joannis Laurentii Barbiellini, 1751. 207 p.

359
Catholic Church. Congregatio pro ecclesia orientali. Codificazione canonica orientale: fonti. [Roma] Tipografia Poliglotta Vaticana, 1931–
"Bibliographia": v. 11, p. [xiii].

360
Catholic Church. Pope. Constitutiones pontificiae et romanorum congregationum decisiones ad vicarios utriusque cleri spectantes. Jo. Baptista Pittono collectore. Venetiis, excudebat Leonardus Pittonus, 1715. 196, [2] p.

361
Catholic Church. Decretales summorum pontificum pro regno Poloniae et constitutiones synodorum provincialium et dioecesanarum regni ejusdem ad summam collectae. Cum annotationibus, declarationibus, admonitionibus et additionibus ex historia, jure ecclesiastico universali et jure civili regni, curantibus plerisque sacerdotibus posnaniensibus editae. Posnaniae, Leitgeber, 1883–

362
Catholic Church. Delectus actorum ecclesiae universalis seu nova summa concilioru, epistolarum, decretorum ss. pontificum, capitularium, ecclesiae fides et disciplina niti solent. Cum notis ad canones. Lugduni, sumptibus Joannis Certe, 1706. 2 v. in 1.

363
Catholic Church. Pope, 1227–41 (Gregorius IX). Epistolae decretales d. Gregorii papae IX, svae integritati restitvtae, et passim notis qvae iustarum glossarum fere instar esse possunt, locupletatae: addita Margarita earundem decretalium, summariis, indicibus, &c. Francofvrdi, excudebat I. Wechelus, impensis Sigismundi Feyrabendii, Henrici Thacquii & Petri Fischeri, 1586. 1055, [14] p.

364
Catholic Church. Pope. Magnvm bvllarivm romanvm, ab Leone magno vsqve ad s. d. n. Inno-centivm X opvs absolvtissimvm Laerti Cherubini . . . et a Angelo Cherubino . . . nunc denuo illustratum & recensitum. Editio novissima. Quatuor tomis distributa: vitis et iconibus aeneis omnium pontificum decorata: in qua non solum constitutiones omnes Vrbani VIII quotquot reperii potuerunt, ordine temporis insertae appendicesque duae suis locis restitutae; verum et Innocentiri X constitutiones vsque ad hanc diem emanatae, sunt superadditae, suis rubricis, et scholijs conuenientibus summarijsque marginalibus exornatae, ac tandem vberioribus quam antea indicibus locupletatae. Lvgdvni, Borde, Arnaud & Rigaud, 1655. 4 v. in 3.

365
Catholic Church. Pope. Magnum bullarium romanum ab Urbano VIII, vsqve ad s. d. n. Clementem X opus absolutissimum a Laertii Cherubini; & a Angelo Cherubino, novissime vero a Angelo a Lantusca, & Joanne Paulo a Roma quinti tomi editione illustratum, & auctum. Editio novissima. Quinque tomis distributa, vitis et iconibus aeneis omnium pontificum decorata: in qua non solum constitutiones omnes Urbani VIII, quotquot reperiri potuerunt, ordine temporis insertae, appendicesque duae suis restitutae locis; verum et Innocentii X, Alexandri VII, Clementis IX, & Clementis X constitutiones usque ad hac diem emanatae, superadditae sunt, rubricis suis, et scholiis convenientibus, summariisque marginalibus exornatae, ac tandem uberiribus quam antea indicibus locupletatae. Lugduni, Borde et Arnaud, 1692–97. 5 v.

366
Catholic Church. Pope, 1700–21 (Clemens XI). Orationes consistoriales. Romae, Salvioni, 1722. 353 p.

367
The Catholic encyclopedia; an international work of reference on the constitution, doctrine, discipline, and history of the Catholic Church. Supplementary volume, containing revisions of the articles on canon law according to the Code of canon law of Pius X, promulgated by Pope Benedict XV, by Andrew A. Macerlean. New York, The Encyclopedia Press, Inc., 1917. 82 p.

368
Cathrein, Victor. El derecho natural y el positivo.

Traducción directa de la 2. ed. alemana por Alberto
Jardón y César Barja. 6 ed. Madrid, Instituto
Editorial Reus, 1950. 288 p. (Biblioteca jurídica de
autores españoles y extranjeros, v. 15)

369
Cavalario, Domingo. Instituciones del derecho
canónico, traducidas del latin al castellano por D.
Juan Tejada y Ramiro, e ilustradas con lo corres-
pondiente al derecho canónico español por el Dr.
D. Antonio Rodríguez de Cepeda. 4. ed. en que ha
corregido notablemente la traducción D. Vicente
Salvá. Paris, V. Salvá, 1846. 3 v.

370
Cavalario, Domingo. Instituciones del derecho
canónico, traducidas del latin al español por d. José
Antonio de Ojea. Nueva ed., corr. notablemente,
y aum. con notas importantes sobre la disciplina y
jurisprudencia canónicas de España, por don Juan
B. Guim. Paris, Rosa, Bouret y ca., 1852. 879 p.

371
Cavallari, Domenice. Institutiones juris canonici.
Editio tertia. Conimbricae, Typis Academicis, 1851.
2 v.

372
Cavallario, Domingo. Instituciones del derecho
canónico. Nueva traducción arreglada a los cánones
y leyes de España, e ilustrada con hechos históricos
y autoridades de algunos sabios de la misma. 2. ed.
corregida. Madrid, Fuentenebro, 1843–   . v. 1,
3–

373
Cavallarius, Dominicus. Institvtiones ivris canonici
in tres partes tributae, quibus vetus & noua Eccle-
siae disciplina & mutationum caussae enarrantur.
Neapoli, apvd Simones Fratres, 1764–71. 3 v.
  Includes bibliographical references.

374
Cavigioli, Giovanni. Manuale di diritto canonico.
Torino, Società Editrice Internazionale [1932]. 737
p.

375
Cavigioli, Giovanni. Manuale di diritto canonico.
Torino [etc.], Società Editrice Internazionale
[1934]. 737 p., 1 l.

376
Cavigioli, Giovanni. Manuale di diritto canonico.
2. ed., accresciuta ed integrata della sezione sacra-
mentaria. Torino [etc.], Società Editrice Internazionale [1939]. 920 p.

377
Cavigioli, Giovanni. Manuale di diritto canonico.
3. ed., riv. Torino, Società Editrice Internazionale
[1946]. 827 p.
  Bibliographical footnotes.

378
Cavigioli, Juan. Derecho canónico, prólogo, notas
de derecho español y traducción directa del itali-
ano, por Ramón Lamas Lourido. Madrid, Editorial
Revista de Derecho Privado [1946–   ]. 2 v.
(Manuales de derecho, economia y hacienda. Ser.
G. Vol. XV)

379
Ceccoperio, Francesco. Lucubrationum canonical-
ium bibliotessera. Lucae, Pacius, 1662. 319 p.

380
Cevallos, Gerónimo de. Specvlvm avrevm opi-
nionvm commvnivm contra commvnes. In qvo non
tantvm octingentarvm quaestionum practicarum,
in iure canon. ciuili & regio repertarum resolutiones, ad contractus, vltimas voluntates, delicta &
iudicorum ordinem spectantes: sed etiam ex oppositione, diuersarum communium opinionum,
quaenam ex illis magis commvnis, & in foro receptior sit, ad viuum cernere licet. Tomi dvo. Cvm
privilegio. Venetiis, apud Societatem minimam,
1604. 2 v. in 1.

381
Cevallos, Gerónimo de. Specvlvm avrevm opi-
nionvm commvnivm contra commvnes. In qvo non
tantvm noningentarvm et sex quaestionum practicarum, in iure canonico, ciuili & regio, repertarum
resolvtiones ad contractus, vltimas voluntates, delicta & iudiciorum ordinem spectantes . . . sed etiam
ex oppositione, diuersarum communium opinionum, quaenam ex illis magis commvnis & in
foro receptior sit, cernere licet. Cum gemino indice
generali, vno quaestionum, altero rerum & materiarum copiosissimo. Tomi qvinqve. Antverpiae,
apud Keerbergivm, 1623. 5 v. in 3.

382

Champeaux, Gilbert de. Recueil general du droit civil ecclesiastique français. Paris [1952]. 2 v.

383

Chisilari, Francesco. De indice regularium tractatus. Venetiis. Somachus, 1613. 178 p.

384

Chodorow, Stanley. Christian political theory and church politics in the mid-twelfth century; the ecclesiology of Gratian's Decretum. Berkeley, University of California Press, 1972. 300 p.

385

Choppin, René. De sacra politia forensi libri III. Ad Henricvm III Galliarum & Poloniae regem. Cum indice verborum, rerumque locupletissimo. 3. ed. Parisiis, apud Sonnium, 1609. 644, [96] p.

386

Cicognani, Amleto G., cardinal. Canon law. Authorized English version by the Rev. Joseph M. O'Hara ... and the Rev. Francis Brennan. Philadelphia, The Dolphin Press, 1934. 887 p.
Includes bibliographies.

387

Cimetier, Francisque. Pour étudier le Code de droit canonique; introduction générale, bibliographie, réponses et décisiones, documents complémentaires, 1917–27. Paris, Gabalda, 1927. 245 p.
Includes bibliographies.

388

Ciprotti, Pio. Lezioni di diritto canonico, parte generale. Padova, CEDAM, 1943. 305 p.
Includes bibliographies.

389

Ciprotti, Pio. Observaciones al texto del Codex iuris canonici. 2. ed. refundida. [La traducción del italiano es de Tomás García Barberena] Salamanca, Consejo Superior de Investigaciones Científicas, Instituto "San Raimundo de Peñafort," 1950. 208 p.

390

Ciron, Innocent. Observationes ivris canonici in qvinqve libros digestas. Recensvit et dissertationem de vtilitate ex historia atqve antiqvitatibvs sacris in ivrisprvdentiae ecclesiasticae stvdio capienda praemisit Io. Salom. Brvnnqvell. Ienae, apvd Rittervm, 1726. 137 p.

391

Claro, Giulio. Receptarvm sententiarvm opera hactenus per eum in lucem edita. Cum eruditis D. Hieronymi Giacharii, Manfredi Goveani & Ioannis Gviotii clarissimorum jurisconsultorum notis & additionibus haud poenitendis. Accesserunt eiusdem D. H. Giacharii consilia seu responsa duo: primum de syndicatv, alterum de moneta marchisana multa eruditione referta ... Postrema ed. longè priobus auctior ac emendatior. Lvgdvni, apvd Harsy, 1600. 2 v. in 1.

392

Clercq, Carlo de. Fontes iuridici ecclesiarum orientalium. Studium historicum, Romae, Pont. Institum orientalium studiorum, 1967. 191 p.
Includes bibliographical references.

393

Cocchi, Guido, *ed.* Commentarium in Codicem iuris canonici ad usum scholarum. Taurinorum Augustae, ex officina libraria Marietti, 1931–[36]. [7] v.
"Elenchus scriptorum" at beginning of each volume.

394

El Código eclesiástico primitivo; o las leyes de la iglesia ... Traducción del italiano ... por un diputado a cortes. Madrid, de Burgos, 1822. 49 p.

395

Collectio Vetus Gallica. Kirchenrecht und Reform im Frankenreich: die collectio vetus Gallica: die älteste systematische Kanonessammlung des fränkischen Gallien: Studien und Edition/von Hubert Mordek. Berlin, New York, de Gruyter, 1975. 723 p. (Beiträge zur Geschichte und Quellenkunde des Mittelalters; Bd. 1)
Includes bibliographical references and indexes.

396

Conte, Matteo. Institutiones iuris canonici ad usum utriusque cleri et scholarum. Taurini (Italia) ex officina libraria Marietti, 1928–36. 5 v.

397

Conte, Matteo. Institutiones iuris canonici ad usum utriusque cleri et scholarum. De sacramentis tractatus canonicus. Ed. altera emendata et aucta. [Torino] Marietti [1951–   ].

398

Conte, Matteo. Interpretatio authentica codicis iuris canonici et circa ipsum sanctae sedis iurisprudentia 1916–1940. Taurini, Domus Editorialis Marietti, 1960. 452 p.

399

Contelori, Felix. Questiones duae: I. De praecedentia. II. De Societatibus officiorum. Lugduni, Durand, 1628. 131 p.

400

Conway, William. Problems in canon law: classified replies to practical questions. Dublin, Browne and Nolan [1956]. 345 p.

401

Conway, William. Problems in canon law: classified replies to practical questions. Westminster, Md., Newman Press [1957]. 345 p.

402

Corral Salvador, Carlos M. La noción metafísica del derecho en el Código de derecho canónico. Madrid, 1962. 64 p.
    Bibliography: p. [11]–17.

403

Corso, Rinaldo. De privata reconciliatione liber, qvi pridem Ethrvscvs, nvnc vero in lvcem Latinvs exit. Romae, apud A. Bladum impressorem cameralem, 1563. 26 l.

404

Corvinus, Arnoldus. Ivs canonicvm, per aphorismos strictim explicatumn. Amstelodami, apud Ludovic. Elzevirium, 1651. 380, [12] p.

405

Corvinus, Arnoldus. Ivs canonicvm per aphorismos strictim explicatum. Amstelodami, apud Iohannem Ianssonium, 1657. 380, [12] p.

406

Corvinus, Arnoldus. Jus canonicum, per aphoris-

mos strictim explicatum. Amstelodami, ex officina Elzeviriana, 1663. 362, [19] p.

407

Covarrubias y Leyva, Diego de, abp. Didaci Covarrvvias a Leyva Toletani . . . In quartum Decretalium librū epitome. Item in titul. de testament. & cōstit. Bonifacii VIII vltimā, quae incipit, Alma mater. de senten. excom. interpretatio. Lvgdvni, apud haeredes Iacobi Iuntae, 1558. 549, [1] p.

408

Covarrubias y Leyva, Diego de, abp. Omnia opera mvlto qvam privs emendatiora, ac multis in locis auctiora. Ad finem appositvs est rervm insignivm index vtriqve tomo communis, & locupletissimus. Ea vero omnia, qvae ab ipso avctore etiam pavlo ente obitum suum addita sunt, & hactenus typis mandata, in hac postrema omnium ed. comprehensa, & suis locis apposita, atque ideo nihil penitus deesse lector reperiet. Venetiis, apud haeredem H. Scoti, 1604. 2 v.

409

Crabbe, Pierre. Conciliorvm omnivm tam generalivm qvàm particvlarivm, qvae iam inde ab apostolis in hvnc vsqve diem celebrata, ex vetvstissimis diuersarum regionum bibliotheqis haberi potuerunt, in tres nunc tomos ob recentē multorum additionē diuisa, tomvs primvs[-tertivs] . . . Cvm indice novo copiosissimo. Coloniae Agrippinae, ex officina Ioannis Quentel, 1551. 3 v.

410

Criscito, Angelo. Diritto pubblico e diritto privato nell'ordinamento canonico. Torino [i.e. Torino] Giappichelli [1948]. 173 p.

411

Crivelli, Girolamo. Recitatio solemnis ad tris juris praecepta. Avenione, Bramerau, 1654. 38 p.

412

Croce, Giovanni della. Opera spirituali. Venetia, Brigna, 1683. 496 p.

413

Curtius, Rochus. Tractatus de jurepatronatus. Tractatus perutilis et q̊uotidian₉ de jurepatronat⁹ clarissimi vtriusq₃ censure doctoris dñi Rochi de Curte Papieñ. jura canonica ordinarie legētis in alma ticinensi academia: per eum editus: super rubrica de jurepatronatus: cum lectioni iuris canonici vespertine prefectus esset. Summarijs in hac vltima impressione cuilibet verbo prepositis. Tabulaq₃ singularis reposita est abundãtissime singulas materias: per totum hunc tractatum dispersas: complectens. [Lugduni] Vincentivs de Portonariis, 1532.

414

Czajka, Stanislaw. Bibljoteka katolickiego uniwersytetu lubelskiego wydzial prawa kanonicznego Nr. 7. Przedawnienie w prawie karnem kanonicznem. Lublin, [odbito czcionkami drukarni "Popularnej"] 1934. 192 p.

415

Dalhammer, Patritio. Canona rohrensis documentis, monumentis et observationibus historico-crotocis. Ratisbonae, Literis Johannis Michaelis Englerth, 1784.

416

Daoiz, Esteban. Juris pontificii summa, seu Index copiosus, continens conclusiones, ac summam omnium materiarum, quae exponuntur in textu, & glossis totius juris canonici, Concilii tridentini, in regulis cancellariae, & quibusdam bullis extravagantibus, maxima distinctione contextus. In hac editione accuratè recognitus, & emendatus. Mediolani, sumptibus Jo. Baptistae Cetti, 1745. 2 v.

417

Dausend, Hugo, pater. Das interrituelle Recht im Codex iuris canonici; die Bedeutung des Gesetzbuches für die orientalische Kirche. Paderborn, Schöningh, 1939. 189, [1] p. (Görres-gesellschaft. Veröffentlichungen der Sektion für Rechts- und Staatswissenschaft . . . 79. hft.)
"Quellen- und Literaturverzeichnis": p. [11]–16.

418

Decius, Philippus. Nova ac (per quam) solemnia commentaria super titu. decre. prelato c. j. de elec. de testibus de fi. instru. et de preben. . . . Colof. Lugduni, Io. Oylin alias Cambray, 1527.

419

Deeters, Walter, Die Bambergensisgruppe der Dekretalensammlungen des 12. Jhdts. [Bonn, 1956] 386 p.
Bibliography: p. 358–62.

420

Delvaux, André. Andreae Vallensis Paratitla juris canonici; sive Decretalium Gregorii Papae IX summaria ac methodica explicatio; opus, scholae ac fore, & decretis Concilii Tridentini accommodatum. Cui accesserat Annonis Schnorremberg commentarium in ejusdem juris regulas. Editio secunda Matritensis. [Madriti] Barco Lopez, 1796. 504, 131 p.

421

Delvaux, André. Andreae Vallensis vvlgo del Vavlx Andanensis . . . Paratitla ivris canonici, sive, Decretalivm d. Gregorii papae IX summaria ac methodica explicatio; opus nouum, scholae ac foro, & decretis Concilij Tridentini accommodatum. Sexta editio multò accuratiùs quàm antehac emendata, & necessarijs indicibus nunc demùm locupletata. Lvgdvni, sumptibus Anisson & Devenet, 1658. 688, [20] p.

422

Derecho canónico. [Alberto Bernárdez Cantón et al.] 2. ed. Pamplona, EUNSA [1975]. 811 p. (Colección Canónica de la Universidad de Navarra: Manuales)
Includes bibliographies.

This book, intended for law students and those who are interested in the subject by reason of their profession or culture, offers a general view of canon law by several outstanding Spanish professors. The authors in this collection cover not only the traditional and accepted doctrine but also problems being debated currently and canon law's prospects for the immediate future. The work opens with a comprehensive bibliography covering different topics within the discipline and then proceeds with an analysis of canon law and its relationship to civil law; the structure of canonical legislation; the constitution of the Church; theory and analysis of ecclesiastical magistery; various aspects of canonical marriage, as well as its dissolution and the separation of spouses; penal canon law; procedural canon law; evolution of the doctrines on the relationship between Church and State; and finally, elements of Spanish ecclesiastical law.

423

Des Graviers, Jean. Le droit canonique. 2. ed. mise

à jour. Paris, Presses univeristaires de France, 1967. 128 p. (Que sais-je? No. 779)
Bibliography: p. [127]

424
Desing, Amsel. Spiritus legum bellus, an & solidus? disquisitio. Nolite omni spiritui credere. X. Joan. IV v. L. Pedeponti, Gastl, 1752. 2 v. in 1.

425
Deusdedit, cardinal. Die Kanonessammlung des Kardinals Deusdedit. 1. ⟨einziger⟩ Band: Die Kanonessammlung selbst. Neu hrsg. von Victor Wolf von Glanvell. Mit 3 Tafeln. Neudruck der Ausg. Paderborn 1905. Aalen, Scientia-Verlag, 1967. 656 p.

426
Devoti, Giovanni, abp. Instituciones canónicas de Juan Devoti ... puestas en castellano y reducidas puramente a la parte doctrinal, en beneficio de los jóvenes que se dedican al estudio del derecho canónico. Nueva ed., revista, corregida y sumentada con notas secadas del mismo autor y de otros. Paris, Libreria de Rosa y Bouret, 1862. 404 p.

427
Devoti, Giovanni, abp. Institutionum canonicarum libri IV. Matriti, ex Typographia Regia, 1833. 2 v.

428
Devoti, Giovanni, abp. Institutionum canonicarum libri IV. 3. ed. Gandensis. Gandae, Vander Schelden, 1836–

429
Devoti, Giovanni, abp. De notissimis in jure legibus libri duo. Accedunt adv. Gregorii Fierli observationes practicae ad Curiam florentinam praesertim accomodatae. Aeditio altera locupletior. Florentiae, ex typographia Bonducciana, 1796. 279 p.

430
Diaconia et ius; Festgabe für Heinrich Flatten zum 65. Geburtstag, dargebracht von seinen Freunden und Schülern. Hrsg. von Heribert Heinemann, Horst Herrmann [und] Paul Mikat. München, Schöningh, 1973. 419 p.
Includes bibliographical references.

431
Diana, Antonino. Coordinati; seu, Omnium reso-

lutionum moralium, ejus ipsissimis verbis ad propria loca, & materias, per v. p. Martinum de Alcolea ... fideliter dispositarum, tomus puimus–[decimus]. Editio novissima, mvltis in locis avcta, & à quampluribus, quibus caeterae scatebant erroribus, purgata; cui de novo accessit tomus decimus, veluti totius operis summa. Venetiis, apud Balleonium, 1698. 10 v.
"Syllabus authorum": v. 1, 23d–26th prelim. leaves.

432
Dinus de Rossonibus, de Mugello. Commentarii in regulas iuris pontificij: cum additionibus Nicolae Boerii ... aliorúmque doctissimorum iurisconsultorum: iam quartò & vltimò studio & industria C. M. iurisconsulti & clarissimi aduocati accuratissimè recogniti, natiuae integritati, suóque nitori restituti, ac multis in locis eiusdem annotationibus analyticis illustrati & locupletati, vt nihil penitus ad eorum splendorem possit desiderari. Cvm indice rervm et verborum locupletissimo. Lvgdvni, apud Bartholomaeum Vincentium, 1577. 328 p.

433
Dinus. de Rossonibus, de Mugello. Commentarius in regulas iuris pontificii. Coloniae Agrippinae, Baum, 1578. 479 p.

434
Dinus de Rossonibus, de Mugello. De reg[ulis] iur[is] Commentarius mirabilis super titulo De regulis iuris Dyni Muxellani, multo plus q̆₃ vnq̆₃ annotationibus auctus & recognitus. Vbi preter Nicolai Boerij et Celsi Hugonis additiones, multa nouissime per doctorem anonymum sunt addita, pleraq₃ deprauata in hac vltima impressione restituta. Ludg., Venundantur p Iacobū Giuncti, 1537.
Includes text of the title De regulis iuris from Liber Sextus Decretalium.

435
Dodd, Joseph. A history of canon law in conjunction with other branches of jurisprudence: with chapters on the royal supremacy and the report of the Commission on ecclesiastical courts. London, Parker and Co., 1884. 278 p.

436
Donoso, Justo, bp. Derecho público eclesiástico. (En 40 lecciones.) Para el uso de las universidades, academias i seminarios de la república. 2. ed.

notablemente aumentada i mejorada. Cochabamba, Imprenta del Siglo, 1873. 217 p.

437

Donoso, Justo, bp. Instituciones de derecho canónico. 3 ed., corr. y completada con las más recientes disposiciones canónicas, por Carlos Silva Cotapos. Friburgo de Brisgovia (Alemania) San Luis [etc.], Herder, 1909. 715 p.

438

Donoso, Justo, bp. Instituciones de derecho canónico americano, para el uso de los colejios en las repúblicas de la América española. Valparaiso, Imprenta y Librería del Mercurio, 1848–49. 2 v.

439

Donoso, Justo, bp. Instituciones de derecho canónico americano, para el uso de los colegios de las repúblicas americanas. Nueva edición. Paris, Rosa y Bouret, 1854. 3 v.

440

Donoso, Justo, bp. Instituciones de derecho canónico americano, para el uso de los colegios en las repúblicas americanas. Nueva ed. Paris, Rosa y Bouret, 1868. 3 v.

441

Donoso, Justo D. Instituciones de derecho canónico americano. Paris, Librería de Rosa, Bouret y Cie., 1852.

442

Doskocil, Walter. Der Bann in der Urkirche; eine rechtsgeschichtliche Untersuchung. München, Kommissionsverlag K. Zink, 1958. 220 p. (Münchener theologische Studien. III. Kanonistische Abt., 11 Bd.)

443

Doujet, Jean. Specimen juris ecclesiastici apud Gallos usu recepti. Paris, Alliot, 1671. 2 v. in 1.

444

Duardo, Leonardo. Commentaria in extravag. Pii Papae Qvinti, de cambiis. In quibus tota cambiorum materia facilè, ac exactissimè traditur. Additis quamplurimis casibus, per Sacram Congregationem à S. D. N. D. Vrbano Papa VIII ad id specialiter deputatam, nouissime resolutis. Cum duplici indice qq. & materiarum copiosissimo. Nae-

poli [sic], apud Octauium Beltranum impress., 1641. 311 p.

445

Duardo, Leonardo. Commentariorvm in extravag. Pii Papae v. de forma creandi censvs. [Genevae] Ex Typographia I. Stoer, 1635. 2 v. in 1.

446

Du Moulin, Charles. In regulas cancellariae romanae hactenus in regno Franciae vsv receptas commentarivs analyticvs ... Quae huic editioni praeter accesserunt, sequens pagina indicabit. Cum indice et summariis locupletissimis. Parisiis, apud Sevestre, 1608. 844, [34] p.

447

Duprat, Pardoux. Lexicon ivris civilis et canonici: sive potivs, commentarivs de verborvm quae ad vtrumque ius pertinent significatione, antiquitatum romanarum elementis, & legum pop. rom. copiosissimo indice, adauctus: abhinc septem annis Pardulphi Prateij diligentia delineatus: nunc verò ita constructus, & supra omnes omnium editiones, tot tamque praeclaris & graecis & latinis dictionibus illustratus, vt parum ad eius eximium splendorem desiderari possit. Quid praeterea in hac secunda editione praestitū sit, epistola ad lectorem docebit. Lvgdvni, apvd Gulielmvm Rovillivm, 1574. 638 p.

448

Duranti, Jean É. Qvaestiones notatissimae, ex vtroque iure decisae, & in suprema Tholosani Senatus curia collectae; quarum nonnullae iam antea quidem in lucem editae, nunc autem ex cod. ms. ab omni labe emaculatae, & LXXIX quaestionibus, quae priùs deerant, auctae. His adduntur notae, siue dissertationes Iacobi Ferrerii ... Cum summariis, & duplici indice, vno quaestionum, altero rerum singularium locupletissimo. Studio & operâ Io. Fehii. Lvgdvni, Charlot, 1624. 403, [27] p.

449

Duranti, Jo. Stephan. Questiones notatissimae ex utroque iure decisae, et in suprema Tholosani Senatus Curia collecta. Lugduni, Charlot. 1624.

450

Durantis, Gulielmus, bp. of Mende. Prochiron, vvlgo rationale divinorvm officiorvm. . . . Opus iam recens diligenti fidelique opera castigatum, adnotationibus illustratum. . . . Adhaec summa rerum

& vocum capita nunc primum adiecta, cum indice duplici. Lvgdvni, Haeredes Iacobi Giuntae [excvdebat Theobaldvs Paganvs], 1551. 296 1.

451

Ebenstein, William. La teoría pura del derecho, versión directa de J. Malagón y A. Pereña. [1. ed. en español] México, Fondo de Cultura Económica [1947]. 241 p. (Sección de obras de ciencia política [del Fondo de Cultura Económica])

452

Ebers, Godehard J. Grundriss des katholischen Kirchenrechts; Rechtsgeschichte und System. Wien, Manz, 1950. 479 p.
Bibliography: p. [xiii]–xv.

453

Ecclesia et ius; Festgabe für Audomar Scheuermann zum 60. Geburtstag. Dargebracht von seinen Freunden und Schülern. Hrsg. von Karl Siepen, Joseph Weitzel und Paul Wirth. München, Schöningh, 1968. 784 p.
Bibliographical footnotes.

454

Eck, Cornelii van. Epistola ad amicum de praefatione, quam suis dissertationibus juridico-theologicus. Franequerae, apud Amama et Taedama, 1688. 45 p.

455

Eck, Cornelii van. Vindiciae juris academici. Franequerae, apud Amama et Taedama, 1688. 129 p.

456

Eichmann, Eduard, Lehrbuch des Kirchenrechts auf Grund des Codex juris canonici, für Studierende. Paderborn, Schöningh, 1923. 752 p. (Added t.-p.: Wissenschaftliche Handbibliothek, 1 reihe. Theologische Lehrbücher, XXXIV)
"Literatur": p.22–23, and in footnotes.

457

Eichmann, Eduard. Lehrbuch des Kirchenrechts auf Grund des Codex iuris canonici . . . 4. verb. und verm. Aufl. Paderborn, Schöningh, 1934. 2 v. (Added t.-p.: Wissenschaftliche Handbibliothek, eine Sammlung theologischer Lehrbücher)
"Literatur": v. 1, p. 42–44.

458

Eichmann, Eduard. Lehrbuch des Kirchenrechts auf Grund des Codex iuris canonici. Neu bearb. bon Klaus Mörsdorf. Völlig veränderte 6. Aufl. Paderborn, Schöningh, 1950. 3 v. (Wissenschaftliche Handbibliothek)
Bibliography: v. 1, p. 41–43.

459

Eichmann, Eduard. Lehrbuch des Kirchenrechts auf Grund des Codex iuris canonici. Neu bearb. und hrsg. von Klaus Mörsdorf. 7. verb. und verm. Aufl. Paderborn, Schöningh, 1953–54. 3 v. (Wissenschaftliche Handbibliothek; eine Sammlung theologischer Lehrbücher)
Bibliography: v. 1, p. 40–53.

460

Eichmann, Eduard. Lehrbuch des Kirchenrechts auf Grund des Codex iuris canonici. Neu bearb. und hrsg. von Klaus Mörsdorf. 9. verb. Aufl. Paderborn, Schöningh [1959–   ]. (Wissenschaftliche Handbibliothek; eine Sammlung theologischer Lehrbücher)
Includes bibliography.

461

Eichmann, Eduard. Lehrbuch des Kirchenrechts auf Grund des Codex iuris canonici . . . fortgeführt von Klaus Mörsdorf. 11. verb. und verm. Aufl. München, Schöningh [1964–   ]. (Wissenschaftliche Handbibliothek)
Bibliography: v. 1, p. 39–42.

462

Eichmann, Eduard. Manual de derecho eclesiástico, a tenor del Codex juris canonici . . . Traducción de la 3. edición alemana, por T. Gómez Piñán. Barcelona, Librería Bosch, 1931. 2 v.
"Bibliografía": t. I, p. 24–25.

463

Elías de Molins, Antonio. Legislación canónica, civil y administrativa vigente en España y sus posesiones de ultramar sobre cementerios. Madrid, Suarez [188?]. 310 p.

464

Elroy Ramírez, Guillermo. Derecho eclesiástico conforme al nuevo código. Trujillo, Impr. Comercial-Loyer Hoyle, 1922. 409 p.

465

Engel, Ludovico. Collegium universi juris canonici . . . nunc vero servato ordine Decretalium accuratius translatum, et indice copioso locupletatum. Editio quinta. Venetiis, apud Michaelem Hertz, 1718.

466

Engel, Ludwig. Collegium universi juris canonici, ante hac juxta triplex juris objectum partitum. Nunc vero servato ordine decretalium accuratius translatum, et indice copioso locupletatum. Omnibus tam in foro quàm in scholis apprimè utile, ac necessarium. Ed. 6. cui accessit ejusdem authoris Tractatus de privilegiis monasteriorum. Venetiis, apud Giavarina, 1723. 527 p.

467

Engel, Ludwig. Collegium universi juris canonici antehac juxta triplex juris objectum partitum; nunc verò servato ordine decretalium accuratius translatum & indice copioso locupletatum, omnibus tam in foro, quam in scholis apprimè utile, ac necessarium. Ed. 7. prioribus longè accuratior, cui praeter Tractatum de privilegiis monasteriorum novissimè accessit aureus liber ejusdem auctoris, qui inscribitur Manuale parochorum. Venetiis, apud Bettinelli, 1733. 2. v. in 1.

468

Engel, Ludwig. Jvs canonicvm, pars I[–V]. Vindobonae, typis Joannis Thomae Trattner, 1761. 3 v.

469

Eppler, Hans. Quelle und Fassung katholischen Kirchenrechts; mit einem Anhang über seinen zeitlichen Geltungsbereich. Zürich und Leipzig, Füssli, 1928. 181 p.
"Literatur": p. xiii–xix.

470

Escobar, D. Joannes. A corro U. J. D. . . . Tractatus prior, de utroque foro. Lugduni, apud Fratres Deville, 1737. 2 v.

471

Escobar, D. Joannes. Tractatus bipartitus de puritate et nobilitate probanda, secundum statuta S. officii inquisitionis regii ordinum senatus. Editio novo. Lugduni, Fratrum de Tournes, 1761. 448 p.

472

Espen, Zeger B. van. Commentarius in canones et decreta juris veteris ac novi et in jus novissimum, opus posthumum. . . . Lovanii, sumptibus Societatis, 1759. 620 p.

473

Espen, Zeger B. van. Commentarius in canones juris veteris ac novi et in jus novissimum opus posthumum. Coloniae Agrippinae, sumptibus et typis viduae Francisci Wilhelmi Metternich, 1777.

474

Espen, Zeger B. van. Jus ecclesiasticum in epitomen redactum a. d. p. Benedicto Oberhauser . . . additis brevibus ss. patrum sententiis, aliisque ad novissimos mores, ac praxin spectantibus. Bassani, prostant Venetiis apud Remondini, 1784–

475

Espen, Zeger B. van. Jus ecclesiasticum universum. Coloniae Agrippinae, sumptibus et typis viduae Francisci Wilhelmi Metternich, 1777. 5 v.

476

Espen, Zeger B. van. Jus ecclesiasticum universum caeteraque scripta omnia . . . Editio recentissima omnibus anteactis longe praestantior, & nitidior, plurimis tractatibus hactenus ineditis, litteris, & monumentis passim suo loco positis, praesertim vero selectis adnotationibus. Venetiis, ex typographia Joannis Gatti, 1781–82. 10 v. in 5.

477

Espen, Zeger B. van. Jus ecclesiasticum universum hodiernae disciplinae accommodatum. Ex ipsis Sacrae Scripturae litteris, SS. canonibus, conciliorum, tum oecumenicorum, tum synodalium decretis, pontificum rescriptis, SS. patrum sententiis, principum edictis, & magistratûs tàm ecclesiastici, quam civilis judicatis depromptum . . . In hac editione, prima hispana, suo loco inserta reperientur supplementa, quae in aliis ad calcem operis apposita erant, & notantur hoc signo*, opera et studio licent. d. Francisci Mariae Vallarna. Matriti, in typographia regía, vulgò de la Gazeta, 1778. 3 v.

In this three-volume treatise on the entire body of ecclesiastical law, Espen presents a synthesis of ancient and modern Church law, indicating when, on what occasion, and to what degree changes have occurred. He offers not only an exegesis of the provisions, but also the history of the Church vis-á-vis its legislation. The author develops several themes: the use of ancient discipline and the method of its assimilation into more modern customs; the authority of the Decree of Gratian; the intention of Pope Gregory IX in ordering a collection of the Decretals; the place of the other collections in the *Corpus Juris Canonici;* and the contribution of the Council of Trent (1545–1563) and the local synods. The first part of the treatise is devoted to persons; the second, to things; the third, to trials, crimes, and punishments; the fourth, to such subjects as simony, the office of the canons, and dispensations; and the fifth is a historico-canonical treatise on the canons of Greek and Latin councils which were approved by both churches, and on the best known codes or collections of old and recent canons.

478

Espen, Zeger B. van. Jus ecclesiasticum universum hodiernae disciplinae accommodatum. Ex ipsis Sacrae Scripturae litteris, SS. canonibus, conciliorum, tum oecurenicorum, tum synodalium decretis, pontificum rescriptis, SS. patrum sententiis, principum edictis, & magistratus tam ecclesiastici, quam civilis judicatis depromptum. Opus, in quinque partes distributum . . . 2 ed. Hispana priori accuratior & mendis quamplurimis, quae in prima passim occurrunt, praecipue in indicibus, diligenter expurgata. In ea aeque ac in prima studio & cura Francisci Mariae Vallarna facta, quae in aliis ad calcem operis apposita erant supplementa, suo loco inserta reperientur, & notantur hoc signo*. Matriti, in typographia Ruiz, 1791, 3 v.

479

Espen, Zeger B. van. Jus ecclesiasticum universum hodiernae disciplinae, praesertim Belgii, Galliae, German, et vicinarum provinciarum accommodatum . . . Editio in Germania secunda, Belgicâ venustior & gallici idiomatis in latinum subjecta versione, ut & monumentis ab authore in fine tantùm appositis suis nunc classibus insertis commodior reddita. Coloniae Agrippinae, sumptibus Wilhelmi Metternich, 1715. 3 v. in 2.

480

Espen, Zeger B. van. Operum quae hactenus in lucem prodierunt, pars prima[-sexta]. Lovanii, sumptibus Societatis, 1732. 6 v. in 3.

481

Espen, Zeger B. van. Supplementum ad varias collectiones operum clar. viri Zegeri Bernardi Van-Espen, J. U. D. et SS. canonum professoris in academia Lovaniensi. Coloniae Agrippinae, Viduae Francisci Wilhelmi Metternich, 1777.

482

Espen, Zeger B. van. Tractatus historico-canonicvs exhibens scholia in omnes canones conciliorum, tam graecos, quam latinos, unanimi utriusque ecclesiae graecae & latinae consensu probatos. . . . Coloniae, Metternich, 1709. 195 p.

483

Estratto delle fonti vigenti di diritto canonico. Bari, Cacucci, 1972. 203 p.

484

Études de droit et d'histoire: mélanges Mgr. H. Wagnon. Leuven, Bibliothèque centrale de l'U. C. L., 1976. 680 p.
Includes bibliographical references.

485

Études d'histoire du droit canonique, dediées à Gabriel Le Bras, doyen honoraire de la Faculté de droit et de sciences économiques de Paris, membre de l'Institut. Paris, Sirey, 1965. 2 v. (1491 p.)
"Bibliographie des travaux de Gabriel Le Bras": v. 1, p. [ix]–xxxiii.

486

Fagnani, Prospero. Jus canonicum: sive commentaria absolutissima in V libros Decretales, cum indice. Coloniae Agrippinae, Widenfelt, 1681. 2 v. in 1.

487

Falco, Mario. Introduzione allo studio del "Codex iuris canonici." Torino, Fratelli Bocca, 1925. 326 p.
Bibliography: p. [xix].

488

Falenciak, Jerzy. Studia nad prawem rzymsko-kanonicznym w "Księdze henrykowskiej." [Wyd. 1.]

Wrocław, Zakład Narodowy im. Ossolińskich, 1966. 74 p. (Monografie Śląskie Ossolineum, 11)
Bibliography: p. [68]–71.

489

Fargna, Francesco de. Commentaria in singulos canones de jurepatronatus, qui sparsim tam intrà, quàm extra Corpus juris canonici vagantur . . . Et quibus accedunt quamplures decisiones Sacrae Rotae Romanae nullibi adhuc impressae, & recentissima decreta Sacrae Congregationis concilii, unà cum votis auctoris in causis in eadem Sacra Congregatione ventilatis, & ad materiam jurispatronatus spectantibus. Montisfalisci, ex typographia Seminarii, 1717–19. 3 v.

490

Farinacci, Prospero. Tractatvs de haeresi. In qvo per qvaestiones, regvlas, ampliationes, & limitationes; quid à iure ciuili, & canonico; quid à sacris concilijs, summorumq́. pontifcum constitutionibus statutum; quid verius, 7 magis communiter in hac materia receptum sit; et quid demum in practica seruetur, solito authoris ordine explicatur. In hac postrema editione a mvltis mendis, quibus scatebat, expurgatus. Cvm argvmentis, svmmariis, et indice locvpletissimo. Ad Pavlvm V pont. opt. max. Cvm priviliegiis. Venetiis, apud Ioannem, & Variscum Variscos, 1620. 63 p. 1., 456 p.

491

Febei, Francesco A. Institvtionvm ivris canonici, sive, Primorum totius sacrae iurisprudentiae elementorum libri qvatvor. Romae, Corbelletti, 1698. 640 p.

492

Fedele, Pio. Discorso generale sull'ordinamento canonico. Padova, CEDAM, 1941. 170 p.
"Estratto da Annali della Facoltà di giurisprudenza della R. Università di Perugia, vol. LV, 1941, serie VI, vol. VI."

493

Feine, Hans E. A. Kirchliche Rechtsgeschichte. 1. Bd. Die Katholische Kirche. 2. durchgearb. und ergänzte Aufl. Weimar, H. Böhlaus Nachf., 1954. 715 p.
Includes bibliographies.

494

Feine, Hans E. A. Kirchliche Rechtsgeschichte. 1. Bd. Die Katholische Kirche. 3. unveränderte, aber durch einen Nachtrag ergänzte Aufl. Weimar, Böhlaus Nachfolder, 1955. 722 p.
Includes bibliographies.

495

Feine, Hans E. A. Kirchliche Rechtsgeschichte, auf der Grundlage des Kirchenrechts von Ulrich Stutz. 1. Bd. Die Katholische Kirche. Weimar, Böhlaus Nachfolger, 1950. 662 p.
Includes bibliographies.

496

Feine, Hans E. A. Kirchliche Rechtsgeschichte; die katholische Kirche. 5., durchgesehene Aufl. Köln, Böhlau, 1972. 788 p.
Includes bibliographies.

497

Feliciani, Giorgio. L'analogia nell'ordinamento canonico. Milano, Giuffrè, 1968. 235 p.
Bibliographical footnotes.

498

Feloaga y Ozcoide, Antonio. Ex temporaria, sed florulenta, ac matura relectio ad Alexand. III in cap. 1. De ijs quae vi metusvè causa fiunt . . . Pro obtinenda primaria decretalium cathedra. Salmanticae, Tabernier, 1638. 20 p.

499

Fermosinius, Nicolas R. Tractatus III, tomus I, de probationibus, ad titulum VII, libri II de Decretalium Gregorii Pontificis IX . . . Nunc primum in lucem prodit. Lugduni, sumptibus Boissat & Remeus, 1662. 427 p.

500

Fermosinius, Nicholas R. Tractatus XV . . . ad lib. II Decretalium Gregorii Pontificis IX . . . Nunc primum prodit. Lugduni, Borde, Arnaud & Rigaud, 1657. 642 p.

501

Fernández y Concha, Rafael. Derecho público eclesiástico. Santiago de Chile, Imprenta del Correo, 1872. 2 v.

502
Fernández y Concha, Rafael. Derecho público eclesiástico. 2. ed. aum. y corr. Santiago de Chile, Perez L., 1894. 2 v.

503
Ferraris, Lucius. Bibliotheca canonica iuridica moralis theologica nec non ascetica polemica rubricistica historica. Ed. novissima mendis expurgata et novis additamentis locupletata. Romae, ex typ. polyglotta S. C. de Propaganda fide, 1885–99. 9 v.

504
Ferraris, Luicius. Prompta bibliotheca canonica, juridica, moralis, theologica nec non ascetica, polemica, rubricistica, historica de principalioribus, & fere omnibus, quae in dies occurrunt, nec penes omnes facile, ac prompte reperiri possunt, ex utroque jure, summorum pontificum constitutionibus . . . ac probatissimis et selectissimis auctoribus accurate collecta, adaucta, in unum redacta, & ordíne alphabetico congesta, ac in octo tomos distributa. Post plures italicas editio postrema absolutissima . . . r. p. Philippi a Carboneano . . . notis criticis; nec non supplementis & additionibus luculentissimis a clariss. anonymo jurisconsulto romano hactenus, in lucem editis . . . illustrata . . . Adduntur auctoris vindiciae in easdem notas, & additiones, una cum indice generali accuratissimo. Romae, curis et sumptibus Societatis Venetae, 1766. 8 v.

505
Ferraris, Lucius. Prompta bibliotheca canonica, juridica, moralis, theologica nec non ascetica, polemica, rubricistica, historica de principalioribus, & fere omnibus, quae in dies occurrunt, nec penes omnes facile, ac prompte reperiri possunt, ex utroque jure, summorum pontificum constitutionibus . . . ac probatissimis et selectissimis auctoribus accurate collecta, adaucta, in unum redacta, & ordíne alphabetico congesta, atque in decem tomos distributa. Post plures italicas editio postrema absolutissima . . . r. p. Philippi a Carboneano . . . notis criticis; nec non supplementis & additionibus luculentissimis a clariss. anonymo jurisconsulto romano hactenus in lucem editis . . . illustrata . . . Adduntur auctoris vindiciae in easdem notas, & additiones, una cum indice generali accuratissimo. Romae, Typis modesti Fentii, 1778. 3 v.

506
Ferraris, Lucius. Prompta bibliotheca canonica, juridica, moralis, theologica nec non ascetica, polemica, rubricistica, historica de principalioribus, & fere omnibus, quae in dies occurrunt, nec penes omnes facile, ac prompte reperiri possunt, ex utroque jure, pontificiis constitutionibus. Sacrae Romanae Rotae Decisionibus ac probatissimis et selectissimis auctoribus accurate collecta, adaucta, in unum redacta, & ordine alphabetico congesta, ac in octo tomos distributa. Editio novissima. Locupletior adjecto quoque indice materiarum absolutissimo. Hagae, apud van Duren, 1781–84.

507
Ferraris, Lucius. Prompta bibliotheca canonica, juridica, moralis, theologica, nec non ascetica, polemica, rubricistica, historica. Editio novissima, mendis expurgata . . . opera et studio monachorum ordinis sancti Benedicti . . . abbattiae Montis Casini. Romae, Frid. Lampato, 1844–55. 7 v.

508
Ferraris, Lucius. Prompta bibliotheca canonica, juridica, moralis, theologica, nec non ascetica, polemica, rubricistica, historica. Editio novissima, mendis expurgata . . . opera et studio monachorum ordinis sancti Benedicti, abbattiae Montis Casini . . . accurante rursum et innumeris notis necnon sextuplici indice . . . locupletante J.-P. Migne. Petit-Montrouge [Paris], Migne, 1858. 8 v.
"Index biographicus et bibliographicus auctorum qui in L. Ferraris Bibliotheca referuntur": v. 8, col. 563–704.

509
Ferrière, Claude de. Institutiones iuris canonici, nova et singulari methodo contextae. Parisiis, apud Saugrain Patrem, 1732. 119 p.

510
Flatten, Heinrich. Der Häresieverdacht im Codex iuris canonici. Amsterdam, Schippers, 1963. 338 p. (Kanonistische Studien und Texte, Bd. 21)
Bibliography: p. 11–23.

511
Fleiner, Fritz. Ueber die Entwicklung des katholischen Kirchenrechts im 19. Jahrhundert; Rektoratsrede gehalten am Jahresfeste der Universität

Basel, den 8. November 1901. Tübingen, Mohr, 1902. 31 p.

512

Fleury, Claude. Institutiones juris ecclesiastici, quas latinas reddidit, cum animadversionibus Justi Henningii Boehmeri edidit Joannes Daniel Gruber ... Accedit praefatio altera, ac criticae in notas animadversisones, quibus heteradoxorum praejudicia indicantur, ac dirimuntur. Editio quarta. Lipsiae, apud Ernest Gottl. Crugium, et prostant Venetiis, apud Antonium Zatta, 1762. 255 p.

513

Florent, François. Opera juridica studio J. Doujati antecessoris Parisensis collecta. Venetiis, Typ. Balleoniana, 1763. 366 p.

514

Florez Díaz de Mena, Blasius. Recentiorem practicarvm qvaestionvm ivris canonici, et civilis, ad praxim vtriusque fori spectantium. Libri tres. ... Opvs ... cum duplici indice quaestionum & materiarum summarijs. Metinae à Campi, apud Ioannem Godinez de Millis, expensis Martini á Corduua bibliopolae, 1603.

515

Foerster, Hans. Dionysius Exiguus-Studien; neue Wege der philologischen und historischen Text- und Quellenkritik. Berlin, De Gruyter, 1960. 533 p. (Arbeiten zur Kirchengeschichte, 33)
  "Siglenverzeichnis": p. [xi]–xvi.

516

Fogliasso, Emilio. Il ius publicum ecclesiasticum e il Concilio ecumenico vaticano II. Come si giunse agli odierni trattati di ius publicum ecclesiasticum. Incidenza del Concilio vaticano II sulla scienza del ius publicum ecclesiasticum. Torino, Società editrice internazionale, 1968. 123 p. (Biblioteca del "Salesianum," 75)
  Includes bibliographical references.

517

Fonseca, Cosimo D. Medioevo canonicale. Milano, Vita e pensiero, 1970. 213 p. (Pubblicazioni dell'Università cattolica del Sacro Cuore. Contributi. Ser. 3: Scienze storiche, 12)
  Includes bibliographical references.

This work is of particular interest to students willing to analyze the canonical experience in the framework of the great institutional, social, religious, and spiritual components of "Christian society" in the eleventh and twelfth centuries. The first part is devoted to the formation of the historical canonical conscience through jurisdictional and historiographical polemics. Some of these controversies have a local flavor, and others are more ecumenical in nature, for instance, the "canonical question" between the Councils of Constance and Trent. The second part discusses the contribution to the *corpus* of canonical customs in Italy. An appendix with a commentary on several documents, and indexes of names, codes, and tables close the work.

518

Fontoura, Ezechias G. da. Lições de direito ecclesiastico. Vol. III. São Paulo, Jorge Seckler & Co., 1887. 225 p.

519

Fournier, Édouard. Questions d'histoire du droit canonique. Extraits du cours professé à l'Institut catholique de Paris (année scolaire 1935–36). Paris, Recueil Sirey, 1936. 46 p.

520

Fournier, Paul E. L. Histoire des collections canoniques en Occident depuis les Fausses décrétales jusqu'au Décret de Gratien. Paris, Recueil Sirey, 1931–32. 2 v. (Bibliothèqve d'histoire dv droit, pvbliée sovs les avspices de la Société d'histoire dv droit)

521

Fournier, Paul E. L., and Gabriel Le Bras. Histoire des collections canoniques en Occident: depuis les fausses décrétales jusqu'au Décret de Gratien. Aalen, Scientia-Verlag, 1972. 2 v.
  Bibliography: v. 1, p. [xi]–xv.

522

Franchis, Philipp de. Ad titv. De appella. in volv. Gregor. commentarij elegantissimi argumentis (Summaris vocant) indice locupletissimo, scholijsq́ nouissimè illustrati in lucem emendatiùs quàm anteà prodeunt in pontificii ac caesarei iuris studiosorum gratiam. Lvgdvni, apud haeredes Iacobi Giuntae, 1548. 103 l.

523

Francisco de Vitoria. Relecciones teológicas, edición crítica, con facsímil de códices y ediciones príncipes, variantes, versión castellana, notas e introd. por Luis G. Alonso Getino. [Madrid, Impr. La Rafa] 1933–35. 3 v. (Publicaciones de la Asociación Francisco de Vitoria)

524

Franck, Ad. Philosophie du droit ecclésiastique. Des Rapports de la religion et de l'état. Paris, Germer Baillière, 1864. 192 p.

525

Frantz, Adolph. Lehrbuch des Kirchenrechts. Göttingen, Vandenhoeck und Ruprecht, 1887. 322 p.

526

Friedberg, Emil. Die Canones-Sammlungen zwischen Gratian und Bernhard von Pavia. Leipzig, Tauchnitz, 1897.

527

Friedberg, Emil. Decan und die übrigen Ordentlichen Professoren der Juristischen Facultät verkündigen die feier des andenkens an Hofrath Christian Friedrich Kees . . . Die allgemeine Rechtliche Stellung der Evangelischen Kirche zum Staats. Leipzig, Alexander Edelmann [1887]. 35 p.

528

Friedberg, Emil. Herrn Gustav Friedrich Hänel . . . zur Feier seines Sechzigjährigen Doctorjubiläums am 18 April 1876. Überreicht von der Juristenfaculatät zu Leipzig. Eine Neue Kritische Ausgabe des corpus iuris canonici. Leipzig, Alexander Edelmann [1876]. 39 p.

529

Friedberg, Emil. Die Juristische Facultät der Universität Leipzig verkündigt die feier des andenkens an Dr. Bernh. Friedr. Rud. Lauhn . . . Ueber Meine Ausgabe der quinque compilationes antiquae. Eroerterungen ueber die Entstehungszeit des decretum Gratiani. Leipzig, Druck von Alexander Edelmann [1882]. 17 p.

530

Friedberg, Emil. Die Juristische Fakultät der Universität Leipzig verkündigt die feier des andenkens

an Dr. Christian Friedrich Kees . . . Ueber Meine Neue Ausgabe der Decretalen-Sammlungen und der quinque compilationes antiquae. Leipzig, Alexander Edelmann [1882]. 46 p.

531

Friedberg, Emil A. Trattato del diritto ecclesiastico cattolico ed evangelico . . . Ed. italiana, riveduta in collaborazione con l'autore ed ampiamente annotata per rispetto al diritto italiano dall' avv. Francesco Ruffini. Torino [etc.], Fratelli Bocca, 1893. 864 p.

"Elenco delle opere tedesche citate nel volume": p. [836]–864.

532

Fumus, Batholomaeus. Aurea armillâ Bartholomei Fumi villaurensis placen. ord. praed. ac haereticae pravitatis inquisitoris. Opus vere aurem continens breviter, ac summatim, quaecunque in iure Canonico . . . sparsimque tractantur. Venetiis, apud Altobellum Salicatium, 1596. 524 p.

533

Fusco, Paolo. In ivre caesareo atqve pontificio, ad svbtiliores qvaestiones, ac freqventiores, qvae in foro versantur causas, tam veterum quam recentiorum iurisconsultorum sententiis receptissimis comprobata . . . Item Gomezii Leonii . . . decisionvm singvlarivm et conclvsionvm centvria vna. Francofvrti ad Moenvm, typis Matthaei Beckeri, sumptibus Ioannis Theobaldi Schönvvetteri, 1600. 644, [23] p.

534

The Future of canon law. Edited by Neophytos Edelby, Teodoro Jiménez-Urresti [and] Petrus Huizing. New York, Paulist Press [1969]. 180 p. (Concilium: theology in the age of renewal. Canon law, v. 48)

Bibliographical footnotes.

535

Gailio, Andrea. Novum opus consiliorum, aliisque non minoris authoritatis . . . Simul ac universitatibus celebrioribus conceptorum, questiones canonicas, civilis, matrimoniales, feudales, pro moderno rerum statu solutas, in se complectentium . . . In tres partes divisum. Francofurti, Heyll, 1662. 352, 156, 163 p.

536

Galante, Andreas. Fontes iuris canonici selecti. Oeniponte, Libraria academica Wagneriana, 1906. 677 p.

"Opera quae crebrius afferuntur" (recto of 4th prelim. leaf)

537

Gallicus, Mars. Alexandri patricii armacani, theologi Mars Gallicus seu de iustitia armorum et foederum regis Galliae, libri duo. Editio novissima . . . 1637. 442 p.

538

Garsia [Garzia, Garcia], Fortunius. De ultimo sine Juris canonici et civilis . . . Commentaria . . . super titulo de Justicia et jure . . . Colof. Lugduni, Joannis de Moylin, 1522.

539

García Barberena, Tomás. Un canonista español, el doctor don Remiro de Goñi; su vida, su obra científica (1481–1554). Pamplona, 1947. 91 p. (Pampilonensia, publicaciones del Seminario Diocesano de Pamplona, ser. A, v. 3)

Bibliography: p. [87]–91.

540

García Cruzado, Servando. Gonzalo García de Villadiego, canonista salmantino del siglo XV. Roma [Consejo Superior de Investigaciones Científicas, Delegación de Roma], 1968. 287 p. (Cuadernos del Instituto Jurídico Español, no. 20)

Includes bibliographical references.

541

García Gallo, Alfonso. El Concilio de Coyanza, contribución al estudio del derecho canónico español en la Alta Edad Media. Madrid, 1951. 361 p.

542

García-García, Antonio. Estudios sobre la canonística portuguesa medieval. Madrid, Fundación Universitaria Española, 1976. 295 p. (Publicaciones de la Fundación Universitaria Española: Monografías; 39)

Bibliography: p. [11]–13.

543

Gargiaria, Giovanni B. Tractatvs varii. Cum indice rerum, at uerborum locupletissimo. [Bononiae, 1643] 66, 37, 130 p.

544

Garzadori, Francesco G. Compendivm ivris canonici, in qvo reiicivntvr omnia, quae repetebantur, & quae iam abrogata fuere à constitutionibus rom. pont. à Concilio tridentino, & à catechismo. In septem partes diuisum & explicatdum . . . Vniversvm opvs nvnc primvm typis commissvm . . . Cum rerum summis; & indice locupletissimo. Venetiis, apud Foelicem Valgrisium, 1582. 312 p.

545

Gaze, Th. Le droit concordataire. Marseille, Impr. Marsellaise, 1891. 248 p.

546

Gebhard, Heinrich. De principiis & dignitate jurisprudentiae. Tractatus philosopho-iuridicus longé pulcherrimus. Rutheno, Geran, 1613.

547

Gerbenzon, Pieter. Emo van Huizunge; een vroege decretalist. . . . Groningen, Wolters, 1965. 19 p.

Bibliographical references included in "Noten" (p. 17–19).

548

Gerdil, [Giacinto S.] cardinal. Nouveaux opuscules du cardinal Gerdil publiés pour la première fois d'après les autographes existants au Collége des PP. Barnabites, de Rome. Rome [Bertinelli], 1852. 320 col. (Analecta juris pontificii. Rome, 1855. 1. sér., livr. préliminaire)

549

Geschichte des kanonischen Rechts bis auf die Zeiten des falschen Isidorus. Halle, Gebauer, 1778. 303 p.

550

Gibert, Jean P. Corpus juris canonici, per regulas naturali ordine digestas, usuque temperatas, ex eodem jure, et conciliis, patribus, atque aliunde desumptas, expositi. Opus, tum in rebus obscuris claritate, tum dispersis collectione ac delectu, in contrariis conciliatione, eximium, simulque indicibus ac praefationibus, notisque quamplurimis & exquisitis illustratum. In tres tomos divisum. Coloniae Allobrogum, sumptibus Marci Michaelis Bousquet, 1735. 3 v.

551

Gilbert, Johannes M. Constitutiones . . . ex sanctorum patrum dictis & canonicis institutis. . . . Veronae, Hieronymus, 1599. 294 p.

552

Giordani, Pace, bp. Elvcvbrationes diversae . . . Opus sacrae, et profanae doctrinae varietate iucundum ac vtile. V. 1: De sacra. Patavii, 1650. 3 v.

553

Giordani, Pace, bp. Elvcvbrationvm diversarvm, qvibvs pleraqve ad episcopi mvnvs quocumque modo spectantia, noua, facili, breuique methodo, ex vtroqve iure deprompta, diligenter explicantur. Opvs tvm sacrae tvm profanae doctrinae varietate plane iucundum, ac omnibus praelatis, iudicibus, aduocatis, caeterique iurisprudentiae professoribus, apprime vtile, et necessarium. Venetiis, apud Balleonium, 1693. 3 v.

554

Giraldi di San Cajetano, Ubaldo. Institutioni Canonicae Remigii Maschat a S. Ersmo . . . novissimis pontificum constitutionibus, summarii, decretalium omnium correctionibus. . . . Ferraris, sumptibus Societatis, 1760. 2 v. in 1.

555

Gismondi, Pietro, Il diritto della Chiesa dopo il Concilio. Milano, Giuffrè, 1972. 194 p.
Includes bibliographical references.

556

Gitzler, Ludwig. Geschichte der Quellen des Kirchenrechts; zum Gebrauch bei den Vorlesungen. Breslau, Nischkowsky, 1863. 44 p.

557

Giudice, Vincenzo del. Istituzioni di diritto canonico. V. I. Milano, 1932.

558

Giudice, Vincenzo del. Manuale di diritto ecclesiastico. 8. ed. interamente rifatta e aggiornata. Milano, Giuffrè, 1955. 534 p.
"Cenni di bibliografia generale": p. [xiii]–xiv.

559

Giudice, Vincenzo del. Nozioni di diritto canonico. 5. ed. rinnovata. Milano, Giuffrè, 1941. 195 p.

560

Giudice, Vincenzo del. Nozioni di diritto canonico. 6. ed. rinnovata. Milano, Giuffrè, 1944. 401 p. (Manuali Giuffrè)
"Cenni di bibliografia generale": p. [7]–12.

561

Giudice, Vincenzo del. Nozioni di diritto canonico. 9. ed., modificata a completamente aggiornata. Milano, Giuffrè, 1949. 260 p.
Bibliography: p. [3]–7.

562

Giudice, Vincenzo del. Nozioni di diritto canonico. 12. edizione rifatta e interamente aggiornata in conformità alle disposizioni del Concilio ecumenico vaticano II. Preparata con la collaborazione del prof. Gaetano Catalono. Milano, Giuffrè, 1970. 568 p.
Bibliography: p. [1]–11.

This work contrasts the traditional discipline of the Church with the conclusions reached at Vatican II, as well as the present system of canonical legislation. To explain the extent and limitation of his work, the author recalls the statement made by Pope Paul VI: "the Church is at the beginning of a new and great legislative period, inaugurated by the council, demanded by the *aggiornamento,* and required by the revision of the Code of Canon Law." He devotes a chapter to the Second Vatican Council and thereafter, he attempts to harmonize traditional teaching with the doctrine of the council. This is particularly noticeable in chapter 19, on the Church and her presence in the modern world, where he uses conciliar decrees and declarations extensively.

563

Glavell, Victor W. von. Die letztwilligen Vergügungen nach gemeinem kirchlichen Rechte. Paderborn, Schöningh, 1900. 300 p.

564

Gmeiner, Xaver. Institutiones juris ecclesiastici, ad principia juris naturae et civitatis adonatae, et Germaniae accommodatas. Tomus II complectens jus ecclesiasticum privatum. Viennae & Graecii, Weingand, 1782. v. II only.

565

Goffredo da Trani. Summa super titulis decretalium. Novissime cum repertorio et numeris prici-palium et emergentium questionum impressa. Neudruck der Ausg. Lyon, 1519. Aalen, Scientia Verlag, 1968. 534 p.

566

Goldáraz, Carlos G. El Codice lucense de la colección canónica hispana. [Roma] Consejo Superior de Investigaciones Científicas, Delegación de Roma, 1954. 2 v. in 3. (Biblioteca de la Escuela Española de Historia y Arquelogía en Roma, 10–12)
Bibliography: v. 1, pt. 1, p. [19]–20.

567

Golmayo, Pedro B. Instituciones del derecho canónico. Madrid, Sánchez, 1859. 2 v.

568

Golmayo, Pedro B. Instituciones del derecho canónico. 3. ed. Madrid, Librería de Sánchez, 1870. 2 v.

569

Golmayo, Pedro B. Instituciones del derecho canónico. 4. ed. Madrid, Librería de Sánchez, 1874. 2 v.

570

Golmayo, Pedro B. Instituciones del derecho canónico. 7. ed. Madrid, Librería de Sánchez, 1896. 2 v.

571

Gomez, Luis, bp. Commentarij in iudiciales regulas Cancellariae; Ioannis Millaei, ac aliorum doctissimorum virorum adnotationibus illustrati. Eivsdem vriusque signaturae compendium, cum gemino indice. Lvgdvni, apud Rovilivm, 1575. 474 1.

572

Gómez del Campillo, Francisco. Derecho canónico. Parte general. Rev., ampliado y adaptado a la doctrina actual y a la legislación vigente por Jaime M. Mans Puigarnau. Barcelona, [Bosch] 1949. 299 p.

573

Gómez del Campillo, Francisco. Programa-guía con algunas notas bibliográficas, para el estudio del derecho canónico general y particular de España. Barcelona, Bosch, 1919. 133 p.
Contains bibliographies.

574

Gómez-Salazar, Francisco, bp. Instituciones de derecho canónico. 3. ed. corr. y aum. León, Imp. de herederos de Miñón, 1891. 3 v.

575

Gómez-Salazar, Francisco, bp., and Vicente de la Fuente. Lecciones de disciplina eclesiástica y suplemento al Tratado teórico-práctico de procedimientos eclesiásticos. 2. ed., corr. y aum. Madrid, Gomez Fuentenebro, 1877. 2 v.

576

González del Valle Cienfuegos, José M. La plenitud del derecho canónico. [Pamplona, 1965] 114 p. (Colección canónica de la Universidad de Navarra. Cuadernos 2)
Bibliography: p. 107–114.

577

González Tellez, Emanuel. Commentaria perpetua in singulos textus quinque librorum decretalium Gregorii IX tomus primus[–quintus] . . . Editio Veneta, iuxta editionem Lugdunensem ab ipsomat authore recognita & emendata; cum additionibus, tum prioribus suis locis restitutes, tum etiam aliquot recentionibus. Venetiis, apud Pezzana, 1699. 5 v. in 4.

578

González Tellez, Emanuel. Commentaria perpetua in singulos textus quinque librorum decretalium Gregorii IX . . . Ed. novissima, mendis expurgata. Maceratae, Venetiis, apud haeredes Balleonios, 1766. 5 v. in 4.

579

González Tellez, Emanuelus. Commentaria perpetua in singulos textus quinque librorum decretalium Gregorii IX. . . . Francofurti ad Moenum, 1690. 4 v.

580

Gorino-Causa, Mario. Sui regolamenti in diritto canonico. Torino, Giappichelli [1954]. 181 p. (università di Torino. Memorie dell'Istituto giuridico, ser. 2. Memoria 84)
Bibliographical footnotes.

581

Goris, Lambert. Adversariorum iuris subcisivorum,

ad lucem consuetudinis Ducatus Gelriae et Comitatus Zutphaniae, ac vicinarum Belgii provinciarum. 3. ed. Arnhemii, Johannis Jacobi, 1651. 507 p.

582

Gousset, Thomas M. J., cardinal. Exposition des principes du droit canonique. Paris, Lecoffre, 1859. 674 p.

583

Grabowski, Ignacy. Prawo kanoniczne, wedŧung nowego kodeksu. We Lwowie, Nakŧ. "Przeglądu teologicznego," 1921. 439 p. (Wydawnictwa "Przeglądu teologicznego." Serja D: Podręczniki naukowe)

584

Grabowski, Ignacy. Procedura kanoniczna w sprawach małzeńskich. Warszawa, 1938. 134 p.

585

Graña y Nieto, Antonio. Catena jurium utriusque jurisprudentiae; sive, In librum secundum et tertium Decretalium Gregorii IX. Commentarii per singula capita digesti, in quibus non solùm vera cujusque textus sententia aperitur, sed & plurimis adductis & expositis juribus, difficilia quaeque reserantur, & potioribus doctorum sententiis resolvntur. Nova editio, infinitis prope mendis, quibus scatebant priores, singulari studio expurgata. Lugduni, Huguetan, 1678. 698 (i.e., 696), [46] p.

586

Graña y Nieto, Antonio. Catena jurium utriusque jurisprudentiae; sive, In Decretalium Gregorii IX librum secundum et tertium. Commentarii per singula capita digesti, in quibus non solùm vera cujusque textus sententia aperitur, sed & plurimis adductis & expositis juribus, difficilia quaeque reserantur, & potioribus doctorum sententiis resolvntur. Nova editio, infinitis prope mendis, quibus scatebant priores, singulari studio expurgata. Coloniae Allobrogum, sumpt. fratrum de Tournes, 1734. 698 (i.e., 696), [46] p.

587

Gratianus, Stephanus. Disceptationvm forensivm ivdiciorvm . . . Tomus primus[–quintus] in qvibvs, qvae in controversiam quotidie veniunt secundum doctorum receptas sententias, et veram praxim praecipue Sacrae Rotae Romanae definiuntur. Omnia super Venetiis correctius, & ornatius in lucem prodeunt, duplici indice tam rerum, quam argumentorum decorata. Venetiis, apud Iuntas, 1629. 5 v. (Ex libris Fuerstlich Auersbergsche Fideicommisbibliothek zu Laybach)

588

Gratianus, Stephanus. Disceptationvm forensivm judiciorum . . . tomus primus[-quintus] in qvibvs qvae in controversiam qvotidie veniunt secundum doctorum receptas sententias, & veram praxim praecipuè Sacrae Rotae Romanae definiuntur. Hvic novissimae editioni accessit praeter epitomen capitulorum Clavis, seu Index generalis locupletissimus rerum & materiarum notatu dignarum, quae in quinque tomis . . . continentur, a Iohanne Andrea Cadaeo elaboratvs. Genevae, sumptibus Samuelis Chouet, 1664. 6 v.

589

Gravina, Giovanni V. Institutiones canonicae. Nunc primum in lucem editae. Augustae Taurinorum, ex Typographia Regia, 1742. 240 p.

590

Grégoire, Pierre. Opera omnia ad ius pontificium spectantia, ab ipso paulò ante mortem recognita, duobus distincta voluminibus . . . Vnà cum indicibus capitum, verborum, rerúmque memorabilium locupletissimis. Lvgdvni, svmptibvs Ioannis Pillehotte, svb signo nominis Iesv, 1612. 2 v. in 1.

591

Gregorius IX. Decretales Gregorij noni Pontificis, typorum elegantia ornatius, & emendationis fide, integrius quàm antea, restitutae. Insuper non paucae, nec mediocriter vtiles, cum varijs variè scribentium prelectionibus, preclare accesserunt annotationes. Que omnia, nunc recens labore fideliori illustrata sunt. Lvgdvni, apud de Porta, 1550. 548 p.

592

Gross, Karl. Lehrbuch des katholischen Kirchenrechts mit besonderer Berücksichtigung der partikulären Gestaltung desselben in Österreich. 6. aufl. Wien, Manz, 1911. 443 p.

593

Gundling, Nicolaus H. Allgemeines geistliches

Recht der drey christlichen Haupt-Religionen; oder, Gründliche und gelehrte Anmerckungen über Arnoldi Corvini a Belderen Jus canonicum, ihrer Wichtigkeit halber zum Drucke befördert. Franckfurt am Mayn, Spring, 1743–44. 2 v.

594

Gutiérrez, Juan. Canonicarvm quaestionvm, vtrivsq₃ fori, tam exterioris quàm interioris animae, libri dvo, cum eiusdem Repetitionvm, allegationvm, & consiliorvm volumine vno, in quibus multae quaestiones in praxi admodum vtiles continentur, cum indice rerum & verborum locupletissimo. Antverpiae, apud Petrum & Ioannem Belleros, 1618. 473, [43] p.

595

Gutiérrez, Juan. Canonicarum questionum utriusque fori tam exterioris quàm interioris animae, liber tertius, qui totus circa sponsalia de futuro & matrimonia versatur. Cum indice tam capitulorum quàm rerum locupletissimo. Noribergae, sumptibus Wolfgangi Endteri, 1647.

596

Gutiérrez, Juan. Canonicarum quaestionum, vtrivsqve fori, tam exterioris, quàm interioris animae, libri dvo, in qvibvs mvltae qvaestiones in praxi admodum vtiles continentur, editio nouissima caeteris correctior & auctior, cvm indice rervm et verborvm locvpletissimo. Lvgdvni, sumptibus Lavrentii Anisson, 1661. 512, [67] p.

597

Gutiérrez, Juan. Canonicarum quaestionum, utriusque fori tam exterioris quàm interioris animae, liber primus: in quo multae quaestiones in praxi admodum utiles continentur; cum indicibus argumentorum, rerum & verborum locupletissimis. Nova editio, prioribus correctior et elegantiori ordine disposita. Coloniae Allobrogum, sumptibus Perachon & Cramer, 1730.

598

Haffennecker, Cajetan. Manipulus juridico-canonicus regularum juris in ulto succinctis casibus et rationibus. Pragae, Pruscha, 1754. 110 p.

599

Hagen, August. Prinzipien des katholischen Kirchenrechts. Würzburg, Schöningh [1949]. 399 p.
  Bibliography: p. 395–99.

600

Halfes, Henricus. De impedimento erroris (secundum praecepta juris canonici catholicorum). Dissertatio inauguralis. Creveldiae typis Kleinianis, 1861. 38 p.

601

Hamilton Depassier, Carlos. Derecho canónico; prólogo de don Raimundo del Rio C. Santiago, Chile, Editorial "La Salle" [1944]. 343 p.

602

Hansenius, Joannes B. De ivreivrando vetervm liber. Tolosae, typis Raymvndi Colomerii, 1614. 163, [10] p.

603

Haring, Johann B. Grundzüge des katholischen Kirchenrechtes. Graz, Moser, 1910. 881 p.
  Issued in three parts, 1905–10.

604

Haring, Johann B. Grundzüge des katholischen Kirchenrechtes. 3. nach dem Codex j. c. umgearbeitete Aufl. Graz, Moser, 1924. 1037 p. 2 v.
  Bibliographical footnotes.

605

Hase, Karl A. Libri symbolici ecclesiae evangelicae sive concordia. Lipsiae, Suehring, 1827. Vol. 1 only.

606

Hautesere a Salvaizon, Flavien F. de. Notae and animaduersiones ad indivulos ecclesiasticorum canonum, fulgentii ferrandi Carthaginensis ecclesiae diaconi, et Cresconij afri. Augustoriti Pictonum, sumptibus Iuliani Thorellii, regis et Academiae typographi, 1630. 192 p.

607

Heckel, Johannes. Initia iuris ecclesiastici Protestantium. München, Verlag der Bayerischen Akademie der Wissenschaften, 1950. 128 p. (Sitzungsberichte der Bayerischen Akademie der Wissenschaften, Philosophisch-historische Klasse, Jahrg. 1949, Heft 5)

608

Heggelbacher, Othmar. Geschichte des frühchristlichen Kirchenrechts bis zum Konzil von

Nizäa, 325. Freiburg/Schweiz, Universitätsverlag (1974). 251 p.
Bibliography: p. xi–xxvii.

609
Heiner, Franz X. Katholisches Kirchenrecht. 2. verb. Aufl. Paderborn, Schöningh, 1897. 2 v. (Wissenschaftliche Handbibliothek; 1. Reihe: Theologische Lehrbücher, 5, 6)

610
Heiner, Franz X. Katholisches Kirchenrecht. 3. verb. Aufl. Paderborn, Schöningh, 1901. 2 v. (Wissenschaftliche Handbibliothek, 1. Reihe: Theologische Lehrbücher, 5–6)

611
Heiner, Franz X. Katholisches Kirchenrecht. 5. verb. Aufl. Paderborn, Schöningh, 1909. 2 v. (Wissenschaftliche Handbibliothek; 1. Reihe: Theologische Lehrbücher, 5, 6)

612
Heiner, Franz X. Katholisches Kirchenrecht. 6. verb. Aufl. Paderborn, Schöningh, 1912–13. 2 v. (Wissenschaftliche Handbibliothek. 1. Reihe: Theologische Lehrbücher, 5–6)

613
Helfert, Joseph. Handbuch des Kirchenrechts aus den gemeinen und oesterreichischen Quellen zusammen gestellt. . . . Prag, Thabor, 1849. 888 p.

614
Henrici, Hermann. Das Gesetzbuch der Katholischen Kirche; der neue Codex juris canonici; Vortrag. Basel, Helbing & Lichtenhahn, 1918. 82 p.

615
Henricus de Segusia, cardinal. Avrea svmma, Nicolai Svperlantii adnotationibus, & quibusdam excerptis ex summa . . . Fr. Martini Abbatis (vt ferunt) contemporanei Azonis, & Accursii, illustrata; nunc tandem ad incorruptum authoris exemplar diligentissime restituta. Cum svmmariis, & indice locupletissimis. Venetiis, apud Gratiosum Perchacinum, 1605. 1950 cols.

616
Hera, Alberto de la. Introducción a la ciencia del derecho canónico. Madrid, Editorial Tecnos [1967]. 333 p. (Biblioteca universitaria de Editorial Tecnos)
Bibliographical footnotes.

617
Heredia, Ricardo. Apuntes de derecho privado eclesiástico. Lima, Lira, 1882. 192. p.

618
Heredia, Ricardo. Lecciones de derecho público eclesiástico. Dictadas en la Universidad de San Marcos. Lima, Imp. calle del padre Gerónimo n. 94 y 94 A., 1882. 286 p.
Bibliography: 1 leaf at end.

619
Hergenröther, Philipp. Lehrbuch des katholischen Kirchenrechts. Freiburg im Breisgau, Herder'sche Verlagshandlung, 1888. 552 p.

620
Hergenröther, Philipp. Lehrbuch des katholischen Kirchenrechts. 2., neu bearb. aufl. Von dr. Joseph Hollweck. Freiburg im Breisgau [etc.], Herder, 1905. 949 p.
"Literatur des Kirchenrechts": p. 14–17.

621
Héricourt du Vatier, Louis de. Les loix ecclesiastiques de France dans leur ordre naturel et une Analyse des livres du droit canonique conferez avec les usages de l'Eglise gallicane. Nouv. ed., rev., cor. et augm. Paris, Mariette, 1721. 708, 168, [709]–[740] p.

622
Herrmann, Horst. Kleines Wörterbuch des Kirchenrechts für Studium und Praxis. Freiburg, Herder [1972]. 137 p.

623
Hervada Xiberta, Francisco J. El ordenamiento canónico. Pamplona, Universidad de Navarra, 1966–   . (Colección canónica de la Universidad de Navarra)
Bibliographical footnotes.

624
Hervada Xiberta, Francisco J., and Pedro Lombardía. El derecho del pueblo de Dios; hacia un

sistema de Derecho Canónico. Pamplona, Ediciones Universidad de Navarra, 19– . (Colección canónica de la Universidad de Navarra. Manuales)
Bibliography: v. 3, p. 388–89.

This work is part of a general treatise and is devoted to ecclesiastical matrimonial law. The author explains that the magnitude of the subject of marriage, the most elaborate part of canon law and the richest in doctrine and jurisprudence, requires two volumes, but that he intends to be concise in his exposition, considering only essential elements of the topic. Chapter one is devoted to general concepts, but the remaining chapters deal specifically with marriage's legal structure and social reality, marriage as a mystery and sign, legal matrimonial relation, the content of the matrimonial relation, marriage and canonical legislation, the formation of marriage (which offers the basic elements of its historical evolution), the conjugal contract and its general presuppositions, and assumption of capabilities.

625
Hickey, John J. Irregularities and simple impediments in the new Code of Canon Law. [Gettysburg, Pa., Gettysburg compiler print, 1920] 95, [5] p. (The Catholic University of America. Canon law studies, no. 7)
Bibliography: p. 94–95.

626
Hilling, Nikolaus. Die Allgemeinen Normen des Codex juris canonici. Freiburg i. Br., Waibel, 1926. 163 p.

627
Hilling, Nikolaus. Die Reformen des Papstes Pius X auf dem Gebiete der kirchenrechtlichen Gesetzgebung. Bonn, Hanstein, 1909–15. 3 v.

628
Himmel, Johann. Tractatus de canonicatu, jure canonico, & theologia scholastica. Jenae, Impensis Birknerianis, Typis Weidnerianis, 1632. 886 p.
Includes bibliographical references.

629
Hispana collectio. La colección canónica Hispana. Madrid, [Consejo Superior de Investigaciones Científicas, Instituto Enrique Flórez] 1966– . 1 v.

(Monumenta Hispaniae sacra. Serie canónica, v. 1)
Includes bibliographies.

This is the Spanish canonical collection *par excellence* and the greatest national contribution to the legal universalism of the Church; at the first Week of Canon Law, organized in Salamanca in October 1945, a resolution was adopted to start working on a critical edition of this collection, but it has not been completed. This work represents thorough research on the manuscript tradition and the cataloging and classifying of codes, a first step toward a scientific and critical text of the *Hispana*. It deals with the historiography of the collection; the manuscript tradition in chronological order; the classification of manuscripts; content and structure of the *Hispana;* its author, date, and sources; and its dissemination and influence on subsequent canonical collections.

630
Hobbes, Thomas. Leviathan, sive de materia, forma, & potestate civitatis ecclesiasticae et civilis. Amsteledami, Blaev, 1670. 364 p.

631
Hobza, Antonín. Úvod do práva církevního. Napsal Antonín Hobza za spolupráce Josefa Turečka. Praha, Všehrd, 1936. 480 p.

632
Hoffmann, Pál. Közönséges és mahyar részszerü katholikus egyházjog alapvonalai. Pozsony, 1865. 267 p.
Bibliography: p. 11–15.

633
Hogg, James. Die ältesten Consuetudines der Kartäuser. Repr. Salzburg, Inst. f. Engl. Sprache u. Literatur, Univ. Salzburg, 1973. 252 p. (Analecta cartusiana, 1)
Bibliography: p. [242]–252.

634
Hohenlohe-Schillingsfürst, Constantin, father. Grundlegende Fragen des Kirchenrechts. Wien, Mayer, 1931. 169 p.
Bibliography at head of each chapter.

635
Holböck, Carl. Handbuch des Kirchenrechtes. Innsbruck, Tyrolia [1951]. 2 v.

636

Hollerbach, Alexander. Neuere Entwicklungen des katholischen Kirchenrechts. Karlsruhe, Müller, 1974. 46 p. (Schriftenreihe - Juristische Studiengesellschaft Karlsruhe; Heft 118)
Includes bibliographical references.

637

Honig, Richard M. Beiträge zur Entwicklung des Kirchenrechts. Göttingen, Schwartz, 1954. 62 p. (Göttinger rechtswissenschaftliche Studien, Heft 12)

638

Horoy, César A. Gratien, auteur du Decretum et fondateur de l'enseignement du droit canonique; étude suivie d'un plan et projet d'encyclopédie du droit canon, sous forme de répertoire, comprenant le droit canonique des différentes communions chrétiennes. Paris, Marescq aîné, Chevalier-Marescq, successeur, 1891. 240 p.

639

Horoy, César A. Prolégoménes d'un cours sur le droit canonique et ses relations avec le droit civil; professé à la faculté de droit de Dousi durant l'année scolaire 1883–84. Paris, Librairie A. Marescq Ainé, 1884. 210 p.

640

Hove, Alphonse van. De legibus ecclesiasticis. Mechliniae, Dessain, 1930. xviii, 382 p. (Commentarium Lovaniense in Codicem iuris canonici, v. 1, t. 2)
Bibliographical footnotes.

641

Hove, Alphonse van. Prolegomena. Mechliniae, Dessain, 1928. 373 p. (Commentarium Lovaniense in Codicem iuris canonici, v. 1, t. 1)
Bibliography: p. [1]–2.

642

Huber, Ulricus. De jure popularis optimatium & regalis imperii sine vi & à sui juris populo constituti ... Dissertatio. Franequerae, apud Henricum Amama, et Zachariam Taedama, 1689. 55 p.

643

Hubertus van Groessen, father. Het kerkelijk recht, commentaar op den Codex met vermelding van het particulier kerkelijk recht voor Nederland en België door Hubertus van Groessen en Clementinus van Vlissisgen. Nederlandsch burgerlijk- en strafrecht door L. Keyzer. Belgisch burgerlijk- en strafrecht door W. Leën. Roermond, Romen, 1947. 1441 p. (Romen's compendia)

644

Hübler, Bernhard. Kirchenrechtsquellen. Urkundenbuch zu vorlesungen über kirchenrecht. 4. berichtigte und verstärkte aufl. Berlin, Puttkammer und Mühlbrecht, 1902. 130 p.

645

Hüllmann, Karl D. Ursprünge der Kirchenverfassung des Mittelalters. Bonn, Marcus, 1831. 218 p.

646

Humphrey, George H. The law of the protestant episcopal church and other prominent ecclesiastical bodies. A manual for church officers with forms. 4. ed. with appendix. New York, James Pott and Co., 1895. 226 p.

647

Huth, Adam. Jus canonicum ad libros V Decretalium Gregorii IX explicatum. Augustae Vindelicorum, Wolff, 1748. 218 p.

648

Icard, Henri J. Praelectiones juris canonici habitae in Seminario Sancti Sulpitii. 7. ed. accurate recognita ab auctore. parisiis, apud Lecoffre, 1893. 3 v.

649

Incerti auctoris Ordo judiciarius, pars Summae legum et Tractatus de praescriptione. Nac einer Göttweiger (Stiftsbibliothek. saec. XII ex.) und einer Wiener (Hofbibliothek. saec. XIII ex.) handschrift, hrsg. und bearb. von dr. Carl Gross. Innsbruck, Wagner, 1870. 269, [1] p.

650

Institutiones iuris ecclesiastici publici quas iuxta methodum Card. Tarquini. Romae, Pustet, 1901. 2 v. in 1.

651

Ius et salus animarum: Festschrift f. Bernard Panzram. Ulrich Mosiek; Hartmut Zapp (Hrsg.). Freiburg (im Breisgau), Rombach, 1972. 509 p.

(Sammlung Rombach, n. F.; Bd. 15)
Includes bibliographical references.

652

Ius populi Dei. Miscellanea in honorem Raymundi Bidagor. Roma, Università Gregoriana, 1972. 3 v.
Includes bibliographical references.

653

Ius sacrum; Klaus Mörsdorf zum 60. Geburtstag. Hrsg. von Audomar Scheuermann und Georg May. München, Schöningh, 1969. 944 p.
Bibliographical footnotes.

654

Jannaccone, Costantino. Corso di diritto ecclesiastico. Padova, CEDAM, 1944–

655

Jannaccone, Costantino. Manuale di diritto ecclesiastico. Pisa, Vallerini editore, 1950–

656

Jansen, Raymond J. Canonical provisions for catechetical instruction; an historical synopsis and commentary. Washington, D.C., The Catholic University of Amercia, 1937. 153 p. (The Catholic University of America. Canon law studies, no. 107)
Bibliography: p. 139–42.

657

Johannes Monachus Picardus, card. Glossa aurea. Nobis priori loco super sexto decretalium libro addita. Cum additionibus Philippi Probi Biturici et in supremo parisiensi senatu advocati. Neucruck der Ausg. Paris, 1535. Aalen, Scientia-Verlag, 1968. 1022 p.

This 1968 reprint of the 1535 Paris edition of the *Glossa Aurea* provides a good commentary by Johannes Monachus on the six books of the Decretals, and an extensive contribution by Philippe Probi. To introduce the study the author starts with a philosophical consideration on knowledge: to know is to comprehend the subject by its causes of which there are four—material, formal, efficient, and final. The *finis* or end is the cause of causes intentionally, but is the effect of the causes in the execution. By stating that nothing is cause of itself, the author is ready to proceed with the analysis of the texts of the *Liber Sextus,* the Decretals of Boni-

face VIII, which is divided into five books and subdivided into titles and chapters.

658

Jombart, Émile. Manuel de droit canon; conforme au Code de 1917 et aux plus récentes décisions du Saint-Siège. Paris, Beauchesne, 1949. 564 p.
Bibliographical footnotes.

659

Jombart, Émile. Manuel de droit canon, conforme au Code de 1917 et aux plus récentes décisions du Saint-Siége. Nouv. éd. rev. et complétée. Paris, Beauchesne, 1958. 566 p.
Includes bibliographical references.

660

Jombart, Émile. Mémento de droit canon à l'usage des clercs, religieux, religieuses, et laïcs. Paris, Beauchesne, 1958. 189 p.

661

Jombart, Émile. Summary of canon law. Translated by Raymond F. Bégin. New York, Benziger Bros. [1960]. 232 p.

662

Jone, Heribert, father. Commentarium in Codicem iuris canonici. Paderborn, Schöningh, 1950–
3 v.

663

Jone, Heribert, father. Gesetzbuch der lateinischen Kirche; Erklärung der Kanones. 2., verm. und verb. Aufl. Vol. 1, General norms and persons. Paderborn, Schöningh, 1950–53. 3 v.

664

Jordanus, Ignac. De fontibus juris canonici, et de veteri ecclesiae disciplina dissertatio. Caesar-Augustae, Typographia Regia, 1764. 45 p.

665

Justel, Christophe. Codex canonvm ecclesiae africanae. Christophorvs Ivstellvs ex mss. codicibus edidit, graecam versionem adiunxit, & notis illustrauit. Lvtetiae Parisorvm, apud Pacard, 1614. 379, 160 p.

666

Kaiser, Matthäus. Der gute Glaube im Codex iuris

canonici. München, Hueber, 1965. 246 p.
(Münchener theologische Studien. 3. Kanonistische
Abteilung, 22. Bd.)
  Bibliography: p. xv–xxii..

667
Kelleher, Stephen J. Discussions with non-Catho-
lics; canonical legislation. Washington, D.C., The
Catholic University of America, 1943. 93 p. (The
Catholic University of America. Canon law studies,
no. 180)
  Bibliography: p. 73–77.

668
Keller, Paul V. Die "Normae generales" des Codex
iuris canonici. Calw (Württbg.) A. Oelschläger'sche
buchdruckerei, 1923. 110 p.
  "Hauptsächlich benützte werke": p. [vii]–viii.

669
Keuffel, Georg G. Elenta jurisprudentia ecclesiasticae universalis. Rostochii, Fritsch, 1728. 2 v. in 1.

670
Klein, Joseph. Grundlegung und Grenzen des
kanonischen Rechts. Tübingen, Mohr, 1947. 32 p.
(Recht und Staat in Geschichte und Gegenwart,
130)

671
Knecht, August. Das neue kirchliche Gesetzbuch,
Codex juris canonici; seine Geschichte und Eigen-
art. Mit einem Anhang: Sammlung einschlägiger
Aktenstücke. Strassburg, Trübner, 1918. 71 p.
(Schriften der Wissenschaftlichen Gesellschaft in
Strassburg, 35. Heft)

672
Koeniger, Albert M. Grundriss einer Geschichte
des katholischen Kirchenrechts. Köln, Bachem,
1919. 91 p.

673
Koeniger, Albert M., and Friedrich Giese.
Grundzüge des katholischen Kirchenrechts und
des Staatskirchenrechts. 2. neubearb. und verm.
Aufl. Bonn und Köln, Röhrscheid, 1932. 306 p.
(Der Staatsbürger, Sammlung zur Einführung in
das öffentliche Recht. 6)

674
Koeniger, Albert M., and Friedrich Giese.
Grundzüge des katholischen Kirchenrechts und
des Staatskirchenrechts. 3. neubearb. und verm.
Aufl. Augsburg-Göggingen, Naumann, 1949. 303
p.

675
Kollányi, Ferenc. A magánkegyuri jog hazánkban
a középkorban. Budapest, Magyar Tudományos
Akadémia, 1906. 298 p.

676
Kölner Mediae vistentagung. Lex et sacramentum
im Mittelalter. Hrsg. von Paul Wilpert. Für d.
Druck besorgt von Rudolf Hoffmann. Berlin, de
Gruyter, 1969. 237 p. (Miscellanea mediaevalia,
Bd. 6)
  Includes bibliographical references.

677
Kress, Johann P. Rechts-begründete vollständige
Erläuterung des Archidiaconal-Wesens und der
geistlichen Send-Gerichte, wie sie beyde so wol bey
andern Stifftern, in- und ausser Teutschland, als
absonderlich in den Hoch-Stifft Ossnabrück, von
Zeit zu Zeit beschaffen gewesen und noch sind;
nebst ... Untersuchung der von verschiedenen
Capitulis und Archidiaconis dessfalls angemasster
weit-aussehender Praetensionen &c. &c. Wobey
zugleich von denen bischöflichen Juramentis, Of-
ficialat-Gerichten, so dann von dem Instrumento
Pacis Westphal. und besonders desselben Artic.
XIII wie auch der Ossnabrückischen Capitulatione
perpetua, nicht weniger von den vorzeitigen
teutschen weltlichen Gerichten verschiedene ...
Nachrichten ... mitgetheilet werden. Helmstedt,
Gedruckt bey P. D. Schnorrn, Univ. Buchdr., 1725.
369, 212 p.

678
Kreutzwald, Peter C. A. De canonica iuris consue-
tudinarii praescriptione. Dissertatio inauguralis.
Berolini, Schade (L. Schade), 1873. 94 p.

679
Krüger, Gerda. Die Rechtsstellung der vorkon-
stantinischen Kirchen. Amsterdam, Rodopi, 1969
[1970]. 336 p. (Kirchenrechtliche Abhandlungen,
Heft 115, 116)
  Includes bibliographical references.

680
Księżopolski, Józef. Kremacjonizm w świetle prawa kanonicznego. Poznań, 1947. 23 p.

681
Kurtscheid, Bertrand, father. Historia iuris canonici. Ad usum scholarium. Tomus 1[-2, volumen 1] Romae, Officium Libri Catholici, 1941–43 [v. 1, 1943]. 2 v.
Includes bibliographies.

682
Kurtscheid, Bertrand, father. Das neue Kirchenrecht, Zusammenstellung der wichtigsten Neubestimmungen; zugleich als Ergänzung zu Heiners Katholisches Kirchenrecht, sechste Auflage. Paderborn, Schöningh, 1919. 163 p.

683
Kuttner, Stephan G. Harmony from dissonance; an interpretation of medieval canon law. Latrobe, Pa., Archabbey Press [1960]. 64 p. (Wimmer lecture, 10)

684
Lacerte, Henry. The nature of canon law according to Suarez. Ottawa, University of Ottawa Press, 1964. 186 p. (Universitas Catholica Ottaviensis. Dissertationes ad gradum laureae in facultatibus ecclesiasticis consequendum con scriptae. Series canonica nova, t. 6) Les Publications sériées de l'Université d'Ottawa, 72.
Bibliography: p. [177]–180.

685
Lacoste, Jean de. In Decretales Gregorii IX PP. summaria et commentaria. Neapoli, sumptibus M. Guarracini, ex Typographia Raymundiana, 1770. 2 v. (613 p.) in 1.

686
Laemmer, Hugo. Zur Codification des canonischen Rechts. Freiburg im Breisgau, St. Louis, Mo. [etc.], Herder, 1899. 223, [1] p.

687
Laemmer, Hugo. Institutionen des katholischen Kirchenrechts. Freiburg im Breisgau, Herder'sche Verlagshandlung, 1886. 553 p.

688
Laemmer, Hugo. Institutionen des katholischen Kirchenrechts. 2., vielfach verm. und verb. Aufl. Freiburg im Breisgau, Herder, 1892. 742 p.

689
Laeuchli, Samuel. Power and sexuality; the emergence of canon law at the Synod of Elvira. Philadelphia, Temple University Press [1972]. 143 p.
Includes bibliographical references.

690
Lagarde, Paul A. de. Reliquiae iuris ecclesiastici antiquissimae. Graece et Syriace Edidit Paulus de Lagarde. Osnabrück, Zeller; Wiesbaden, Harrassowitz, 1967. 96 p., 72 l.

691
Lakits, György Z. Juris publici ecclesiastici. Venetiis, Orlandelli, 1790. 2 v.

692
Lakits, György Z. Juris publici ecclesiastici pars generalis, de ecclesia christiana potestatisque sacrae cum civili nexu . . . Editio prima matritensis. Matriti, typis Societatis, praela regente Joanne Josepho Sigüenza et Vera, 1822. 204 p.

693
Lakits, György Z. Praecognita juris ecclesiastici universi. Editio prima matritensis. Matriti, typis Societatis praela regente Joanne Josepho Sigüenza et Vera, 1822. 271 p.
"Historia juris ecclesiastici" (p. 266–68) contains bibliography.

694
Lancelotti, Giovanni P. Institutiones juris canonici. Venetiis, Typ. Balleoniana, 1750. 588 p.

695
Lauder, John, comp. St. Andrews Formulare, 1514–46. Edinburgh, Printed for the Stair Society by Skinner, 1942–44. 2 v. (The Stair Society. Publications, 7, 9)

696
Lauer, Artur. Index verborvm Codicis ivris canonici. [Rome] Typis Polyglottis Vaticanis, 1941. 936 p.

697

Laurin, Franz. Introductio in Corpus juris canonici cum appendice brevem introductionem in Corpus juris civilis continente exaravit dr. Franciscus Laurin. Friburgi Brisgoviae et Vindobonae, sumptibus Herder, typographi editoris pontificii, 1889. 284 p.

698

Law for liberty, the role of law in the church today. James E. Biechler, editor. Foreward by Ernest J. Primeau. Baltimore, Helicon [1967]. 221 p.
    Bibliography: p. 209–13.

699

Le Bras, Gabriel, ed. Histoire du droit et des institutions de l'Église en Occident. Paris, Sirey [1955–   ].
    Bibliography: v. 1, p. [247]–264.

700

Lega, Michele, cardinal. Praelectiones in textum iuris canonici in scholis Pont. Seminarii Rom. habitae. De delictis et poenis. Ed. altera. Romae, Ex Typographia Pontificia in Instituto Pii IX, 1910. 475 p.

701

Leges ecclesiae post Codicem iuris canonici editae/ collegit, digessit notisque ornavit Xaverius Ochoa. Roma, Commentarium pro Religiousis, 1966–74. 4 v.

    The compiler notes that anyone wanting to know the rule that applies to a particular case should take into account not only the code but also the laws and documents issued after the promulgation of the code, for they amend or complete the codified laws in many instances. These new laws and documents, however, are scattered throughout several volumes of the *Acta Apostolicae Sedis* and periodicals. These facts prompted the writer to compile, in chronological order, the documents issued after the code. All the documents are collected in four impressive volumes covering the years 1917 to 1972. The selection is legal in a broad sense, and includes constitutions and decrees of the Popes and Ecumenical Councils; pontifical documents issued as *motu proprio;* and resolutions, decrees, norms, *responsa,* instructions, privileges, declarations, etc., of the Roman Curia. The collection offers the documents in their complete form

and shows their influence upon the universal Church. The compiler had in mind, as criteria for his selection, the documents' condition (public or official, particular or private), author, and nature. Volumes one through four offer chronological indexes, and volume four also provides a very useful analytical index of laws from the first four volumes.

702

Leitmaier, Charlotte. Die Kirche und die Gottesurteile; eine rechtshistorische Studie. Wien, Verlag Herold [1953]. 139 p. (Weiner rechtsgeschichtliche Arbeiten. Bd. 2)
    "Literatur": p. 135–38.

703

Lely, John M. The Church of England position as appearing from statutes, articles, canons, rubrics, and judicial decisions: a compilation for general use. London, Cox, 1899. 228 p.

704

León, Luis Ponce de. De legibus; o, tratado de las leyes, 1571. Introducción y edición crítica bilingüe por Luciano Pereña. Madrid, Consejo Superior de Investigaciones Científicas, 1963. 138, 138, [139]–148 p. (Corpus Hispanorum de pace, v. 1)
    Bibliography: p. [lxxxiii]–lxxxviii.

705

Leonelius, Johannes B. Compendivm ivris canon, et ordinis librorvm eivsdem, per modvm introdvctionis. Desvmptvm ex doctrina. . . . Pervsiae, typis Petri Iacobi Petrutij, 1598. 39 p.

706

Leonelli, Giovanni B. Tractatvs de praecedentia hominis. Cum tribus indicibus. Pervsiae, apud P. Petrutium, 1601. 230 p.

707

Lesage, Germain. La nature du droit canonique. Ottawa, Éditions de l'Université d'Ottawa, 1960. 224 p. (Les Publications sériées de l'Université d'Ottawa, 61)
    Includes bibliography.

708

Leurenio, R. P. Petro. Forum ecclesiasticum in quo jus canonicum universum librorum ac titulorum ordine per questiones et responsa, tam canonistarum veterum & recentiorum, quam legistrarum, in iis, quae utrique juri, canonico et civili communia sunt. Editio secunda. Augustae Vindelicorum, sumptibus Martini Veith & Jodoci Henrici Müller, 1737. 5 v.

709

Lewald, Ursula. An der Schwelle der Scholastik, Bonizo von Sutri und das Kirchenrecht seiner Tage. Weimar, Böhlaus Nachfolger, 1938. 104 p.

710

Lex ecclesiae fundamentalis. Roma, Officium Libri Catholici, 1974. 131 p. (Annali di dottrina e iurisprudenza canonica; 3) (Studia et documenta juris canonici; 6)
Includes bibliographical references.

This book, the third volume of the *Annals of Canonical Doctrine and Jurisprudence,* edited by the *Arcisodalizio* of the Roman Curia, contains several studies on the fundamental law of the Church, considered from three different aspects: the theological interpretation of canon law; the distinction between common law and particular legislation; and the relationships between charisma of the Holy Spirit and the institutional church. The book contributes to the search for the doctrine and formulation of a fundamental law of the Church.

711

Las leyes eclesiásticas, sacadas del Nuevo Testamento. Traducción del italiano al español por Agustin de Arrieta. Madrid, Cano, 1793. 159 p.

712

Liber amicorum Monseigneur Onclin: actuele thema's van kerkelijk en burgerlijk recht—thèmes actuels de droit canonique et civil/J. Lindemans, H. Demeester. Gembloux, Duculot, [1976]. 398 p. (Bibliotheca ephemeridum theologicarum Lovaniensium, 42)
"Bibliografie van Mgr. Onclin": p. [xv]–xxii.
Includes bibliographical references.

713

Likhachev, N. Pis'mo papy Piia piatage. . . . [in Russian] 1906. 175 p.

714

Limburch, Arnoldus a. Disputationum iuris feudalis. 140 p.

715

Llamazares Fernández, Dionisio. Sacramento-Iglesia-derecho en el pensamiento de R. Sohm. Prólogo del Dr. D. Alfonso Prieto Prieto. Oviedo, Instituto de Estudios Jurídicos, 1969. 351 p.
Includes bibliographical references.

716

Loening, Edgar. Geschichte des deutschen Kirchenrechts. Vol. 1, Das Kirchenrecht in Gallien von Constantin bis Chlodovech. Strassburg, Trübner, 1878. 2 v.

717

Lombardía, Pedro. Escritos de derecho canónico. Pamplona, Ediciones Universidad de Navarra, 1973–. 3 v. (Colección canónica de la Universidad de Navarra)
Includes bibliographical references.

718

López y Lleras, Rudesindo. Compendio de instituciones de derecho canónico. 2. ed. Bogotá, Editorial Santafé, 1958. 334 p.

719

Luca, Luigi de. Il concetto del diritto ecclesiastico nel suo sviluppo storico. Padova, CEDAM, 1946. 201 p.

720

Lydon, Patrick J. Ready answers in canon law, a practical summary of the Code for the parish clergy. 3d ed. enl. and rev. in accordance with latest decrees. New York, Benziger Bros., 1948, 636 p.
Includes bibliographies.

721

Lydon, Patrick J. Ready answers in canon law; a practical summary of the Code for the parish clergy. 4th ed., enl. and rev. in accordance with latest decrees. New York, Benziger Bros. [1954]. 638 p.
Includes bibliographies.

722

Maassen, Friedrich B. C. Geschichte der Quellen und der Literatur des canonischen Rechts im Abendlande bis zum Ausgange des Mittelalters. 1. bd. Gratz, Leuschner & Lubensky, 1870. 981, [1] p.

723

Maassen, Friedrich B. C. Glossen des canonischen Rechts aus dem Carolingischen Zeitalter. Wien, Gerold, 1877. 68 p.

724

Maassen, Friedrich B. C. Paucapalea. Ein Beitrag zur Literargeschichte des canonischen Rechts im Mittelalter. Wein, Aus der k. k. Hof- und Staatsdr., Gerold, 1859, 70 p.

725

Mager, Martin. De advocatia armata siue clientelari patronorvm irve et potestate clientvmqve officio, vulgo Schutz vnd Schirms—Gerechtigkeit dicto, in & extra Romano-Germanicum imperium, moribus priscis & hodiernis recepto. Tractatus iuridico-historico-politicus . . . Cum indice triplici, qvaestionvm explicatarum, diplomatvm, rerum et materiarvm locupletissimo. Francofvrti, Egenolphi, König, 1625. 826, [111] p.

726

Magni, Cesare. Corso di diritto ecclesiastico; diritto canonico. Milano, Giuffrè, 1944. 615 p.

727

Magonus, Joannes B. Lucerna moralis, biparte constituta. Cvivs prima pars notariatus auctoritatem, causidicorumq; nobile officium continet. Secvnda vero, eiusdem notariatus fidelitatem indicat. His breue, circa causidicorum praecedentiam compendium accommodatur. Index postremo titulorum duplex adijcitur. Ticini, ex typographia P. Bartoli, sumptibus O. Bordoni bibliopolae papiensis, 1602. 2 v. in 1.

728

Mahl-Schedl-Alpenburg, Franz J. Grundrisz des katholischen Kirchenrechts. Mit Berücksichtigung de österreichischen Gesetzgebung. 2. verb. Aufl. Wien, Hölder, 1905. 280 p.

729

Maitland, Frederic W. Roman canon law in the Church of England; six essays. London, Methuen, 1898. 184 p.

730

Maitland, Frederic W. Roman canon law in the Church of England; six essays. New York, Franklin [1968]. 184 p. (Burt Franklin research and source works series, 340)
Bibliographical footnotes.

731

Maldonado y Fernández del Torco, José. Curso de derecho canónico para juristas civiles; parte general. Madrid, 1967. 535 p.
"Orientación bibliográfica": p. [17]–26.

732

Maldonado y Fernández del Torco, José. Curso de derecho canónico para juristas civiles: parte general. Reimpresión de la 2. ed. Madrid, Grafoffset, 1975. 503 p.
Bibliography: p. [13]–22.

The author's intention is to provide lawyers who are not theologians with a manual of canon law to complement their education. The book, divided into two main parts—general theory and history of canon law—stresses the important contribution of canon law to law in general and to that of Spain in particular. The author also presents briefly the laws of other Christian and non-Christian religions, their relationship to canon law, and the possibility of an interconfessional law. Of great value is the analysis, in chapter eight of the second part, of the law of Vatican II. The work ends with an appendix on the ecclesiastical law of the Spanish State covering fundamental laws, the law on religious freedom, and the Concordat of August 27, 1953, with complementary agreements.

733

Mandosi, Quintiliano. Signatvrae gratiae praxis. Secvnda aeditio. Romae, apud Antonium Bladum, 1561. 143, [2] p.

734

Manenti, Carlo. Concetto ed importanza dello studio del diritto ecclesiastico. Discorso letto il 20 novembre 1892 per l'inaugurazione dell'anno accademico nella R. Università di Macerata. Macerata, Stab. tip. Bianchini, 1892. 57 p.

735

Manrique Ferro, Michael. Tractatus de praecentiis et praelationibus ecclesiasticis. Lugduni, Prost, 1635. 242 p.

736

Marchesi, Francesco M. Summula iuris publici ecclesiastici. Neapoli, d'Auria, 1948. 172 p.
Bibliography: p. [13]–14.

737

Maroto, Filippo. Instituciones de derecho canónico de conformidad con el nuevo código. Tr. al castellano por el R. P. Jesús López Alijarde, rev. por el doctor D. Felipe Clemente de Diego . . . seguida de las lecciones de disciplina eclesiástica de España, por el R. P. Juan Portíus. Madrid, Editorial del corazón de María, 1919–   1 v.

738

Martín, Isidoro. Tres estudios de derecho canónico. Madrid, Sección de Publicaciones de la Facultad de Derecho de la Universidad, 1961. 123 p.
Bibliographical footnotes.

739

Martin, Konrad, bp. Katechismus des römisch-katholischen Kirchenrechts. Münster, Verlag der Aschendorfs'schen Buchhandlung, 1875. 240 p.

740

Maschat, Remigius. Institutiones canonicae Remigii Maschat a S. Erasmo, cl. reg. Scholarum Piarum, novissimis pontificum constitutionibus, summariis decretalium omnium correctionibus ex posteriori jure, et Consilio Tridentino collectis, bullarum ad ejusdem Concilii decreta spectantium compendio augtae et illustrate ab Ubaldo Giraldi a S. Cajetano. Ed. 1. Florentina. Florentiae, Conti, 1854–55. 2 v. in 4.

741

Massa, Antonio. Ad formulam cameralis obligationis liber. Romae, Zannetti, 1607. 381 p.

742

Masseo da Casola, padre. Compendio di diritto canonico. Aggiornato alle ultime disposizioni canoniche e civili. [Torino], Marietti, 1967. 1477 p.

743

Mastricht, Gerhard. Historia juris ecclesiastici et pontificii, seu De ortu, progressu, incrementis, collectionibus, auctoribusque juris ecclesiastici & pontificii tractatio. Cum praefatione Christiani Thomasii, de neglectu studii juris canonici, ejusq; usu frequente & methodo. Halae, Zeitler, 1705. 464, [28] p.

744

Mathis, Burkhard, father. Das katholische Kirchenrecht für den Laien. Paderborn, Schöningh [c1940] 661 p.

745

Matthaeus, Antonius. Manuductio ad jus canonicum, quae eiusdem originem, institutiones, ac fundamenta, & quicquid in eo primum ac praecipuum, complectitur. Lvgdvni Batavorvm, apud Fredericum Haaring, 1696. 471, [28] p.

746

Maupied, François L. M. Juris canonici universi, per faciliorem methodum ad veram praxim sincere redacti, compendium ex probatissimis auctoribus catholicis. Accurante J. P. Migne, Lutetiae Parisiorum, apud J. P. Migne editorem, 1861. 2 v.

747

Maurize, I. P. Iuris canonici selecta, et eorum, quae ad usum fori Gallicani pertinent. Parisiis, Clousier, 1659. 239 p.

748

Mayer, Suso, ed. and tr. Neueste Kirchenrechts-Sammlung. Die Gesetze der Päpste, die authentischen Auslegungen der kirchlichen Gesetze und die anderen Erlasse des Heiligen Stuhles seit Erscheinen des Codex iur. can. (1917) gesammelt, nach den Kanones des Cod. iur. can. geordnet und ins Deutsche übersetzt. Freiburg, Herder [1953–   ] v.

749

Meerman, Gérard. Novus thesaurus juris civilis canonici, continens varia et rarissima optimorum interpretum, inprimis Hispanorum et Galloru, opera tam edita antehac quam inedita, apud Petrum de Hondt, 1751–53. 7 v.

750

Mentzer, Balthasar. Analysis capitis noni epistolae d. Pauli ad Romanos: de que divina adspirante gratia. Francofurti a. M., Becker, 1603.

751

Metz, René. L'Église a ses lois, le droit canon. Paris,

Librarie Fayard [1959] 126 p. (Je sais, je crois; encyclopédie du catholique au XXeme siècle, 79. 8. ptie: L'Église dans son organisation)

752

Metz, René. Das Kirchenrecht. [Aus dem Französischen übertragen von Knüppel] Aschaffenburg, Pattloch [1963, c1959] 149 p. (Der Christ in der Welt. 12. Reihe: Bau und Gefüge der Kirche. 1. Bd.)
Bibliography: p. 136–138.

753

Metz, René. What is canon law? Translated from the French by Michael Derrick. [1st ed.] New York, Hawthorne Books [1960] 157 p. (Twentieth century encyclopedia of Catholicism, v. 80. Section 8: The organization of the church)
Includes bibliography.

754

Metz, René, and Jean Schlick. La Mise en ordinateur du vocabulaire canonique et juridique du "Décret" de Gratien: recherches préliminaires, communication au IVe Congrès international de droit canonique médiéval, Toronto, 21–25 août 1972. Strasbourg (Palais universitaire, 9, place de l'Université, 67084): C.E.R.D.I.C. [Centre de recherche et de documentation des institutions chrétiennes], 1972. 44 1. (Université des sciences humaines de Strasbourg. Mémoires du Cerdic; 3)
Includes bibliographical references.

755

Michiels, Gommar. Normae generales juris canonici; commentarius libri I Codicis juris canonici. Lublin-Polonia, Universitas catholica, 1929. 2 v.
"Index praecipuorum commentariorum libri I Codicis juris canonici": v. 2, p. [537]–541.

756

Michiels, Gommar. Normae generales juris canonici; commentarius libri I Codicis juris canonici. Ed. 2, penitus retractata et notabiliter aucta. Tornacum, Typis Societatis S. Joannis Evangelistae, 1949. 2 v.
"Literatura generalis praecipua": v. 1, p. xvi–xxii.

757

Migliorucci, Lazarus B. Institutiones juris canonici, cum explicationibus, in quibus universum jus pontificium proponitur et notitia historiae ecclesiasticae passim illustratur, nec non variis disputationibus aliqua novitate ad usum shcolasticum [sic] excitatis discussisque elucitatur. Pisis, Bindi, 1712–23. 4 v.

758

Miguélez Domínguez, Lorenzo, Sabino A. Morán, and Marcelino Cabreros de Anta, comps. Derecho canónico posconciliar; suplemento al Código de derecho canónico bilingüe de la Biblioteca de autores cristianos. Madrid, [Editorial Católica] 1967. 216 p. (Biblioteca de autores cristianos, 7 bis)

759

Miguélez Domínguez, Lorenzo, *et al.* Derecho canónico posconciliar: suplemento al Código de Derecho Canónico bilingüe. 4. ed. Madrid, [Editorial Católica] 1974. 649 p. (Biblioteca de autores cristianos)

760

Mirkovič, Mirko. Pravni položaj i karakter srpske crkve, 1459–1766. [In Russian] 223 p.
Bibliography: p. [212]–221.

761

Mittelstaedt, Ludvig O. De iuris patronatus, quod reale dicitur, origine. Dissertatio inauguralis. Vratislaviae, Lindner, [1856] 2 p. 1., 32 p.

762

Mocchegiani, Petro. Iurisprudentia ecclesiastica ad usum et commoditatem utriusque cleri. Ad Claras Aquas (Quaracchi), Ex Typ. Colegii S. Bonaventurae, 1904–1905. 3 v.

763

Molitor, Wilhelm. Die Decretale per venerabilem von Innocenz III, und ihre Stellung im öffentlichen Rechte der Kirche; kanonistische Studie. Münster, Russell, 1876. 247 p.

764

Montero y Gutiérrez, Eloy. Instituciones de derecho canónico. Madrid, Fontana, 1928–1930. 3 v.
Contains bibliographies.

765

Montero y Gutiérrez, Eloy. Instituciones de derecho canónico; derecho canónico constitucional, administrativo y penal, libros II, III y V del código.

3. ed., corr. y aumentada. Madrid, Sáez, 1948. 466 p.
Bibliographical footnotes.

766

Montero y Gutiérrez, Eloy. Manual de derecho canónico. Buenos Aires, Perrot, 1950. 2 v.

767

Móra, Mihály. Magister Gratianus mint perjogász. Budapest, 1938. 43 p.

768

Mörsdorf, Klaus. Die Rechtssprache des Codex juris canonici; eine kritische Untersuchung. Paderborn, Schöningh, 1937. 424 p. (Görres gesellschaft zur pflege der wissenschaft im katholischen Deutschland. Veröffentlichungen der Sektion für rechts und staatswissenschaft . . . 74. hft.)
"Quellen und schrifttum": p. [11]–15.

769

Mortimer, Robert C., Bp. of Exeter. Western canon law. London, Black [1953] 92 p.

770

Moser, Johann J., comp. Corpvs jvris evangelicorvm ecclesiastici, oder Sammlung evangelisch-luterisch- und reformirter kirchen-ordnungen, wie auch dergleichen armen-, classical-, consistorial-, ehe-, gerichts-, gymnasien-, hochzeit-, hospital-, inspections-, leichen-, presbyterial-, schul-, super-intendentz-, tauf-, visitations-, universitäts-, waisenhaus- und andere solche ordnungen, nebst denen von dergleichen dingen, oder auch von causis et delictis mixtis handelnden edicten, generalre-scripten u. d. Züllichau, Frommann, 1737–38, 2 v.

771

Mosiek, Ulrich. Verfassungsrecht der lateinischen Kirche. 1. Aufl. Freiburg (im Breisgau), Rombach, 1975– 1 v. (Rombach Hochschul Paperback; Bd. 72)
Includes bibliographies.

772

Murillo Velarde, Pedro. Cursus juris canonici, hispani, et indici, in quo, juxta ordinem titulorum. ed. 3. notis, et constitutionibus bened XIV illustrata. Matriti, In typographia Ulloae a Ramone Ruiz, 1791. 2 v.

773

Naogeorgus, Thomas. Rvbricae sive Svmmae capitvlorvm iuris canonici. Thomae Naogeorgi Straubingensis opera in lucem editae. Adiunctus quoque est in calce, praecipuorum locorum, qui in decretis tractantur, index. Lvgdvni, apvd Rovillivm, 1578, 286 p.

774

Narbona, Didacus de. Horographia iuris seu de legitimis horarum intervallis iuridica descriptio. Matriti, Coello, 1652. 271 p.

775

Naz, Raoul, ed. Traité de droit canonique. Paris, Letouzey et Ané [1948–]
Bibliographies at beginning of most chapters.

776

Naz, Raoul, ed. Traité de droit canonique. 2. éd. rev. Paris, Letouzey et Ané [1955] 4 v.
Includes bibliographies.

777

Nemes, Antal. Egyházi törvénykezési rendtartás. Budapest, Athenaeum Könyvnyomdája, 1895, 288 p.

778

Neuberger, Nicolas J. Canon 6 or The relation of the Codes Juris Canonici to preceding legislation. Washington, D.C., The Catholic University of American Press, 95 p. (Catholic University of America. Canon law studies, no. 44)

779

Neumann, Johannes. Das Kirchenrecht. Chance und Versuchung. Graz, Wien, Köln, Verl. Styria, 1972. 63 p. (Reihe X)
Includes bibliographical references.

780

Nicollis, Laurentius V. de, abp. Praxis canonica sive jus canonicum casibus practicis explanatum. Salisburgi, Mayr, 1729, 2 v.

781

Nociones de derecho canónico en conformidad con el novísimo código de Pío X. Valparaíso, Curso Universitario de los Sagrados Corazones, 1919. 152 p.

782

Novati, Girolamo. Hieronymi Novati Mediolanen, advocati pro serenissima, d. Catherina de Castiglia de Aragonia Angliae regina Allegationes. [1532]

783

Ochoa Sanz, Javier. Vincentius Hispanus; canonista boloñes del siglo XIII. Roma, 1960. 184 p. (Cuadernos del Instituto Jurídico Español, no. 13)
Bibliographical footnotes.

784

Ogle, Arthur. The canon law in mediaeval England; an examination of William Lyndwood's "Provinciale," in reply to the late Professor F. W. Maitland. London, Murray, 1912. 220 p.

785

Ogle, Arthur. The canon law in mediaeval England; an examination of William Lyndwood's "Provinciale," in reply to the late Professor F. W. Maitland. New York, Franklin [1971] 220 p. (Burt Franklin research and source works series, 731. Selected essays, in history, economics and social science, 262)

786

Olmo, Cesare. Il diritto ecclesiastico vigente in Italia; esposto. 2 ed. riv. ed ampliata dall'autore. Milano, Hoepli, 1903. 483 p. (Manuali Hoepli. Serie scientifica, 108–109)

787

Ordo "Invocato Christi nomine". Der Ordo "Invocato Christi nomine". Mit Unterstützung der Forschungsgemeinschaft der deutschen Wissenschaft und des Ministeriums für Schulwesen und Volkskultur in der Tschechoslovakischen Republik. Heidelberg, Winter, 1931. 165 p. (Quellen zur geschichte des römisch-kanonischen processes im mittelalter, hrsg. von Dr. Ludwig Wahrmund . . . v. bd. hft. 1)

788

Orlet, Rainer. Die Anfänge Kirchlicher Rechtsetzung bis in das sechste Jahrhundert. München, Schön, 1976. 193 p.
Bibliography: p. v–vi.

789

Ortíz, Ramón. A Ação Católica no direito eclesias-tico. Québec, Faculté de droit canonique, Université Laval, 1947. 104, [1] p. (Les thèses canoniques de Laval)
Bibliography: p. v–vii.

790

Ourliac, Paul, and Henri Gilles. La période post-classique, 1378–1500. [Paris, Cujas, 1971–] (Histoire du droit et des institutions de l'Église en Occident, t. 13)
Includes bibliographical references.

791

Owen, Robert. Institutes of canon law. London, Hayes, 1884. 178 p.
Includes bibliographical references.

792

Pachmann, Theodor, ritter von. Lehrbuch des Kirchenrechtes, mit Berücksichtigung der auf die kirchlichen Verhältnisse bezug nehmenden österreichischen Gesetze und Verordnungen. 3. ganz umbearb. aufl. Wien, Braumüller, 1863–66. 3 v.

793

Pacichelli, Giovanni B. De jure hospitalitatis universo. Coloniae Ubdorum, Friess, 1675. 322, [10] p.

794

Palazzini, Pietro. Il diritto strumento di riforma ecclesiastica in S. Pier Damiani. Romae, Officium Libri Catholici, 1956. 104 p.
Includes bibliography.

795

Paleolus, Michael A. Praxis succincta ad sous adjutores studii super rite. Romae, de Rubeis, 1752. 146 p.

796

Paquet, Louis A. Droit publique de l'église. L'organisation religieuse et le pouvoir civil. Québec, Imprimé par la compagnie de l'Événement, 1912. 315 p.

797

Paquet, Louis A. Droit public de l'église; principes généraux. 2. éd., ouvrage précédé d'une lettre-préface de monseigneur Paul-Eugène Roy. Québec, Laflamme, 1916. 368 p.

798
Parexa, Gabrielis de. Praxis edendi, sive tractatus de universa instrumentorum editione. Editio novissima. Lugduni, sumtibus Lavrentii Anisson, 1668. 2 v. in 1.

799
Paris, Institut catholique. Faculté de droit canonique. Actes du congrès de droit canonique; cinquantenaire de la Faculté de droit canonique, Paris, 22–26 avril 1947. Paris, Letouzey & Ané [1950] 414 p. (Bibliothèque de la Faculté de droit canonique de Paris)
"Bibliographie sommaire de la Faculté de droit canonique": p. [117]–137. Bibliographical footnotes.

800
Parisio, Flaminio. Consvultatio Parisii cvivsdam de controversia inter sanctitatem Pauli quinti & serenissimam Rempublicã venetam. 114 p.

801
Passerini, Pietro M. Commentaria in primum [–secundum] librum sexti decretalium. Cvm ipso textv svis locis disposito et indicibus necessariis. Venetiis, apud Balleonium, 1698. 2 v. in 1.

802
Passerini, Silvio, cardinal. Statuta reuerendissimi dñi Syluij cardinalis cortonensis legati. [Perusie, 1526]

803
Paucapalea. Die Summa des Paucapalea über das Decretum Gratiani. Hrsg. von dr. Joh. Friedrich von Schulte. Giessen, Roth, 1890. 146 p.

804
Pellegrini, Marco A. Tractstvs varij, selecti, practici, omnibvs absoluti nvmeris, & vt vsu frequentes, sic vtilitate referti, in sex libros. Nvnc primvm in lvcem editi. Venetiis, apud Polum, 1611. 151 l.

805
Perathoner, Anton. Das kirchliche Gesetzbuch; sinngemäss wiedergegeben und mit Anmerkungen versehen. 4., verb. und stark verm. Aufl. Bressanone, Weger, 1926. 763 p.

806
Perathoner, Anton. Kurze Einführung in das neue kirchliche Gesetzbuch (Corpus juris canonici). Brizen, Weger, 1919. 191 p.

807
Périn, Carlos. Las leyes de la sociedad Cristiana. Versión castellana de Francisco Morena. Barcelona, Diario de Barcelona, 1876. 331 p.

808
Pesendorfer, Marianne. Partikulares Gesetz und particularer Gesetzgeber im System des geltenden lateinischen Kirchenrechts. Wien, Herder, 1975. 134 p. (Kirche und Recht; 12)
Bibliography: p. 13–15.

809
Petroncelli, Mario. Corso di diritto ecclesiastico. 2. ed. Milano, Giuffrè, 1946. 303, [1] p.
"Bibliografia": p. 11–12.

810
Petroncelli, Mario. Corso di diritto ecclesiastico; anno accademico 1948–1949. Napoli, Pellerano [1949–]

811
Petroncelli, Mario. Diritto canonico. 7. ed. aggiornata con le disposizioni post conciliar. Napoli, Società editrice napoletana, 1976. 406 p.

812
Petroncelli, Mario. Il diritto canonico dopo il Concilio Vaticano II. Napoli, Libreria scientifica editrice, [1969] 478 p.

This manual analyzes canon law's close relationship with theology. In its introduction it presents many elements of historical importance for the life of the Church, including Vatican II, already in the minds of Popes Pius XI and XII. The council was finally announced on January 25, 1959, by John XXIII, convened under Him, and concluded under Paul VI on December 8, 1965. Besides the basic elements found in canon law textbooks, included in this manual are other decisions and documents which greatly affected the discipline of the Church, for instance, the authority of the synods of the bishops, and the contribution of laymen in the government of the universal Church.

813

Petroncelli, Mario. Diritto ecclesiastico. Napoli, Società editrice napoletana, [1975] 300 p.

814

Petroncelli, Mario. Lineamenti di diritto canonico. 2. ed. Napoli, Humus, 1947. 255 p. (Manuali di scienze giuridice ed economiche)

815

Petroncelli, Mario. Lineamenti di diritto canonico. 3. ed. [Napoli] Humus, 1949. 271 p. (Manuali di scienze giuridiche ed economiche)
Bibliography: p. [237]–261.

816

Petroncelli, Mario. Il principio della non retroattivita delle leggi in diritto canonico. Milano, Pensiero, 1931. 73 p.

817

Phillips, George. Du droit ecclésiastique dans ses sources, considérées au point de vue élements législatifs que les constituent, traduit par l'abbé Crouzet, suivi d'un essai de bibliographie du droit canonique. Paris, Lecoffre, 1852. 550 p.
Includes bibliographies.

818

Phillips, George. Du droit ecclésiastique dans ses principes généraux, traduit par J. P. Crouzet. 2. ed. Paris, Lecoffre, 1855, 3 v.

819

Phillips, George. Kirchenrecht. Graz, Akademische Druck- u. Verlagsanstalt, 1959–. (Orbis literarum)

820

Piacenti, Lorenzo. Ambarum legum institutiones in septem libros divisas quatuor tribunalia continentes canonicum, morale, civile et criminale. Bononiae, Borzaghi, 1714. 391 p.

821

Picasso, Giorgio. Collezioni canoniche milanesi del secolo XII. Milano, Vita e pensiero, 1969. 310 p. (Pubblicazioni dell'Università cattolica del S. Cuore. Saggi e ricerche. Serie 3: Scienze storiche, 2)
Bibliography: p. [3]–14.

822

Pichler, Veit. Jus canonicum practice explicatum, seu Decisiones casuum selectorum centum octoginta quinque ad singulos Decretalium Gregorii papae IX. titulos, et ad consuetum referendi modum accommodatae. Opus novum, prius in duas partes divisum, nunc verò redactum in unum volumen, ut in pari forma respondeat Praxis Theoriae, jam antecedenter editae in Candidato jurisprudentiae sacrae, vel potiùs in Summa jurisprudentiae sacrae, quem titulum praesefert idem liber in folio impressus. Ingolstadii, de la Haye, 1746. 720, [10] p.

823

Pichler, Vitus. Summa jurisprudentiae sacrae universae seu jus canonicum, secundum quinque Decretalium Gregorii Papae IX titulos explicatum. Augustae Vindelicorum, Sumptibus Martini Veith, 1741. 686, 430 p.

824

Pickett, R. Colin. Mental affliction and church law; an historical synopsis of Roman and ecclesiastical law and a canonical commentary. Ottawa, University of Ottawa Press, 1952. 220 p. (Universitas Catholica Ottaviensis. Series canonica, 25)
Bibliography: p. [207]–218.

825

Pictet, Benedict. Motifs de la conversion de Noble Joachim Frideric Minuteli. Modane, 1714. 180 p.

826

Pietrzyk, Stanley. A practical formulary in accordance with the Code of canon law. 2d. rev. ed. Rome, Officium libri catholici, Catholic Book Agency, 1959. 278 p.

827

Pignatelli, Giacomo. Consultationes canonicae, in quibus praecipuae controversiae quae ad sanctorum canonizationem ac sacros ritus . . . ac hujusmodi alia potissimum pertinent non solum ex utroque jure scripto, sed etiam ex sacrarum congregationum decretis, rebus judicatis . . . breviter ac perspicue dirimuntur. Ed. ultima ab authore recognita, multis in locis aucta, & a mendis expurgata. Coloniae Allobrogum, de Torunes, 17—.

828

Pira, Karl. Satser till kritisk belysning af R. Sohms kyrkorätt. Stockholm, Tryckt hos P. Palmquists aktiebolag, 1897. 46 p.

829

Pirhing, Ennricus. Jus canonicum in V libros decretalium distributum. Omnis capitulis titulorum . . . promiscue et confuse prositis, in ordinem doctrinae digesti . . . Tomus primus. Venetiis, Remondini, 1759.

830

Pius VII. Sanctissimi domini nostri Pii septimi pontificis maximi allocutiones consistoriales habitae sacri principatus ejus anno primo. Romae, apud Lazzarinum Rev. Camerae Apost. Typographum, 1801. 33 p.

831

Plassmann, Engelbert. Staatskirchenrechtliche Grundgedanken der deutschen Kanonisten an der Wende vom 18. zum 19. Jahrhundert. Freiburg, Herder, 1968. 191 p. (Freiburger theologische Studien, 88. Heft)
   Bibliography: p. 171–186.

832

Plettenberg, Hunold. Introductio ad jus canonicum. Hildesii, typis Joan. Leonardi Schlegelii, episc. & Summi capit. typog., prostant Coloniae de Berges, 1692. 387, [16] p.

833

Plöchl, Willibald M. Geschichte des Kirchenrechts. Wien, Verlag Herold [1953–69] 5 v.
   Includes bibliographies.

834

Pole, Reginald, cardinal. Reformatio Angliae ex decretis Reginaldi Poli Cardinalis, Sedis Apostolicae legati, anno 1556. Romae, Manut, 1562. 27 1.

835

Politi, Vincenzo. Diritto ecclesiastico; appunti ad uso degli studenti. [Palermo] Università di Palermo, Facoltà di giurisprudenza [1955] 238 p.

836

Pometti, Francesco. Il Decretum di Graziano nei suoi precedenti storici e nelle sue conseguenze storico-ecclesiastiche, contributo alla storia della Chiesa; note. Corigliano Calabro, Dragosei, 1910. 234 p.

837

Pomey, François A. Pantheum mythicum, seu Fabulosa deorum historia hoc primo epitomes eruditionis volvmine breviter dilucideque comprehensa. Ed. novissima, prioribus correctior, variisque aeneis figuris ornata. Francofurti, Rönnagel, 1738. 282 p.

838

Porubszky, József. Katholikus egyházjogtan, főleg a jogakademiai ifjúság számára. Egerben, Erseki Lyceum könyv- és Kőnyomdájában, 1863. 239 p.

839

Pöschl, Arnold, Kurzgefasstes Lehrbuch des katholischen Kirchenrechtes auf Grund des neuen kirchlichen Gesetzbuches. 2. umgearbeitete Aufl. Graz, Moser, 1921. 370 p.

840

Pöschl, Arnold. Kurzgefasetas Lehrbuch des Katholischen Kirchenrechtes auf Grund das neuen kirchlichen Gesetzbuches. 3. umgearb. Aufl. Graz, Mosers, 1931.

841

Posoborowe prawodawstwo kościelne: dokumenty prawno-liturgiczne, zebrał i przetłumaczył Edward Sztafrowski. Warszawa, Akademia Teologii Katolickiej, 19—.
   Includes bibliographical references and indexes.

842

Posoborowe prawodawstwo kościelne: za okres styczeń 1963—czerwiec 1967 r., zebrał i przetłumaczył Edward Sztafrowski. Warszawa, Akademia Teologii Kotolickiej, 1968–1975. 6 v. in 18.
   Includes bibliographical references and indexes.

843

Pospishil, Victor J. Interritual canon law problems in the United States and Canada. Chesapeake City, Md., St. Basil's, 1955. 248 p.
   Bibliography: p. 7–9.

844

Postconciliar thoughts; renewal and reform of canon law. Edited by Neophytos Edelby, Teodoro Jiménez Urresti [and] Petrus Huizing. New York, Paulist Press [1967] 183 p. (Concilium: theology in the age of renewal, v. 28)

Includes bibliographical references.

845

Postíus, Juan. El Código canónico aplicado a España en forma de instituciones. 5. ed refundida por el autor, rev. por Felipe Clemente de Diego. Madrid, Editorial del Corazón de María, 1926. 1111 p.

846

Pragmatische Geschichte der so berufenen Bulle in coena domini und ihren fürchterlichen Folen für den Staat und die Kirche, zur Beurtheilung aller Streitigkeiten unseres Jahrhunderts mit dem römischen Hof. Frankfurth und Leipzig, 1772. 2 v. in 1.

847

Proposed norms for considerations in the revision of the canons concerning religious. [Washington], Conference of Major Religious Superiors of Women's Institutes in the United States of America. [1968]. 99 p.

848

El Proyecto de ley fundamental de la Iglesia; texto y análisis crítico. Pamplona, Ediciones Universidad de Navarra, 1971] 226 p. (Cuadernos de la Colección canónica, 13)

Includes bibliographical references.

849

Prümmer, Dominicus M. Manuale iuris canonici in usum scholarum. Ed. 6 quam curavit Engelbertus M. Münch. Friburgi Brisgoviae, Herder, 1933. 756 p.

"Brevis catalogus auctorum qui de iure ecclesiastico scripserunt": p. [xvii]–xiv.

850

Quaestiones regulares et canonicae enucleatae. Salmanticae, Ramirez, 1628. 880 p.

851

Questioni attuali di diritto canonico; relazioni lette nella Sezione di diritto canonico del Congresso internazionale per il IV centenario della Pontificia Università gregoriana, 13–17 ottobre 1953. Romae, apud Aedes Universitatis Gregorianae, 1955. 496 p. (Analecta Gregoriana, v. 69. Series Facultatis Iuris Canonici, sectio A, n. 4)

Bibliographical footnotes.

852

Quigley, Joseph A. M. Condemned societies. Washington, D.C., The Catholic University of America Press, 1927. 139 p. (The Catholic University of America, Canon law studies, no. 46).

853

Ramstein, Matthew, father. A manual of canon law. Hoboken, N.J., Terminal Print. and Pub. Co., 1947. 747 p.

Bibliography: p. 44–86.

854

Ravà, Anna. I trapiantidi organi da individuo a individuo nel diritto canonico. Milano, Giuffrè, 1956. 125 p.

Includes bibliography.

855

Raymundus de Pennaforte, saint. Opera omnia. Curante Rmo. Dre. Josepho Rius et Serra. Barchinonae, 1945—

856

Raynaldus, Joannes D. Vota Io. Dominici Raynaldi ... Opus posthumum. Romae, ex typographia reverendae Camerae apostolicae, 1714. 356 p.

857

Rechtsgeschichtlich-diplomatische Studien zu frümittelalterlichen Papsturkunden, von Egon Boshof u. Heinz Wolter. Köln, Wien, Böhlau, 1976. 264 p. (Studien und Vorabeiten zur Germania pontificia, Bd. 6)

Includes bibliographical references and index.

858

Reformatio legum ecclesiasticarum, ex authoritate primum regis Henrici 8. inchoata: deinde per regem Edovardum 6. provecta, adauctáque in hunc modum, atq$_3$ nunc ad pleniorem ipsarum reformationem in lucem edita. Londini, typis T. H. & R. H., impensis Danielis Frere, 1640. 303 p.

859

Regatillo, Eduardo F. Interpretatio et iurisprudentia Codicis iuris canonici. 3. ed. Santander, Sal terrae, 1953. 719 p. (Biblioteca Comillensis, serie canónica)

860

Regino, abbot of Prüm. De synodalibus causis et disciplinis ecclesiasticis. Ed. F. G. A. Wasserschleben. (Photomechanischer Nachdruck [der Ausg. von] 1840) Graz, Akademische Druck- u. Verlagsanstalt, 1964. 526 p.

861

Regulae omnes, ordinationes, & constitutiones Cancellariae S. D. N. d. Pauli papae III. vndiq collecte, ac in hunc vsq diem editae, mendis innumeris expurgate. Addito etiam indice regularum, quae omissa, ac negligenter in aliis impressionibus obseruata fuere. Festa palatii apostolici, & capitolina. Romae, apud de Carulariis, impensis Lilii Veneti, 1541.

862

Regulae omnes, ordinationes, et constitutiones Cancellariae S. d. n. d. Pauli diuina prouidentia papae IV. Parisiis, apud Renauld, 1555. 32 l.

863

Regulae ordinationes, et constitutiones Cancellariae apostolicae sanctissimi d. n. d. Clementis divina providentia papae XIV. Romae, typis reverendae Camerae apostolicae, 1769. 90 p.

864

Regulae ordinationes, et constitutiones Cancellariae apostolicae sanctissimi d. n. d. Pii divina providentia papae VI. Romae, typis reverendae Camerae apostolicae, 1776. 90 p.

865

Reichel, Oswald J. The elements of canon law. London, Bosworth, 1887. 306 p.

866

Reicke, Siegfried. Kirchenrecht. Marburg, Lahn, Elwert [1950] 361–392 p.
  Bibliography: p. 392.

867

Reiggenstuel, Anaklet, Father. Jus canonicum universum clara methodo juxta titulos quique librorum decretalium in quaestiones distributum, solidisque responsionibus, & objectionum solutionibus dilucidatum: cui in hac novissima editione accessit tomus sextus complectens tractatum de regulis juris. Venetiis, apud Antonium Bortoli, 1735. 6 v. in 4.

868

Reims (Archdiocese). Status synodaux, publiés en 1960 par Louis-Augustin Marmottin, archevêque de Reims. Reims, Impr. Matot-Braine, 1960. 217 p.

869

Repertorium super Lectu. Panor. Index, aut si mauis Repertorium admodum solennis super Comentarijs ... Nicolai de Tudeschis ... in quinq$_3$ libros Decretalium, summo labore ac vigilantia recognitus examusimq$_3$ castigatus. [Lugduni, Impressum in edibus Antonij du Ry, sumptibus Iacobi q. Francisci de Giuncta, ac sociorum] 1527. [422] p.

870

Repetitionum iuris canonci volumina sex. Coloniae Agrippinae, Cymnicus, 1618. 3 v. in 1.

871

Retzbach, Anton. Das Recht der katholischen Kirche nach dem Codex iuris canonici, für die Praxis bearb. 3., verb. und verm. Aufl, hrsg. von Franz Vetter. Freiburg im Br., Herder, 1947. 580 p.

872

Retzbach, Anton. Das Recht der katholischen Kirche nach dem Codex iuris canonici für die Praxis bearbeitet. 4., verb. u. verm. Aufl. hrsg. von Franz Vetter. Freiburg, Herder, 1953. 540 p.

873

Retzbach, Anton. Das Recht der katholischen Kirche nach dem Codex Iuris Canonici, für die Praxis bearbeitet. 5., verb. und verm. Aufl., hrsg. von Franz Vetter. Basel, Herder, 1959. 553 p.

874

Riccio, Giovanni L., bp. Praxis avrea, et qvotidiana novissimae probationis ivrispatronatvs, eiusdemque existentiae, & pertinentiae, ivxta Sacri concilii tridentini seriam. Rotaeq; romanaeq; curiae, aliorumq; ecclesiasticorum tribunalium inueteratum stylum, atque ritum. Opvscvlvm sane avrevm, nvnc primvm prodit ... Cvm gemino indice ... Neapoli, Maccarano, 1631.

875

Richter, Aemilius L. Lehrbuch des katholischen und evangelischen Kirchenrechts. Mit besonderer Rücksicht auf deutsche Zustände. 5. umgearb. aufl. Leipzig, Tauchnitz, 1858. 835, [2] p.

"Ausgewählte literatur des kirchenrechts": p. 8–18.

876

Richter, Ämilius L. Lehrbuch des katholischen und evangelischen Kirchenrechts. 8. Aufl, bearb. von Dove und Kahl. Aalen, Scientia, 1975. 2 v. (1410 p.)

Includes bibliographical references and index.

877

Riegger, Paul J. Lecciones de disciplina eclesiastica general traducidas, anotadas y adicionadas con la particular de la iglesia española ... sobre la obra que con el título de instituciones de jurisprudencia eclesiástica dio a luz en latin Pablo José de Rieger ... por el Dr. D. Joaquín Lumbreras. Madrid, Calero, 1838–41. 6 v.

878

Riegger, Paul J., ritter von. Institvtionvm ivrisprvdentiae ecclesiasticae pars I.–[IV.] ... Editio nova, et emendata. Vindobonae, typis I. Thomae nob. de Trattnern, caes. reg. avlae typogr. et bibliop., 1777. 4 v.

879

Riesco Terrero, Angel. Las causas pías en la legislación civil y canónica. Vitoria, Editorial ESET, 1962. 58 p.

Bibliographical footnotes.

880

Rinander, Viktor A. Kanonisk rätt och nutida offentlig rätt; klerus och offentlig tjänst. Uppsala, Almqvist & Wiksells boktryckeri-a.b., 1927. 180 p.

"Litteratur": p. [v]–viii.

881

Robert of Flamborough. Liber poenitentialis; a critical edition with introduction and notes, edited by J. J. Francis Firth. Toronto, Pontifical Institute of Mediaeval Studies, 1971. 364 p. (Pontifical Institute of Mediaeval Studies. Studies and texts, 18)

Bibliography: p. [ix]–xxiv.

882

Robilant, Enrico di. Significato del diritto naturale nell'ordinamento canonico. Torino, Giappichelli [1954] 211 p. (Università di Torino. Memorie dell'Istituto giuridico. Ser. 2., memoria 85)

883

Roboredo, Giulio A. Dissertationes ad praecepta primae tabulae. Florentiae, Guiducci, 1715. 427, [5] p.

884

Rocca, Fernando della. Diritto canonico. Padova, CEDAM, 1961. 677 p.

Bibliographical footnotes.

885

Rocca, Fernando della. Manual of canon law. Translated by Anselm Thatcher. Milwaukee, Bruce Pub. Co. [1959] 624 p.

886

Rodriguez Fermosino, Nicolás, Bp. Tractatvs III. De probationibvs, ad titvlvm VII. libri II. decretalivm Gregorii pontificis. IX. Ad titulos de confessis, probationibus, testibus, & testibus cogendis. Cum indice multiplici titulorum, capitum, quaestionum, canonum, legum iurium, locorum, rerum & verborum hoc tractatu contentorum. Nvnc primvm in lvcem prodit. Lvgdvni, Boissat & Remevs, 1662. 2 v. in 1.

887

Romani, Silvio. Jus privatum comparatum. Romae, Rassegna di morale e diritto. 1937.

888

Romani, Silvio. Studia juris canonici. [Romae, apud auctorem, 1939—]

Includes bibliographies.

889

Romani, Silvio. Studia juris canonici. Romae, apud auctorem, 1940. (Studia juris canonici, no. 4)

890

Rösser, Ernst. Göttliches und Menschliches, unveränderliches und veränderliches Kirchenrecht von der Entstehung der Kirche bis zur mitte des 9. jahrhunderts; untersuchungen zur Geschichte des Kirchenrechts mit besonderer Berücksichtigung der Anschaungen Rudolph Sohms. Paderborn, Schöningh, 1934. 192 p. (Görres gesellschaft zur pflege der wissenschaft im katholischen Deutschland. Veröffentlichungen der Sektion für rechts und staatswissenschaft . . . 64 hft).
"Quellen- und literaturverzeichnis": p. [vii]–xvi.

891

Rosshirt, Konrad E. F. Aeussere encyclopädie des Kirchenrechts; oder, Die Haupt- und Hilfswissenschaften des Kirchenrechts. Heidelberg, Weiss, 1865–67. 2 v.
Contains bibliographies.

892

Rosshirt, Konrad E. F. Canonisches Recht. Schaffhausen, F. Hurter, 1857. 1047, [1] p.

893

Rosshirt, Konrad E. F. Lehrbuch des Kirchenrechts. 3. ganz umgearb. aufl. Schaffhausen, Hurter, 1858. [1], 160 p.

894

Rossi, Gaspare de. Tractatus valde utilis et necessarius de reservationibus apostolicis, compositus per R. P. D. Gasparem de Perusio quondam episcopu Frequentinum, nunc primu in luce aeditus. Romae, 1539. 22 p.

895

Roye, François de. Canonici juris institutiones . . . Additvr Ioannis Dujati Historia de eodem jure ex gallico in latinum idioma nunc primum versa. Venetiis, Pazzana, 1771. 392 p.

896

Roye, François de. Canonici juris institutionum libri tres. Parisiis, Dezallier, 1717. 358 p.

897

Rubeus, Theodosius. Singvlaria ex Sacrae Rotae Romanae decisionibvs selecta. Romae, Mascardi, 1624–37. 2 v.

898

Ruck, Erwin. Kirchenrecht. 2. Aufl. Berlin, Springer, 1931. 88 p. (Enzyklopädie der Rechts- und Staatswissenschaft, Abt. Rechtswissenschaft, 29)

899

Rufinus, bp. of Assisi. Die Summa decretorum. Herausgegeben von dr. Heinrich Singer . . . Mit unterstützung der Gesselschaft zur förderung deutscher wissenschaft, kunst und litteratur in Böhmen. Paderborn, Schöningh, 1902. 570 p.

900

Rufinus, bp. of Assisi. Summa decretorum. Hrsg. von Heinrich Singer. Aaelen, Scientia Verlag, 1963. 570 p.
Includes bibliographical references.

901

Rufinus, bp. of Assisi. Die Summa magistri Rufini zum Decretum Gratiani. Mit einer erörterung über die bearbeitungen derselben hrsg. von dr. Joh. Friedrich von Schulte. Giessen, Roth, 1892. 496 p.

902

Ryan, John J. Saint Peter Damiani and his canonical sources; a preliminary study in the antecedents of the Gregorian reform. With a pref. by Stephen Kuttner. Toronto, Pontificum Institutum Studiorum Mediae Aetatis, 1956. 213 p. (Pontifical Institute of Mediaeval Studies. Studies and texts, 2)
Bibliography: p. 205–213.

903

Ryder, Raymond A. Simony, an historical synopsis and commentary. Washington, D.C., The Catholic University of America Press, 1931. (The Catholic University of America. Canon law studies, no. 65)

904

Rynthelen, Cornelius von. Ivrista romano-catholicvs, id est, Ivridica romanae catholicae fidei confessio, qva clarissimis Ivstiniani maximi imperatoris ante mille et plvres annos pvblicatis II. praecipua ss. Romanae ecclesiae hodie controuersa dogmata apertè probantur, sectariorum verǒ, i. Lutheranorum, Caluinistarum & Anabaptistarum, &c. errores damnantur, avthore Cornelio à Rynthelen . . . Coloniae Agrippinae, apud Stephanum Hemmerden, 1618. 299 p.

905

Sacco, Vincenzo, conte. Institutionum juris canonici libri quatuor, ubi de personis, rebus, nec non jurdiciis civilibus, ac criminalibus; quibus praemittitur introductio ad studium juris canonici. Parmae, Borsi, 1664. 336 p.

906

Salamanca. Pontificia Universidad Eclesiástica. Investigación y elaboración del derecho canónico; trabajos de la V semana de derecho canónico. Barcelona, Flors, 1956. 336 p.

907

Salazar Abrisquieta, José de. Lo jurídico y lo moral en el ordenamiento canónico. Vitoria, Editorial Eset, Seminario Diocesano, 1960. 276 p. (Victoriensia; publicaciones del Seminario de Vitoria, 11)

908

Salis-Mayenfeld, Ludwig R. von. Die Publikation des tridentinischen Rechts der Eheschliessung. Basel, Detloff, 1888. 74 p.

909

Salzano, Tomm. M. V. Lezioni di diritto canonico pubblico, e privato considerato in sè stesso e secondo l'attual polizia del Regno delle due Sicilie. Napoli, Giordano, 1838. 2 v. in 1.

910

Salzano, Tomm. M. V. Lezioni di diritto canonico, pubblico, e privato considerato in sè stesso e secondo l'attual polizia del Regno delle Due Sicilie. 3. ed., corretta, novelle aggiunzioni. Napoli, Giordano, 1841. 4 v. in 2.

911

Sandeo, Felino M., bp. Commentaria Felini Sandei in V lib. Decretalivm longè utilissima, doctissimorvm virorvm Benedicti à Vadis [et al.] adnotationibus, rerumq₃ summis illustrata, ac innumeris locis, collatione ad uetustissimorum codicum fidem facta, integritati suae fideliter restituta. Pars prima[–tertia]. Basileae, Ex Officina Frobeniana, 1567. 4 v. in 2.

912

Sandeo, Felino M., bp. Commentariorum Felini Sandei ad quinque libros Decretalium pars prima[–tertia]. Eruditorum virorum adnotationi-

bus atque rerum summis illustrata, innumerisq₃ prope mendis nunc denuò collatione vetustorum exemplarium expurgata. Venetiis. 1600–01. 3 v. in 2.

913

Sandeo, Felino M., bp. Consilia Felini Sandei Ferrariensis, qua fieri potuit diligentia abinnumeris prope erroribus vindicata. His subiectus est Index in omnia eiusdem Felini opera locupletissimus. Venetiis, 1601. 157 p.

914

Sanguineti, Sebastiano. Iuris ecclesiastici institutiones in usum praelectionum. Ed. 2. aucta et expolita. Romae, Ex Typographia Polyglotta, 1890. 587 p.

915

Sarmiento de Mendoza, Francisco, bp. Selectarvm interpretationvm libri tres ad S. D. N. Pivm v. pontificem maximvm. Romae, apud Iulium Accoltum, 1571. 460 p.

916

Sarpi, Paolo. Petri Svavis Polani Historiae Concilii Tridentini libri octo. Ex Italicis summa fide & accuratione Latini facti. Avgustae Trinobantvm primum. Francofvrti, Tampachio, 1621. 924 p.

917

Sarpilius, Johann. Compendiosa delineatio totius Juris canonici et civilis, in utroque tam allegandi quàm abbreviationes legendi modum exhibens. [Jenae, Nisi] 1675. 67 p.

918

Sauter, Josef A. Fvndamenta ivris ecclesiastici Catholicorvm. 3. ed. Rotwilae, In officina Libraria Herderiana, 1825. 2 v.

919

Sauter, Josef A. Fundamenta juris ecclesiastici Catholicorum. Friburgi, Herder, 1840. 3 v. in 1.

920

Saviano, Renato. Le fonti canoniche del diritto comune. 2. ed., riv. e ampliata. Napoli, Libreria scientifica editrice [1958?] 159 p.

Bibliography: p. [133]–153.

921

Scharnagl, Anton. Das neue kirchliche Gestzbuch; eine Einführung mit besonderer Berücksichtigung des bayerischen Rechtes. 2. vielfach verm. Aufl. München, Manz, 1918. 142 p.

922

Schelstrate, Emmanuel. Tractatvs de sensv et avctoritate decretorvm constantiensia concilii sessione qvarta et qvinta circa potestatem ecclesiasticam editorvm cvm actis et gestis ad illa spectantibvs et ex m. ss. italicis, germanicis, ac gallicis nvnc primvm in lvcem ervtis opera et stvdio d. Emanvelis a Schelstrate. Romae, typis s. congregationis de propaganda fide, 1686. 302 p.

923

Schenkl, Maurus. Synopsis juris ecclesiastici. Passavit, Winkler, 1834. 172 p.

924

Scheuermann, Audomar. Die Exemtion nach geltendem kirchlichen Recht mit einem Überblick über die geschichtliche Entwicklung. Paderborn, Schöningh, 1938. 255 p. (Görres-gesellschaft; veröffentlichungen der Sektion für rechts- und staatswissenschaft. 77. hft.)
"Quellen und literaturabkürzungen": p. [13]–22.

925

Schiappoli, Domenico. Manuale di diritto ecclesiastico. Napoli, Pierro, 1913. 623 p.
"Elencho delle principali opere che si possono consultare": p. [xi]–xii.

926

Schilling, Bruno. Der Kirchenbann nach canonischem Rechte, in seiner Entstehung und allmäligen Entwickelung. Leipzig, Graefe, 1859. 213 p.

927

Schilling, Bruno, *and* C. F. F. Sintenis. Das Corpus juris canonici in seinem Wichtigsten und Anwendbarsten Theilen, in's Deutsche Übersetzt und Systematisch zusammengestellt. Leipzig, Focke, 1834–37. 2 v.

928

Schilter, Johann. Io. Schilteri Institvtiones ivris canonici ad ecclesiae veteris et hodiernae statum accommodatae, cvm praefatione Ivsti Henningii Bohmeri. Editio sexta, correctior & magna parte auctior. Francofurti et Lipsiae, apud heredes Bircknerianos, 1718. 558, [34] p.

929

Schmalz, Theodor A. H. Handbuch des canonischen Rechts und seiner Anwendung in den deutschen evangelischen Kirchen. 3. unveränderte Aufl. Berlin, Rücker, 1834. 300 p.
Includes bibliographies.

930

Schmalzgrueber, Franz X. Jus ecclesiasticum universum brevi methodo ad discentium utilitatem explicatum seu lucubrationes canonicae in quinque libros secretalium Gregorii IX Pontificis Maximi. Romae, ex typographia Rev. Can. Apostolicae, 1843–45. 12 v.

931

Schmid, Caspar. Discussio theologico-juridica. Augustae Vindelicorum, Nopperschmid, 1698. 300 p.

932

Schneider, Philipp. Die Lehre den Kirchenrechtsquellen. Eine Einleitung in das Studium des Kirchenrechts. 2 (vollständige Aufl. Regensburg, New York, Pustet, 1892. 212 p.
Contains bibliographies.

933

Schnell, Anselmus. Jus canonicum abbreviatum, id est, quinque librorum decretalium Gregorii IX Pont. Max. summa seu compendium. Augustae Vindelicorum, Mauracher, 1749. 5 v.

934

Schulte, Johann F., *Ritter* von. Die Geschichte der Literatur über das Dekret Gratians. 1.[–2.] Wien, In commission bei K. Gerold's sohn, 1870. 2 v.

935

Schulte, Johann F., *Ritter* von. Die Geschichte der Quellen und Literatur des canonischen Rechts von Gratian bis auf die Gegenwart. Stuttgart, Enke, 1875–80. 3 v. in 4.

936

Schulte, Johann F., *Ritter* von. Handbuch des katholischen Eherechts nach dem gemeinen katholischen Kirchenrechte und dem österreichischen, preussischen, französischen Particularrechte, mit Rücksichtnahme auf noch andere Civilgesetzgebungen. Giessen, Ferbersche Universitäts-Buchhandling, 1855. 622 p.

937

Schulte, Johann F., *Ritter* von. Das katholische Kirchenrecht; dessen Quellen und Literaturgeschichte, System, Einfluss auf die verschiedenen Rechtsdisciplinen überhaupt. Giessen, Verlag der Ferber'schen Universitäts-Buchhandlung, 18—. 2 v.

938

Schulte, Johann F., *Ritter* von. Lehrbuch des katholischen Kirchenrechts auf Grundlage der kirchlichen Quellen und der Staatsgesetze in Oesterreich und den übrigen deutschen Bundesstaaten, nebst dessen Literaturgeschichte und einer Statistik der Katholischen Kirche in Oesterreich, mit Ausschluss Italiens, und den übrigen deutschen Bundesstaaten. Giessen, Ferber'sche Universitäts-Buchhandlung, 1863. 517 p.

939

Schulte, Johann F., *Ritter* von. Lehrbuch des katholischen Kirchenrechts nach dem gemeinen, dem deutschen und österreichischen Partikularrechte und dessen Literaturgeschichte. 2. gänzlich umbearb. und verm. Aufl. Giessen, Roth, 1868. 584 p.

940

Schulte, Johann F., *Ritter* von. Lehrbuch des katholischen und evangelischen Kirchenrechts nach dem gemeinen Rechte, dem Rechte der Deutschen Länder und Oesterreichs. 4. Aufl. des Katholischen, 1. des Evangelischen. Giesen, Roth, 1886. 559 p.

941

Schulte, Johann F., *Ritter* von. Lehrbuch des katholischen Kirchrechts nach dem gemeinen und partikularrechte in Deutschland und Oesterrich und dessen Literaturgeschichte. 3. verb. und verm Aufl. Giessen, Roth, 1873. 642, [2] p.
   "Die literaturgeschichte des kirchenrechts": p. 40–141.

942

Schulte, Johann F., *Ritter* von. Die summa magistri Rufini zum Decretum Gratiani. Mit einer erörterung über die bearbeitungen derselben hrsg. Giessen, Roth, 1892. 496.

943

Schultes, Reginald M., *father*. Was beschwören wir im Antimodernisteneid? Theologische Erklärung des Antimodernisteneides. Mainz, Verlag von Kirchheim, 1911. 85 p.

944

Schwering, Josef. Zur Lehre vom kanonischen Gewohnheitsrecht. Warendorf, J. Schnell'sche buchdr., 1888. 53 p.

945

Sehling, Emil. Derecho canónico; traducido de la 2. ed. alemana y anotado por Juan Moneva y Puyol. 2. ed. Barcelona, Buenos Aires, Editorial Labor, S. A., [1933] 203 p. (Colección Labor. Sección VIII: Ciencias Jurídicas, no. 91).
   "Bibliografía": p. [197]–203.

946

Semana de Derecho Canónico. *10th, Pamplona, 1964.* Iglesia y derecho; trabajos de la X Semana de Derecho Canónico. Salamanca, 1965. 370 p.
   Bibliographical footnotes.

947

Semana Española de Teología. *14th, Madrid, 1954.* Los fundamentos teológicos del derecho público eclesiástico; teología del laicado; otros estudios. Madrid, 1955. 530 p.

948

Silbernagl, Isidor. Lehrbuch des katholischen Kirchenrechts; zugleich mit Rücksicht auf das im jetzigen deutschen Reiche geltende Staatskirchenrecht. Verlags-Anstalt, 1890. 716 p.

949

Silbernagl, Isidor. Lehrbuch des katholischen Kirchenrechts; zugleich mit Rücksicht auf das im jetzigen deutschen Reiche geltende Staatskirchenrecht. 4. verb. Aufl. Regensburg. Manz, 1903. 797 p.

950

Silva Carneiro, Bernardino J. da. Elementos de direito ecclesiastico portuguez e seu respectivo processo. 3. ed. rev. e corr. Coimbra, Impr. da Universidade, 1882. 463 p.

951

Sipos, István. Az új egyházi törvénykönyv főbb vonási és ujitási. 2., bőv. és jav kiad. Pécs, Nyomatott a "Dunántúl" R. Tnál, 1918. 266 p.

952

Sipos, István. Enchiridion iuris canonici. Ad usum scholarum et privatorum concinnavit Stephanus Sipos. Pécs, Ex Typographia "Haladás R. T.," 1926. 1019 p.
Bibliographical footnotes.

953

Sipos, István. Enchiridion iuris canonici. Ad usum scholarum et privatorum. Ed. 4. Pécs, Ex typographia "Haladás," 1940. 1076 p.
Bibliographical footnotes.

954

Smejkal, Miroslav. Právo církevní a právo kanonické. V Brně, Č. a. s. Právník, 1947. 118 p.
Bibliography: p. [115]–118.

955

Smith, Sebastian B. Compendium juris canonici ad usum cleri et seminariorum hujus regionis accomodatum. Neo-Eboraci, Cincinnati, Benziger fratres, 1890. 427 p.

956

Smith, Sebastian B. Compendium juris canonici. Neo-Eboraci, Cincinnati, Chicago, Benzinger fratres, 1892. 435 p.

957

Smith, Sebastian B. Elements of ecclesiastical law. Compiled with reference to the Syllabus, the "Const. Apostolicae sedis" of Pope Pius IX, the Council of the Vatican and the latest decisions of the Roman congregations. Adapted especially to the discipline of the church in the United States. 2. ed. rev. and enl. New York, Cincinnati, Benzinger brothers printers, 1878—

958

Soglia, Giovanni, *cardinal*. Institutiones juris privati ecclesiastici, libri III. Edition 2. prima Parisiensis ab ipso auctore recognita et aucta. Paris, Courcier [1860] 581 p.

959

Soglia, Joannis Cardinalis. Institutiones juris privati ecclesiastici libri III. Editio quinta. Paris, Courcier [1860]. 581 p.

960

Soglia, Joannis Cardinalis. Institutiones juris publici ecclesiastici. Editio quinta. Paris, Courcier [1860]. 406, 40 p.

961

Sohm, Rudolf. Das altkatholische Kirchenrecht und das Dekret Gratians. München, Leipzig, Duncker & Humblot, 1918. 674 p.

962

Sohm, Rudolf. Das altkatholische Kirchenrecht und das Dekret Gratians. Im Anhang: Rezension von Ulrich Stutz. (Unveränderter reprografischer Nachdruck München und Leipzig 1918). Darmstadt, Wissenschaftliche Buchgesellschaft, 1967. 685 p.
Bibliographical footnotes.

963

Sohm, Rudolf. Kirchenrecht. München und Leipzig, Duncker & Humblot, 1923. 2 v. (Systematisches handbuch der deutschen rechtswissenschaft . . . begründet von dr. Karl Binding . . . 8 abt., 1–2 bd.)
Bibliography: v. 1, p. [xix]–xxiii.

964

Sokolich, Alexander F. Canonical provisions for universities and colleges; a historical synopsis and a commentary. Washington, D.C., Catholic University of America Press, 1956. 180 p. (Catholic University of America. Canon law studies, no. 373)
Bibliography: p. 166–173.

965

Somerville, James W. Gratianus in jurisprudence, with translations. Washington, D.C., Law reporter printing company, 1934. 31 p.

966
Souto, José A. Notas para una interpretación actual del derecho canónico. [Pamplona] EUNSA [1973] 210 p. (Colección canónica de la Universidad de Navarra)
Includes bibliographical references.

967
Spinelli, Lorenzo. Prospettive canonistiche nella Chiesa di oggi. 2. ed. riveduta ed ampliata. Modena, S.T.E.M., 1975. 219 p.
Bibliography: p. [195]–216.

968
Stachow, Maximianus. De juris canonici, quod ad just patronatus spectat in terris protestantium usu ac non usu. Berlin, Lange [1865]. 80 p.

969
Stephanus Tornacensis, *bp.* Die Summa des Stephanus Tornacensis über das Decretum Gratiani. Hrsg. von der. Joh. Friedrich von Schulte. Giessen, Roth, 1891. 280 p.

970
Stevick, Daniel B. Canon law, a handbook. New York, Seabury Press [1965] 241 p.
Bibliography: p. 229–235.

971
Stickler, Alphonsus. Historia juris canonici latini. Institutiones academicae. I Historia fontium. Torino, Apud Custodiam Librariam Pontif. Athenaei Salesiani, 1950. 468 p.

972
Stiegler, Anton. Der kirchliche Rechtsbegriff; Elemente und Phasen seiner Erkenntnisgeschichte. München, Schnell & Steiner, 1958. 171 p.
Bibliography: p. x–xvi.

973
Struvius, Georg A. Notae et observationes theoreticae, canonicae et practicae, ad Antonii Matthaei . . . tractationum de successionibus ejusque auctarium de divortio legum et usus in materia successionis. Jenae, sumptib. Matthaei Birckneri, bibl. Jen. et Helmst, 1677. 532 p.

974
Stryk, Samuel. Samuelis Stryckii JCti. consumma-

tissimi Annotationes succinctae in Johannis Schilteri Institutiones juris canonici, ad Ecclesiae veteris & hodiernae statum accommodatae, in quibus multa rationibus & exemplis illustrantur, obscura declarantur, atque dubia resolvuntur. nunc primúm publicatae. Norimbergae, Sumptibus W. M. Endteri Haeredum & J. A. Engelbrechti Viduae, 1732. 240 p.

975
Studi di diritto canonico in onore di Marcello Maglicchetti. Roma, Officium libri catholici, 1974. (Studia et documenta iuris canonici; 3)
Includes bibliographical references.

976
Studia Gratiana, post octava Decreti saecularia. [Bononiae] Institutum Iuridicum Universitatis Studiorum Boniensis, 1953.
Includes bibliographies.

977
Summa Coloniensis. Summa "Elegantius in iure diuino" seu Coloniensis. Edidit Gerardus Gransen, Adlaborante Stephano Kuttner. New York, Fordham University Press, 1969. (Monumenta iuris canonici. Series A: Corpus glossatorum, v. 1, t. 1)

978
Svatoš, Ludwig. Rechtsberater für die Seelsorge. Warnsdorf, Opitz [1933] 2 v.

979
Sztafrowski, Edward. Prawo kanoniczne w okresie odnowy soborowej: podrecznik dla duchowieństwa. Warszawa, Akademia Teologii Katolickiej, 1976.
Includes bibliographical references.

980
Tardif, Adolphe F. L. Histoire des sources du droit canonique. Paris, Picard, 1887. 409, [1] p.

981
Tarquini, Camillo, *cardinal.* Instituciones de derecho eclesiastico publico, virtiólas del latin al español, para uso del Seminario conciliar del arzobispado de la Plata, el p. fr. Manuel Murga. Sucre, Tipografía del Cruzado, 1878. 130 p.

982
Tarquini, Camillo, *cardinal.* Iuris ecclesiastici pu-

blici institutiones. Accedit dissertatio eiusdem de regio placet habita in academica religionis catholicae die 2 Septembris 1852 nunc primum latine reddita. Editio XVII. Romae, Ex Typographia Polyglotta S.C. de Propaganda Fide, 1898. 170 p.

983
Taunton, Ethelred L. The law of the church; a cyclopaedia of canon law for English-speaking countries. London, Paul, Trench, Trübner, 1906. 652 p.
  Bibliography: p. [647]–652.

984
Tedeschi, Niccolò, *abp of Palermo.* Commentaria super prima[–secunda] parte primi [prima–tertia parte secundi, tertii, quarti & quinti] Decretalium libri, nunc recens ab innumeris ferè mendis uindicata, suóq; nitori restituta. Quibus accessere doctissimorum iurisconsultorum adnotamenta. Avgvstae Tavrinorvm, apud haeredes Nicolai Beuilaquae, 1577. 7 v.

985
Thomasius, Christian. Cavtelae circa praecognita jurisprudentia ecclesiasticae in usum auditorii Thomasiani. Halae Magdeburgicae, prostat in officina Rengeriana, 1712. 307, [82] p.

986
Thomasius, Christian. Dissertatio juris canonici, De usu practico denunciationis evangelicae, ad cap. 13. X De juridiciis. Quam . . . publico eruditorum examini subjicit die XVI. aprilis MDCCXII. H.L.Q.C. Wilhelmus Irwing. Halae Magdeburgicae, Zeitler, [1712] 48 p.

987
Thorkelin, Grimur J. Jus ecclesiasticum novum sive Arnaeanum constitutum 1275. Kristinnrettr inn nyi edr Arna Biskups. Hafniae, typis Hallagerianis, 1777. 256 p.

988
Tobón R., Octavio. Compendio de derecho público eclesiástico. Bogotá, Editorial Temis, 1954. 111 p.

989
Torre, Joannes. Variarvm ivris qvaestionvm tomi tres. Placentiae, In ducali typographia L. L. Bazachij, sumptibus Pincij, 1705. 3 v.

990
Torrecilla, Martín de. Propugnaculum ortodoxae fidei, adversvs qvosdam veritatum catholicarum hostes, eas labefactare conantes. Matriti, Ròman, 1707. 514 p.

991
Torrubiano Ripoll, Jaime. Novísimas instituciones de derecho canónico, acomodadas al nuevo "Código" ordenado por s. s. el papa Pío X y promulgado por la santidad de Benedicto XV. 2 ed., corr. y notablemente aum., con todas las disposiciones nuevas desde el 19 de mayo de 1918 hasta el 1° de julio de 1934. Madrid, "Librería Universidad," Otero-Portela, 1934. 2 v.

992
Tortosa Nicolás, Diego. El nuevo Código de derecho canónico, su necesidad, su preparación, su contenido, sus reformas principales. Prólogo del Excmo., Sr. Dr. D. Enrique Reig. Madrid, Editorial Reus, 1921. 241 p. (Biblioteca de la "Revista general de legislación y jurisprudencia," v. 24)

993
Traictez des droicts et libertez de l'Eglise gallicane. Paris, Chevalier, 1609. 391 p.

994
Turner, Cuthbert H., *ed.* Ecclesiae Occidentalis monumenta iuris antiquissima. Canonum et conciliorum Graecorum interpretationes Latinae. Post Christophorum Iustel [et al.] edidit Cuthbertus Hamilton Turner. Oxonii, E Typographeo Clarendoniano, 1899–1939. 2 v. in 7.

995
Uría, José M. Apuntes sobre cuestiones selectas de derecho canónico. [Bogotá] Imp. del Corazón de Jesús, 1932. 538 p.

996
Urquhart, David. Rétablissement du droit canon. Vindication de l'Eglise catholique contre un dominicain. Londres, Diplomatic review office; Paris, Blériot, 1870. 111, [1] p.

997
Valletta, Nicola, Partitiones juris canonici . . . concinnatae. Neapoli, Morelli, 1785. 38 p.

998

Vasconcillos, Felipe de la Cruz. Tratado vnico de intereses. Sobre si se puede llevar dinero por prestallo. Madrid, Martínez, 1637. 27, [5] p.

999

Vatican Council. Fontes juris ecclesiastici novissimi. Decreta et canones sacrosancti oecumenici Concilii vaticani una cum selectis constitutionibus pontificiis aliisque documentis ecclesiasticis. Edidit atque illustravit Philippus Scheider. Ratdisbonae, Pustet, 1895. 136 p.

1000

Vecchis, Petrus A. de. Collectio constitutionum, chirographorum, et brevium diversorum Romanorum pontificum, pro bono regimine universitatum, ac communitatum status ecclesiasti, & pro ejusdem status felici gubernio promulgatorum, ac specialiter disponentium ... edita sub clementissimis auspiciis Sanctissimi Domini Nostri, Domini Clementis XII. P. M. ac zelo, & cura Josephi Renati Imperialis per materias, marginalibus, annotatonibus, & alphabetico ordine disposita, ac multiplici indice. Romae, Mainardi, 1731.

1001

Vega, Gabriel de. Hic liber continet sacrorum canonum, lecturas, quas audiuit ed scripsit Gabriel de Vega. 1605. 377 1.

1002

Venatorius, Daniel. Analysis methodica ivris pontificii: qvas [sic] svb titvlis decretalivm antiqvarvm distinctis qvinqve libris ... continetur quicuid in decretalibus, decretis, & todo iure pontificio sparsim traditur ... Explicantvr etiam plane methodica tractatione omnia iudicia tam ciuilia quam criminalia, & processus iudiciarius. Mogvntiae, Breem, 1596. 696, 301 p.

1003

Vering, Friedrich H. T. H. Lehrbuch des katholischen, orientalischen und protestantischen Kirchenrechts, mit besonderer Rücksicht auf Deutschland, Oesterreich und die Schweiz. 3., umgearb., sehr verb. und verm. aufl. Freiburg im Breisgau, Herder, 1893. 1031 p. (Theologische bibliothek)
  "Uebersicht der allgemeinen literatur des kirchenrechts": p. 16–36.

1004

Vering, Friedrich H. T. H. Lehrbuch des katholischen und protestantischen Kirchenrechts, mit besonderer Rücksicht auf das Vaticanische Concil, sowie auf Deutschland, Oesterreich und die Schweiz. Freiburg im Breisgau, Herder, 1876. 815 p.

1005

Vermeersch, Arthur. Epitome juris canonici cum commentariis ad scholas et ad usum privatum. 3. ed. Mechliniae, Dessain, 1927–28. 3 v. (Museum Lessianum. Section theologique, no. 5)

1006

Vermeersch, Arthur, *and* Joseph Creusen. Epitome iuris canonici cum commentariis ad scholas et ad usum privatum. Mechliniae, Dessain, 1940–49. 3 v. (Museum Lessianum. Section théologique)
  Includes bibliographies.

1007

Vestri, Ottaviano. In Romanae aulae actionem & iudiciorum mores, ad Iacobū Pellaeum eisagogé. [Venice, apud Tramezinū, 1547] 224 1.

1008

Vestri, Ottaviano. In Romanae avlae actionem, et ivdiciorvm mores, ad Iacobvm Pellaevm eisagogé. Habes hîc, humanissime lector, officia ac officiales, qui & in camera gratiae & iustitiae, ad resignaturas, bullas, aliáque rescripta concipienda praefecti sunt, & in quibus eorum uersetur officium: quae omnia hoc breui libello constant, ut in sequenti folio uidere cuique liberum est. Parisiis, le Preux, 1553. 160 p.

1009

Vetulani, Adam. Prawo kościelne - Część I: Organizacja kościoła; Część II: Organizacja kościoła; Część III: Prawo małzeńskie; Część IV: Historja stosunku kościoła do państwa. Kraków, 1937. 4 v.

1010

Vetus canonum codex Lusitanae Ecclesiae notis illustratus a'Thoma ab Incarnatione. Colimbriae, Ex typographia Academiae Liturgicae, 1764. 348 p.

1011

Viau, Roger. Doubt in cannon law; a historical synopsis and a commentary. Washington, D.C., The Catholic University of America Press, 1954. 119 p. (The Catholic University of America. Canon law studies, No. 346)

Bibliography: p. 107–111.

1012

Vidaurre y Enclada, Manuel L. de. Vidaurre Contro Vidaurre. Volumen 1°: Curso de derecho eclesiastico. Lima, Impr. del Comercio, Monterola, 1839. 195 p.

1013

Vigelius, Nicolaus. Methodvs vniversi ivris pontificii absolutissima, in quinq$_3$ libros distincta: nvnc demvm additionibvs methodi ivris controuersi aucta. Ex qua patet, in quibus ius pontificum cum iurè ciuili consentiat. Basileae, König, 1616. 916 p.

1014

Villarosa, Carlo A. de Rosa, *marchese* di. Civilis decretorum praxis plurimis, ac recentissimis s. c. decisionibus illustrata. Cum observationibus, et additionibus u. j. d. Leonardi Riccii. Neapoli, expensis Thomae Alphano, 1750. 335 p.

1015

Vinton, Francis. A manual commentary on the general canon law and the constitution of the Protestant Episcopal Church in the United States. New York, Dutton and Company, 1870. 223 p.

1016

Vitaliano Berroa, J. Derecho público de la iglesia. Lima, 1934. 111 p.

Bibliography: p. 111.

1017

Viterbo, Council of. Viterbiensis synodi vindicatio quam . . . Jacobus tit. S. Laurentii in Lucina S. R. E. primus presbyter cardinalis Oddi Viterbii et Tuscanelae publici juris facit. Viterbii, Zenti, 1764. various pagings.

1018

Vives Estévez, Francisco. Nociones de derecho canónico; lo que un seglar debe saber de derecho canónico. [Santiago] Editorial Jurídica de Chile [1959] 171 p.

1019

Viviani, Giovanni B. Rationale ivris pontificii, quinque libris distinctum. Opvs, in qvo omnivm, qvae asvmmis pontificibus constituta sunt in libris decretalium, sexti, clementinarum, et extrauagantium, viua et fundamentalis ratio redditur. Coloniae Agrippinae, Cholini, 1628. 5 v. in 1.

1020

Voellius, Gulielmus. Bibliotheca ivris canonici veteris in dvos tomos distribvta. Qvorvm vnvs canonvm eccliastivorvm codices antiqvos, tum graecos, tum latinos complectitur . . . alter vero insigniores ivris canonici veteris collectores graecos exhibet. Ex antiquis codicibus mss. bibliothecae Christorphori Ivstelli. Horvm maior pars nunc primvm in lvcem prodit, cum versionibus latinis, praefationibus, notis, & indicibus huic editioni necessariis. Opera & studio Gvlielmi Voelli . . . et Henrici Ivstelli, Christophori f. Lvtetiae Parisiorvm, apud Lvdovicvm Billaine, in maiori aula Palatij, ad insigne magni Caesaris, & sancti Augustini, 1661. 2 v.

1021

Voellius, Gulielmus. Biblioteca ivris canonici veteris in dvos tomos distribvta qvorvm vnvs canonvm ecclesiastivorvm codices antiqvos, tum graecos, tum latinos complectitur . . . alter vero insigniores ivris canonici veteris collectores graecos exhibet. Ex antiqvis condicibus mss. bibliothecae Christophori Ivstelli. Horum maior pars nvnc primvm in lvcem prodid, cum versionibus latinis . . . Opera et studio Gvlielmi Voellii et Henrici Ivstelli, Christophori F. Lvtetiae Parisiorvm, apud Joannem Jombert, 1685. 2 v.

1022

Vogt, Alfons. Strafverhängung und Strafbemessung im Strafrecht des Codex iuris canonici. Frankfurt A. M., Schack, 1929. 49 p.

1023

Waechter, Eberhard, *freiherr* von. Die Quellen des katholischen Kirchenrechtes für österreichische Universitäten. Graz, Leuschner & Lubensky, 1912. 95 p.

1024

Waesberghe, J. F. A. M. van. De Akense regels voor canonici en canonicae uit 816. Een antwoord

aan Hildebrand-Gregorius VII en zijn geestver-
wanten. Assen, Van Gorcum, 1967. 529 p. (Van
Gorcum's historische bibliotheek, nr, 83)
Bibliography: p. xx–xxxix.

1025
Wagnereck, Henricus. Commentarius exegeticus
ss. canonum; seu, expositio brevis et clara omnium
pontificiarum decretalium Gregorii IX [et al.] extrauagantium Ioannis XXII & communium, atque
etiam concordatorum Germaniae, & primariarum
precum suo loco insertarum quinqve libris ad
mentem et literam summorum pontificum comprehensa & per singula capitula sic elucubrata, vt
iuris canonici studiosis & in foro ecclesiastico oc-
cupatis lucis plurimum afferre queat. Dilingae,
Apud J. Federle, 1672. 1082 p.

1026
Wahl, Johannes. Die Stellung der Spanier zu dem
Problem der klandestinen Ehen in den Verhand-
lugen aus dem Konzil von Trient. Bonn, 1958. 69
p.
Bibliography: p. 7–9.

1027
Wahrmund, Ludwig. Quellen zur geschichte des
römisch-kanonischen Processes im Mittelalter. Mit
Unterstützung der Kais. Akademie der Wissenschaften in Wien und des K. K. Ministeriums für
Cultus und Unterricht. Innsbruck, Wagner, 1905.
3 v.

1028
Walter, Ferdinand, *comp*. Fontes iuris ecclesiastici
antiqui et hodierni. Bonn, Marcus, 1862. 599 p.

1029
Walter, Ferdinand, *ed*. Fontes iuris ecclesiastici
antiqui et hodierni. Aalen, Scientia, 1966. 599 p.
Bibliographical footnotes.

1030
Walter, Ferdinand, Lehrbuch des Kirchenrechts
aller christlichen Confessionen. 7. völlig
umgeänderte Aufl. Bonn, Marcus, 1836. 688, 111
p.
Bibliographical footnotes.

1031
Walter, Ferdinand. Lehrbuch des Kirchenrechts

aller chrislichen Confessionen. 10. verb. Aufl.
Bonn, Marcus, 1846. 818 p.

1032
Walter, Ferdinand. Lehrbuch des Kirchenrechts
aller christlichen Confessionen. 14., sehr verb. und
verm. ausg. Im auftrage des verfassers besorgt von
Hermann Gerlach. Bonn, Marcus, 1871. 792 p.

1033
Walter, Ferdinand. Lehrbuch des Kirchenrechts,
aus den älteren und neueren Quellen bearbeitet.
3., sehr veränderte und verm. Aufl. Bonn, Marcus,
1825. 610 p.

1034
Walter, Ferdinand. Manual del derecho eclesiástico
universal, traducido al español por D. Joaquin
Escriche. Edición en que además de haberse corregido algunos descuidos del traductor y las inu-
merables erratas y errores del impresor Calleja, se
han añadido en un apéndice: las disposiciones
notables que en los puntos relativos al derecho
eclesiástico han adoptado las repúblicas de Méjico,
el Perú, Colombia, Venezuela, la Nueva Granada
y Chile. Paris, Salva, 1845. 522 p.

1035
Wasserschleben, Hermann. Beitraege zur Geschichte der vorgratianischen Kirchenrechtsquellen. Leipzig, Tauchnitz jun., 1839. 191 p.

1036
Weber, J. Kompendium des katholischen Kirchenrechts, mit Berücksichtigung des Staatskirchenrechts in Deutschland, Oesterreich und der
Schweiz. Zunächst für Studierende der Theologie
und des Rechts. 3. verb. Aufl. Augsburg, B.
Schmid'sche Verlagsbuchhandlung, 1888. 654 p.

1037
Weinzierl, Karl. Rückgabepflicht nach kanonischem Recht; rechtshistorische, rechtsdogma-
tische Darstellung. Freiburg im Breisgau, Herder,
1932. 143 p.

1038
Werle, Johann M. Album juridicum, seu Tabella
jurisprudentiae et aliorum quoruncunque, doctri-
nalium A. B. C. Daria. Augusta Vindel, Wolff,
bibliopol., 1733. 311 p.

1039

Wernz, Franz X. Ius canonicum ad Codicis normam exactum opera p. Petri Vidal. Romae, apud aedes universitatis Gregorianae, 1927. 7 v.

1040

Wernz, Franz X. Ius canonicum ad Codicis normam exactum opera Petri Vidal. Romae, apud aedes Universitatis Gregorianae, 1933.

1041

Wiener, Harold M. Studies in Biblical law. London, Nutt, 1904. 128 p.

1042

Wiener Hispana-Handschrift. Vollst. Faks.-Ausg. im Originalformat des Codex Vindobonensis 411. Einf.: Otto Mazal. Graz, Akadem. Druck- u. Verlagsanst, 1974. 72 p., 314 l. (Codices selecti phototypice impressi, v. 41)
Bibliography: p. 72.

1043

Wigand, Johann. De Schwenck-feldismo, Dogmata et argumenta, cum succintis solutionigus. Lipsiae, Berwald, 1596. 392 p.

1044

Winckworth, Peter. A simple approach to the canon law. London, S. P. C. K., 1951. 39 p.

1045

Wohlhaupter, Eugen. Aequitas canonica: eine studie aus dem kanonischen recht. Paderborn, Schöningh, 1931. 207 p. (Görres-gesellschaft zur pflege der wissenschaft im katholischen Deutschland. Veröffentlichungen der Sektion für rechts- und staatswissenschaft, 56 hft.)

1046

Wojnar Meletius M. De regimine Basilianorum Ruthenorum a Metropolita Josepho Velamin Rutskyj instauratorum. Romae, Sumptibus PP. Basilianorum, 1949. 3 v. (Analecta OSBM. Ser. 2, sectio 1: Opera, v. 1, 3–9)

1047

Wolf, Jacob G. Institutiones jurisprudentiae ecclesiasticae, in usum tractatus Brunnemanniani De jure ecclesiastico adornatae. Lipsiae, Meyer, 1713. 927 p.

1048

Wood, Edmund G. de Salis. The regal power of the church; or, The fundamentals of the canon law. With a pref. and a Supplementary bibliography by E. W. Kemp. Westminster [London] Dacre Press [1948] 86 p.

1049

Woywod, Stanislaus, *father*. The new canon law; a commentary and summary of the new Code of canon law; with a preface by Right Rev. Mgr. Philip Bernardini. New ed., augm. by recent decrees and declarations. New York, Wagner [c1918] 133 p.

1050

Woywod, Stanislaus, *father*. A practical commentary on the Code of canon law, with a preface by Most Rev. Philip Bernardini. 5th rev. ed. New York, Wagner; London, Herder, 1939. 2 v.
Bibliography: v. 2, p. 709–713.

1051

Woywod, Stanislaus, *father*. A practical commentary on the Code of canon law. Rev. by Callistus Smith. Rev. and enl. ed. New York, Wagner, 1948. 2 v.
Bibliography: v. 2, p. 831–835.

1052

Woywod, Stanislaus, *father*. A practical commentary on the Code of canon law. Revised by Callistus Smith. [Rev. and enl. ed.] New York, Wagner [1952] 833, 905 p.
Bibliography: p. 831–835 (2nd group).

1053

Wulffen, Arndt-Siegfried von. Die Stellung des Patronats in heutigen Staatskirchenrecht. Osnabrück, Gedruckt in der werkdrickerei Kleinert, 1929. 93 p.

1054

Wurm, Hubert. Studien und texte zur Dekretalensammlung des Dionysius Exiguus. Bonn, Röhrscheid, 1939. 304 p. (Kanonistische studien und texte, hrsg. von dr. A. M. Koeniger, bd. 16)
"Schrifttum": p. [x]–xix.

1055

Wurtzbacher, Ingrid. Das Reichsrecht und die Rechtswirklichkeit im Fall Dr. Martin Luther am Beispiel des Repräsentanten Kursachsens Friedrich

III. Bern, Lang; Frankfurt, Lang, 1976. 199 p. (Europäische Hochschulschriften: Reihe 3, Geschichte und ihre Hilfswissenschaften; Bd. 74)
Bibliography: p. 157–199.

1056

Wypler, Carolus. Consensus legislatoris pro consuetudine in Ecclesia, doctrina Medii Aevi ac doctoris Fr. Suarez. Roma, Pontificia Universitas Gregoriana, Facultas Iuris Canonica, 1974. 46 p.

1057

Zabarella, Francesco, *cardinal*. In Clementinarum volumen commentaria, Philippi Franchi, et Nicolai Superantii antiquis, ac etiam nouis Vincentij Godemini adnotationibus illustrata. Cum summarijs, & indice. Hac in ed. ab erroribus repurgata. Venetiis, Apud Iuntas, 1602. 212 p.

1058

Zabarella, Francesco, *cardinal*. Super primo[–secundo] Decretalium subtilissima commentaria. Cum additionibus, summariis, ac repertorio Ioannis Thierry: nunc autem recens cum additionibus alijs, & summarijs, magis quàm antea erant, auctis & amplificatis, per Brunorum à sole, illustrata. Et in hac postrema ed. recognita & expurgata. Cum nouo pariter, & reformato indice. Venetiis, Apud Iuntas [1602] 2 v.

1059

Zabarella, Francesco, *cardinal*. Super IV. & V. Decretalium, subtilissima commentaria. Cum additionibus, summarijs, ac repertorio Ioannis Thierry. In hac postrema ed. a multis mendis expurgata. Venetiis, Apud Iuntas, 1602. 167 p.

1060

Zachariae von Lingenthal, Karl E. Ueber die quellen des sogenannten Photianischen Nomokanon. Athens, Perris, 1879. 23 p.

1061

Zallinger zum Thurm, Jakob A. von. Juris ecclesiastici publici; compendium. Bononiae, Ex Typog. Archiepiscopali, 1817. 231 p.

1062

Ziegler, Kaspar. Jus canonicum notis & animadversionibus academicis ad Joh. Pauli Lancellotii. Institutiones enucleatum, & quale sit, remoto velamento publicae luci expositum. Praemittitur dissertatio de juris canonici origine & incrementis. Wittebergae, Quensted, 1696. 58, [14], 1072, [213] p.

1063

Zoesius, Henricus. Commentarius in jus canonicum universum sive ad decretales epistolas Gregorii IX. Coloniae Agrippinae, Metternich, 1691. 682 p.

1064

Zoesius, Henricus. Commentarius in Jus canonicum universum; sive, Ad decretales epistolas Gregorii IX. P. M. Pluribus nunc additamentis ab Joanne Nabben & Mauritio a Geismaer; illustratus ac locupletatus cum indicibus titulorum, rerum, quaestionumque notabilium. Venice, Pezzana, 1757. 813 p.

1065

Zype, Franciscus van der. Ivris pontificii novi analytica enarratio. Editio auctior. Coloniae Agrippinae, Hierati, 1624. 538, [44] p.

PERSONS

CLERGY AND RELIGIOUS

1066

Adam, René. Le pouvoir coercitif de l'évêque. Québec, Faculté de droit canonique, Université Laval, 1946. v. (Les Thèses canoniques de Laval. Thèse no. 4)
Notes bibliographiques.

1067

Agius, Laurentio M. Manuale de ecclesiarum rectoribus ad normam Codicis iuris canonici. Taurini (Italia) Marietti, 1931. 118 p.

1068

Agius, Lorenzo M. Summarium iurium et officiorum parochorum ad normam Codicis iuris canonici. Neapoli, d'Auria, 1953. 258 p.

1069

Albani, Giovanni Girolamo, cardinal. De cardinalatv liber ad Pavlvm. III. pon. max. Romae [apud Antonium Bladum Asulanum] 1541. 109 numb. 1.

1070

Alonso, Santiago. El pensamiento regalista de Francisco Salgado de Somoza (1595–1665). Contribución a la historia del regalismo español. Salamanca, 1973. 288 p. (Monografías canónicas Peñafort, no. 16)

Bibliography: p. [275]–279.

1071

Amort, Eusebius. Vetus disciplina canonicorum regularium & saecularium: ex documentis magna parte hucusque ineditis a temporibus apostolicis usque ad saeculum XVII critice, & moraliter expensa a Eusebio Amort. Farnborough, Gregg, 1971. 2v. 1094 p.

1072

Anfossi, Filippo. La restituzione de' beni ecclesiastici necessaria alla salute de quelli che ne han fatto acquisto senza il consenso e l'autorità della S. Sede apostolica. Roma, Bourlié, 1824. 161 p.

1073

Anton, Hans Hubert. Studien zu den Klosterprivilegien der Päpste im frühen Mittelalter: unter bes. Berücks. d. Privilegierung von St. Maurice d'Agaune. Berlin, New York, de Gruyter, 1975. 172 p. (Beiträge zur Geschichte und Quellenkunde des Mittelalters; Bd. 4)

1074

Antonelli, Giovanni Carlo, bp., d. 1694. Tractatus posthumus de juribus, & oneribus clericorum in duos libros distributus in quibus utriusque juris controversiae difficiliores, & in foro frequentiores singulariter tractantur. Opus judicibus tàm ecclesiasticis, quàm saecularibus advocatis . . . maximè necessarium. Cui accedunt quamplurima recentissima decreta Sacrae concregationis concilii, bullae regnantis s. d. n. Innocentii XII ac Decisiones Sacrae rotae romanae nullibi adhuc impressae. Cum duplici indice scilicet Tractatus, & decisionum locupletissimo. Rome, Zenobii & Plachi; sumptibus Aloysii & Francisci de Comitibus, 1699. 203, 165 p.

1075

Apostolic constitution "Sponsa Christi" and instruction of the Sacred Congregation of Religious. [Derby, N.Y.] Daughters of St. Paul, Apostolate of the Press [c1955] 75 p.

[Pope, 1939–1958 (Pius XII) Sponsa Christi (21 Nov. 1950) English.]

1076

Argento, Gaetano, duca. De re beneficiaria dissertationes tres vbi Caroli III . . . edictum quo fructuum capionem in sacerdotiis externorum, & vagantium clericorum, jubet, tum summo, tum optimo jure, recte, atque ordine factum, demonstratur. 1708.

1077

Astrath, Willi. Die vita communis der Welpriester. Amsterdam, Grüner, 1967 [1968] 264 p. (Kanonistische Studien und Texte, Bd. 22)

Bibliography, p. 13–17.

1078

Baccari, Renato. Le chiese ricettizie. Milano, Giuffrè, 1948. 191 p.

1079

Barbosa, Agostinho, bp. De canonicis et dignitatibvs, aliisqve inferioribvs beneficiariis cathedralium . . . tractatvs. Vltima ed., ab ipsomet auctore multis in locis locupletata. Lvgdvni, Sumptibus L. Dvrand, 1634. 407 p.

1080

Barbosa, Agostinho, bp. Pastoralis salicitudinis, sive De officio at potestate episcopi, tripartita descriptio. Nunc ultimum ab ipso auctore recognita, variis resolutionibus exornata, & multis doctorum citationibus, aliisque accessionibus illustrata. Lugduni, sumptibus Borde & Arnaud, 1698. 2 v.

This is a comprehensive treatise, divided into three parts or books, on the functions and authority of the bishop. The first book deals with the appointment, election, consecration, and duties of the bishop, the creation of patriarchal Sees, and archiepiscopal superiority. The second book is devoted to the authority of the bishop in relation to the sacraments, ordination, and his faculty to grant dispensation. The third examines a variety of subjects, including reservation of cases, residence of the bishop, granting of benefices, visiting the parishes, and appointment of vicars. It also offers a *formularium episcopale* (episcopal formulary) in which many methods are suggested for the proper and useful exercise of episcopal jurisdiction, as well as apostolic constitutions and decrees, bulls and letters *in forma brevis*.

1081

Barbosa, Agostinho, bp. Tractatus de canonicis, et dignitatibus, aliisque inferioribus beneficiariis cathedralium, & collegiatarum ecclesiarum, eorumque officiis, tam in choro, quam in capitulo. Hac ultimia editione ab ipso authore recognitu, & quamplurimorum additamemtorum accessione locupletatus. Cum summariis, et indicibus copiosis. Lugduni, sumptibus Borde & Arnaud, 1700. 263 p.

1082

Barry, Garrett F. Violation of the cloister; an historical synopsis and commentary. Washington, D.C., The Catholic University of America Press, 1942. 260 p. (The Catholic University of America. Canon law studies, no. 148)
Bibliography: p. 237–243.

1083

(Basilica) Sanctus Petrus de Urbe. Privilegia avctoritates, facvltates, indvlgentiaeq fabricae basilicae principis apostoloru Sancti Petri de Vrbe, a quàmpluribus ro. pontificibus concessae: et per sanctissimvm d. n. dominum Pavlvm diuina prouidentia papam IIII, confirmatae. Romae, 1559. 131 numb. 1.

1084

Bastien, Pierre. Directoire canonique à l'usage des congrégations à voeux simples. 5. éd. Bruges, Beyaert, 1951. 591 p.
Bibliography: p. [xiv]–xvi.

1085

Bastnagel, Clement V. The appointment of parochial adjutants and assistants. Washington, D.C., The Catholic University of America Press, 1930. (The Catholic University of America. Canon law studies, no. 58)

1086

Beil, Josef. Das kirchliche vereinsrecht nach dem Codex juris canonici, mit einem staatskirchenrechtlichen anhang. Paderborn, Schöningh, 1932. 134 p. (Görres-gesellschaft zur pflege der wissenschaft im katholischen Deutschland. Veröffentlichungen der Sektion für rechtsund staatswissenschaft. 60. hft.)
"Quellen und literatur": p. 18–20.

1087

Benedictus XIII, pope, 1724–1730. Constitvtio sev motvs proprivs . . . papae Benedicti XIII, svper controversiis inter episcopum juvenacensem, et archipresbyterum, capitulum, et clerum terlitiensem. Romae, Typis Reuerendae Camerae Apostolicae, 1728, 11 p.

1088

Benko, Matthew. The abbot nullius. Washington, D.C., The Catholic University of America Press, 1943. 147 p. (The Catholic University of America. Canon law studies, no. 173)
Bibliography: p. 125–131.

1089

Bernier, Paul. De patrimonio paraeciali. Quebeci, apud auctorem, 1938–   v.
"Bibliographia": v. 1, p. [11]–30.

1090

Bleynianus, Antonius Fabricius. In theoriam et praxim beneficiarum ecclesiasticorum methodica et familiaris introductio. Turnani, Michael, 1616. 498 p.

1091

Boelens, Martin. Die Klerikerehe in der Desetzgebung der Kirche unter besonderer Berücksichtigung der Strafe. Eine rechtsgeschichtliche Untersuchung von den Anfängen der Kirche bis zum Jahre 1139. Paderborn, Schöningh, 1968. 192 p.
Bibliography: p. 11–15.

1092

Boffa, Conrad H. Canonical provisions for Catholic schools (elementary and intermediate). Washington, D.C., The Catholic University of America Press, 1939. 211 p. (The Catholic University of America. Canon law studies, no. 117)
Bibliography: p. 193–200.

1093
Böhmer, Justus Henning. Ius parochiale ad fundamenta genuina revocatum a spuriis principiis purgatum atqeita adornatum ut ius ecclesiasticum protestantium illustrare et usum modernum, et supplemento novo, editio sexta. Halae Magdeb., Litteris et Impensis Orphanotrophei, 1760. 552 p.

1094
Boileau, Jacques. De antigvo ivre presbyterorvm in regimine ecclesiastico, autore Clavdio Fontejo [pseud.] Tavrini, Typis Zappatae, 1676. 162 p.

1095
Bonner, Dismas W. Extern sisters in monasteries of nuns. Washington, D.C., Catholic University of America, 1963. 253 p. (Catholic University of America. Canon law studies, no. 430)
Bibliography: p. 239–242.

1096
Borkowski, Aureliusz L., *ojciec*. De confraternitatibus ecclesiasticis. Washingtonii, D.C., Universitas Catholica Americae, 1918. 130 p. (The Catholic University of America. Canon law studies, no. 3)
"Fontes et scriptores": p. 130.

1097
Bossuet, Jacques B., *bp. of Meaux*. Defensio declarationis conventus cleri gallicani an. 1682. de ecclesiastica potestate. Lugani, sumptibus Agnelli & Soc., 1768. 2 v.

1098
Bovini, Giuseppe. La proprietà ecclesiastica e la condizione giuridica della Chiesa in età precostantiniana. Milano, Giuffrè, 1948. 164 p. (Università di Roma. Pubblicazioni dell'Instituto di diritto romano, dei diritti dell'Oriente mediterraneo e di storia del diritto, 28)
Bibliographical footnotes.

1099
Braschi, Giovanni Battista, abp. De metropolitano per episcopos eligendo, qui nulli archiepiscopo subjiciuntur. Ad tramites sacri Concilii Tridentini sess. 24 cap. 2. Proecthesis d. Jo: Baptistae Braschii. Romae, Ex Typographia Joseph de Martiis, 1725. 24 p.

1100
Brockhaus, Thomas A., Father. Religious who are known as conversi, an historical synopsis and commentary. Washington, D.C., The Catholic University of America Press, 1946. 127 p. (The Catholic University of America. Canon law studies, no. 225)
Bibliography: p. 106–111.

1101
Brown, Brendan F. The canonical juristic personality with special reference to its status in the United States of America. Washington, D.C., The Catholic University of America, 1927. 212 p. (The Catholic University of America. Studies in canon and civil law, no. 39)
Bibliography: p. 197–200.

1102
Brunini, Joseph B. The clerical obligations of canons 139 and 142, and historical synopsis and commentary. Washington, D.C., The Catholic University of America, 1937. 121 p. (The Catholic University of America. Canon law studies, no. 103)
Bibliography: p. 109–112.

1103
Buisson, Ludwig. Potestas und Caritas; die päpstliche Gewalt im Spätmittelalter. Köln, Böhlau Verlag, 1958. 448 p. (Forschungen zur kirchlichen Rechtsgeschichte und zum Kirchenrecht, 2. Bd.)
Bibliography: p. [401]–423.

1104
Byrne, Harry J. Investment of church funds; a study in administrative law. Washington, D.C., Catholic University of America Press, 1951. 206 p. (Catholic University of America. Canon law studies, no. 309)
Bibliography: p. 181–187.

1105
Calcaterra, Mannes M. De vicario adiutore. Neapoli, d'Auria, 1955. 178 p.
Bibliography: p. [8]–12.

1106
Campagna, Michael Angelo. Il vicario generale del vescovo; una sinossi storica e commento; dissertazione sottoposta. Washington, D.C., The Catholic University of America, 1931. 205 p. (The Catholic

University of America. Canon law studies, no. 66)
"Bibliografia": p. 189–192.

1107
Capelle, Germaine Catherine. Law voeu
d'obéissance des origines au XIIᵉ siècle; étude
juridique. Paris, Librairie générale de droit et de
jurisprudence, 1959. 261 p. (Bibliothèque
d'histoire du droit et droit romain, t. 2)
Bibliography: p. [245]–257.

1108
Capuchins. Schema provisorium capitis tertii constitutionum O. F. M. Cap. A commissione capitulari
legislationis elaboratum et iudicio provinciarum
submissum. (Pro manuscripto). Ad usum esclusi-
vum Fratrum ordinis nostri. Roma, Officium se-
cretariatus C. C. L., [1969?] 240 p.

1109
Carlo, Camillus de. Jus religiosorum. Tornaci,
Typis Societatis S. Joannis Evangelistae, Desclée,
1950. 622 p.
Bibliography: p. xxvi.

1110
Caron, Pier Giovanni. La rinuncia all'ufficio ecclesiastico nella storia del diritto canonico dalla età
apostolica alla riforma cattolica. Milano, Società
editrice "Vita e pensiero," 1946. 413 p. (Università
cattolica del Sacro Cuore, Saggi e ricerche, nuova
ser., v. 2)
Bibliographical footnotes.

1111
Carr, Aidan. Vocation to the priesthood: its canonical concept; a historical synopsis and a commentary. Washington, D.C., Catholic University of
America Press, 1950. 124 p. (The Catholic University of America. Canon law studies, no. 293)
Bibliography: p. 101–104.

1112
Carreri, Alessandro. De potestate Romani pontificiis adversus impios politicos. Patavii, Bolzeta,
1599. 86 l.

1113
Carroll, James J. The bishop's quinquennial report;
a historical synopsis and a commentary. Washington, D.C., Catholic University of America Press,

1956. 149 p. (Catholic University of America.
Canon law studies, no. 359)
Bibliography: p. 140–145. Bibliographical foot-
notes.

1114
Carthusians. Directorium novitiorum utriusque
sexus ordinis cartusiensis. De quo fit mentio in
ordinatione capituli generalis anni 1679. sub n. 6
cap. 17. II. partis relata. 77, [3] p. (Nova collectio
statutorum ordinis cartusiensis. Correriae, 1736)

1115
Carthusians. Nova collectio statutorum ordinis cartusiensis. Ea quae in antiquis et novis statutis, ac
tertia compilatione dispersa & confusa habebantur
simul ordinate disposita complectens. A S. Sede
Apostolica examinata, atque in forma specifica
confirmata. Editio quarta. Cura et jussu . . . patris
Domini Stephani, totius ordinis generalis moderatoris. Correriae, 1736. 359, [53], 42, 77, [3] p.

1116
Casarino, Nicolás. Apuntes y estudios de derecho
comprendiendo el patronato, las capellanías, el
matrimonio, las personas jurídicas, etc.; precedidos
de una introducción por el dr. d. Juan José Montes
de Oca. Buenos Aires, Lajouane, 1883. 228, 207
p.

1117
Catholic Church, Pope. Casus papales episcoplaes
& . . . Photostat facsimile reproduced from the
copy in the Henry E. Huntington Library.

1118
Chantre y Herrera, José. Dissertatio theologico-
dogmatica de infallibilitate summi pontificis in
rebus fidei definiendis, . . . Accedunt Theses de
fide, spe, et charitate quas in hoc primo erecti
convictus anno dictavit ipse, et explanavit pome-
ridiano tempore. Parmae, typis Philippi Carmignani, 1794. 154, [2] p.

1119
Chiericato, Giovanni. Discordiae forenses. Editio
secunda. Venetiis, Poleti, 1718–26. 6 v. in l.

1120
Chimy, Hieronymus. De figura iuridica archiepiscopi maioris in iure canonico orientali vigenti. Ed.

2. Romae, PP. Basiliani, 1968. 222 p. (Analecta OSBM, ser. 2. Sectio 1: Opera, v. 23)
Bibliography: p. [11]–19.

1121
Chyang, Peter Byong-bo. Decennial faculties for ordinaries in quasi-dioceses. Washington, D.C., Catholic University of America Press, 1961. 368 p. (Catholic University of America. Canon law studies, no. 402)
Bibliography: p. 338–356.

1122
Ciesluk, Joseph E. National parishes in the United States. Washington, D.C., Catholic University of America Press, 1944 [i.e., 1947] 178 p. (Catholic University of America. Canon law studies, no. 190)
Bibliography: p. 151–158.

1123
Claeys Bouuaert, Ferdinandus. De canonica cleri saecularis obedientia. Tomus prior. Lovanii, van Linthout, 1904. 359, 13 p.
"Index bibliographicus": p. [xiii]–xxiv.

1124
Clancy, Patrick M. J. The local religious superior; an historical conspectus and commentary on the rights and duties of the minor local superior in religious orders of men. Washington, D.C., The Catholic University of America Press, 1943. 229 p. (The Catholic University of America. Canon law studies, no. 175)
Bibliography: p. 201–208.

1125
Clarke, Thomas J. Parish societies. Washington, D.C., The Catholic University of America Press, 1943. 147 p. (The Catholic University of America. Canon law studies, no. 176)
Bibliography: p. 127–132.

1126
Cleary, Joseph F. Canonical limitations on the alienation of church property, an historical synopsis and commentary. Washington, D.C., The Catholic University of America Press, 1936. 141 p. (The Catholic University of America. Canon law studies, no. 100)
Bibliography: p. 127–132.

1127
Coady, John J. The appointment of pastors. Washington, D.C., The Catholic University of America Press, 1929. 150 p. (The Catholic University of America. Canon law studies, no. 52)
Bibliography: p. 140–143.

1128
Cohelli, Giacomo. De bono regimine rervm ad vniversitates spectantivm in bullam X. Clementis papae VIII. commentaria multiplici doctrina, & eruditione repleta, ac diu exoptata Caroli Cartharii studio nunquam intermisso ab interitu vindicata. Romae, Sumptibus I. Casonij, 1656. 539 p.

1129
Colegio de Abogados. Saragossa. Universidad. El papa y los problemas actuales del mundo. Curso de conferencias en el ilustre Colegio de Abogados de Zaragoza. Madrid, Instituto Editorial Reus, 1947. 240 p.

1130
Confetti, Giovanni Battista. Privilegiorvm sacrorum ordinum fractrvm Mendicantivm & non Mendicantium, collectio, ivxta sacri Concilii trid. reformationem, & sum. pont. nouissimas confirmationes, & innouationes; cum summario eorum omnium, que in ipsis priuilegijs apostolicis & decretis Concilij tridentini continentur. Qvarta hac editione ab erroribus pene. innvmeris quibus prior typographorum incuria impressio scatebat, summo studio, diligentissimoq; quarundam virorum cura candori pristino veterum collatione exemplorum integre restituta. Venetiis, apud Baglionum, 1610. 398 p.

1131
Connolly, John P. Synodal examiners and parish priest consultors; an historical synopsis and commentary. Washington, D.C., The Catholic University of America Press, 1943. 223 p. (The Catholic University of America. Canon law studies, no. 177)
Bibliography: p. 199–203.

1132
Connolly, Nicholas P. The canonical erection of parishes; an historical synopsis and commentary. [Washington, D.C.] The Catholic University of America Press, 1938. 132 p. (The Catholic University of America. Canon law studies, no. 114)
Bibliography: p. [115]–119.

1133

Connor, Maurice. The administrative removal of pastors, an historical synopsis and commentary. Washington, D.C., The Catholic University of America Press, 1937. 159 p. (Catholic University of America. Canon law studies, no. 104)
Bibliography: p. 145–147.

1134

Consejo Superior de Investigaciones Científicas. Instituto San Raimundo de Peñafort. El patrimonio eclesiástico; estudios de la tercera semana de derecho canónico. Salamanca, 1950. 474 p.

1135

Conte, Matteo. Il Terzordine francescano; legislazione canonica. Torino-Roma, Casa editrice Marietti, 1933. 530 p.

1136

Conte, Matteo. El Terzordine francescano; legislazione canonica. 2. ed., riv. Torino-Roma, Casa editrice Marietti, 1937. 530 p.

1137

Cook, John P. Ecclesiastical communities and their ability to induce legal customs; a historical synopsis and a commentary. Washington, D.C., The Catholic University of America Press, 1950. 132 p. (The Catholic University of America. Canon law studies, no. 300)
Bibliography: p. 129–132.

1138

Costello, John M. Domicile and quasi-domicile. Washington, D.C., The Catholic University of America Press, 1930. (The Catholic University of America. Canon law studies, no. 60)

1139

Cox, Joseph G. The administration of seminaries; historical synopsis and commentary. Washington, D.C., The Catholic University of America Press, 1931. 124 p. (The Catholic University of America. Canon law studies, no. 67)
Bibliography: p. 112–115

1140

Creusen, Joseph. Religiosos y religiosas según la disciplina del código de derecho canónico. Adaptación española. Bilboa, El Mensajero del Corazón de Jesús, 1947. 313 p.
Bibliography: p. [7]–8.

1141

Creusen, Joseph. Religieux et religieuses d'après le droit ecclésiastique. 6. éd. corr. et augm. Bruxelles, Edition universelle, 1950. 320 p. (Museum Lessianum. Section théologique, no. 11)

1142

Creusen, Joseph. Religious men and women in the Code. 5th English ed., rev. and edited to conform with the 6th French ed. by Adam C. Ellis. Milwaukee, Bruce Pub. Co. [1953] 322 p.
Bibliography: p. vii–viii.

1143

Creusen, Joseph. Religious men and women in church law. 6th English ed., rev. and edited to conform with the 7th French ed., by Adam C. Ellis. Milwaukee, Bruce Pub. Co. [1958] 380 p.

1144

Cuva, Armando. De juridicis relationibus inter ordinarios locales et religiones clericales exemptas ad cultum quod attinet. Torino, Società editrice internazionale [1955] 87 p. (Biblioteca del "Salesianum," 37)

1145

Delgado, Gregorio. Desconcentración orgánica y potestad vicaria. Pamplona, Edio. Universidad de Navarra, 1971. 339 p. (Colección canónica de la Universidad de Navarra)
Bibliography: p. 321–329.

1146

Dello Iacono, Cletus J. A commentary on the canonical legislation for solemn profession and sacred ordinations of friars. New York, 1960. 186 p.
Bibliography: p. ix–xiii.

1147

Demers, Francis L. The temporal administration of the religious house of a non-exempt, clerical, pontifical institute. Washington, D.C., The Catholic University of America Press, 1961. 147 p. (The Catholic University of America. Canon law studies, no. 396)
Bibliography: p. 129–135.

1148

De Reeper, John. A missionary companion; a commentary on the apostolic faculties. Dublin, Browne and Nolan [1952] 245 p.

1149

De Reeper, John. A missionary companion; a commentary on the apostolic faculties. Westminster, Md., Newman Press, 1952. 245 p.

1150

De Witt, Max G. The cessation of delegated power; a canonical commentary with historical notes. Washington, D.C., The Catholic University of America. (Canon law studies, no. 330)
Bibliography: p. 137–144.

1151

Díaz Moreno, José María. La regulación jurídica de la cura de almas en los canonistas hispánicos de los siglos XVI–XVII. Granada, Facultad de Teología, 1972. 517 p. (Biblioteca Teológica granadina, v. 14)

1152

Diederichs, Michael F. The jurisdiction of the Latin ordinaries over their oriental subjects; a historical synopsis and a commentary. Washington, D.C., 1946 [i.e. 1947] 153 p. (Catholic University of America. Canon law studies, no. 229)
"Sources for the oriental code": p. 127–128.
Bibliography: p. 131–135.

1153

Dlouhy, Maur J. The ordination of exempt religious; a history and a commentary. Washington, The Catholic University of America Press, 1955. 146 p. (Catholic University of America. Canon law studies, no. 271)
Bibliography: p. 134–140.

1154

Doheny, William J. Church property: modes of acquisition. Washington, D.C., 1927. 118 p. (The Catholic University of America. Studies in canon and Roman law, v. 41)
"Bibliographia": p. 107–112.

1155

Dougherty, Thomas D. The vicar general of the episcopal ordinary. Washington, D.C., The Catholic University of America Press, 1966. 124 p.

(Catholic University of America. Canon law studies, no. 447)
Bibliography: p. 115–120.

1156

Duren, François. Francisci Dvareni icti De sacris ecclesiae ministeriis ac beneficiis libri VIII. In quibus quicquid ad plenam iuris pontificii cognitionem necessarium est, breuiter ac dilucide explicatum continetur. Item pro libertate ecclesiae gallicae aduersus romanum aulam defensio Parisiensis curiae, Ludouico XI. Gallorum regi quondam oblata. Accedunt Concordata Nationis germanicae, cum notis Io. Schilteri. [n.p.] 1718. 515, [9] p.

1157

Dugan, Henry F. The judiciary department of the diocesan curia. Washington, D.C., The Catholic University of America, 1925. 87 p.
Bibliography: p. 78–79.

1158

Ebers, Godehard J. Der papst und die Römische kurie. Paderborn, Schöningh, 1916– v. (Quellensammlung zur kirchlichen rechtsgeschichte und zum kirchenrecht . . . 3)

1159

Ebers, Godehard J. Sammlung kirchlicher Erlässe und Verordnungen für die Apostolische Administratur Innsbruck-Feldkirch. In amtlichem Auftrage herausgegeben von Dr. Godehard Jos. Ebers. Innsbruck, Universitätsverlag Wagner, 1952, 236 p.

1160

Ebers, Godehard J. Devolutionsrecht vornehmlich nach katholischem Kirchenrecht. Eine von der juristischen Fakultät der Universität Breslau preisgekrönte historisch-dogmatisch Studie zum kirchlichen Benefizialwesen. (Stuttgart, Enke, 1906) Nachdruck. Amsterdam, Schippers, 1965. 448 p. (Kirchenrichtliche Abhandlungen, Heft 37/38)
Bibliography: p. [xvi]–xx.

1161

Eguren, Juan Antonio. De condicione iuridica missionarii. Neapoli, d'Auria, 1962. 340 p.
Bibliography: p. [ix]–xv.

1162

Erler, Adalbert. Mittelalterliche Rectsgutachten zur

Mainzer Stiftsfehde, 1459–1463. Wiesbaden, Steiner, 1964. 326 p. (Schriften der Wissenschaftlichen Gesellschaft an der Johann Wolfgang Goethe-Universität Frankfurt/Main. Geisteswissenschaftliche Reihe, Nr. 4)

Biographical footnotes.

1163

Escudero, Gerardo. El nuevo derecho de los religiosos. Madrid, Claune, 1971. 294 p.

1164

Escudero, Gerardo. El nuevo derecho de los religiosos. 2. ed., puesta al día. Madrid, Claune, 1975. 383 p.

"Documentos principales": p. [17]–19.
Includes indexes.

The Church finds itself at the beginning of a new legislative era now, involving the revision and updating of the entire Code of Canon Law as proposed by the popes and urged by Vatican II. Consequently, parts of the code have changed completely, and the canons devoted to men and women religious are no exceptions. The Sacred Congregation for the Religious and Secular Institutes has been introducing on its own those changes required by the spirit of the Council and the needs of the times, in some instances *motu proprio*, and in others by petitions of the superiors, General Chapters, or representative groups of religious. This book, a second edition of a 1971 publication (see entry 1163), covers all the amendments introduced as well as the current legislation on the subject. This is a manual for study and easy reference, and deals with facts and concrete problems. The triple index at the end is a very valuable contribution.

1165

Espinosa, Bernabé. Breve exposición de las facultades concedidas por cordillera, a los señores curas y vicarios de la diocesis de México. México, Torres, 1843. 174 p.

1166

Esswein, Anthony. The extrajudicial coercive powers of ecclesiastical superiors. Washington, D.C., The Catholic University of America Press, 1941. 144 p. (Catholic University of America. Canon law studies, no. 127)

1167

Falconi, Enea. Tractatus vtilissimvs reservationvm papalium, ac legatorum, . . . Nunc primum in lucem aeditum per r. p. d. Ludouicum Gomesium. Romae, [impensis d. Michaelis Tramezini] 1539. 71 l.

1168

Fanfani, Lodovico Giuseppe. De iure parochorum ad normam Codicis iuris canonici. Editio altera, notabiliter aucta. Taurini-Romae, Marietti, 1936. 558 p.

1169

Fatinellis, Fatinelli de. De referendariorvm votantium Signaturae justitiae collegio. Romae, typis Joannis Jacobi Komarek Bohemi, 1696. 214 p.

1170

Fermosinius, Nicholas Rodríquez. Tractatus secundus de officiis et sacris ecclesiae. Ad titulum XXII, libri I Decretalium Gregorii Pontificis IX . . . Editio prima in duos tomos distributa. Lugduni, Sumptibus Boissat & Remeus, 1662. 2 v. in 1.

1171

Ferroglio, Giuseppe. Circoscrizioni ed enti territoriali della Chiesa. Torino, In vendita presso: Giappichelli [1946] 111 p. (Università di Torino. Memorie dell'Istituto giuridico, ser. 2. Memoria 59)

Bibliographical footnotes.

1172

Figueras, Caesarius M. De impedimentis admissionis in religionem; usque ad Decretum Gratiani. [Montserrat, In Abbatia Montisserrati] 1957. 184 p.

"Scripta et documenta": p. 9.

1173

Figueroa, Rafael. La persona standi in iudicio en la legislación eclesiástica. Roma, Universitá Gregoriana, 1971. 292 p. (Analecta Gregoriana, v. 179. Series Facultatis Iuris Canonici: Sectio B, no. 29)

Bibliography: p. [xv]–xxii.

1174

Flinn, Robert J. Admission to vows; recent directives and trends. Techny, Ill., Divine Word Publications, 1965. 157 p.

Bibliography: p. 143–150.

1175

Foesser, Iustus R. De unione speciatim de incorporatione beneficiorum. Dissertatio inauguralis. Moguntiae, typis Francisci Sausen, 1869. 66 p.

1176

Freking, Frederick W. The canonical installation of pastors; a historical synopsis and a commentary. Washington, D.C., The Catholic University of Washington Press, 1948 [i.e., 1949] 210 p. (The Catholic University of America. Canon law studies, no. 273)

Bibliography: p. 184–192.

1177

Freriks, Celestine A. Religious congregations in their external relations. [Washington, D.C., Columbia Polytechnic Institute for the Blind] 1916. 114, [5] p. (The Catholic University of America. Canon law studies, no. 1)

"Sources and bibliography": p. 111–114.

1178

Frey, Wolfgang N. The act of religious profession; a brief historical synposis and commentary. Washington, D.C., The Catholic University of America, 1931. 174 p. (The Catholic University of America. Canon law studies, no. 63)

Bibliography: p. 159–162.

1179

Fürst, Carl G. Cardinalis; Prolegomena zu einer Rechtsgeschichte des römischen Kardinalskollegiums. München, Fink, 1967. 261 p.

Bibliography: p. 212–246.

1180

Gaffaro, Caesare. Disputationis tiranensis inter pontificios et ministros verbi dei in Rhaetis, anno 1595 & 1596. habitae partes IV. Basilae, Waldkirch, 1602.

1181

Gagliardi, Carlo, fl. Tractatus de jure congrui. Editio prima. Cum indice copiosissimo. Neapoli, excudebat Mazzola-Vogola, sumptibus Marotta, 1782. 101 p.

1182

Galliher, Daniel M. Canonical elections. [Somerset, O., The Rosary Press] 1917. 116 p.

"Sources and bibliography": p. [111]–112.

1183

Galvin, William A. The administrative transfer of pastors; an historical synopsis and commentary. Washington, D.C., The Catholic University of America Press, 1946. 288 p. (The Catholic University of America. Canon law studies, no. 232)

Bibliography: p. 265–271.

1184

Gambaro, Pietro Andrea. Tractatvs de officio, atque avctoritate legati de latere, per r. Petrvm Andream Gambarvm . . . conscriptus, & in decem libros digestus, in qvo praeter alia complvra, qvae ad ipsius legationis officij munus pertinent; casus omnes pontifici maximo reseruati, beneficiorum permutationes, pensiones . . . pertractantur . . . Ab Avgvstino Ferentillo i. v. d. summo studio, summaque diligentia recognitus. Venetiis, apud Vincentium Valgriaium, 1572.

1185

Gannon, John M. The interstices required for the promotion to orders. Washington, D.C., The Catholic University of America Press, 1944. 100 p. (The Catholic University of America. Canon law studies, no. 196)

Bibliography: p. 85–87.

1186

Ganter, Bernard J. Clerical attire; a historical synopsis and a commentary. Washington, D.C., The Catholic University of America Press, 1955. 194 p. (Catholic University of America. Canon law studies, no. 361)

Bibliography: p. [157]–180.

1187

Ganzer, Klaus. Papsttum und Bistumsbesetzungen in der Zeit von Gregor IX bis Bonifaz VIII; ein Beitrag zur Geschichte der päpstlichen Reservationem. Köln, Böhlau, 1968. 469 p. (Forschungen zur kirchlichen Rechtsgeschichte und zum Kirchenrecht, Bd. 9)

Bibliography: p. [417]–429.

1188

García, Nicolao. Additiones, ad primvm et secvndvm tomvm De beneficijs, nunquam anteà editae, ab ipso authore adhuc viuo relictae. Madriti, excudebat Ludouicus Sanctius typographus regius, sumptibus Ioannis Hasrey, 1615. 101 1.

1189

García, Nicolao. Tractatus de beneficiis amplissimus at doctissimus declarationibus cardinelium Sacrae Congregationis Concilii Tridentini. Coloniae Allobrogum, Chonst, 1701. 2 v. in 1.

1190

Gass, Sylvester F. Ecclesiastical pensions; an historical synopsis and commentary. Washington, D.C., The Catholic University of America Press, 1942. 206 p. (The Catholic University of America. Canon law studies, no. 157)
Bibliography: p. [175]–186.

1191

Geser, Fintan. The canon law governing communities of sisters. St. Louis, Mo. and London, Herder, 1938. 415 p.

1192

Giganti, Girolamo, d. Tractatvs de pensionibvs ecclesiasticis, Hieronymo Gigante Forosemproniensi autore. Adiecta est in calce operis tabula quaestionum secundum ordinem quo sunt annotatae. Lvgdvni, Apud G. Rouillium, 1553. 461 p.

1193

Giganti, Girolamo. De pensionibvs ecclesiasticis, tractatvs vere aureus Hieronymi Gigantis ... Eivsdem avctoris responsa quinqvaginta in materia pensionum ecclesiasticarum, vna cum epithomate de intrvso. Cum indicibus quaestionuum. Coloniae Agrippinae, sumptibus Henningij, 1619. 2 v. in 1.

1194

Gill, Nicholas. The spiritual prefect in clerical religious houses of study, an historical synopsis and commentary. Washington, D.C., The Catholic University of America Press, 1945. 140 p. (The Catholic University of America. Canon law studies, no. 216)
Bibliography: p. 121–125.

1195

Gillet, Pierre. La personnalité juridique en droit ecclésiastique, spécialement chez les décrétistes et les décrétalistes et dans le Code de droit canonique. Malines, Godenne, 1927. 282 p.
"Bibliographie": p. [viii]–xii.

1196

Girardet, Klaus M. Kaisergericht und Bischofsgericht: Studien zu den Anfängen des Donatistenstreites (313–315) und zum Prozess des Athanasius von Alexandrien (328–346). Bonn, Habelt, 1975. 183 p. (Antiquitas: Reihe 1, Abhandlungen zur alten Geschichte; Bd. 21)
Bibliography: p. [163]–170.

1197

Gonzáles de Vallejo, Pedro. Discurso canónico-legal sobre los nombramientos de gobernadores ... hechos por los cabildos en los presentados por S.M. para obispos de sus iglesias. Madrid, Repullés, 1839. 274 p.

1198

González, Hieronymus. Dilvcicvm ac pervtile glossema seu commentatio ad Regulam octauam Cancellariae, de reservatione sensivm et alternativa episcoporvm. Nunc rursum post autoris obitum ex ipsius manuscripto exemplari multis additionibvs locupletius, & emendatius editum. Romae, Ex Typographia Mascardi, 1611. 680, 83 p.

1199

Gossler, Friedrich Franz Theodore Heinrich. Pro memoria; oder, Theologisches Gutachten über den Rechts-Zestand des erzbischöflichen Stuhles zu Köln seit dem 21 November 1837; geschichtlich-kirchentliche Abhandlung. Augsburg, Kollmann, 1838. 44 p.

1200

Gossman, Franics J. Pope Urban II and canon law. Washington, D.C., The Catholic University of America Press, 1960. 208 p. (Catholic University of America. Canon law studies, no. 403)
Bibliography: p. 194–200.

1201

Goyeneche, Servo. Quaestiones canonicae de iure religiosorum. Neapoli, d'Aurea, 1954–55. 2 v.
Bibliographical footnotes.

This work on the law of the religious provides the answers given by the author in the periodical *Commentarium pro Religiosis* to consultations on the subject during a period of over more than thirty years. They are presented in the order adopted by the code: general provisions, persons (clergy [especially religious and such related matters as foundation and suppression of province; superiors and chapters; confessors and chaplains; secular assets and their administration; novitiate; religious profession; the duties and privileges of the religious, etc.] and laymen), things (sacraments, sacred places and times, divine worship, etc.), trials, and crimes and punishments. The book also offers the jurisprudence practiced by the Sacred Congregations and by the Pontifical Commission for the authentic interpretation of the Code of Canon Law.

1202

Grassis, Carlo de. Tractatvs de effectibvs clericatvs, in qvo praeter ecclesiasticam ivrisdictionem, & clericorum priuilegia, omnes fere casus ad materiam pertinentes eruditissime declarantur, & resoluuntur. Cum summarijs, ac indice locupletissimo. Accesservnt praeterea additiones ad Tract. de effectibvs clericatvs, & in fine operis eiusdem authoris singularis. Tractatus de amicitia. Venetiis, apud Bertanum, 1639. 426 p.

1203

Grassis, Carlo de. Tractatus de effectibus clericatus ... Cum summarijs, ac indice ... Accesserunt praeterea additiones ad tractatus de effectibus clericatus, & in fine operis eiusdem auctoris singularis Tractatus de amicitia. Venetiis, Bertanorum sumptibus, 1674. 328, 28 p.

1204

Gross, Karl. Das Recht an der Pfründe; zugleich ein Beitrag zur Ermittlung des Ursprunges des jus ad rem. Graz, Leuschner & Lubensky, 1887. 318 p.
  Bibliographical footnotes.

1205

Gutiérrez Martín, Luis. También los clérigos bajo la jurisdicción del Estado. Roma, Commentarium pro Religiosis [1968] 270 p.
  Bibliography: p. [263]–266.

1206

Hannan, Philip M. The canonical concept of congrua sustentatio for the secular clergy. Washington, D.C., The Catholic University of America Press,

1950. 237 p. (The Catholic University of America. Canon law studies, no. 302)
  Bibliography: p. 212–219.

1207

Hanstein, Honorius. Ordensrecht, ein Grundriss für Studierende, Seelsorger, Klosterleitungen, und Juristen. Paderborn, Schöningh, 1953. 335 p.
  Bibliography: p. 11–12.

1208

Hay, Romanus, fl. Astrvm inextinctvm sive ivs agendi antiqvorvm religiosorvm ordinvm, pro recipiendis svis monasteriis ... & bonis ecclesiasticis, per S.C. Mtis. edictum generale, vel ius belli, &c restituendis, e sacri canonibus, eorumq; interpretibus clare demonstratvm. Editio prima. [n. p.], 1636. 425, [19] p.

1209

Haydt, John Joseph. Reserved benefices. Washington, D.C., The Catholic University of America Press, 1942. 148 p. (The Catholic University of America. Canon law studies, no. 161)

1210

Heintschel, Donald E. The mediaeval concept of an ecclesiastical office; an analytical study of the concept of an ecclesiastical office in the major sources and printed commentaries from 1140–1300. Washington, D.C., The Catholic University of America Press, 1956. 108 p. (The Catholic University of America. Canon law studies, no. 363)
  Bibliography: p. 101–103.

1211

Henry, Charles W. Canonical relations between the bishops and abbots at the beginning of the tenth century. Washington, D.C., The Catholic University of America Press, 1957. 220 p. (The Catholic University of America. Canon law studies, no. 382)
  Bibliography: p. 200–211.

1212

Hermes, Heinrich J. R. Dissertatio historico-canonica de capitulo sede vacante vel impedita et de vicario capitulari, quam ... publice propugnabit Henricus Josephus Ludolphus Hermes. Lovanii, Excudebant Vanlinthout Fratres [1873] 182 p.

(Universitas Catholica in oppido Lovaniensi. S. Facultas Theologica, 1872–1875, no. 394)
Bibliographical footnotes.

1213
Hilling, Nikolaus. Das personenrecht des Codex iuris canonici. Paderborn, Schöningh, 1924. 271 p.
Includes bibliographies.

1214
Hourlier, Jacques. L'âge classique, 1140–1378: les religieux. [Paris] Cujas, 1974. 567 p. (Histoire du droit et des institutions de l'Église en Occident; t. 10)
Includes bibliographical references and index.

1215
Hubertus van Groessen, Father. De Apostolische faculteiten voor missiegebieden; tekst met commentaar. Roermond, Romen [1949] 128 p.

1216
Hynes, Harry G. The privileges of cardinals, commentary with historical notes. Washington, D.C., The Catholic University of America Press, 1945. 183 p. (The Catholic University of America. Canon law studies, no. 217)
Bibliography: p. 157–164.

1217
Incarnato, Fabio. Scrvtinivm sacerdotale, sive modvs examinandi, tam in visitatione episcopali, quam in susceptione ordinum. Nunc postremo ab infinitis mendis. quibus vitio impressorum scatebat, a Liuio a Lege diligentissime repurgatum. Venetiis, apud Iacobum Sarzinam, 1620. 23 p. l., 252 l.

1218
De institutione ad vitam religiosam ducendam iuxta instructionem "Renovationis causam," cura et studio Commentarii pro religiosis. Roma, Commentarium pro religiosis, 1969. 322 p.
Includes bibliographical references.

1219
Jäger, Johann W. De concordia imperii et sacerdotii, sive de jure potestatum supremarum circa sacra. Tubingae, Cotta, 1711. 374 p.

1220
Jansen, Josef M. Ordensrecht; kurze Zusammenstellung der geltenden kirchenrechtlichen Bestimmungen für die Orden und religiösen Kongregationen. Paderborn, Schöningh, 1911. 146 p.

1221
Jesuits. Canones. Canones trivm congregationvm generalivm Societatis Iesv. Auctoritate tertiae Congregationis confecti. Romae, in Collegio Societatis Iesv, 1573. 83 p.

1222
Jura sacerdotum vindicata. The rights of the clergy vindicated; or, A plea for canon law in the United States by a Roman Catholic priest. New York, Sheehy, 1883. 388 p.

1223
Kealy, Thomas M. Dowry of women religious, an historical synopsis and commentary. Washington, D.C., The Catholic University of America Press, 1941. 152 p. (The Catholic University of America, Canon law studies, no. 134)

1224
Kearney, Raymond A. The principles of delegation. Washington, D.C., The Catholic University of America Press, 1929. 148 p. (The Catholic University of America. Canon law studies, no. 55)
Bibliography: p. 140–144.

1225
Kelliher, Jeremiah F. Loss of privileges. Washington, D.C., The Catholic University of America Press, 1964. 117 p. (The Catholic University of America. Canon law studies, no. 364)
Bibliography: p. 111–112.

1226
Kelly, James P. The jurisdiction of the simple confessor, a dissertation to the faculty of canon law of the Catholic University of America. Washington, D.C., The Catholic University of America Press, 1927. 208 p. (The Catholic University of America. Canon law studies, no. 43)

1227
Kilcullen, Thomas J. The collegiate moral person as party litigant; a historical synopsis and commentary. Washington, D.C., The Catholic University of America Press, 1947. 150 p. (The Catholic University of America. Canon law studies, no. 251)
Bibliography: 122–131.

1228

Klingel, Valentin. Die päpstliche Autorität nach Johann Caspar Barthel (1697–1771): ein Beitrag zur Würzburger Kanonistik des 18. Jahrhunderts. Excerptum e dissertatione ad lauream. Rome, Pontificium Athenaeum Salesianum, 1972. 103 p. (Theses ad lauream. Pontificium Athenaeum Salesianum, Facultas Juris Canonici, no. 121)
Bibliography: p. 5–14.

1229

Koch, Walter. Die klerikalen Standesprivilegien nach Kirchen und Staatsrecht unter besonderer Berücksichtigung der Verhältnisse in der Schweiz. Freiburg, 1949. 274 p.
Bibliography: p. x–xi.

1230

Koesler, Leo. Entrance into the novitiate by clerics in major orders; a historical synopsis and a commentary. Washington, D.C., The Catholic University of America Press, 1953. 176 p. (The Catholic University of America. Canon law studies, no. 327)
Bibliography: p. 164–170.

1231

Konrad, Joseph G. The transfer of religious to another community; an historical synopsis and a commentary. Washington, D.C., The Catholic University of America Press, 1949. 284 p. (The Catholic University of America. Canon law studies, no. 278)
Bibliography: p. 253–260.

1232

Kook, Matthias de. De potestatis civilis episcoporum praecipue Trajectinorum in regno Francorum initiis atque incrementis. Trajecti ad Rhenum, Natan, 1838. 200 p.

1233

Kop, František. Vývoj Metropolitní pravomoci v církvi Západní. Příspěvek k dějinám monarchického zřízení církevního. Praha, nákladem České Akademia věd a uměni, 1941. 2 v.

1234

Kowalski, Romuald E. Sustenance of religious houses of regulars. Washington, D.C., The Catholic University of America Press, 1944. 174 p. (The Catholic University of America. Canon law studies, no. 199)
Bibliography: p. 153–159.

1235

Krimmel, Arthur. Die Rechtesstellung der ausserhalb ihres Verbandes lebenden Ordensleute. Paderborn, Schöningh, 1957. 214 p.
Includes bibliography.

1236

Krzemieniecki, Jan. Procedura administracyjna w Kodeksie prawa kanonicznego, kan. 2142–2194. Kraków, Skład główny: Księgarnia Krakowska, 1925. 246 p.
Bibliography: p. [7]–10.

1237

Kubelbeck, William J. The sacred Penitentiaria and its relations to faculties of ordinaries and priests. [Somerset, O., The Rosary Press] 1918. 124, [4] p. (The Catholic University of America. Canon law studies, no. 5)
"Sources and bibliography": p. [122]–124.

1238

Kujawa, George M. von. De incorporatione beneficiorum. Dissertatio inauguralis. Glacii, typis Schirmeri, 1872. 4 p. 1., 72 p.

1239

Labhart, Verena. Zur Rechtssymbolik des Bischolfsrings. Köln, Böhlau, 1963. 116 p. (Rechtshistorische Arbeiten, Bd. 2)
Bibliography: p. [110]–116.

1240

Lafontaine, Germain. Relations canoniques enter le missionnaire et ses supérieurs; abrégé historique et commentaire canonique. Sherbrooke, Que., Messager Saint-Michel, 1947. 115 p. (The Catholic University of America. Canon law studies, no. 252)
"Bibliographie": p. [100]–103.

1241

Lafontaine, Paul H. Les conditions positives de l'accession aux ordres dans la première législation ecclésiastique (300–492) Ottawa, Editions de l'Université d'Ottawa, 1963. 398 p. (Les Publications sériées de l'Université d'Ottawa, 71)
Bibliography: p. [373]–383.

1242

Lahidalga, José M. de. La coacción en la ordenación sagrada, estudio histórico-jurídico del canon 214. Vitoria [España] Eset, 1960. 388 p. (Victoriensia, v. 10)

Includes bibliography.

1243

Lancelot, J. P. Institutiones iuris canonici, quibus jus Pontificium singulari methodi Libris quatuor comprehenditur. 3. ed. Parisiis, apud Langlois, 1679. 452, 58 p.

1244

Lancellotti, Giovanni P. Institvtionvm ivris canonici libri qvatvor . . . Ab Io. Pavlo Lancelotto . . . Nunc primum in lucem editi. Venetiis [apud cominum de Tridino Montisferrati] 1564. 111 1.

1245

Lancellotti, Giovanni P. Institvtiones ivris canonici qvibvs ivs pontificivm singvlari methodo libris quatuor comprehenditur. His accesserunt interpretationes, quas glossas vocant. Nouissimè accesserunt casuum, vt appellant, positiones, adnotationesque nonnullae quae ad huius iuris scientiam expeditiorem studiosis praebent aditum. Io. Baptista Bartolino auctore. Necnon adnotationes paucae, quibus nonnulla ad sensum theologorum exactius explicatur Antonio Timotheo auctore. Item commentariolum, quo conscripti operis, & ratio & historia quaedam continetur. Accessit etiam ipsius Lancelotti opusculum, De comparatione utriusque iuris. Venetiis, Apud Bertanum, 1613. 453, 84 p.

1246

Lancellotti, Giovanni P. Institvtiones ivris canonici, qvibus ivs pontificivm singulari methodo libris quator comprehenditur: aIo. Pavlo Lancelotto Perusino conscriptae & in Aula romana, mandato pon. max. ab illustrib. viris olim recognitae: nunc primùm annotatis in margine locis, vnde sumpti sunt. Vnà cum indicibus locupletissimis. Lvgdvni, apvd Rovillivm, 1578. 420, [75] p.

1247

Lancellotti, Giovanni P. Institvtiones ivris canonici, qvibus ivs pontificivm singvlari methodo libris qvattvor comprehenditur; ab Ioan. Pavlo Lancelotto, conscriptae, His accedderunt interpretationes, quas Glossas vocant, Nouissime accesserunt casuum, vt appellant, positiones, annotationes que nonnullae, quae ad huius iuris scientiam expeditiorem studiosis praebent aditum. Io. Baptista Bartolino, auctore. Necnon adnotationes paucae quibus nonnula ad sensum theologorum exactius explicantur, Antonio Timotheo. Accessit etiam ipsius Lancelotti opusculum de comparatione vtrivsque. Lvgdvni, apud Rouillium, 1588. 513, 80, [32] p.

1248

Lancellotti, Giovanni P. Institvtiones ivris canonici, qvibus ivs pontificivm singvlari methodo libri quatuor comprehenditur, a Ioanne Pavlo Lancelotto, conscriptae, Cum interpretationibus, quas glosas vocant, quibus loca omnia, vnde contextus desumptus est, indicantur, pleraque declarantur, non nulla per sacrosanctum concilium hodie immutata adnotantur. Et his accesserunt casuum, vt appellant, positiones, adnotationesque nonnullae, quae ad huius iuris scientiam expenditiorem studiosis praebent aditum, Ioannis Baptistae, nec non adnotationes, Antonii Timothei, Ac Tandem nouiter additiones, et adnotationes, Ioannis Aloysii Riecij. Venetiis, apvd Ivntas, 1630. 504 p.

1249

Lancelotti, Giovanni P. Institutiones juris canonici, quibus jus pontificium singulari methodo comprehenditur. Parisiis, Dezallier, 1685.

1250

Lancelotto, Paulo. Institutiones Iuris Canonici, quibus ius Pontificium singulari methodo libris quatuor comprehenditur. Nunc primum annotatis in margine locis, unde sumptisunt. Lugduni, apud Gulielmum, 1587. 500 p.

1251

Lariccia, Sergio. Considerazioni sull'elemento personale dell'ordinamento giuridico canonico. Milano, Giuffrè, 1971. 135 p. (Università di Cagliari. Pubblicazioni della Facultà di giurisprudenza. Serie 1 (Giuridica) v. 9)

Bibliography: p. [89]–124.

1252

Larraona, Arcadio M. La nuova disciplina canonica sulle monarche, la costituzione apostolica "Sponsa Christi" e la istruzione "Inter praeclara," commentate dall'ecc. no p. Arcadio Larraona ed altri collaboratori di "Commentarium pro religiosis." Roma, Desclée [1952] 319 p.

1253

Lavelle, Howard D. The obligation of holding sacred missions in parishes; a historical synopsis and a commentary. Washington, D.C., The Catholic University of America Press, 1949. 142 p. (The Catholic University of America. Canon law studies, no. 295)
Bibliography: p. 113–120.

1254

Laymann, Paul. Qvaestiones canonicae de praelatorvm ecclesiasticorvm electione, institvtione, et potestate. Ex lib. I. Decretalium. Quas . . . in celebri Catholica vniuersitate Dilingana. Praeside Pavlo Laymann . . . In pvblicam dispvtationem prodvxit p. f. Leonardvs Caesar . . . Dilingae, formis academicis, apud Jacobvm Sermondi, 1627.
201, [4] p.

1255

Leclerc, Gustave. Zeger-Bernard van Espen (1646–1728) et l'autorité ecclésiastique; contribution a l'histoire des théories gallicanes et du jansénism. Zürich, PAS, 1964. 451 p. (Studia et textus historia juris canonici, v. 2)
Bibliography: p. 415–430.

1256

Lee, S. van der. Clerus en medicijnen in de geschiedenis van het kereklijk recht. Utrecht, Dekker & Van de Vegt, 1951. 142 p.
Bibliography: p. ix–xiv.

1257

Lenz, Paul. Die diözesan- und ortskirchlichen juristischen Personen des kanonischen Rechtes im privaten und öffentlichen Recht der Schweiz. [Wil, 1949] 73 p.
"Literatureverzeichnis": 4th–7th prelim pages.

1258

Leoni, Marco P. De auctoritate, et usu pallii pontifici. Romae, Grignani, 1649. 178 p.

1259

Lesage, Germain. L'accession des congrégations à l'état religieux canonique. Ottawa, Éditions de l'Université d'Ottawa, 1952. 240 p. (Universitas Catholica Ottaviensis. Dissertationes ad gradum laureae in facultatibus ecclesiasticis consequendum conscriptae. Series canonica, 19)
"Bibliographie utile": p. [223]–237.

1260

Lewis, Gordian. Chapters in religious institutes; an historical synopsis and commentary. Washington, D.C., The Catholic University of America Press, 1943. 109 p. (The Catholic University of America. Canon law studies, no. 181)
Bibliography: p. 145–149.

1261

Link, Ludwig. Die Besetzung der kirchlichen Ämter in den Konkordaten Papst Pius' XI. Bonn, Röhrscheid, 1942. Amsterdam, Schippers, 1964. 624 p. (Kanonistische Studien und Texte, Bd. 18–19)
Includes bibliographical references.

1262

Liotta, Fillippo. La continenza die chierici nel pensiero canonistico classico. Da Graziano a Gregorio IX. Milano, Giuffrè, 1971. 401 p. (Quaderni di "Studi senesi," 24)
Includes bibliographical references.

1263

Lo Castro, Gaetano. Personalità morale e soggettività giuridica nel diritto canonico: (contributo allo studio delle persone morali). Milano, Giuffrè, 1974. 251 p. (Pubblicazioni della Facoltà di giurisprudenza, Università di Catania; 73)
Includes bibliographical references.

1264

Lochbronner, Pfarrer. Das katholische Pfarrergesetz; nach dem Dekrete Sr. Heiligkeit des Papstes Pius X. vom 20. August 1910 und nach dem neuen kirchlichen Gesetzbuch (Codex juris canonici vom Jahre 1917) 2 verb. und verm. Ausg. des Amotionsgesetzes. München, Verlag Veritas, 1918. 61 p.

1265

López de Prado, Joaquín. Derecho de misión y libertad religiosa en los juristas clásicos de la Compañía de Jesús; lección inaugural del curso en la Facultad de Derecho Canónico, 1964–1965. Madrid, Universidad Pontificia de Comillas [1964] 64 p.

Bibliography: p. 7.

1266

Lotteri, Melchiorre. De re beneficiaria. Romae, Corbelletti, 1629–35. 2 v. in 1.

1267

Lover, James F. The master of novices; an historical synopsis and commentary. Washington, D.C., The Catholic University of America Press, 1947 [i.e., 1948] 168 p. (The Catholic University of America. Canon law studies, no. 254)

Bibliography: p. 141–147.

1268

Luca, Giovanni Battista de, cardinal. Theatrum veritatis & justitiae, sive Decisivi discursus per materias, seu titulos distincti, & ad veritatem editi in forensibus controversiis canonicis & civilibus, in quibus in urbe advocatus pro una partium scripsit, vel consultus respondit; Repertorium seu index generalis rerum notabilium, quae continentur in Theatro veritatis & justitiae cardinalis de Luca, a Nicolao Falconio, elaboratum. Accedit in fine hujus voluminis index decisionum, constitutionum, ac allegationum additarum in hac veneta impressione. Venetiis, ex typographia Balleoniana, 1726. 15 v. in 10.

1269

Luca, Giovanni Battista de, cardinal. Tractatus de officiis venalibus vacabilibus Romanae curiae; cum juribus, seu documentis, informationibus, responsis, & decisionibus super suppressione Collegii sacretariorum apostolicorum. Accedit alter Tractatvs de locis montium non vacabilium urbis. Cvm novissimis svmmorvm pontificvm constitutionibus; nec non sacrae Rotae romanae decisionibus ad materiam facientibus, suis locis optimè adjectis. Venetiis, apud Paulum Balleonium, 1716. 264, 52, [4] p.

1270

Lynch, George E. Coadjutors and auxiliaries of bishops; a historical synopsis and a commentary. Washington, D.C., The Catholic University of America Press, 1947. 107 p. (The Catholic University of America. Canon law studies, no. 238)

Bibliography: p. 89–92.

1271

Madrenys Caballé, Pedro. La impericia y la enfermedad como causas de remoción del párroco. [Pamplona, Rialp Navarra, 1965] 178 p. (Colección canónica de la Universidad de Navarra. Cuadernos, 5)

Bibliography: p. 175–178.

1272

Mahoney, Gerard M. The academic curriculum in minor seminaries. Washington, D.C., The Catholic University of America Press, 1965. 192 p. (Catholic University of America. Canon law studies, no. 440)

1273

Manfredi, Girolamo. De cardinalibvs Sanctae Rom. eccles. liber, in qvo omnia, qvae ad hanc materiam pertinent, copiosissime tractantur. Bononiae, excudente Ioanne Rubrio, 1564. 126 p.

1274

Manning, Joseph. The free conferral of offices; a historical synopsis and commentary. Washington, D.C., The Catholic University of America Press, 1945. 116 p. (The Catholic University of America. Canon law studies, no. 219)

Bibliography: p. 96–101.

1275

Marositz, Joseph J. Obligations and privileges of religious promoted to episcopal or cardinalitial dignities; a historical synopsis and commentary. Washington, D.C., The Catholic University of America Press, 1948. 179 p. (The Catholic University of America. Canon law studies, no. 256)

Bibliography: p. 149–154.

1276

Martínez Díez, Gonzalo. El patrimonio eclesiástico en la España visigoda; estudio histórico jurídico. Comillas, 1959. 200 p. (Universidad Pontificia de Comillas. Publicaciones anejas a "Miscelánea Comillas." Serie canónica, v. 2)

Bibliography: p. [9]–12.

1277

Martini, Giuseppe. Parroco e parrocchia personale in diritto canonico; studio di diritto canonico. Torino, Tip La Salute, 1950. 163 p.

1278

Mathis, Marcian J. The constitution and supreme administration of regional seminaries subject to the Sacred Congregation for the Propagation of the Faith in China; a historical synopsis and a commentary. Washington, D.C., The Catholic University of America Press, 1952. 172 p. (Catholic University of America. Canon law studies, no. 331)
  Bibliography: p. 159–162.

1279

Mayer, Heinrich Suso. Benediktinische Ordensrecht in der Beuroner Kongregation. Beuron/Hohenzollern, Beuroner Kunstverlag, 1932–36. v.
  Includes bibliographies.

1280

Mazón, Cándido. Las reglas de los religiosos, su obligación y naturaleza jurídica. Romae, apud aedes Universitatis gregorianae, 1940. [3]–360 p. (Analecta Gregorianna, cura Pontificiae universitatis Gregorianae edita. v. XXIV. Series Iuris Canonici, sectio A (n. 3))
  "Bibliografia": p. [xiii]–xiv

1281

McDonough, Thomas J. Apostolic administrators, an historical synopsis and commentary. Washington, D.C., The Catholic University of America Press, 1941. 217 p. (The Catholic University of America. Canon law studies, no. 139)

1282

McElroy, Francis J. The privileges of bishops; commentary with historical notes. Washington, D.C., The Catholic University of America Press, 1951. 142 p. (Catholic University of America. Canon law studies, no. 282)
  Bibliography: p. 130–137.

1283

McFarland, Norman F. Religious vocation, its juridic concept; a historical synopsis and a commentary. Washington, D.C. The Catholic University of America Press, 1953. 132 p. (Catholic University of America. Canon law studies, no. 328)
  Bibliography: p. 121–126.

1284

McGrath, James. The privilege of the canon; a historical synopsis and commentary. Washington, D.C., The Catholic University of America Press, 1946. 156 p. (The Catholic University of America. Canon law studies, no. 242)
  Bibliography: p. 129–137.

1285

McGrath, John J. Catholic institutions in the United States; canonical and civil law status. Washington, D.C., Catholic University of America Press, 1968. 48 p.
  Bibliography: p. 45–48.

1286

McManus, James E. The administration of temporal goods in religious institutes. Washington, D.C., The Catholic University of America Press, 1937. 196 p. (The Catholic University of America. Canon law studies, no. 109)
  Bibliography: p. xiii–xvi.

1287

Ménard, Pierre. L'exemption des séminaires de la juridiction paroissiale. Ottawa, Éditions de l'Université d'Ottawa, 1950. 192 p. (Universitas Catholica Ottaviensis. Dissertationes ad gradum laureae in facultatibus ecclesiasticis consequendum conscriptae. Series canonica, t. 30)
  Bibliography: p. [167]–173.

1288

Mengoni, Pietro. De eminentiori parochorum dignitate supra canonicos praesertim collegiatarum, forensis disceptatio authore Petro Mengonio. Florentiae, typis regiae celsitud. apud Tartinium & Granchium, 1732. 87, [1] p.

1289

Metz, John E. The recording judge in the ecclesiastical collegiate tribunal; a historical synopsis and a commentary. Washington, D.C., The Catholic University of America Press, 1949. 115 p. (The Catholic University of America. Canon law studies, no. 287)
  Bibliography: p. 109–111.

1290

Meyer, Louis G. Alms-gathering by religious; an historical conspectus and commentary. Washington, D.C., The Catholic University of America Press, 1946. 163 p. (The Catholic University of America. Canon law studies, no. 220)
  Bibliography: p. 142–147.

1291

Michal, Jaroslav J. Komentář k druhé knize Kodexu. O osobách. Zprac. Jaroslav Michal. Skriptum pro stud. účely Cyrilometodějské bohosl. fak. v Praze-Litoměřice. 1. vyd. Praha, ÚCN, rozmn. ST, 1969. 172 p.

Bibliography: p. 6–8.

1292

Michiels, Gommar. Principia generalia de personis in ecclesia; commentarius libri II Codicis juris canonici, canones praeliminares 87–106. Ed. 2, penitus retracta et notabiliter aucta. Parisiis, Typis Societatis S. Joannis Evangelistae, 1955. 708 p.

Includes bibliographies.

1293

Mock, Timothy. Disqualification of electors in ecclesiastical elections. Washington, D.C., The Catholic University of America Press, 1958. 210 p. (The Catholic University of America. Canon law studies, no. 365)

Bibliography: p. 194–199.

1294

Moeder, John M. The proper bishop for ordination and dismissorial letters; an historical synopsis and commentary. Washington, D.C., The Catholic University of America, 1935. 135 p. (The Catholic University of America. Canon law studies, no. 95)

Bibliography: p. 124–126.

1295

Molitor, Wilhelm. Ueber kanonisches Gerichtsverfahren gegen Kleriker; ein rechtsgeschichtlicher Versuch zur Lösung der praktischen Frage der Gegenwart. Mainz, Kirchheim, 1856. 284 p.

1296

Moroni, Attilio. La volantà nell' "Ordo sacer." Milano, Giuffrè, 1957. 244 p. (Biblioteca degli "Annali dell'Università de Macerata," 4)

1297

Motry, Hubert L. Diocesan faculties according to the code of canon law. Washington, D.C., The Catholic University of America Press, 1922. 167 p.

Bibliography: p. 157–160.

1298

Motu proprio su facoltà e privilegi concessi ai vescovi Pastorale munus. Costituzione del Sinodo dei vescovi Apostolicam sollicitudo. Norme date ai vescovi circa la facoltà di dispensare De episcoporum muneribus. Facoltà delegate ai superiori generali Cum admotae. Padova, Gregoriana, 1967. 51 p. (Collana Concilio ecumenico vaticano II. Norme di applicazione, 2)

[Pope, 1963–1978 (Paulus VI)]

1299

Moynihan, James M. Papal immunity and liability in the writings of the medieval canonists. Roma, Gregorian University Press, 1961. 151 p. (Analecta Gregoriana, v. 120. Series Facultatis Iuris Canonici, sectio B, n. 9)

Bibliography: p. [145]–151.

1300

Murphy, Edwin J. Suspension ex informata conscientia. Washington, D.C., The Catholic University of America Press, 1932. 138 p. (The Catholic University of America. Canon law studies, no. 76)

Bibliography: p. 123–126.

1301

Naeve, Johann K. Jus clericorum, oder Das priesterrecht, in welchem, wie die kirche und deren diener anfangs beschaffen gewesen, hernach zugenommen, und wieder in abfall kommen, auch was insonderheit die kirchen-diener heute zu tage vor befügnüss und privilegien haben, kürtzlich vorgestellet und zum andern mahl viel vermehrter herausgegeben von d. Io. Carol. Naevio. Wittenberg, Zimmermann, 1713. 786, [52] p.

1302

Nissl, Anton. Der gerichtsstand des clerus im Frankischen reich. Innsbruck, Wagner, 1886. 247 p.

"Verzeichniss der abgekürzt angeführten werke": p. [xi]–xv.

1303

Nothum, Alfred. La rémunération du travail inhérent aux fonctions spirituelles et la simonie de droit divin. Roma, Libreria editrice dell'Università gregoriana, 1969. 262 p. (Analecta Gregoriana, v. 176. Series Facultatis Iuris Canonici: sectio B, no. 27)

Bibliography: p. [ix]–xx.

1304

Nugent, John G. Ordination in societies of the common life; a historical synopsis and a commentary. Washington, D.C., The Catholic University of America Press, 1958. 240 p. (Catholic University of America. Canon law studies, no. 341)
Bibliography: p. 220–231.

1305

O'Brien, Kenneth R. The nature of support of diocesan priests in the United States of America; a historical synopsis and a commentary. Washington, D.C., The Catholic University of America Press, 1949. 162 p. (The Catholic University of America. Canon law studies, no. 286)
Bibliography: p. 135–141.

1306

O'Brien, Romaeus W. The provincial religious superior; a historical conspectus and a commentary on the rights and duties of the provincial religious superior in religious orders of men. Washington, D.C., The Catholic University of America Press, 1947 [i.e., 1948] 294 p. (The Catholic University of America. Canon law studies, no. 258)
Bibliography: p. 261–268.

1307

O'Leary, Charles G. Religious dismissed after perpetual profession; an historical conspectus and commentary. Washington, D.C., The Catholic University of America Press, 1943. 213 p. (The Catholic University of America. Canon law studies, no. 184)
Bibliography: 189–196.

1308

Olivares, Estanislao. Los votos de los escolares de la Compañía de Jesus, su evolución jurídica. Roma, Institutum Historicum S. I., 1961. 250 p. (Biblioteca Instituti Historici S. I., v. 19)

1309

O'Neill, Francis J. The dismissal of religious in temporary vows; an historical conspectus and commentary. Washington, D.C., The Catholic University of America Press, 1942. 220 p. (The Catholic University of America. Canon law studies, no. 166)
Bibliography: p. 191–204.

1310

Ordnung der Bischofssynode. Ordo Synodi episoporum celebrandae. (Lateinisch-deutsch) (Mit) Motuproprio über die Errichtung einer Bischofssynode für die ganze Kirche. Von den deutschen Bischöfen approbierte Übersetzung. Eingeleitet von Hubert Jedin. Trier, Paulinus-Verlag, 1968. 61 p. (Nachkonziliare Dokumentation, Bd. 12)
[Catholic Church. Synodus Episcoporum]

1311

Dell'origine delle immunità del clero cattolico e d'ogni altro sacerdozio creduto dagli uomini legittimo e santo. Libri due. Cesena, Eredi Biasini all Insegna di Pallade, 1791. 428 p.

1312

Orth, Clement R. The approbation of religious institutes. Washington, D.C., The Catholic University of America Press, 1931. 170 p. (The Catholic University of America. Studies in canon law, no. 71)
Bibliography: p. [159]–161.

1313

Pallavicino, Sforza, cardinal. Vindicationes Societatis Iesv quibus multorum accusationes in eius institutum, leges, gymnasia, mores refelluntur. Romae, typis Dominici Manelphi, 1649. 407 p.

1314

Palombo, Joseph. De dimissione religiosorum; commentarium theoretico-practicum ad tit. XVI libri II Codicis iuris canonici. Taurini-Romae, Marietti, 1931. 296 p.
"Bibliographia": p. [ix]–xi.

1315

Papi, Hector. Religious in church law; an exposition of canon law concerning religious, with a preface by the Right Rev. Msgr. Philip Bernardini. New York, Kenedy & sons, 1924. 355 p.

1316

Parecer sobre o privilegio qve a Bvlla da Crvzada concede a todos os religiosos mendicantes, & não mendicantes para elegerem confessor que os absolua dos reseruados, mandado fazer pello Conselho da Cruzada. Composto por hvm religioso deputado ordinario do Sancto Officio, & dado a estampa pello licenciado R. Mendez. Lisboa, 630 [i.e., 1630] 33 l.

1317

Parisius, Flaminius. De resignatione beneficiorvm tractatvs. Venetiis, Apud haeredem Scoti, 1605–07. 2 v. in l.

Includes bibliographical references.

1318

Parisio, Flaminio. De resignatione beneficiorvm tractatvs. Complectens totam fere praxim beneficiariam. Decisionibus Rotae romanae, & receptis doctorum opinionibus attestatam, & copiose comprobatam. Indice primo quaestionum, altero deinde sententiarum, ao verborum copiosissimo adiecto. Venetiis, apvd Scotvm, 1619. 2 v. in l.

1319

Parsons, Anscar. Canonical elections. Washington, D.C., The Catholic University of America Press, 1939. 236 p.

1320

Pater, Januarius. Die bischöfliche visitatio liminum ss. apostolorum. Eine historisch-kanonistische studie. Paderborn, Schöningh, 1914. 152 p. (Görresgesellschaft zur pflege der wissenschaft im katholischen Deutschland. Veröffentlichungen der Sektion für rechtsund sozialwissenschaft, 19. hft.)

"Verzeichnis der quellen und literatur": p. [vi]–xii.

1321

Paulo Romano. Tractatus non minvs necessarivs q̃ utilis pensionu ecclesiasticaru. Pauli de Roma no antea in lucem aeditus. Discutiutur etia hoc in opusculo multa ad permutationes beneficioru spectantia, que omnia vidisse lectore no mediocriter iuuabit. Romae [impensis domini Michaelis Tramezini] 1539. 48 l.

1322

Paulus III, pope. Tractatus non minvs necessarivs vtilis pensionu ecclesiasticaru excel. I. V. D. domini Pauli de Roma, no antes in lucem aeditus, quem si legeris nihil amplius in persionu materia desiderabis. Disscutiutur etia hoc in opusculo multa ad permutatices beneficioru spectantia, que omnia vidisse lectore no mediocriter iuuabit. Cum priuilegio summi pontificis, Venetorum senatus. Romae, 1539. 48 p.

1323

Pawlina, Leon. Dymisorje w rozwoju historycznym. Lublin, Tow. Nautokowe Katolickiego Uniwersytetu Lubelskiego, 1936. 147 p. (2. Wydzial Prawa Kanonicznego. Rozprawy kodtorskie, t. 5)

Bibliography: p. [141]–147.

1324

Pellegrini, Carlo, bp. Praxis vicariorum, et omnium in utroque foro jusdicentium, quatuor partibus comprehensa. Cum observationibus itriusque juris, imo et municipalis Regni neapolitani, necnon formulis singulorum actorum judicialium. Omnia fere complectens, quae per ponteficias, ac caesareas leges, conciliorum decreta, sacrarum congregationum declarationes, ac Sacra rotae decisiones haec sancita juerunt. Cum triplivi indice copiosissimo. Venetiis, apud Bonifacium Viezzeri, 1743. 472 p.

1325

Pellizzari, Francesco. Tractatio de monialibvs in qva resolvvntvu omnes fere qvaestiones (& ex his plurime adhuc non tractatae) quae de ijs excitari solent in communi, & in particulari; nimirvm de receptione, nouitatu, dote. Accessit Formvlarivm licentiarvm, quarum vsus in monialium gubernatione solet esse frequentior. Editio secvnda ab ipsomet avthore recognita, et multis additionibvs. ijsq; vtilissimis aucta. Venetiis, Apud Baleonium, 1646. 590 p.

1326

Perathoner, Anton. Das kirchliche Sachenrecht nach dem Codex juris canonici (drittes Buch). Brixen, Weger, 1919. 187 p.

A paraphrase, with comments, of the 3d book (c. 725–1551) of Codex juris canonici.

1327

Pereira, António da S. Sacramento da ordem e ofício eclesiástico. Problemática hodierna do sacramento e poder na Igreja. Roma, Libreria editrice dell'Università gregoriana, 1969. 260 p. (Analecta Gregoriana, v. 175. Series Facultatis Iuris Canonici; Sectio B, n. 26)

Bibliography: p. [xii]–xvi.

1328

Peterson, Casimir M. Spritual care in diocesan seminaries; a historical synopsis and a commentary. Washington, D.C., The Catholic University of

America Press, 1966. 193 p. (Catholic University of America. Canon law studies, no. 342.)
Bibliography: p. 175–184.

1329

Petroncelli, Mario. La "deputatio ad cultum publicum"; contributo allo dotrina conanica degli edifici pubblici di culto. Napoli, Pellerano-Del Guadio [1952] 174 p.

1330

Pfaller, Benedict A. The ipso facto effected dismissal of religious; a historical conspectus and a commentary. Washington, D.C., The Catholic University of America Press, 1948. 225 p. (The Catholic University of America. Canon law studies, no. 259)
Bibliography: p. 195–204.

1331

Pfurtscheller, Friedrich. Die Privilegierung des Zisterzienserordens im Rahmen der allgemeinen Schutzund Exemtionsgeschichte vom Anfang bis zur Bulle Parvus Fons (1265). Ein Überblick unter besonderer Berücksichtigung von Schreibers Kurie und Kloster im 12. Jahrhundert. Bern, Herbert Lang; Frankfurt, Peter Lang, 1972. 184 p. (Europäische Hochschulschriften. Reihe 23: Theologie, Bd. 13)
Bibliography: p. xi–xv.

1332

Piasecio, Paolo. Praxis episcopalis ea quae officium, et potestatem episcopi concernunt continens. Venetiis, Dusinellus, 1613. 356 p.

1333

Piatti, Girolamo. De cardinalis dignitate, et officio. Hieronymi Plati. Romae, apud Gulielmum Facciottum, 1602. 245 p.

1334

Piñero Carrión, José M. La sustentación del clero; síntesis histórica y estudio jurídico. Sevilla, 1963. 549 p.
"Notas bibliográficas": p. [xxiii]–iv.

1335

Piontek, Cyril. De indulto exclaustrationis necnon saecularizationis. Washingtonii, D.C., 1925. 273 p.
"Bibliographia": p. vii–xiii.

1336

Pistocchi, Mario. De bonis ecclesiae temporalibus (Cod. i. c. lib. III, p. vi) Taurini, Italia, ex Officina Libraria Marietti, 1932. 489 p.

1337

Plocque, Auguste. De la condition juridique du prêtre catholique. Paris, Larose et Forcel, 1887. 282 p.

1338

Polacco, Giorgio. De potestate praelatorvm im foro interno, relectio Georgii Polacchi. Venetiis, 1629. 94 p.

1339

Popek, Alphonse S. The rights and obligations of metropolitans; a historical synopsis and commentary. Washington, D.C., The Catholic University of America Press, 1947 [i.e., 1948] 460 p. (The Catholic University of America. Canon law studies, no. 260)
Bibliography: p. 425–434.

1340

Postconciliar thoughts; renewal and reform of canon law. Edited by Neophytos Edelby, Teodoro Jiménez Urresti [and] Petrus Huizing. New York, Paulist Press [1967] 183 p. (Concilium: theology in the age of renewal, v. 28)
Includes bibliographical references.

1341

Pöschl, Arnold. Bischofsgut und mensa episcopalis, ein beitrag zur geschichte des kirchlichen vermögensrechtes. Bonn, Hanstein, 1908. v.

1342

Postious, Luigi. De svbhastatione tractatus non superfluus, sed necessarius, & ad praxim aptatus, & ordinatus. Iunctis ad materiam Decisionibus Rotae romanae vltra centum alibi non impressis. Maceratae, ex officina Carboniana, 1644. 308, [4], 163, 32 p.

1343

Prince, John E. The Diocesan Chancellor, an historical synopsis and commentary. Washington, D.C., The Catholic University of America Press, 1942. 136 p.

1344

Pugliese, Agostino. I poteri dei superiori generali degli instituti laicali di diritto pontificio. Presentazione di S. E. mons. Edoardo Heston. Milano, Àncora; Roma, Centro studi U. S. M. I., [1969] 109 p. (Collana "Studi e sussidi")

Includes bibliographical references.

1345

Pujol, Clemente. De religiosis orientalibus ad normam vigentis iuris. Roma, Pont. Institutum Orientalium Studiorum, 1957. 590 p.

Bibliography: p. [xv]–xvii.

1346

Quinn, John S. The extraordinary minister of confirmation according to the most recent decrees of the sacred congregations. Romae, Officium Libri Catholici, Catholic Book Agency, 1951. 137 p.

Bibliography: p. 131–136.

1347

Quinn, Joseph J. Documents required for the reception of orders; a historical synopsis and commentary. Washington, D.C., The Catholic University of America Press, 1948 [i.e., 1949] 207 p. (The Catholic University of America. Canon law studies, no. 266)

Bibliography: p. 181–187.

1348

Quinn, Stephen. Relation of the local ordinary to religious of diocesan approval; a historical synopsis and a commentary. Washington, D.C., The Catholic University of America Press, 1949. 153 p. (The Catholic University of America. Canon law studies, no. 283)

Bibliography: p. 129–133.

1349

Rainer, Eligius G. Suspension of clerics, an historical synopsis and commentary. Washington, D.C., The Catholic University of America, 1937. 249 p. (The Catholic University of America. Canon law studies, no. 111)

Bibliography: p. [xiii]–xvii.

1350

Rebuffi, Pierre. Praxis beneficiorvm, cvi apposvimvs bvllam coenae domini, bvllam item lejuniorum ac supplicationum, Pavli III. additiones praeterae ad regulas cancellariae, cura Audomari Rebuffi, diligentissime excultas; necnon practicam Cancellariae apostolicae Hieronymi Pauli Barchim, adjecimus concordatorvm tractatvm inter, papam Leonem X. ac Sedem Apostolicam, & Franciscvm, francorum regem ac regnum, editum cum glossis eiusdem Petri Rebuffi. Item svper coneordatis inter Sanctam sedem apostolicam et inclitam nationem Germaniae collectanea per Georgivm Branden Adjunctis nunnulas aliis ad executionem literarum apostolicarum pertinentibus. Coloniae, sumptibus Lazari Zetzneri, 1610. 750 p.

1351

Regatillo, Eduardo Fernández. De statibus particularibus tractatus. Santander, Editorial Sal Terrae, 1954. 267 p.

Includes bibliographies.

1352

Regatillo, Eduardo Fernández. Derecho parroquial. 3. ed. Santander, Editorial Sal Terrae, 1959. 640 p. (Biblioteca Comillensis)

Bibliography: p. [7]

1353

Regolamento generale della Curia Romana. [Città del Vaticano] Tip. poliglotta vaticana, 1968. 46 p.

1354

Regulae seu constitutiones communes congregationis missionis. Lisbonae, 1743. 2 v. in 1.

1355

Reig y Casanova, Enrique. Cuestiones canónicas (Colección de artículos) El derecho canónico en España y su influencia. Las Falsas decretales y su influencia en la doctrina de la iglesia. El derecho canónico no escrito. El clérigo en los tribunales civiles. El estado religioso y la patria potestad. Cementerios y sepultura eclesiástica. Toledo, Rodríguez [1907] 323, [4] p.

1356

Reilly, Peter. Residence of pastors; an historical synopsis and commentary. Washington, D.C., The Catholic University of America, 1935. 81 p. (The Catholic University of America. Canon law studies, no. 97)

Bibliography: p. 69–70.

1357

Reilly, Thomas F. The visitation of religious. Washington, D.C., The Catholic University of America, 1938. 195 p. (The Catholic University of America. Canon law studies, no. 112)
Bibliography: p. 179–183.

1358

Reina, Víctor de. El sistema beneficial. Pamplona, Universidad de Navarra, 1965. 397 p. (Colección canónica de la Universidad de Navarra)
Bibliography: p. 387–397.

1359

Reinmann, Gerald J. The third order secular of St. Francis. Washington, D.C., The Catholic University of America Press, 1928. 200 p. (The Catholic University of America. Studies in canon law, no. 50)
Bibliography: p. 189–195.

1360

Reiss, John C. The time and place of sacred ordination; a historical synopsis and a commentary. Washington, D.C., The Catholic University of America Press, 1953. 124 p. (Catholic University of America. Canon law studies, no. 343)
Bibliography: p. 108–112.

1361

Riedl, Richard. Der Sachbegriff des Codex iuris canonici. 1950. 75 l.

1362

Robleda, Olis. Quaestiones disputatae iuridico-canonicae. Romae, Libreria editrice Università gregoriana, 1969. 172 p.
Includes bibliographical references.

1363

Rodrigues, Manuel. Nova collectio et compilatio privilegiorvm apostolicorvm regvlarivm mendicantivm, et non mendicantivm: praesertim in qvibvs ipsae religiones commvnicant, edita a Emmanvele Roderico. Editio vltima. Antverpiae, apud Petrum & Belleros, 1623. 546 p.

1364

Rodrigues, Manuel. Qvaestiones regvlares, et canonicae, in quibus vtriusque iuris, et priuilegiorum, et apostolicarum constitutionum, nouae, et veteres difficultates dispersae, et confusae. Tomvs primvs [-qvartvs]. Editio vltima. Antverpriae, apud Petrum & Belleros, 1628. 4 v. in 1.
v. 4 has title: Praxis criminalis regvlarivm.

1365

Rodriguez Fermosino, Nicolás, Bp. Tractatvs dvo de ivdiciis, et foro competenti. Ad lib. II. decretalium Gregorii pontificis IX. Sub quibus agitur de iudiciis, ac iudicum competentia, & de personis spectantibus ad iudicia tam ecclesiastica quam saecularia, & aliis practicabilibus dubiis. Opus multiplici exornatum, cui etiam post generalem rerum & verborum, adiecta est. Nvnc primvm prodit. Lvgdvni, sumptibus Ph. Borde, Lavr. Arnavd, & C. Rigavd, 1657. 2 v. in 1.

1366

Rodriguez Fermosino, Nicolás, Bp. Tractatvs secvndvs de officiis et sacris ecclesiae. Ad titvlvm XXII, libri I. decretalivm Gregorii pontificis IX. A titulo de postulatione praelat. ad titulum de officio vicarij. Cum indice multiplici titulorum, capitum, quaestionum, canonum, legum, iurium, locorum, rerum & verborum in hoc tractatu contentorum. Editio primi in dvos tomos distribvta. Lvgdvni, sumptibus H. Boissat & G. Remevs, 1662. 2 v. in 1.

1367

Romita, Fiorenzo. Le chiese ricettizie nel diritto canonico e civile dalle origini ai giorni nostri. Roma, Monitore ecclesiastico [1947] 252 p.
Bibliography: p. [9]–14.

1368

Romo, Judas J. Discurso canónico acerca de la congrua del clero y de las fabricas. Madrid, Aguado, 1846. 277 p.

1369

Rosa, Thomas de, Bp. Tractatus de executoribus litterarum apostolicarum tam gratiae, quam justitiae. Cum additionibus ad quaelibet capita, secrsim alias impressis; necnon Tractetu de executoribus litterarum remissorialium in ordine ad processus pro sanctorum canonizatione, una cum Praxi, suis locis apprimè accomodatis. Cum nonnullis decisionibus Sacrae rotae romanae, & indice materiarum locupletissimo. Venetiis, apud Paulum Balleonium, 1697. 472 p.

1370

Rosignoli, Gregorio. Novissima praxis theologico-legalis in vniversas de cambiis et permvtationibvs qvaestiones. Mediolani, Apud Agnellum, 1680. 492 p.

1371

Rosignoli, Gregorio. Novissima praxis theologico-legalis in vniversas de societatibvs, simonia et de commodato et deposito controversias. Mediolani, Apud Maiettam, 1682. 518 p.

1372

Rosignoli, Gregorio. Teoremata theologicoivridica de restitvtione opus omnibus tum moralis, tum sacrae theologiae, & iuris prudentiae professoribus nedum vtile, sed pene necessarium. Cum duplici indice, altero titulorum, altero rerum locupletissimo. Mediolani, typis Malatestae, 1688. 527 p.

1373

Rosignoli, Gregorio. Novissima praxis theologico-legalis in universas, de contractibus controversias, Editio secunda. Mediolani, Ex Typographia Malatestae, 1719. 608 p.

1374

Ryan, Gerald A. Principles of episcopal jurisdiction. Washington, D.C., The Catholic University of America Press, 1939. 172 p. (The Catholic University of America. Canon law studies, no. 120)
Bibliography: p. [147]–150.

1375

Sadlowski, Erwin L. Sacred furnishings of churches. Washington, D.C., The Catholic University of America Press, 1951. 176 p. (The Catholic University of America. Canon law studies, v. 315)
Bibliography: p. 161–167.

1376

Sägmüller, Johannes B. Die Papstwahlen und die Staaten von 1447 bis 1555 (Nikolaus V. bis Paul IV) Eine kirchenrechtlich-historische Untersuchung über den Anfang des staatlichen Rechtes der Exklusive in der Papstwahl. Tübingen, Laupp, 1890. 238 p.

1377

Sánchez Aliseda, Casimiro. Memoriale sacerdotum; índice de los deberes sacerdotales sacado del Código de derecho canónico con comentarios pas-torales de los últimos paps. Toledo, Editorial Católica Toledana, 1955. 35 p.

1378

Santos Díez, José L. La encomienda de monasterios en la Corona de Castilla, siglos X–XV. Con un prólogo de Rafael Gibert. Roma, 1961. 238 p. (Cuadernos del Instituto Jurídico Español, no. 14)

1379

Sarpi, Paolo. Traité des benefices. Troisième edition, revüe, corrigée, et augmentée de notes. Amsterdam, Vvestein, 1699. 271 p.

1380

Saurmann, Johann F. Tractatus historico-juridica de jure circa sepulchra et hominum demortuorum cadavera. Bremae, Saurmann, 1737. 2 v. in 1.

1381

Sbrozzi, Giacomo. Tractatvs de vicario episcopi, officio eivs, et potestate constitvenda, exercenda, et finienda. Cvm svmmariis, ao indice. Venetiis, Apud I. Somaschum, 1592. 163 l.

1382

Scanaroli, Giovanni B., abp. De visitatione carceratorum libri tres. Summorum pontificum hac super re constitutiones, iura, Rotae romanae decisiones passim toto opere allegatae in calce, appendicis loco, subiungutur. Opus . . . cum indicibus. Romae, typis reverendae Camerae apostolicae, 1655. 588 p.

1383

Schaefer, Karl H. Pfarrkirche und Stift im deutschen Mittelalter; eine kirchenrechtsgeschichtliche Untersuchung. Stuttgart, Enke, 1903. Amsterdam, Schippers, 1962. 210 p. (Kirchenrechtliche Abhandlungen, 3 Heft)
Includes bibliography.

1384

Schelstrate, Emmanuel. Dissertatio de avctoritate patriarchali et metropolitica adversvs ea, qvae scripsit Edvardvs Stillingfleet, in libro de originibvs britannicis. Romae, typis, & sumptibus Dominici Antonij Herculis, 1687. 114 p.

1385

Schierse, Paul J. Laws of the State of Delaware affecting church property. Washington, D.C., The

Catholic University of America Press, 1963. 240 p. (The Catholic University of America. Canon law studies, no. 428)

Bibliography: p. 218–228.

1386

Schmid, Heinrich F. Die rechtlichen Grundlagen der Pfarrorganisation aug Westslavischam Boden und ihre Entwicklung während des Mittelalters. Weimar, Hermann Böhlhaus Nachrolger, 1938. 1292 p.

1387

Schneider, Edelhard L. The status of secularized exreligious clerics. Washington, D.C., The Catholic University of America Press, 1948 [i.e., 1949] 155 p. (The Catholic University of America. Canon law studies, no. 284)

Bibliography: p. 128–136.

1388

Schrod, Joseph L. De jure supremi in civitate imperantis circa sacra. Opus posthuma. Pragae, Glatz, 1782. 230 p.

1389

Schulte, Johann F., ritter von. Die macht der römischen päpste über fürsten, länder, völker und individuen, nach ihren lehren und handlungen seit Gregor VII. zur würdigung ihrer unfehlbarkeit beleuchtet von Friedrich v. Schulte. 3. umgearb. aufl. Giessen, Roth, 1896. 127 p.

1390

Schulz, Winfried. Zum Schutz des geistigen Eigentums im System des kanonischen Rechts: eine rechtsvergleichende Untersuchung z. Problemkreis d. Urheberrechts u. seiner Aufgabe u. Bedeutung im kanon. Recht. München, Vahlen, 1973. 227 p. (Internationale Gesellschaft für Urheberrecht. Schriftenreihe; Bd. 49)

Bibliography: p. [211]–222.

1391

Schuyler, David H. De sodalibus laicis in congregationibus clericalibus. Studium de iure religiosorum comparato. Roma, Pontificía università lateranense, 1969. 69 p.

Bibliography: p. vi–x.

1392

Scot, Giulio C. De obligatione regularis extra re-

gularem dumum commorantis ob lustrum metum, opuscula tria. Coloniae, Duglass, 1647. 256 p.

1393

Semana de Derecho Canónico. *7th, Granada, 1958.* La potestad de la Iglesia; análisis de su aspecto jurídico; trabajos de la VII Semana de Derecho Canónico. Barcelona, Flors, 1960. 526 p.

Bibliographical footnotes.

1394

Sentis, Franz J. Die iure testamentorum a clericis saecularibus ordinandorum. Dissertatio inauguralis. Bonnae, formis Georgi, [1862] 76 p.

1395

Setién, José M. Naturaleza jurídica del estado de perfección en los institutos seculares. Introd. por R. Bidagor. Romae, Apud Aedes Universitatis Gregorianae, 1957. 207 p. (Analecta Gregoriana, v. 86. Series Facultatis Iuris Canonici. Sectio B, no. 5)

Includes bibliography

1396

Sheehan, Joseph G. The obligation of respect and obedience of clerics toward their ordinary (canon 127); a historical synopsis and a canonical commentary. Washington, D.C., The Catholic University of America Press, 1954. 132 p. (Catholic University of America. Canon law studies, no. 344)

Bibliography: p. 123–127.

1397

Shuhler, Ralph V. Privileges of regulars to absolve and dispense; an historical conspectus and commentary. Washington, D.C., The Catholic University of America Press, 1943. 195 p. (The Catholic University of America. Canon law studies, no. 186)

Bibliography: p. 171–175.

1398

Siegle, Bernard A. Choral obligation of religious. Romae, Officium Libri Catholici, 1954. 82 p.

Bibliography: p. [79]–82.

1399

Siepen, Karl, Vermögensrecht der klösterlichen Verbände. Paderborn, Schöningh, 1963. 399 p.

Bibliography: p. [376]–384.

1400

Simon, Erwin. Die katholische Militärseelsorge

nach dem Codex iuris canonici und den dazu ergangenen Sonderbestimmungen unter besonderer Berücksichtigung der Militärseelsorge in der Bundeswehr. [Erlangen, 1962] 131 p.

Bibliography: p. viii–xiv.

1401

Spinelli, Lorenzo. La vacanza della Sede apostolica dalle origini al Concilio tridentino. Milano. Giuffrè, 1955. 254 p.

1402

Squillante, Paulo. Tractatvs de privilegiis clericorvm in qvo qvidqvid circa privilegia clericorvm in curijs vtriusque fori in dubium reuocari potest, distinctè, & quam breuissimè dilucidatur. Nuper in secunda hac editione à multis mendis, expurgatus, Indice duplici, altero priuilegiorum, & altero materiarum. Neapoli, per Vincentium de Francho; expensis Dominici Vecchi bibliop. sub signo sanctiss. nominis, 1635. 340, [36] p.

1403

Stadalnikas, Casimir J. Reservation of censures; a commentary with historical notes on the nature of the reservation of censures. Washington, D.C., The Catholic University of America Press, 1944. 141 p. (The Catholic University of America. Canon law studies, no. 208)

Bibliography: p. 121–127.

1404

Stafileo, Giovanni, bp. Secvnda edictio tractatvs De gratijs expectatiuis, ac alijs literis ad uacatura beneficia. De stiloq$_3$, ac usu signature r. p. d. Io. Staphielei episcopi siginiben, ac de brevibvs eivsdem, ac r. p. d. Lvdovici Gomesig, cum summarijs & additionibus, necnon cum quibusdam notabilibus de officio legati apostiloci, ex diuersis locis collectis, & sub certis capitibus dispostiis, ac in unum nouiter redactis. Venetiis, 1549. 171 1.

1405

Stenger, Joseph B. The mortgaging of church property; a historical synopsis and commentary,. Washington, D.C., The Catholic University of America Press, 1942. 186 p. (The Catholic University of America. Canon law studies, no. 169)

Bibliography: p. 162–170.

1406

Stiegler, Maria A. Dispensation, dispensations-

wesen und dispensationsrecht kirchenrecht, geschichtlich, dargestellt. Mainz, verlag von Franz Kirchheim, 1901. 375 p.

1407

Stingl, Richard A. Grundfragen der kirchlichen Ämterorganisation. München, Hueber, 1960. 188 p. (Münchener theologische Studien. 3. Kanonistische Abteilung, 13. Bd.)

Bibliography: p. xi–xxii.

1408

Stocchiero, Giuseppe. Il beneficio ecclesiastico. Vicenza, Editrice S. A. T., 1942–46. 2 v.

"Principali fonti giuridiche e dottrinali": v. 1, p. [ix]–xv.

1409

Sweeny, Francis P. The reduction of clerics to the lay state; an historical synopsis and commentary. Washington, D.C., The Catholic University of America Press, 1945. 199 p. (Catholic University of America. Canon law studies, no. 223)

Bibliography: p. 175–181.

1410

Tabera Araoz, Arturo, *and* Gregorio Martínez de Antoñana y Gerardo Escudero. Derecho de los religiosos; manual teórico práctica; prólogo del Rvmo. P. Arcadio Larraona. 3. ed. Madrid, Editorial Coculsa, 1957. 701 p.

Includes bibliography.

1411

Thomassin, Louis. Vetus et nova ecclesiae disciplina circa beneficis, et beneficiarios. Lucae, Venturini, 1728. 2 v.

1412

Thomassin, Louis. Vetus et nova ecclesiae disciplina circa beneficia, & beneficiarios, in tres partes distributa, variisque animaversionibus locupletata; authore, eodemque interprete Ludovico Thomassino. Accedit Tractatus beneficiarius fr. Caesarii Mariae Sguanin pro indemniter salvandis juribus sanctae matris ecclesiae quoad beneficia ecclesiastica. Editio postrema, cum parisiensi accuratissime collata. Venetiis, typis Petri Savioni, 1773. 3 v.

1413

Tobin, Thomas J. De officiali curiae dioecesane.

Romae, Apud aedes Pontificiae Universitatis Gregorianae, 1936. 252 p.

1414

Tonduti, Pietro F. Tractatvs de pensionibvs ecclesiasticis, ad stylvm cvriae romanae, et ad praxim tribunalium Galliae accommodatus. Adiicitur in fine operis selectarum atque recentissimarum Rota romanae decisionum centuria pro confirmatione eorum, quae ab authore resoluta sunt in materia pensionum & beneficiorum. Cum notis quibusdam ad praecedentia opera. Secvnda editio. Lugduni, Arnaud & Borde, 1671. 238 p.

1415

Torrente, Camilo. Las procesiones sagradas; síntesis histórica y comentario. Washington D.C., 1932. 149 p. (Universidad católica de América. Estudios canónicos, no. 75)
"Bibliografía": p. 135–137.

1416

Uccella, Fulvio. Le conferenze episcopali in diritto canonico. Napoli, Jovene, 1973. 240 p. (Pubblicazioni della Facoltà giuridica dell'Università di Napoli, 138)
Bibliography: p. [227]–233.

1417

Ugolinus, Bartholomaeus. Tractatvs de irregvlaritatibvs. Ad forum conscientiae, pontificium, ac ciuile perutilis. Nunc primum in lucem editus. Ad Clementem VIII. pont. max. Venetiis, apud haeredem Hieronymi Scoti, 1601. 254 p.

1418

Urrutia, José L. de. Régimen de las órdenes religiosas a mediados del S. XVI y aportación de san Ignacio. Madrid, 1962. 62 p.
Bibliography: p. [9]–13.

1419

Usodimare, Stefano. Privilegia per complvres svmmos pontifices ordini fratrum praedicatoru concessa, & communicata, non quidem omnia; sed ea tantu, quae ex archetypis, aut eorum authenticis trasumptis haberi potuerunt iussu, impensis, & opera reuerendiss. pris. f. Stephani Vsusmaris Genuen. eiusdem ordinis magistri generalis, transumpta, & impressa. [Romae, apud Antonium Bladum impressorem cameralem, 1556]

1420

Valenti, Ferdinando. Ferdinandi de Valentibus Trebiensis. Opera omnia selectiora. Romae, sumptibus Venantii Monaldini, ex typographia Johannis Baptistae Bernabò & Josephi Lazzarini, 1744–46. 3 v. in 4.

1421

Vecchis Romano, Petro Andrea de. Decisiones Diversorum Sacrae Rotae Romanae Auditorum Ad Materiam Boni Regiminis, Universitatum, & Communitatum, signanter Status Ecclesiastici, Spectantes Editae Sub Auspiciiis Sanctissimo Domini Nostri, Domini Clementis XII. P. M. Zelo & Cura. Cardinalis Josephi Renati Imperiales. Ac quadruplici Indice exornatae. Tomus Tertius. De Bono Remimi ne. Romae, Ex Typographia Hieronymi, Mainardi, 1732. 726 p.

1422

Viceconte, Giuseppe N. Parrocchia, Chiesa e fabbriceria nel diritto canonico. Milano, Giuffrè, 1963. 82 p.
Bibliographical footnotes.

1423

Victor a Iesu Maria, Fr. De iurisdictionis acceptione in iure ecclesiastico praemittitur eiusdem notio in iure romano. Romae, Collegium internazionale, ss. teresive a Iesu et Ioannis a cruce, 1940. 244 p.

1424

Vincioli, Giovanni C. De illegitimis clericorvm ac regvlarivm ad intellectum bullae Pij V. contra eosdem illegitimos editae tractatus avthore Io. Nicolao Lvcidoro [pseud.] Pervsiae Avgvstae, apud haeredes Angeli Bartoli, & Angelum Laurentium, 1648. 264, [29] p.

1425

Vinuesa, Joseph de. Diesmos de legos en las iglesias de España: Discursos histórico-jurídicos. Madrid, en la oficina de don Benito Cano, 1791. 262 p.

1426

Vogelpohl, Henry J. The simple impediments to holy orders, an historical synopsis and commentary. Washington, D.C., The Catholic University of America Press, 1945. 190 p. (The Catholic University of America. Canon law studies, no. 224)
Bibliography: p. 168–173.

1427

Waddilove, Alfred. Church patronage historically, legally, and morally considered. In connection with the offense of simony. London, Longman, Brown, Green, and Longmans, 1854. 185 p.

1428

Wagner, Peter. Die geschichtliche entwicklung der metropolitangewalt bis zum zeitalter der dekretalgesetzgebung. Offenbach a. M., Buchdr. Scherz, 1917. 123 p.

"Literatur": p. [121]–123.

1429

Walsh, Donnell A. The new law on secular institutes; a historical synopsis and a commentary. Washington, D. C., Catholic University of America Press, 1953. 145 p. (Catholic University of America. Canon law studies, no. 347)

Bibliography: p. 129–139.

1430

Walsh, Maurice B. Mission faculties; a commentary on the decennial faculties granted by the Sacred Congregation of Propaganda Fide, 1961–1970. Washington, D.C., Mission Secretariat [c1960] 32 p.

1431

Waterhouse, John M. The power of the local ordinary to impose a matrimonial ban; a historical synopsis and a commentary. Washington, D.C., Catholic University of America Press, 1952. 134 p. (p. 134 advertisement) (The Catholic University of America. Canon law studies, no. 317)

Bibliography: p. 122–128.

1432

Waters, Joseph L. The probation in societies of quasi-religious; a historical synopsis and a commentary. Washington, D.C., The Catholic University of America Press, 1951. 135 p. (The Catholic University of America. Canon law studies, v. 306)

Bibliography: p. 111–116.

1433

Welsh, Thomas J. The use of the portable altar; a historical synopsis and a commentary. Washington, D.C., The Catholic University of America Press, 1950 [i.e., 1951] 141 p. (The Catholic University of America. Canon law studies, v. 305.)

Bibliography: p. 118–122.

1434

Wiest, Donald H. The precensorship of books (canons 1384–1386, 1392–1394, 2318, par. 2) a history and commentary. Washington, D.C., The Catholic University of America Press, 1953. 194 p. (Catholic University of America. Canon law studies, no. 329)

Bibliography: p. 172–183.

1435

Winslow, Francis J. Vicars and prefects apostolic. [Maryknoll, N.Y., Catholic Foreign Mission Society of America, Inc.] 1924. 148 p.

Bibliography: p. 139–141.

1436

Woltersdorf, Th. Die rechtsverhältnisse der Greifswalder pfarrkirchen im mittelalter, nach den quellen untersucht. Greifswald, 1888. 79 p.

1437

Zaecherl, Anselmus. Figmentum jurium status politici in res ac personas status ecclesiastici. Amstelodami, 1764. 116 p.

1438

Zaplotnik, John L. De vicariis foraneis. Washingtonii, D.C., Catholica universitas Americae, 1927. 142 p. (The Catholic University of America. Canon law studies, no. 47)

"Bibliographia": p. v–ix.

1439

Zech, Franz Xaver. Rigor moderatus doctrinae pontificiae circa usuras. ASS. D. N. Fenedicto XIV. Per epistolam encyclicam episcopis Italiae traditus. Dissertatio III, Ingolstadii, etc., sumptibus Joannis Francisci Xaverii Graz, 1751. 260 p.

1440

Zenk, Richard E. The office of the deacon in ecclesiastical law. Excerpta ex dissertatione ad lauream in Facultate iuris canonici Pontificiae universitatis Gregorianae. Roma, 1969 [i.e., 1970] 67 p.

Bibliography: p. [63]–67.

1441

Ziegler, Kaspar. De dote ecclesiae eivsqve ivribvs et privilegiis, tractatvs canovicvs. Vitembergae, Apvd Lvdovicvm, 1717. 284 p.

1442

Żuk, Petrus. De iure proprietatis privatae. Romae, 1971. 140 p.

Bibliography: p. [5]–13.

LAITY

1443

Adversi, Aldo. Il laicato cattolico: lineamenti storico-canonistici. Roma, Editrice Studium [1961] 118 p. (Cultura, 26)

Bibliography: p. [103]–110.

1444

Bahima, Matilde. La condición jurídica del laico en la doctrina canónica del siglo XIX. [Pamplona] EUNSA [1972] 215 p. (Colección canónica de la Universidad de Navarra. Cuadernos, 15)

Includes bibliographical references.

The main concern of the author is to answer this question: Why do modern canonists who deal with the reality of the layman neglect to provide references concerning the doctrine of the previous centuries? At the outset it seems of little use to deal with such doctrine; it appears that the almost complete silence of the Code of Canon Law on the legal condition of the layman, in the canons explicitly devoted to him, is a reflection and consequence of the doctrine which was in effect immediately preceding the code. Unfortunately, the code does not reflect the reality of time; for in the nineteenth century and the years immediately before 1917, the date of the code's promulgation, the layman enjoyed a much broader and more positive legal position in the Church than that actually expressed in the code. The author aims to discover the cause of the imbalance between the ideas of the doctrine and the formulations of the code.

1445

Benucci, Giuseppi M. Gli istituti secolari nella nuova legislazione canonica. Con lettera dell'Ecc.mo. P. Arcadio Larraona. Roma, Tip. Regionale, 1955. 66 p.

Includes bibliography.

1446

Canals Navarrete, Salvador. Institutos seculares y estado de perfección. Madrid, Ediciones Rialp, 1954. 200 p. (Patmos; libros de espiritualidad, 34)

"Apendices: Constitución apostólica 'Provida Mater Ecclesia,' Motu proprio 'Primo feliciter,' Instrucción 'Cum sanctissimus' ": p. [151]–195.

1447

Caron, Pier G. I poteri giuridici del laicato nella Chiesa primitiva. Milano. Giuffrè, 1948. 228 p.

Bibliographical footnotes.

1448

Chelodi, Giovanni. Ius canonicum de personis, praemissis notionibus de iure publico ecclesiastico de principiis et fontibus iuris canonici. Vicenza, Società anonima tipografica, 1942. 501 p.

1449

Gómez Carrasco, Mercedes. La condición jurídica del laico en el Concilio Vaticano II. [Pamplona] EUNSA [1972] 307 p. (Colección canónica de la Universidad de Navarra. Cuadernos, 16)

Includes bibliographical references.

The doctrine of the Second Vatican Council, which gave greater impulse to the movement of renewal in the life of the laity, has been the subject of much theological research; but there has been little focus on the notion of duties and rights of laymen as presented in the documents of the council, namely in the constitution *Lumen gentium* and the decree *Apostolicam actuositatem*. The author exposes the legal elements which are present in the studied documents, concerning the new understanding of the constitution of the Church as People of God; the typological description of laymen; and the rights and obligations peculiar to them. The work also offers a vision of the present status of canonical doctrine on the subject, pursuant to the new ecclesiastical stance assumed by the council.

1450

Gómez de Ayala, Alfredo. Gli infedeli e la personalità nell'ordinamento canonico. Milano, Giuffrè, 1971. 1 v. (Collana degli Annali della Facoltà di giurisprudenza dell'Università di Genova, 24)

1451

González del Valle Cienfuegos, José M. Derechos fundamentales y derechos públicos subjetivos en la Iglesia. [Pamplona] Eunsa, 1971. 305 p.

Bibliography: p. [279]–305.

The author determines as clearly as possible the concepts of "fundamental right" and "subjective public right" by establishing a proper distinction between them and other related concepts, and stresses the importance of incorporating these concepts into the canonical system. Only after the Second Vatican Council did the expression "fundamental rights of the faithful" appear, and only after the promulgation of the constitution *Regimini ecclesiae universae,* which introduces in the Church the appeal to the courts against acts of Church government, did "subjective public rights" come into force. These changes reflect a new ecclesiological perspective and are not just changes in terminology or concepts. The work is divided into four parts: canonical doctrine on the subject, secular doctrine, fundamental rights pursuant to the secular doctrine, and conclusions.

1452

Heftrich, Walter. Die Stellung der Instituta saecularia im System des katholischen Kirchenrechts. [n. p.] 1959. 77 p.
Bibliography: p. 73–176.

1453

Keller, Heinrich, and Oswald von Nell-Breuning. Das Recht der Laien in der Kirche. Heidelberg, Kerle, 1950. 92 p.

1454

Kinney, John F. The juridic condition of the people of God. Their fundamental rights and obligations in the Church. Roma, Officium libri catholici, 1972. 99 p.
Bibliography: p. [87]–96.

1455

Ledesma, Ana. La condición jurídica del laico: Del C. I. C. al Vaticano II. [Pamplona] EUNSA [1972?] 184 p. (Colección canónica de la Universidad de Navarra. Cuadernos, 14)
Includes bibliographical references.

1456

Pistocchi, Mario. Il codice dei laici; il Concordato lateranense. Milano, Hoepli, 1930. 144 p. (Manuali Hoepli)

1457

Portillo y Diéz de Sollano, Alvaro del. Faithful and laity in the Church; the bases of their legal status. Shannon, Ireland, Ecclesia Press [1972] 200 p.
Includes bibliographical references.

1458

Ricciullo, Antonio. Tractatvs de ivre personarvm extra ecclesiae gremivm. Libris nouem distinctus, cvi propter argvmenti similitvdinem annexus est alter tratatus de neophitis, opvs plane speciosvmfacili, elegantiq. methodo dispositum, vsuiq. inprimis forensi accomodatum. Cvm triplici indice. Prodit nunc primum. Romae, sumptibus Io. Angeli Riffinelli & Angeli Manni, 1623. 630, [52] p.

1459

Sabater March, Joaquín. Derechos y deberes de los segulares en la vida social de la Iglesia. Barcelona, Herder, 1954. 1002 p.
Includes bibliographies.

1460

Zapico, Marcelino. Estado laico o estado confesional. [Madrid, Ediciones Euramérica, 1968] 239 p. (Centro de Estudios Universitarios. Hombres Nuevos)
"Apéndice" (p. 213–233): Declaración sobre la libertad religiosa. Ley reguladora del ejercicio del derecho civil a la libertad en materia religiosa. Bibliography: p. 235–239.

WOMEN

1461

Fanfani, Lodovico, and Kevin D. O'Rourke. Canon law for religious women. Dubuque, Iowa, Priory Press [1961] 393 p.

1462

Giner Sempere, Santiago. La mujer y la potestad de jurisdicción eclesiástica. Alcoy [España, Instituto Alcoyano de Cultura "Andrés Sempere"] 1959–61. 2 v. (Ediciones del Instituto Alcoyano de Cultura "Andrés Sempere," 6, 10)
"Fuentes y bibliografía": p. [13]–21, v. 1.

1463

Melchior, Albert W. Sicilimentorum variorum. Libri duo. In quibus de rebus variis, inprimis miliere sota ac goele Sanguinis. Harlingae, Jongma, 1740. 662 p. 2 v. in 1.

1464

Morrison, David J. The juridic status of women in canonical law and in the United States law: a

comparative socio-juridical study. Romae, Pontificia Universitas Lateranensis, 1965. 98 p.
　　Bibliography: p. [ix]–xviii.

1465
Otto, Nicolás S.de. La mujer según el derecho y la doctrina de la iglesia. Zaragoza, Tip. "La Académica," 1943. 37 p.

1466
Raming, Ida. Der Ausschluss der Frau vom priesterlichen Amt; gottgewollte. Tradition oder Diskriminierung? Eine rechtshistorisch-dogmastische

Untersuchung der Grundlagen von Kanon 968 § 1 des Codex Iuris Canonici. Köln, Böhlau, 1973. 232 p.
　　Bibliography: p. [xi]–xvii.

1467
Raming, Ida. The exclusion of women from the priesthood: divine law or sex discrimination? An historical investigation of the juridical and doctrinal foundations of the code of canon law, canon 968, 1. Translated by Norman R. Adams; with a pref. by Arlene & Leonard Swidler. Metuchen, N.J., Scarecrow Press, 1976. 263 p.

THINGS

SACRAMENTS (EXCEPT MARRIAGE)

1468
Allgeier, Joseph L. The canonical obligation of preaching in parish churches; a historical synopsis and a commentary. Washington, D.C., Catholic University of America Press, 1949 [c1959] 115 p. (The Catholic University of America. Canon law studies, no. 291)
　　Bibliography: p. 91–97.

1469
Amort, Eusebius. De origine, progressu, valore, ac fructu indulgentiarum, nec non de dispositionibus ad eas lucrandas requisitis, accurata notitia historica dogmatica, polemica, critica. Accedunt quaestiones practicae, & responsa Sacrae congregationis indulgentiarum recentissima. Venetiis, Recursi, 1738. 508 p.

1470
Anglin, Thomas F. The eucharistic fast; an historical synopsis and commentary. Washington, D.C., The Catholic University of America Press, 1941. 183 p. (The Catholic University of America. Canon law studies, no. 124)
　　Bibliography: p. 167–173.

1471
Angulo Martínez, Luis. Legislación de la iglesia sobre la intención en la aplicación de la santa misa. Breve sinopsis histórica y comentario canónico. Washington, D.C., The Catholic University of

America Press, 1931. 103, [1] p. (The Catholic University of America. Canon law studies, no. 62)
　　"Bibliografía": p. 92–96.

1472
Bassett, William W. The determination of rite. Roma, Gregorian University Press, 1967. 281 p. (Analecta Gregoriana, v. 157. Series Facultatis Iuris Canonici, sectio B, n. 21)
　　Bibliography: p. 259–274.

1473
Bennington, James C. The recipient of confirmation; a historical synpsis and a commentary. Washington, D.C., The Catholic University of America Press, 1952. 153 p. (p. 141–153 advertisements) (The Catholic University of America. Canon law studies, v. 267)
　　Bibliography: p. 129–135.

1474
Bieler, Ludwig. The Irish penitentials. With an appendix by D. A. Binchy. Dublin, Dublin Institute for Advanced Studies, 1963. 367 p. (Scriptores Latini Hiberniae, v. 5)

1475
Bliley, Nicholas M. Altars according to the Code of Canon Law. Washington, D.C., The Catholic University of America Press, 1927. 132 p. (The Catholic University of America. Canon law studies, no. 38)

1476

Bohm, Walter. Acatholicus; eine untersuchung über die stellung der ungetauften und der apostaten, häretiker und schismatiker sowie der sonstigen exkommunizierten christen im geltenden kanonischen recht. Hamburg, Friederichsen, de Gruyter, 1933. 59 p. (Hamburger rechtsstudien, hrsg. von mitgliedern der Rechts und staatswissenschaftlichen fakultät der Hamburgischen universität, hft. 18)

"Quellen- und literaturverzeichnis": p. 58–59.

1477

Borowski, Antoni. Sakramentologja w świetle nowego prawa kóscielnego. Nowe wyd. uzup. Włocławek, Nakł. Księgarni Powszechnej, 1920. 144, 2 p.

1478

Bvlla lecta in Cena Domini continens mvltorvm excomvnicationes, svspensiones &c̄. per S. D. N. Ivlivm. II. Pont. Max. edita. Et in calce eivsdem bvlle execvtio. [Bononie, 1511] [12] p.

[Pope, 1503–1513 (Julius II) Consueverunt Romani Pontifices (16 April 1511)]

1479

Bvlla in Cena Domini. M.D.XX. [Rome, 1520] [8] p.

[Pope, 1513–1521 (Leo X) Consueverunt Romani Pontifices (5 April 1520)]

1480

Cabassut, Jean. Ivris canonici theoria et praxis, ad forvm tam sacramentale quam contentiosum, tum ecclesiasticum, tum seculare. Opvs exactvm non solvm ad normam iuris communis & romani, sed etiam iuris francici. Nvnc primvm in lvcem prodit. Lvgdvni, Arnaud & Borde, 1675. 704, [66] p.

1481

Campbell, Joseph E. Indulgences, the ordinary power of prelates inferior to the Pope to grant indulgences; an historical synopsis and a canonical commentary. Ottawa, University of Ottawa Press, 1953. 199 p. (Universitas Catholica Ottaviensis. Dissertationes ad gradum laurae in facultatibus ecclesiasticis consequendum conscriptae. Series canónica, t. 19)

1482

Cappello, Felice M. De sacramentis in genere, de baptismo, confirmatione et eucharistia. Ed. 7. accurate emendata et aucta. [Torino] Marietti, [1962] 726 p. (His Tractatus canonico-moralis de sacramentis: v. 1)

Includes bibliographical references and index.

1483

Cappello, Felice M. Tractatus canonico-moralis de sacramentis. Ed. 7. accurate emendata et aucta. [Torino] Marietti, [1962–   ] 2 v.

Includes bibliographical references and indexes.

The sacraments can be considered from many points of view—dogmatic theology, moral theology, canon law, and liturgy—but the author studies them from the perspective of moral theology and canon law. Volume one analyzes the sacraments in general, the sacramentals, and in particular, baptism, confirmation, and the eucharist. Volume two contains an extensive study on penance. Both volumes offer appendices on the law and discipline of the Oriental Church.

1484

Cavanaugh, William T. The reservation of the blessed sacrament. Washington, D.C., The Catholic University of America, 1927. 101 p. (The Catholic University of America. Canon law studies, no. 40)

"Sources": p. 93. Bibliography: p. 94–95.

1485

Clinton, Connell. The paschal precept; an historical synopsis and commentary. Washington, D.C., The Catholic University of America Press, 1932. 108 p. (The Catholic University of America. Canon law studies, no. 73)

Bibliography: p. 92–96.

1486

Coleman, John J. The minister of confirmation; an historical synopsis and commentary. Washington, D.C., The Catholic University of America Press, 1941. 153 p. (The Catholic University of America. Canon law studies, no. 125)

Bibliography: p. [137]–143.

1487

Conway, Walter J. The time and place of baptism; a historical synposis and a commentary. Washing-

ton, D.C., The Catholic University of America Press, 1954. 155 p. (The Catholic University of America. Canon law studies, no. 324)
Bibliography: p. 146–152.

1488
Crotty, Matthew M. The recipient of first Holy Communion; a historical synposis and commentary. Washington, D.C., The Catholic University of America Press, 1947 [i.e., 1948] 142 p. (The Catholic University of America. Canon law studies, no. 247)
"The decree Quam singulari, issued by the Sacred Congregation of the Sacraments of August 8, 1910 . . . [is] the core about which the dissertation is built."
Bibliography: p. 117–122.

1489
Edelby, Neophytos, Teodoro Jimenez-Urresti, and Petrus Huizing. Canon Law; the sacraments in theology and Canon Law. New York, Paulist Press [c1968] 183 p. (Concilium theology in the age of renewal, v. 38)

1490
Fanfani, Lodovico G. De indulgentiis; manuale theorico-practicum ad normam Codicis iuris canonici. Editio altera, notabiliter aucta. Taurini-Romae, ex officina libraria Marietti, 1926. 150 p.

1491
Fazzalaro, Francis J. The place for the hearing of confessions; a historical synopsis and a commentary. Washington, D.C., The Catholic University of America Press, 1950. 150 p. (The Catholic University of America. Canon law studies, no. 301)
Bibliography: p. 124–130.

1492
Ferry, William A. Stole fees. Washington, D.C., The Catholic University of America Press, 1930. (The Catholic University of America. Canon law studies, no. 59)

1493
Fuchs, Vinzenz. Der Ordinationstitel von seiner Entstehung bis auf Innozenz III; eine Untersuchung zur kirchlichen Rechtsgeschichte mit besonderer Berücksichtigung der Anschauungen Ru-

dolph Sohms. Amsterdam, Schippers, 1963. 291 p. (Kanonistische Studien und Texte, Bd. 4)
Bibliography: p. [viii]–xxiv.

1494
Gallagher, Joseph M. The celebration of Mass outside churches and oratories. Saint John [N. B.] 1949. 158 p. (Canonical theses of Laval, thesis no. 10)
Bibliography: p. [xvi]–xxii.

1495
Gasparri, Pietro, cardinal. Tractatus canonicus de sacra ordinatione. Paris, Lyon, Delhomme et Briguet, 1893. 2 v.

1496
Godley, James. Time and place for the celebration of Mass; historical synopsis and commentary. Washington, D.C., The Catholic University of America, 1948. 205 p. (The Catholic University of America. Canon law studies, no. 275)
Bibliography: p. 179–186.

1497
Goodwine, Joseph G. The reception of converts. Commentary with historical notes. Washington, D.C., The Catholic University of America Press, 1944. 326 p. (The Catholic University of America. Canon law studies, no. 198)

1498
Guiniven, John J. The precept of hearing Mass; a historical conspectus and commentary. Washington, D.C., The Catholic University of America Press, 1942. 188 p. (The Catholic University of America. Canon law studies, no. 158)
Bibliography: p. 165–171.

1499
Heinemann, Heribert. Die rechtliche Stellung der nichtkatholischen Christen und ihre Wiederversöhnung mit der Kirche. München, Hueber, 1964. 222 p. (Münchener theologische Studien. 3. Kanonistische Abteilung, 20. Bd)
Bibliography: p. xiii–xx.

1500
Heiner, Franz X. Die kirchlichen Censuren; oder, Praktische Erklärung aller noch zu Recht beste-

henden Exkommunicationen, Suspensionen und Interdikte l. s. der Bulle "Apostolicae Sedis", des Konzils von Trient und der Konstitution "Romanus Pontifex". Paderborn, Druck und Verlag der Bonifacius-Druckerei, 1884. 437 p.

1501
Henry, Joseph A. The mass and holy communion: interritual law; commentary with historical notes. Washington, D.C., The Catholic University of America Press, 1946. 138 p. (The Catholic University of America. Canon law studies, no. 235)
Bibliography: p. 107–111.

This is a very interesting work on canons related to the sacrament of the Holy Eucharist affecting the Oriental as well as Latin Churches. It deals with interritual laws, i.e., laws affecting a priest of one Rite wishing "to celebrate Mass in another Rite, or to distribute communion consecrated in another Rite, or to perform these functions in a Church of a different Rite;" and laws affecting "the faithful who desire to receive Holy Communion in a Rite different from their own." The author presents a historical look at the celebration and distribution of the Eucharist from the Last Supper to the promulgation of the code in 1917 and comments on the interritual laws contained in the code, and the decrees of the popes, the Roman congregations, and the synods.

1502
Hermés (l'Abbé). Entretien d'un paroissien avec son curé, sur le serment exigé des ecclésiastiques fonctionnaires publics. Paris, Grapart, 1791. 73 p.

1503
Holböck, Carl. Die Bination; rectsgeschichtliche Untersuchung. Romae, Officium Libri Catholici, 1941. 132 p.
Bibliography: p. [vii]–xi.

1504
Hyland, Francis E. Excommunication, its nature, historical development and effects. Washington, D.C., The Catholic University of America Press, 1928. 181 p. (Catholic University of America. Canon law studies, no. 49)
Bibliography: p. 168–175.

1505
Indelicato, Salvatore. Le basi giuridiche del pro-

cesso di beatificazione; dottrina e giurisprudenza intorno all'introduzione delle cause dei servi di Dio. Romae, Officium Libri Catholici, 1944. 122 p.
"Bibliografia": p. [11]–12.

1506
Indelicato, Salvatore. Il processo apostolico di beatificazione. Roma, Scientia Catholica, 1945. 396 p.
"Note bibliografiche": p. [7]–[8]

1507
Jacobi, Erwin. Einfluss der exkommunikation und der delicta mere ecclesiastica auf die fähigkeit zum erwerb und zur ausübung des patronatrechts. Leipzig, Veit & Co., 1908. 76 p.
"Literaturverzeichnis": p. [vi]–viii.

1508
Johannes von Freiburg. Summa confessorum reuerendi patris Joannis de Friburgo sacre theologie lectoris; ordinis predicatorum; non modo vtilis; sed Christi omnium pastoribus perõ necessaria; summo studio ex Raymundo; Guilhelmo; Innocentio; Hostiensi; Goffredo. alijsq viris perdoctis; in vinea dñi laborarũ cõuexa; antea prelũ nõ passa; luculento atq euoluto adhibito repertorio; ab innumeris insuper mendis per egregiu iuris vtriusq liceniatum dñm Henricum Uortomã de Norémberga emaculata; marginarijsq doctorum notis insignita. Adhibitus est preterea epilogus totius ferme iuris canonici puncta complectens. Lugduni, Saccon & Koberger, 1518. 254 l.

1509
Kappel, Kurt. Communicatio in sacris; die gottesdienstliche Gemeinschaft zwichen Katholiken und Nichtkatholiken (nach dem Codex iuris canonici) Winterthur, Keller, 1962. 87 p.
Bibliography: p. ix–xi.

1510
Lafontaine, Paul H. L'évêque d'ordination des religieux des débuts du monachisme à la mort de Louis le Pieux (840) Étude historico-juridique. Ottawa, Ontario, Éditions de l'Université d'Ottawa, 1951. 267 p. (Universitas Catholica Ottaviensis. Dissertationes ad gradum laureae in facultatibus ecclesiasticis consequendum conscriptae. Series canonica, t. 22)
"Bibliographie": p. [243]–253.

1511

Linahen, Leo J. De absolutione complicis in peccato turpi. Washingtonii, D.C., Universitas Catholica Americae, 1942. 114 p. (The Catholic University of America. Canon law studies, no. 164)
"Index bibliographicus": p. [99]–102.

1512

Lowry, James M. Dispensation from private vows; a historical synopsis and a commentary. Washington, D.C., The Catholic University of America Press, 1946 [i.e., 1947] 266 p. (The Catholic University of America. Canon law studies, no. 237)
Bibliography: p. 239–244.

1513

Łuczak, Józef. Ofiary mszalne w ustawodawstwie kanonicznym do soboru trydenckiego. Warszawa [Nakł. Polskiego Tow. Teologicznego] 1939. 165 p. (Warszawskie studia teologiczne, 19)
Bibliography: p. [xi]–xxi.

1514

Masi, Giovanni Domenico, abp. Tractatus de casibus, et excommunicationibus episcopis reservatis, confectus ad normam tabellae lucanae. Lucae, Cappuri, 1724. 397 p.

1515

Matulenas, Raymond A. Communication. A source of privileges. An historical synopsis and commentary. Washington, D.C., The Catholic University of America Press, 1943. 225 p. (The Catholic University of America. Canon law studies, no. 183)

1516

Medici, Zenobio. Trattato vtilissimo on conforto de condennati a morte per via di givstitia. Roma, Dorico, 1565. 91 p.

1517

Miller, Newton T. Founded masses according to the Code of canon law. Washinton, D.C., 1926. 92 p. (The Catholic University of America. Canon law studies, no. 34)
"Bibliography": p. 84–85.

1518

Moriarty, Francis E. The extraordinary absolution from censures; an historical synopsis and commentary. Washington, D.C., The Catholic University of America, 1938. 334 p. (The Catholic University of America. Canon law studies, no. 113)
Bibliography: p. 305–313.

1519

Parra Herrera, Antonio. Legislación eclesiástica sobre el ayuno y la abstinencia; síntesis histórica y comentario. Washington, D.C., The Catholic University of America, 1935. 199 p. (Universidad católica de América. Estudios canónicos, no. 92)
"Bibliografia"; p. [177]–185.

1520

Raymundus de Pennaforte, Saint. Summa Sti. Raymundi de Peniafort Barcinonensis de poenitentia, et matrimonio; cum glossis Ioannis de Friburgo ad S. D. N. Clemen. PP. VIII nunc primum in lucem edita. [1st ed. reprinted] Farnborough (Hants.), Gregg P., 1967. 606 p.

1521

Reed, Albert A. The juridical aspect of incorporation into the church of Christ—Canon 87. Carthagena, Ohio, 1960. 123 p.

1522

Regatillo, Eduardo F. Ius sacramentarium. Santander, Sal Terrae, 1945. 2 v. (Biblioteca Comillensis. Serie canonica)
Includes bibliographies.

1523

Reichel, Oswald J. A complete manual of canon law. v. 1: The sacraments. London, Hodges, 1896. 2 v.

1524

Renati, Charles G. The recipient of extreme unction. Washington, D.C., The Catholic University of America Press, 1961. 189 p. (The Catholic University of America. Canon law studies, no. 419)
Bibliography: p. 175–182.

1525

Roos, John R. The seal of confession. Washington, D.C., The Catholic University of America Press, 1960. 123 p. (The Catholic University of America. Canon law studies, no. 413)
Bibliography: p. 116–121.

1526
Roye, François de. De missis dominicis eorum officio et potestate. Venetiis, Zatta, 1773. various pagings.

1527
Schorr, George F. The law of the celebret; a historical synopsis and a commentary. Washington, D.C., The Catholic University of America, 1952. 116 p. (p. 116 advertisements) (The Catholic University of America. Canon law studies, v. 332)
   Bibliography: p. 103–109.

1528
Solowij, M. M. De reformatione liturgica Heraclii Lisowskyj, Archiepiscopi Polocensis, 1784–1809. Ed. 2. Romae, Sumptibus PP. Basilianorum, 1950. 128 p. (Analecta OSBM. Ser. 2, section 1: Opera, v. 2)

1529
Stadler, Joseph N. Frequent Holy Communion; a historical synopsis and a commentary. Washington, D.C., The Catholic University of American Press, 1947.·158 p. (The Catholic University of America. Canon law studies, no. 263)
   Bibliography: p. 135–140.

1530
Sullivan, Eugene H. Proof of the reception of the sacraments; an historical synopsis and commentary. Washington, D.C., The Catholic University of America Press, 1944. 165 p. (The Catholic University of America. Canon law studies, no. 209)
   Bibliography: p. 146–151.

1531
Szal, Ignatius J. The communication of Catholics with schismatics, a historical synopsis and a commentary. Washington, D. C., Catholic University of America Press, 1948. 217 p. (The Catholic University of America. Canon law studies, no. 264)

1532
Tenbörg, Erwin. Die messstipendien nach dem Codex iuris canonici. Paderborn, Schöningh, 1934. 199 p. (Görres gesellschaft zur pflege der wissenschaft im katholischen Deutschland. Veröffentlichungen der Sektion für rechts und staatswissenschaft . . . 66. hft.)
   "Quellen und literatur": p. [6]–9.

1533
Uhrmann, Johann. Das Geständnis im kanonischen Prozess. Paderborn, Schöningh, 1968. 162 p.
   Bibliography: p. 11–15.

1534
Vanyo, Leo V. Requisites of intention in the reception of the sacraments. Washington, D.C., Catholic University of America, 1965. 127 p. (Catholic University of America. Canon law studies, no. 391)
   Bibliography; p, 120–123.

1535
Vigilio da S. Michele S., Father. La confessione delle parti nel processo canonico; storia e dottrina. Milano, Giuffrè, 1957. 162 p.
   Includes bibliography.

1536
Wenner, Joseph. Kirchliches Lehrapostolat in Wort und Schrift. 2., verm. Aufl. Paderborn, Schöningh, 1953. 126 p.

1537
Zeliauskas, Josephus. De excommunicatione vitiata apud glossatores (1140–1350). Zürich, Pas-Verlag, (1967). [Auslfg.: Libreria Ateneo Salesiano, Piazza Ateneo Salesiano 1, Roma.] 346, 337 p. (Studia et textus historiae juris canonici, v. 4)
   "Appendix; textus inediti vel etiam editi rariores, qui in opere occurrunt": p. [1]–313 (2d group)
   Bibliography: p. [xxiii]–xliii.

1538
Ziolkowski, Thaddeus S. The consecration and blessing of churches; a historical synopsis and commentary. Washington, D.C., The Catholic University of America Press, 1943. 151 p. (The Catholic University of America. Canon law studies, no. 187)
   Bibliography: p. 129–135.

1539
Zirkel, Adam. "Executio potestatis": zur Lehre Gratians von der geistlichen Gewalt. St. Ottilien, Eos Verlag, 1975. 190 p. (Münchener theologische Studien: 3 Kanonistische Abt.; Bd. 33)
   Bibliography: p. xiii–xvi.

1540
Zirkel, Adam. Schliesst das Kirchenrecht alle

wiederverheirateten Geschiedenen von den Sakramenten aus? 1. Aufl. Mainz, Matthias-Grünewald-Verlag, 1977. 64 p.
Includes bibliographical references.

1541
Zürcher, Wolfgang. Die Teilnahme von Katholiken an akatholischen christlichen Kulthandlungen. Basel, Helbing, u. Lichtenhahn, 1965. 105 p. (Basler Studien zur Rechtswissenschaft, Heft 73)
Bibliography: p. xi–xiv.

MARRIAGE

1542
Alford, Culver B. Jus matrimoniale comparatum; jus civile matrimoniale in Statibus Foederatis Americae septentionalis cum jure canonico comparatum. Roma, Anonima libraria cattolica italiana; New York, Kenedy & Sons, 1937. 550 p.
"Bibliographia": p. [531]–543.

1543
Alonso Alija, Honorio, and Belarmino Alonso Alija. Observaciones al nuevo texto De matrimonio: (la reforma del Código de derecho canónico). Madrid, Los autores, 1976. 167 p.
Bibliography: p. 113–115.

1544
Amo, León del. La defensa del vínculo. Madrid, Editorial Revista de Derecho Privado [1954] 657 p. ([Biblioteca de la Revista de derecho privado] Serie B. Monografías fundamentales de derecho privado y público, v. 30)

1545
Amo, León del. Interrogatorio y confesión en los juicios matrimoniales. [Pamplona] EUNSA [1973] 594 p. (Colección canónica de la Universidad de Navarra)
Includes bibliographical references.

It is a well-known fact, the author states, that in matrimonial proceedings it is of the utmost importance to hear the spouses who are the parties in the trial; the degree of difficulty in properly appraising their depositions is equally well known. How can one avoid the risk of falling into extremes, i.e., of giving the parties absolute credit or of contending their worthlessness because of their partiality? This book offers a deep and complete analysis of the elements related to the examination of the parties and to the community of life of the spouses; it also stresses the effectiveness of judicial examination and confession.

1546
Amo, León del. La demanda judicial en las causas matrimoniales. Pamplona, Ediciones Universidad de Navarra, 1976. 205 p.
Includes bibliographical references and index.

This work was originally a series of lectures given by the author at the Rotal Studies of the Apostolic Nuntiature in Madrid, Spain, to postgraduate students holding masters and doctoral degrees in law. Its purpose is primarily a practical one: to train lawyers who are involved or will be involved in matrimonial trials and whose first concern will be to introduce claims and handle the initial phase of the proceedings. It also offers practical exercises on the most important issues discussed.

1547
L'Amore coniugale. Città del Vaticano, Libreria editrice vaticana, c 1971. 285 p. (Annali di dottrina e giurisprudenza canonica; 1)
Includes bibliographical references.

1548
Angelis, Carlo N. de. La natura del vincolo matrimoniale e il privilegio paolina, con note processuali; dissertazione canonica. Napoli, Jovene, 1941. 131 p., 2 l.
"Bibliografia": p. [xi]–xii.

1549
Arboleda Valencia, Hernán. Derecho matrimonial eclesiásitco en relación con la legislación civil y concordataria de Colombia. Bogotá, Editorial Temis, 1970. 257 p.
Includes bibliographical references.

The work analyzes ecclesiastical matrimonial law itself and in relationship to the civil legislation of Colombia and the concordat in force. It presents the principles and laws of the Church and then examines the dual matrimonial legislation existing in Colombia for Catholics and non-Catholics. Ecclesiastical legislation is strengthened by a concordat which declares that Catholicism is the religion of the Republic of Colombia, and religious marriage becomes mandatory for all Catholics. This study raises the question of how to harmonize this principle with the new teaching of the Church on religious freedom.

1550
Arnisasus, Henning. De jure connubiorum commentarius politicus. Francofurti, Thimÿ, 1613. 388, [4] p.

1551
Arquer y Ferrer, Miguel de, and Santiago de Semir y de Arquer. Derecho matrimonial; el matrimonio como institución natural, como sacramento. Barcelona, Editorial Poliglota, 1949. 290 p.

1552
Arza Arteaga, Antonio. Nuevo concepto del matrimonio. Bilbao, Mensajero, c1975. 179 p. (Colección Matrimonio y familia, 25)
Includes bibliographical references.

1553
Ayrinhac, Henry A. Marriage legislation in the new Code of canon law. New York, Cincinnati, Benziger Brothers, 1919. 335 p.
Bibliography: p. 10–11.

1554
Baccari, Renato. L'efficacia civile del matrimonio canonico. Milano, Giuffrè, 1939. 187 p. (Pubblicazioni dell'Instituto di scienze giuridiche, economiche, politiche e sociali della R. Università di Messina, n. 11)

1555
Badii, Cesare. Il procedimento matrimoniale davanti ai tribunali diocesani: secondo la istruzione della S. C. dei sacramenti, 15 agosto 1936. 3. ed. col testo dell'istruzione. Roma, Aequa, 1938. 239 p. (Biblioteca di cultura giuridica e sociale; n. 2)

1556
Balogh, Elemér. Die Eheformvorschriften der Dekrete 'Tametsi' und 'Ne temere' und die Bestrafung des Religionsdieners wegen Vollzugs der Trauung vor dem Nachweis der Zivilehe. Stuttgart, Enke, 1910. 85 p.

1557
Bassibey, René. Le mariage devant les tribunaux

ecclesiastiques. Procédure matrimoniale générale. Paris, Oudin, 1899. 452, 246 p.
Forms v. 12 of B. Duballet's Grand cours de droit canonique.

1558
Batzill, Hartmann. Decisiones Sanctae sedis de usu et abusu matrimonii. Taurini (Italia) Marietti, 1937. 39, [1] p.

1559
Bechstedt, Johann. De conditionibus sponsalium tractatus, in quo materia earundem ex utroq.; jure scripto, tum observationibus Consistoriorum practicis repetita, perque suos effectus, declarationes, ampliationes ac limitationes deducta & enucleata. Ed. altera. Coburgi, Impresus typis ducalibus, Impensis Georgii Friderici Gruneri, bibliopolae viduae & haeredum, 1669. 349 p.

1560
Bender, Ludovicus. De matrimonio commentarius. Torino, L. I. C. E., Berruti [1958] 123 p.

1561
Berger, Joseph. Rejection of the introductory libellus in matrimonial causes, with special reference to the ecclesiastical of the United States of America. Rome, Officium Libri Catholic, 1964 [c1963] 120 p.
Bibliography: p. [111]–118.

1562
Bernárdez Cantón, Alberto. Curso de derecho matrimonial canónico. Madrid, Editorial Tecnos, 1966. 492 p.
Bibliography: p. [491]–492.

1563
Bernárdez Cantón, Alberto. Curso de derecho matrimonial canónico. 3. ed., 3. reimp. Madrid, Tecnos, 1975. 456, [7] p. (Biblioteca universitaria de Editorial Tecnos)
Bibliography: p. [457]

1564
Bernardini, Enrico. Il motu proprio Causas matrimoniales. Roma, Montagnoli, 1972. 91 p.

1565
Bertola, Arnaldo. Matrimonio religioso. Roma, So-

cietà editrice "Athenaeum", 1936. 115 p. (Collana di monografie di diritto privato, [6])
"Bibliografia": p. 113–115.

1566

Bertola, Arnaldo. Il matrimonio religioso; diritto matrimoniale canonico. 2. ed. ampliata. Torino, Giappichelli [1946] 220 p.
"Fonti e letteratura del diritto matrimoniale canonico": p. [17]–25

1567

Bertola, Arnaldo. Il matrimonio religioso; diritto matrimoniale canonico. 3. ed. ampliata e rinnovata. Torino, Giappichelli [1953] 308 p.
"Fonti e letteratura del diritto matrimoniale canonico": p. [17]–26.

1568

Bevilacqua, Americo, abp. Trattato dommatico, giuridico e morale sul matrimonio cristiano secondo la dottrina di S. Tommaso, di S. Alfonso e dei migliori autori in conformità dei documenti più recenti della S. Sede e coll'aggiunta di una parte speciale riguardante le leggi civili e le disposizoni del codice civile italiano sul matrimonio e la filiazione. Roma, Desclée, Lefebvre, 1900. 358 p.

1569

Bézac, Robert. Dispense et mariage; contribution à l'étude de la législation canonique du mariage. Toulouse, Soubiron [1958] 141 p. (Mémoires de l'Académie de législation)

1570

Bézae Vezelii, Théodore. Tractatio de polygamia, in qua et ochini apostatae pro polygamia. Genevae, Vignon, 1573. 260 p.

1571

Biermann, Albert. Der irrtum im kanonischen eherecht, insbesondere der error de qualitate in personam redundans. Rheine i. W., von Kopczynski, 1928. 61 p.
"Literaturverzeichnis": p. [5]–7.

1572

Binder, Matthäus J. Praktisches Handbuch des katholischen Eherechtes; für Seelsorger im Kaiserthume Oesterreich. Mit einer reichlichen Sammlung von Formularien. 2. umgearb. Aufl. St. Pölten, Verlag von Passy & Sydy, 1865. 1052 p.

1573

Bini, Mario. La Chiesa e la libertà di stato in ordine al matrimonio. [Varese, 1951] 143 p.
Bibliography: p. 3–4.

1574

Biskupski, Stefan. Prawo małżeńskie Kościoła Rzymskokatolickiego. Przygotował i uzup. zgodnie z prawem posoborowym Marian Żurowski. Wyd. 2. Warszawa, Akademia Teologii Katolickiej, 1971. 2 v. (Zarys prawa kanonicznego, t. 3. Prawo rzeczowe, zesz. 2)
Bibliography: v. 2, p. [235]–244.

1575

Bober, Piotr. Pojęcie tajnej przeszkody małżeńskiej w prawie kanonicznem. Lublin, Tow. Naukowe Katolickiego Uniwersytetu Lubelskiego, 1935. 284 p. (Katolicki Uniwersytet Lubelski. Rozprawy doktorskie, magisterskie i seminaryjne. 2. Wydział prawa kanonicznego. Rozprawy doktorskie, t. 2)
Bibliography: p. [269]–281.

1576

Boccafola, Kenneth E. The requirement of perpetuity for the impediment of impotence. Roma, Università Gregoriana editrice, 1975. 156 p. (Analecta Gregoriana, v. 200. Series Facultatis Iuris Canonici, sectio B, 35)

1577

Boggiano-Pico, Antonio. Il matrimonio nel diritto canonico con riferimenti alla legislazione concordataria. Torino, Unione tipografico-editrice torinese, 1936. 714 p.

1578

Bonacina, Martino. Tractatvs de magno matrimonii sacramento. In qvo difficvltates, ac quaestiones ferè omnes ad hanc rem pertinentes, breui oratione disseruntur. Ad Deiparam Virginem Mariam, coeli, terrarúmque imperatricem. Lvgdvni, Lavrentii Dvrand, 1621. 289, [38] p.

1579

Brennan, James H. The simple covalidation of marriage, an historical synopsis and commentary. Washington, D.C., The Catholic University of

America Press, 1937. 135 p. (The Catholic University of America. Canon law studies, no. 102)
Bibliography: p. 121–124.

1580
Bressani, Aldo. Volontà degli sposi e trascrizione del matrimonio canonico. Udine, Arti grafiche friulane, 1969. 90 p.
Bibliography: p. 85–90.

1581
Brouwer, Henrici. De jure connubiori, libri duo. In quibus jura naturae, divinum civile, canonicum, prout de nuptiis agunt, referuntur, expenduntur, explicantur. Editio secunda. Delphis, Beman, 1714. 778 p.

1582
Buonocore, Giuseppe. Il sacramento del matrimonio nel diritto canonico; dottrina e legislazione. Roma, Pustet, 1929. 447 p.
Bibliographical footnotes

1583
Cabruni, Alberto. Inspectiones juris diversae super materia de dote; opusculum Alberti Cabruni ... aliàs ad usum auctoris elaboratum, nunc verò in lucem editum ad commodum studiosorum maximè in foro practicantium, in quo multa ab aliis sparsìm tradita ad praxim spectantia in unum collecta, & aliqua ab authore excogitata continentur. Parmae, Gozzi, 1740. 104 p.

1584
Canon law on civil action in marriage problems; lectures delivered under the auspices of the Catholic lawyers guild in the rooms of the Chicago bar association. [Chicago, 1944] 98 p.

1585
Cantelar Rodríguez, Francisco. El matrimonio de herejes; bifurcación del impedimentum disparis cultus y divorcio por herejía. Salamanca, Consejo Superior de Investigaciones Científicas. Instituto San Raimundo de Peñafort, 1972. 204 p. (Monografías canónicas Peñafort, no. 15)
Bibliography: p. [xiii]–xxi.

1586
Carberry, John J. The juridical form of marriage; an historical conspectus and commentary. Washington, D.C., The Catholic University of America Press, 1934. 177 p. (The Catholic University of America. Canon law studies, no. 84)
Bibliography: p. 159–163.

1587
Carpzov, Benedict. Usus practicus arboris consanguinitatis affinitatis in foro saconico tribus disputationibus. Lipsiae, Ritzschiano, 1663. 100 p.

1588
Carroll, Marie T. Ad summum pontificem, santitatem Suam Leonem XIII, gloriossime regnantem, re petitionis Mariae Teresiae Carroll, natae Nolan, pro dissolutione matrimonii rati et non consummati. Literae pro oratrice [Albany] 1885. 53 1.

1589
Carroll, Mariae T. Versio latina curiae albanensis actorum, com autem testimoniorum, re petitionis Mariae Theresiae Carroll, natae Nolan, pro dissolutione matrimonii rati et non consummati, habitae albaniae, A. D. 1885. [Albany] 1886. 16 1.

1590
Castañeda Delgado, Eudoxio. La locura y el matrimonio; psiquiatría y jurisprudencia de la Sagrada Rota Romana. Valladolid, Editorial Sever-Cuesta [1955] 292 p.
Includes bibliography.

1591
Catholic Church. Pope, 1740–1758 (Benedictus XIV). Constitutio sanctissimi domini nostri Benedicti pp. XIV. qua praescribitur ordo, & fora in judiciis causarum matrimonalium super matrimoniorum validitate vel nullitate declaranda servandus. Juxta exemplar romanum reimpressum. Augustae Vindelicorum, in Officina Wolffiana, 1748. 14 p.

1592
Catholic Church. Pope, 1903–1914 (Pius X) Ne temere (2 Aug. 1907) Die neuen eherechtlichen dekrete "Ne temere" (v. 2. august 1907) und "Provida" (v. 18. januar 1906) Dargestellt und kanonistisch erläutert von dr. theol. et iur. utr. August Knecht. Köln, Bachem, 1907. 74 p. (Görresgesellschaft zur pflege der wissenschaft im kath. Deutschland. Sektion für rechts- und sozialwissenschaft. [Veröffentlichungen] 2 hft.)

1593

Catholic Church. Pope, 1922–1939 (Pius XI) El matrimonio cristiano; comentarios y glosas a la carta encíclica de S. S., sobre el matrimonio cristiano, por colaboradores de "Razón y fe". Madrid, Editorial "Razón y fe" [1931] 295 p. (Biblioteca "Razón y fe" de cuestiones actuales, 15)

1594

Cattaneo, Ezio. Annuallamento o scioglimento nel diritto civile svizzero del matrimonio dichiarato nullo in diritto canonico per impedimento dirimente. Lugano, 1964. 317 p.

1595

Chelodi, Giovanni. Ius matrimoniale iuxta Codicem iuris canonici. Editio 3. Trento, Ardesi [1934] 218 p.

1596

Chelodi, Giovanni. Ius matrimoniale iuxta Codicem iuris canonici. Ed. 4., recognita et aucta a Vigilio Dalpiaz. Tridenti, Ardesi, 1937. 238 p.

1597

Chelodi, Giovanni. Ius canonicum de matrimonio et de iudiciis matrimonialibus; ed. 5. recognita et aucta a Pio Ciprotti. Vicenza, Società anonima tipografica editrice, 1947. 296 p.
 Bibliographical footnotes.

1598

Chelodi, Giovanni. El derecho matrimonial conforme al Código de derecho canónico. Barcelona, Bosch [1959] 357 p.

1599

Choveronius, Bermondus. In sacrosanctioris lateranensis concilij titulum de publicis concubinarijs commentarij. Lugduni, ad Salamandrae, apud Sennetonios fratres, 1550. 416 p.

1600

Cloran, Owen M. Previews and practical cases on marriage. v. 1: Preliminaries and impediments, Canons 1012–1080. Milwaukee, Bruce [1960] 1 v.

1601

Coburn, Vincent P. Marriages of conscience, an historical synopsis and commentary. Washington, D.C., The Catholic University of America Press,

1944. 172 p. (The Catholic University of America. Canon law studies, no. 191)
 Bibliography: p. 145–151.

1602

Colección diplomática de varios papeles, antiguos y modernos, sobre dispensas matrimoniales y otros puntos de disciplina eclesiástica. Madrid, Ibarra, 1809. 272, 8 p.

1603

Collet, de M. Dissertation sur la réhabilitation des mariages nuls, corrigé par M. Compans. 2. ed. Paris, Chez Méquignon Junior, 1834. 119 p.

1604

Coriden, James A. The indissolubility added to Christian marriage by consummation: an historical study of the period from the end of the patristic age to the death of Pope Innocent III. Romae, Catholic Book Agency, 1961. 75 p.
 Bibliography: p. [64]–75.

1605

Cosci, Cristoforo. De sponsalibus filiorum familias, vota decisiva. Quibus in fine additum est & aliud votum ejusdem auctoris super matrimonio siue denunciationibus clandestinè celebrato, simulque additiones, pluresque circa sponsalia, & matrimonia Sacrae Rotae Romanae decisiones. Romae, Typis Grossi, prostant venalia apud Barbiellini, 1763. 529 p.

1606

Cosci, Cristoforo. De sponsalibus filiorumfamilias, sive verbaliter, sive in scriptis, vota decisiva Christophori Cosci. Qvibus in fine additvm est ejusdem auctoris aliud votum super matrimonio sine denunciationibus clandestine celebrato. Accedunt etiam additiones sex ad magis confirmandas sententias in opere stabilitas, necnon plures tum editae, tum ineditae S. Rotae romanae decisiones circa sponsalia, & matrimonia. Romae, Sumptibus Remondinianis, 1766. 228, 43 p.
 "Sacrae Rotae romanae decisiones", with special t. p.: p. [145]–228.

1607

Cosci, Cristoforo. De separatione tori conjugalis tam nullo existente, seu soluto, quam salvo vinculo matrimonii, ejusque effectibus. Opus cum summariis, & indice locupletissimo. Romae, Salvioni, 1773.

1608

Curso de derecho matrimonial y procesal canónico para profesionales del foro. Salamanca, Universidad Pontificia, 1975. 267 p. (Biblioteca Salmanticensis; 12: Estudios, 10)
Includes bibliographical references.

1609

Curtin, William T. The plaint of nullity against the sentence; a historical synopsis and a commentary. Washington, D.C., The Catholic University of America Press, 1956. 163 p. (Catholic University of America. Canon law studies, no. 360)
Bibliography: p. 151–155.

1610

Cushieri, Andreas. Morbus mentis in iure matrimoniali canonici. (Pars dissertationis: De lucidis intervallis in iure matrimoniali) Romae, 1968. 132 p. (Pontifium Athenaeum Antonianum. Facultas Iuris Canonici. Theses ad lauream, no. 79)
Includes bibliographical references.

1611

Cutelli, Mario. Tractationvm De donationibvs contemplatione matrimonii, aliisqve de cavsis inter parentes, et filios factis. Tomus primvs—[secvndvs] Panormi, Cyrilli, 1630–41. 2 v.

1612

Cutelli, Mario. Tractationvm de donationibus contemplatione matrimonij, alijsque de causis inter parentes, & filios factis. Tomus primus—[secundus] Nvnc primvm Venetiis excvssvs, cui in hac impressione additae fuerunt in fine operis quamplurime Sac. rom. rotae decisiones, non antea euulgatae, ad materiam conferentes. Venetiis, sumptibus Bertanorum, 1661. 2 v. in 1.

1613

Daudet, Pierre. Études sur l'histoire de la juridiction matrimoniale. Les origines carolingiennes de la compétence exclusive de l'église (France et Germanie) Paris, Librairie du Recueil Sirey, 1933. 183 p.
"Bibliographie": p. [175]–179.

1614

Dauvillier, Jean. Le mariage dans le droit classique de l'église, depuis le Décret de Gratien (1140) jusqu'à la mort de Clément V (1314). Paris, Recueil Sirey, 1933. 517 p.
"Bibliographie": p. [491]–510.

1615

Dauvillier, Jean, and Carlo de Clercq. Le mariage en droit canonique oriental. Préface de Gabriel Le Bras. Paris, Recueil Sirey, 1936. 238 p., 1 l.

1616

Del Corpo, Egidio. De curatore pro mente infirmis in causis matrimonialibus. Napoli, D'Auria, 1970. 114 p.
Bibliography: p. [113]–114.

1617

Del Corpo, Egidio. De retractatione causae matrimonialis post duplicem sententiam conformem. Neapoli, D'Auria, 1969. 179 p.
Bibliography: p. [5]–6.

1618

Delgado, Gregorio. Error y matrimonio canónico. Pamplona, Ediciones Universidad de Navarra, 1975. 328 p.
Includes bibliographical references.

1619

Delphinus, Hieronymus [pseud.] Evnuchi conjvgium. Die capaunen-heyrath/hoc est scripta & judicia varia de conjugio inter evnuchum & virginem juvenculam anno M.DC.LXVI. contracto, t. t. à quibusdam supremis theologorum collegiis petita, postea hinc inde collecta ab Hieronymo Delphino, C. P. Halae, 1697. 159 p.

1620

La Désunion du couple sous l'Ancien Régime: l'exemple du Nord. Alain Lottin, J. R. Machuelle, S. Malolepsy, K Pasquier, ... [etc.] Villeneuve-d'Ascq, Université de Lille III; Paris, Éditions universitaires, 1975. 227 p.
Includes bibliographical references.

1621

Dillon, Robert E. Common law marriage. Washington, D.C., The Catholic University of America Press, 1942. 148 p. (The Catholic University of America. Canon law studies, no. 153)
Bibliography: p. 131–136.

1622
Dodwell, Edward J. The time and place for the celebration of marriage; an historical synopsis and commentary. Washington, D.C., The Catholic University of America Press, 1942. 156 p. (The Catholic University of America. Canon law studies, no. 154)
Bibliography: p. [139]–144.

1623
Doheny, William J. Canonical procedure in matrimonial cases, v. 1: Formal judicial procedure. Milwaukee, Bruce [c1938–44] 2 v.
Bibliography: v. 1, p. xiii–xx.

1624
Doheny, William J. Canonical procedure in matrimonial cases. 2d. ed. rev. and enl. Complete citations added of all the published sentences of the Tribunal of the Sacred Roman Rota, with a pref. by Dennis Cardinal Dougherty. v. 1: Formal judicial procedure. Milwaukee, Bruce, [1948] 1 v.
Bibliography: v. 1, p. 1173–1188.

1625
Dolan, John L. The defensor vinculi, his rights and duties. Washington, D.C., The Catholic University of America Press, 1934. 157 p. (The Catholic University of America. Canon law studies, no. 85)
Bibliography: p. 143–145.

1626
Donohue, John F. The impediment of crime; an historical synopsis and commentary. Washington, D.C., The Catholic University of America, 1931. 110 p. (The Catholic University of America. Canon law studies, no. 69)
Bibliography: p. 95–98.

1627
Donovan, James J. The pastor's obligation in prenuptial investigation; an historical synopsis and commentary. Washington, D.C., The Catholic University of America Press, 1938. 322 p. (The Catholic University of America. Canon law studies, no. 115)
Bibliography: p. 299–307.

1628
Dossetti, Giuseppe. La violenza nel matrimonio in diritto canonico. Milano, Società editrice "Vita e pensiero," 1943. 586 p. (Pubblicazioni del l'Università cattolica del s. Cuora. Ser. 2.: Scienze giuridiche. v. LXVII)

1629
Echeverría, Lamberto de. El matrimonio en el derecho canónico particular posterior al Código. Vitoria, Editorial del Seminario, 1955. 419 p. (Victoriensia, v. 3)
"Fuentes": p. [13]–35.

1630
Egan, Edward M. The introduction of a new "chapter of nullity" in matrimonial courts of appeal. A study of legislation in the Code of Canon Law and the instruction Provida Mater Ecclesia. Rome, Officium libri catholici (Perugia, Grafica), 1967. 214 p.
Bibliography: p. [191]–211.

1631
Eichmann, Eduard. Das katholische Mischehenrecht nach dem Codex Iuris Canonici. Paderborn, Schöningh, 1921. 56 p.

1632
Englmann, Johann A. Katholisches Eherecht. Nach dem hinterlassenen Manuskripte. Mit besonderer Berücksichtigung des in Deutschland geltenden Civil-Eherechts, sowie der Diözesan-Vorschriften der Diözese Regensburg bearb. von Ludwig Stingl. Regensburg, Coppenrath, 1901. 449 p.

1633
Esame del parere de' teologi di corte di s. m. siciliana in risposta a una memoria della corte romana concernte i diritti del sovrano sul matrimonio di sudditi cattolici. Roma, Puccinelli, 1789. 369 p.

1634
Escudero Escorza, Fernando. Matrimonio de acatólicos en España. Vitoria [España] Eset, Seminario Diocesano, 1964. 265 p. (Victoriensia; publicaciones del Seminario de Vitoria, v. 17)
Bibliography: p. [xvii]–xxiii.

1635
Esmein, Adhémar. Le mariage en droit canonique. Paris, Larose et Forcel, 1891. 2 v. (Études sur l'histoire du droit canonique privé)

Esmein, a jurist and historian, devotes his two-volume work to marriage, one of the canonical teachings which has most influenced the development of private law in western European nations. This history of an important and original legal system is divided into three parts: (1) historical development and principles; (2) marriage law until the Council of Trent, with subdivisions covering formation and proof of marriage, and impediments and sanctioning actions; effects of marriage and separation of spouses; second weddings; concubinage; and (3) marriage law after the Council of Trent, with an interesting study on the decision of this Council on the nature and forms of marriage, among other topics.

1636

Esmein, Adhémar. Le mariage en droit canonique; 2. éd. mise à jour par R. Génestal. Paris, Recueil Sirey, 1929. 477 p.

1637

Esmein, Adhémar. Le mariage en droit canonique. New York, Franklin [1968] 2 v. (Essays in history, economics, and social science, 71)
  Bibliographical footnotes.

1638

Ewers, Heinz. Die Nichtigkeitsbeschwerde in dem kanonischen Prozessrecht. München, Zink, 1952. 122 p. (Münchener theologische Studien. 3. Kanonistische Abt., 2. Bd.)
  "Quellen und Schrifttum": p. xi–xv.

1639

Farías Páez, José de J. Consentimiento matrimonial, disertación jurídica. Bogotá [194?] 118 p.

1640

Fässler, Hans N. Die Schizophrenie als Ehenichtigkeitsgrund im kanonischen Recht; Versuch einer Bewertung der Schizophrenie nach der Spruchpraxis der Sacra Romana Rota. Freiburg in der Schwiez, 1951. 173 p.
  "Literatur": p. xv–xx.

1641

Fedele, Pio. L' "ordinatio ad prolem" nel matrimonio in diritto canonico. Milano, Giuffrè, 1962. 556 p.
  Includes bibliography.

1642

Ferreres, Juan B. Derecho sacramental, particular-

mente del matrimonio, y penal especial. Con arreglo al Código de Pío X, promulgado por Benedicto XV a las declaraciones subsigsuientes de la Santa Sede y a las prescripciones de la disciplina española y de la Américal Latina. 3. ed., corregida y aumentada. Barcelona, E. Subirana, Editor-Pontificio, 1923. 595 p.

1643

Flatten, Heinrich. Irrtum und Täuschung bei der Eheschliessung nach kanonischem Recht. Paderborn, Schöningh, 1957. 77 p.
  Anhang: Irrtum und Taüschung im Eherecht der europäischen Staaten: p. [59]–77.

1644

Fleury, Jean. Recherches historiques sur les empêchements de parenté dans le mariage canonique des origines aux Fausses décrétales. [Paris] Recueil Sirey, 1933. 289 p.
  Bibliography: p. [273]–283.

1645

Fraghi, Sebastiano, Abp. De condicionibus matrimonio appositis. Romae, Officium Libri Catholici, 1941. 118 p.
  "Bibliographia": p. [xi]–xv.

1646

Freisen, Joseph. Geschichte des canonischen eherechts bis zum verfall der glossenlitteratur. Tübingen, Fues, 1888. 918 p.
  "Benutzte ausgaben und öfter citirte schriften": p. [xiii]–xvi.

1647

Freisen, Joseph. Geschichte des kanonischen Eherechts bis zum Verfall der Glossenliteratur. Neudruck der 2. Ausg., Paderborn, 1893. Aalen, Scientia Verlag, 1963. 918 p.
  Bibliography: p. [xiii]–xvi.

1648

Frepoli, Federico C. Impotenza psichica congiuntiva nel matrimonio canonico. Varese, Galli, 1973. 93 p. (Studi giuridici dell'Ateneo cattolico di Varese; v. 7)
  Bibliography: p. 89–90.

1649

Fus, Edward A. The extraordinary form of marriage according to canon 1098; a historical synposis and commentary. Washington, D.C., The Catholic University of America Press, 1954. 205 p. (The Catholic University of America. Canon law studies, no. 348)

Bibliography: p. 189–197.

1650

Gallagher, John F. The matrimonial impediment of public propriety; a historical synposis and a canonical commentary. Washington, D.C., The Catholic University of America Press, 1952 [i.e., 1953] 171 p. (Catholic University of America. Canon law studies, no. 304)

Bibliography: p. 146–153.

1651

Galtier, Francisque, ed. and tr. Le mariage, discipline orientale et discipline occidentale; la réforme du 2 mai 1949. [Beyrouth] 1950. 456 p. (Université St. Joseph de Beyrouth. Faculté de théologie. Publications du 75ᵉ anniversaire)

Bibliography: p. 4–9.

1652

García Martínez, Gumersindo. Indisolubilidad del matrimonio rato y consumado entre dos partes bautizadas; discurso inaugural del año 1963–1964. Madrid, 1963. 50 p.

Bibliographical footnotes.

1653

Gasparri, Pietro, Cardinal. Tractatus canonicus de matrimonio. E. nova ad mentem Codicis I. C. [Città del Vaticano] Typis Polyglottis Vaticanis, 1932. 2 v.

"Allegata," v. 2, p. [339]–605, contain fifteen documents including encyclicals of Popes Leo XIII, Pius XI, and Benedict XIV, decrees of the Holy Office, the Congregation of the Council, and the Congregation of the Sacraments.

Bibliographical footnotes.

In this treatise on marriage, the author, who presided over the commission of cardinals for the preparation of the present Code of Canon Law and who was also appointed president of the commission for the Code of Oriental Canon Law, presents an updated version of his teachings on marriage, given while a professor at the *Institut Catholique de Paris*. It is intended for pastors, con-

fessors, and bishops, primarily. Aside from its thorough canonical analysis of marriage, the work is also of great interest because it is preceded by a letter from the then State Secretary of the Vatican, Cardinal Pacelli, the future Pope Pius XII, and another from Pope Leo XIII, praising the method, depth, and faith of the author. Gasparri explains that many elements complicate ecclesiastical matrimonial legislation: the abundance of legislated material; the combination of ecclesiastical positive law with divine law, be it natural or positive, and with civil law. It deals with general notions; premarital conditions; impediments to marriage; consent in marriage; form, place, and time of marriage celebration; divorce; and nullity of marriage.

1654

Génestal, Robert. Histoire de la légitimation des enfants naturels en droit canonique. Paris, Leroux, 1905. 238 p. (*Half-title:* Bibliothéque de l'École des hautes études. Sciences religieuses. 18. v.)

"Principaux ouvrages cités": p. [229]–235.

1655

Gennari, Casimiro, Cardinal. Breve commento della nuova legge sugli sponsali e sul matrimonio. Ed. 4 con nuove giunte e correzioni. Roma, Presso la direzione del Monitore ecclesiastico, 1908. 65 p.

Bibliographical footnotes.

1656

Giacchi, Orio. Lezioni sul consenso nel matrimonio canonico; corso 1948/49. Milano, Vita e pensiero, 1949. 64 p.

1657

Giacchi, Orio. Il consenso nel matrimonio canonico. Milano, Giuffrè, 1950. 210 p.

1658

Giacchi, Orio. Il consenso nel matrimonio canonico. 3. edizione interamente rifatta ed aumentata. Milano, Giuffrè, 1968. 373 p.

Bibliographical footnotes.

The author introduces his study with an analysis of substance and form in ecclesiastical law (the requirement of substantial reality and its formal regulation) and states the need for a method which accounts for the relationship between substance and form in the study of consent in sacramental marriage. This monograph explains the place of consent in canonical matrimonial regulation, the relationship between contract and sacrament, marriage as a consensual contract, and other aspects of marriage. In addition, the book offers a profound and extensive study on the lack of consent in its many manifestations and vitiated consent, as well as a shorter analysis of the essence of marriage, with special reference to the doctrine of Vatican II.

1659
Giménez Fernández, Manuel. La institución matrimonial según el derecho de la Iglesia católica. Madrid, Editorial Católica Española, 1943. 286, [2] p.
"Notas" (bibliographical references) at end of each chapter.

1660
Giudice, Vincenzo del. Sommario di diritto matrimoniale canonico. Estratto dalle Nozioni di diritto canonico del medesimo autore, a cura e con aggiunte del prof. Gaetano Catalono. 3. edizione riveduta e interamente aggiornata. Milano, Giuffrè, 1970. 142 p.
Includes bibliographical references.

1661
Göller, Emil. Das Eherecht im neuen kirchlichen Gesetzbuch, mit einer Einführung in den Kodex kurz dargestellt. 2. ver. Aufl. Freiburg im Breisgau, Herder, 1918. 81 p.

1662
Gómez del Campillo, Francisco. Derecho matrimonial canónico. Rev., completado y adaptado a la legislación vigente por Jaime M. Mans Puigarnau. Barcelona [Bosch] 1948. 152 p.

1663
Gómez-Morán, Luis. Teoría de los impedimentos para el matrimonio. Madrid, Instituto Editorial Reus [194?] 66, 11 p.

1664
Gootlob, Theodor. Grundriss des katholischen Eherechtes. Einsiedeln, Benziger, 1948. 181 p.
Bibliographical footnotes.

1665
Graf, Georg. Die leges irritantes und inhabilitantes in Codex juris canonici. Paderborn, Schöningh, 1936. 119 p. (Görres-gesellschaft zur pflege der wissenschaft im katholischen Deutschland. Veröffentlichungen der Sektion für rechts- und staatswissenschaft . . . 71. hft.)
"Quellen und literatur": p. [6]–10.

1666
Graziani, Ermanno. Volontá attuale e volontá precettiva nel negozio matrimoniale canonico. Milano, Giuffrè, 1956. 208 p. (Pubblicazioni dell'Istituto di scienze giuridiche, economiche, politiche e sociali della Università di Messina, n. 34)

1667
Greco, Joseph. Le pouvoir du Soverain pontife à l'égard des infidèles. Le privilège "Petrinum" peut-il être éntendu au mariage des non baptisés, spécialement à celui des catéchumènes? Jalons historiques: faits et doctrines. Rome, Presses de l'Université grégorienne, 1967. 406 p.
Bibliography: p. [xvii]–xxxi.

The intention of the author is already apparent from the rather long title of his work, which in translation is: "The jurisdiction of the sovereign pontiff concerning the infidels. Does the Petrine privilege extend to the marriage of nonbaptized, especially those of catechumens?" According to the so-called *privilegium Petrinum*, the pope, after pondering the circumstance, can dissolve a first marriage contracted between an infidel spouse and a party baptized in a non-Catholic sect *in favorem fidei* (in favor of faith) by virtue of the apostolic authority, eventually validating a second marriage of the converted party with another Catholic or non-Catholic person. The author had in mind two compelling questions facing missionaries throughout the world: Can the Church accept candidates to baptism, regardless of their previous matrimonial situation, and subject them to a catechumenate, or preparation, of some duration? And in a more pluralistic society, is there a solution for a Catholic deeply involved with a nonbaptized party, who was previously married to another infidel party who has abandoned him or her? The work is divided into three parts: pontifical constitutions of the sixteenth century and other papal acts concerning neophytes; the sovereign pontiffs and the marriages of Jews (1418–1622); and the doctrinal foundations of spiritual power and intervention of the pope regarding any person, especially in the case of *privilegium Petrinum in favorem fidei*.

1668

Gretser, Jacob. Dispvtationes matrimoniales dvae. Altera De cognatione affinitate, et polygamia. Altera De ivdice cavssarvm matrimonialivm, deqve conventientia & differentia sacrorum canonum & legum ciuilium circa impedimenta matrimonji. Propositae olim in Academia ingolstadiensi. Nvnc in gratiam stvdiosorvm denuò euulgatae. Ingolstadii, ex typographeo Adami Sartorii, 1611. 51 p.

1669

Griese, Nicholas O. The marriage contract and the procreation of offspring. Washington, D.C., The Catholic University of America Press, 1946 [i.e., 1947] 224 p. (The Catholic University of America. Canon law studies, no. 226)
Bibliography: p. 195–200.

1670

Grzywacz, Jerzy. Promotor sprawiedliwości i jego udział w sprawach małżeńskich. Lublin, Katolicki Uniwersytet Lubelski, 1974. 340 p.
Bibliography: p. 9–33.

1671

Guerriero, Antonio. Il casus exceptus nel diritto processuale canonico. Napoli, Athena mediterranea, 1970. 261 p. (Contributi all storia del diritto canonico. Nuova serie di studi storico-giuridici, 5)
Bibliography: p. [225]–261.

1672

Guise, Léo de. Le promoteur de la justice dans les causes matrimoniales. Ottawa, Les Éditions de l'Université d'Ottawa, 1944. 331, [1] p. (Universitas catholica ottaviensis. Dissertationes ad gradum laureae in Facultate juris canonici consequendum conscriptae, n. 8)
"Bibliographie": p. [299]–317.

1673

Gutiérrez, Juan. Canonicarvm qvaestionvm vtriusque fori, tam exterioris quàm interioris animae, liber tertivs, qui totus circa sponsalia de fvtvro & matrimonia versatur. Cum indice tam capitulorum quàm rerum locupletissimo. Noribergae, sumptibus Wolffgangi Endteri, 1657. 375, [30] p.

1674

Gutiérrez, Juan. Canonicarum quaestionum, utriusque fori tam exterioris quàm interioris animae ... in quo multae quaestiones in praxi admodum utiles continentur; cum indicibus argumentorum, rerum & verborum locupletissimis. Nova editio, prioribus correctior et elegantiori ordine disposita. Coloniae Allobrogum, Perachon & Cramer, 1729–30 [v. 2, '29] 3 v. in 1.

1675

Hamedinger, Oskar. Die annullierung der katholischen ehe. Wien, Selbstverlag des verfassers, 1928. 63, [1] p.

1676

Hanstein, Honorius. Kanonisches Eherecht; ein Grundriss für Studierende und Seelsorger. 2. Aufl. Paderborn, Schöningh [1948] 256 p.
"Ergänzungen".

1677

Hanstein, Honorius. Kanonisches Eherecht; ein Grundriss für Studierende und Seelsorger. 3., verb. Aufl. Paderborn, Schöningh, 1953. 272 p.
Bibliography: p. 13.

1678

Hanstein, Honorius. Kanonisches Eherecht; ein Grundriss für Studierende und Seelsorger. 5. verb. Aufl. Paderborn, Schöningh [1958] 271 p.
Includes bibliography.

1679

Haring, Johann B. Der kirchliche eheprozess; eine praktische anleitung für kirchliche richter. 3., nach der instruktion der Sakramentenkongregation vom 15. august 1936 umgearb. aufl. Graz, Styria, 1938. 166 p.
"Literatur": p. [vi]

1680

Heggelbacher, Othmar. Kirchenrecht und Fragen der Psychiatrie. Wien, Herder (1967). 44 p. (Kirche und Recht, Bd. 7)
Bibliographical footnotes.

1681

Heggelbacher, Othmar. Kirchenrecht und Psychiatrie. Freiburg, Schweiz, Universitätsverlag, 1975. 93 p.
Includes bibliographical references and indexes.

1682

Heiner, Franz X. Grundriss des katholischen Eherechts. Münster i. W., Schöningh, 1889. 317 p.

(Sammlung von Kompendien für das Studium und die Praxis. II. Serie, 1.)

1683
Heiner, Franz X. Grundriss des katholischen Eherechts. 4. verb, und verm. Aufl. Münster i. W., Schöningh, 1900. 304 p.

1684
Heiner, Franz X. Grundriss des katholischen Eherechts. 5., verb. und verm. Aufl., mit dem neuen Verlöbnis- und Eheschliessungsrecht als Anhang. Müntster i. W., Schöningh, 1908. 319, 73 p.

1685
Heiner, Franz X. Grundriss des katholischen Eherechts. 6 verb. und verm. Aufl. Münster i. W., Schöningh, 1910. 300 p.

1686
Heiner, Franz X. Das neue Verlöbnis- und Eheschliessungsrecht in der katholischen Kirche; für die Praxis dargestellt. Münster i. Westf., Schöningh, 1908. 75 p.

1687
Heneghan, John J. The marriages of unworthy Catholics, canons 1065 and 1066; an historical synopsis and commentary. Washington, D.C., The Catholic University of America Press, 1944. 213 p. (The Catholic University of America. Canon law studies, no. 188)
Bibliography: p. 185–192.

1688
Hera, Alberto de la. Relevancia jurídico-canónica de la cohabitación conyugal. [Pamplona, Universidad de Navarra, 1966] 190 p. (Colección canónica de la Universidad de Navarra. Cuadernos, 7)
Bibliography: p. 185–190.

1689
Herrmann, Horst. Die Stellung unehelicher Kinder nach kanonischem Recht. Amsterdam, Grüner, 1971. 224 p. (Kanonische Studien und Texte, Bd. 26)
Bibliography: p. xv–xxi.

1690
Hervada Xiberta, Francisco J. La impotencia del varón en el derecho matrimonial canónico. Pamplona, 1959. 244 p. (Colección canónica del Estudio General de Navarra, no. 1)
Bibliography: p. 239–244.

1691
Hervada Xiberta, Francisco J. Los fines del matrimonio; su relevancia en la estructura jurídica matrimonial. Prólogo do Pedro Lombardía. Pamplona, Studium Generale, 1960. 227 p. (Colección canónica del Estudio General de Navarra, no. 4)
Includes bibliography.

1692
Hilling, Nikolaus. Das eherecht des Codex juris canonici. Freiburg i. Br., Waibel, 1927. 176 p.

1693
Hörmann zu Hörbach, Walter von. Die desponsatio impuberum. Ein beitrag zur entwicklungsgeschichte des canonischen eheschliessungsrechtes. Innsbruck, Wagner'sche universitätsbuchhandlung, 1891. 269 p.

1694
Hussarek von Heinlein, Max, freiherr. Die bedingte eheschliessung. Eine canonistische studie. Wien, Hölder, 1892. 264 p.

1695
Instructio de quibusdam emendationibus circa normas in processu super matrimonio rato et non consummato servandas: cum adnexis peculiaribus documentis ad rem attinentibus. [Romae]Sacra Congregatio de Disciplina Sacramentorum, 1972. 83 p.
Includes bibliographical references and index.

1696
Instructio Servanda a Tribunalibus Dioecessanis in Pertractandis Causis de Nullitate Matrimonium edita Die 15 Agusti 1936. Typis polyglottis Vaticanus, 1937.

1697
Jeličić, Vitomir. Kanonski ženidbeno pravo katoličke crkve. Sarajevo, Tisak i naklada Hrvatske tiskare d. d., 1930. 240, iv p.

1698
Jemolo, Arturo C. Il matrimonio nel diritto canonico. Milano, Vallardi, 1941. 463 p.
"Cenni bibliografici": p. [xiii]–xiv.

1699

Jornadas Informativas sobre Temática Actual de Derecho Canónico, 1st, Madrid, 1975. Cuestiones matrimoniales y canónicas: temática actual: ponencias, de las I jornadas Informativas sobre Temática Actual de Derecho Canónico de la Asociación Española de Canonistas. Madrid, Eapsa, 1976. 161 p. (Estudios—Universidad Pontificia Comillas; 6: Derecho canónico; I, 1) (Publicaciones de la Universidad Pontificia Comillas. Serie 1)
Includes bibliographical references.

1700

Justis, Vincentius de. Tractatus de dispensationibus matrimonialibus in tres libros digestus, cui accesserunt in calce operis nonnullae annotationes & quamplures recentissimi casus à Sacra congregatione concilii resoluti: cum indice locuplettissimo. Venetiis, Bortoli, 1739. 440 p.

1701

Kay, Thomas H. Competence in matrimonial procedure. Washington, D.C., The Catholic University of America Press, 1929. 163 p., [1] p. (The Catholic University of America. Canon law studies, no. 53)
Bibliography: p. 155–159.

1702

Keating, John R. The bearing of mental impairment on the validity of marriage; an analysis of Rotal jurisprudence. Roma, Gregorian University Press, 1964. 221 p. (Analecta Gregoriana, v. 136. Series Facultatis Iuris Canonici: section B. n. 14)
Bibliography: p. [201]–217.

1703

Kennedy, Edwin J. The special matrimonial process in cases of evident nullity; an historical conspectus and commentary. Washington, D.C., The Catholic University of America Press, 1935. 165 p. (The Catholic University of America. Canon law studies, no. 93)
Bibliography: p. 149–152.

1704

Kérészy, Zoltán. A "Ne temere" decretum tekintettel a jogtörténeti előzményekre. Budapest, Athenáeum nyomása, 1909. 115 p.

1705

Knecht, August. Die neuen ehrechtlichen Dekrete; "Ne temere" vom 2. August 1907 und "Provida" vom 18. Januar 1906, dargestellt und kanonistisch erläutert. Köln, Bachem, 1908. 76 p. (Görres-Gesellschaft zur Pflege der Wissenschaft im katholischen Deutschland. Sektion für Rechts- und Sozialwissenschaft, 2. Heft)

1706

Knopke, Roch F. Reverential fear in matrimonial cases in Asiatic countries: Rota cases; a historical synopsis and a commentary. Washington, D.C., Catholic University of America Press, 1949 [c1950] 112 p. (The Catholic University of America. Canon law studies, no. 294)
Bibliography: p. 86–89.

1707

Knopp, Nikolaus. Vollständiges katholisches Eherecht, mit besonderer Rücksicht auf die practische Seelsorge. Regensburg. Manz, 1850–52. 2 v.

1708

Knopp, Nikolaus. Vollständiges katholisches Eherecht mit besonderer Rücksicht auf die practische Seelsorge. 4. verm. und verb. Aufl. Regensburg, Manz, 1873. 590 p.

1709

Kofler, Anton. Über die Beziehung zwischen Eheunfähigkeit der Personen und dem Ehewillen. Entwicklung des Problems von Sanchez bis in die Gegenwart. Roma, Libreria editrice dell'Università Gregoriana, 1968. 189 p. (Analecta Gregoriana, v. 165. Series Facultatis Iuris Canonici, sectio B, no. 23)
Bibliography: p. [ix]–xv.

1710

König, Robert. Tractatus juridicus de jure matrimoniali principum aeque ac privatorum, jucta ordinem titucrum libri IV. Decretalium Gregorii IX, scientifica methodo concinnatus. Salisburgi, Typis Mayr [1694] 559 p.

1711

Kradepohl, Anton. Stellvertretung und kanonisches Eherecht. Amsterdam, Schippers, 1964. 186 p. (Kanonistische Studien und Texte, Bd. 17)
"Nachdruck der Ausgabe Bonn 1939."
Bibliography: p. [xi]–xvi.

1712

Krukowski, Józef. Wpływ bojanzni z szaounku na wartość umowy małżenskiej w prawie kanonicznym; skrypt dla studentow KUL. Lublin, Katolicki Uniwersytet Lubelski, 1970. 148 p.
Bibliography: p. 7–16.

1713

Krukowski, Józef. Wpływ intencji sprawcy bojaźni na wartość umowy małżeńskiej w prawie kanonicznym: studium prawno-historyczne. Lublin, Katolicki Uniwersytet Lubelski, 1976. 79 p.
Bibliography: p. 73–[77]

1714

Lacey, Thomas A. Marriage in church and state. Fully rev. and supplemented by R. C. Mortimer. London, S. P. C. K., 1947. 219 p.

1715

Lane, Loras T. Matrimonial procedure in the ordinary courts of second instance. Washington, D.C., Catholic University of America Press, 1947 [i.e., 1949] 184 p. (The Catholic University of America. Canon law studies, no. 253)
Bibliography: p. 161–167.

1716

Langohr, Maurits J. Het huwelijk naar Kanoniek recht, bewerkt voor Belgie, Nederland en Kongo met vergelijkingselementen van burgerlijk recht. Met voorwoord door A. van Hove. Antwerpen, 'T Groeit [1947] 227 p.
"Bibliografie": p. 16–18.

1717

Lázaro Benítez, Cecilio. La bendición nupcial y la forma del matrimonio canónico. [Madrid] Reus, 1972. 269 p. (Colección de temas jurídicos-legales)
Includes bibliographical references.

1718

Lázaro Benítez, Cecilio. Influencia del proceso extraordinario en la noción de juicio canónico. [Pamplona, Universidad de Navarra, 1966] 184 p. (Colección Canónica de la Universidad de Navarra. Cuadernos, 8)
Bibliography: p. 181–184.

1719

Leclaire, Roland. La forme canonique ordinaire des mariages interrituels au Canada. [Ottawa] Éditions del'Université d'Ottawa, 1962. 284 p. (Universitas Catholica Ottaviensis. Dissertationes ad gradum laureae in facultatibus ecclesiasticis consequendum conscriptae. Series canonica nova, t. 5)
Includes bibliography.

1720

Leclerc, Gustave. Mariage des vieillards et probati auctores. Torino, Società editrice internazionale, 1968 [i.e., 1967] 99 p. (Biblioteca del Salesianum, 74)
Bibliographical footnotes.

1721

Lefebvre, Carlo. Il motu proprio Causas matrimoniales. A cura di Carlo Lefebvre. Torino, Marietti; Milano, Giuffrè [1972] 77 p. (Ius Ecclesiae novissimum)
Includes bibliographical references.

1722

Leges Ecclesiae de matrimonio sive substantiales sive processuales post promulgatum Codicem I. C. editas collegit Joseph Marcone. Romae, Desclée, [1956] 358 p.

1723

Leite, Antonio. Competência da Igreja e do Estado sobre o matrimónio. Porto, Libraria Apostolado da Imprensa, 1946. 250 p.
Bibliography: p. [xv]–[xxi]

1724

Leitner, Martin. Lehrbuch des katholischen Eherechts. Paderborn, Schöningh, 1902. 648 p. (Wissenschaftliche Handbibliothek, 1. Reihe: Theologische Lehrbücher, 23)

1725

Leitner, Martin. Lehrbuch des katholischen eherechts. 2. aufl. Paderborn, Schöningh, 1912. 635 p. (Wissenschaftliche handbibliothek, 1. Reihe. Theologische lehrbücher, 23)

1726

Leitner, Martin. Lehrbuch des katholischen Eherechts. 3. Aufl. Paderborn, Schöningh, 1920. 455 p. (Wissenschaftliche Handbibliothek. 1. Reihe: Theologische Lehrbücher, 23)
Includes bibliographies.

1727

Le Picard, René. La communauté de la vie conjugale, obligation des époux; étude canonique. Préface par Eugène Duthoit. Paris, Recueil Sirey, 1930.
"Sources, documents, collections": p. [446]–452.
"Auteurs et ouvrages": p. [453]–463.

1728

Lettmann, Reinhard. Die Diskussion über die klandestinen Ehen und die Einführung einer zur Gültigkeit verpflichtenden Eheschliessungsform auf dem Konzil von Trient. Eine kanonistische Untersuchung. Münster/Westf., Aschendorff (1967) 195 p. (Münsterische Beiträge zur Theologie, Heft 31)
Bibliography: p. [v]–vii.

1729

Lindner, Dominikus. Die gesetzliche verwandtschaft als ehehindernis im abendländischen kirchenrecht des mittelalters. Paderborn, Schöningh, 1920. 90 p. (Görres-gesellschaft zur pflege der wissenschaft im katholischen Deutschland. Veröffentlichungen der Sektion für rechts- und sozialwissenschaft, 36. hft.)
"Verzeichnis der öfter wiederkehrenden literatur": p. 9.

1730

Linneborn, Johannes. Grundriss des eherechts nach dem Codex iuris canonici. Paderborn, Schöningh, 1919. 499 p.
Bibliography: p. 5–6.

1731

Linneborn, Johannes. Grundriss des eherechts nach dem Codex iuris canonici, 4. und 5., neubearb. und verm. aufl., besorrgt von dr. theol. et jur. utr. Joseph Wenner. Paderborn, Schöningh, 1933. 502 p. (Added t.-p.: Wissenschaftliche handbibliothek, eine sammlung theologischer lehrbücher)

1732

Litta, Luigi. Del diritto di stabilire impedimenti dirimenti il matrimonio e dispensarne. 2. ed. riv. ed accresiuta. Pavia, Galeazzi, 1783. 2 v.

1733

Lizana et Beaumont, Franciscus X. de. Canonica responsa de matrimonio. Caesar-Augusta, Mereno, 1775.

1734

Llamazares-Fernández, Dionisio. Condición y matrimonio en el derecho canónico. León, Colegio Universitario, 1976. 306 p. (Publicaciones Colegio Universitario de León, Unidad de Investigación, 2)
Bibliography: p. 299–306.

1735

Llorente, Juan A. Colección diplomatica de varios papeles antiguos y modernos sobre dispensas matrimoniales y otros puntos de disciplina ecclesiástica. 2. ed. Madrid, Alban, 1822. 272, 8 p.

1736

Lobethan, Friedrich G. A. Einleitung zur theoretischen ehe-rechts-gelahrtheit. Halle, Waisenhauses, 1775. 220 p.

1737

Lobethan, Friedrich G. A. Einleitung zur theoretischen ehe-rechts-gelahrtheit. 2 verb. aufl. Halle, Waysenhaus, 1785. 216 p.

1738

Löffler, Josef. Die Störungen des geschlechtlichen Vermögens in der Literatur der autoritativen Theologie des Mittelalters. Ein Beitrag zur Geschichte der Impotenz und des medizinischen Sachverständigenbeweises im kanonischen Impotenzprozess. [Mainz? 195?] 128 1.
Bibliography: leaves 111–119.

1739

Lyons, Avïtus E. The collegiate tribunal of first instance with special reference to matrimonial causes. Washington, D.C., The Catholic University of America, 1932. 152 p. (The Catholic Univeristy of America. Canon law studies, no. 78)
Bibliography: p. 137–140.

1740

Magni, Cesare. Gli effetti civili del matrimonio canonico. Padova, CEDAM, 1948. 198 p.
"Nuova edizione ampiament riveduta del mio precedente lavoro 'L'attività degli organi publici in relazione ai matrimoni concordatari.'"

1741

Maida, Adam J. The tribunal reporter, a comprehensive study of the grounds for the annulment of marriage in the Catholic Church, edited by Adam

J. Maida for the Canon Law Society of America. Huntington, Ind., Our Sunday Visitor [1970] 1 v.

1742

Manning, John J. Presumptions of law in marriage cases. Washington, D.C., The Catholic University of America, 1935. 111 p. (The Catholic University of America. Canon law studies, no. 94)
  Bibliography: p. 95–97.

1743

Mans Puigaranau, Jaime M. El consentimiento matrimonial; defecto y vicios del mismo como causas de nulidad de las nupcias. Barcelona, Bosch, 1956. 313 p.

1744

Mans Puigarnau, Jaime M. El error de cualidad en el mattrimonio ante la reforma del Código de derecho canónico. Barcelona, Bosch [1964] 54 p.
  Includes bibliographical references.

1745

Mans Puigarnau, Jaime M. Legislación, jurisprudencia y formularios sobre el matrimonio canónico; textos latino y castellano. Barcelona, Bosch, 1951–52. 3 v.

1746

Manzanedo, Eugenio. El matrimonio: compilación breve, clara y metódica del derecho matrimonial conforme a las disposiciones del Código canónico. Puebla, [México] Escuela Lino-Tip. Salesiana, 1927. 2 v. in 1; 334 p.

1747

Marbach, Joseph F. Marriage legislation for the Catholics of the Oriental rites in the United States and Canada. Washington, D.C., The Catholic University of America Press, 1946. 314 p. (The Catholic University of America. Canon law studies, no. 243)
  Bibliography: p. 275–287.

1748

Marquardt, J. J. The loss of right to accuse a marriage; a treatise on the final clause of C. 1971, § 1, 1° "nisi ipsi fuerint impedimenti causa." Romae, Officium Libri Catholici, 1951. 125 p. (Pontificium Institutum Utriusque Juris, Theses ad lauream, n. 76)
  Bibliography: p. [7]–12.

1749

Marx, Adolph. The declaration of nullity of marriages contracted outside the church. Washington, D.C., The Catholic University of America Press, 1943. 151 p. (The Catholic University of America. Canon law studies, no. 182)
  Bibliography: p. 129–134.

1750

May, George. Die kanonische Frompflicht beim Abschluss von Mischehen. Paderborn, Schöningh, 1963. 69 p.
  Bibliographical footnotes.

1751

May, George. Das neue Mischehenrecht. Werdegang und Inhalt. Trier, Zimmer (1966). 295 p. (Kreuzringbücherei, Bd. 44)
  Bibliographical references included in "Anmerkungen": p. [227]–264.

1752

May, George. Seelsorge an Mischehen in der Diözese Mainz unter Bischof Ludwig Colmar; ein Beitrag zum Kirchenrecht im Rheinland unter französischer Herrschaft. Amsterdam, Grüner, 1974. 172 p. (Kanonistische Studien und Texte, Bd. 27)
  Includes bibliographical references.

1753

Mazzacane, Elio. La justa causa dispensationis nello scioglimento del matrimonio per inconsumazione, contributo all teoria degli atti amministrativi canonici. Milano, Giuffrè, 1963. 176 p.

1754

McClory, Arthur T. The notion of impotence in canon law. Quebec, University of Laval, 1951. 419 p.

1755

McNicholas, Timothy J. The septimae manus witness; a historical synopsis and a commentary. Washington, D.C., The Catholic University of America Press, 1949. 133 p. (The Catholic University of America. Canon law studies, no. 255)
  Bibliography: p. 110–115.

1756

Medrano, Diego de. De consesv connvbiali tractatvs. Nvnc primvm in lvcem emissus, & suis indicibvs pernecessariis insignitus. Lvgdvni, Cardon, 1609. 91 p.

1757

Mellini, Mauro. Così annulla la Sacra Rota. Divorzio di classe nell'Italia clericale. Prefazione di Loris Fortuna. Roma, Samonà e Savelli, [1969]. 157 p. (Saggistica, 23)

1758

Meyer, Diedrich. Das geltende Mischehenrecht der katholischen Kirche. Berlin, Verlag des Evangelischen Bundes, 1929. 99 p. (Protestantische Studien, Heft 16)

1759

Mitterer, Max. Geschichte des ehehindernisses der entiführung im kanonischen recht seit Gratian. Paderborn, Schöningh, 1924. 128 p. (Görres-gesellschaft zur pflege der wissenschaft im katholischen Deutschland. Veröffentlichungen der Sektion für rechts- und sozialwissenschaft. 43 hft.)
"Verzeichnis der quellen und der literatur": p. [vi]–x.

1760

Molano, Eduardo. Contribución al estudio sobre la esencia del matrimonio. Pamplona, Ediciones Universidad de Navarra, 1977. 265 p. (Colección canónica de la Universidad de Navarra)
Bibliography: p. 259–265.

1761

Molins, Francisco. Tractatvs de ritv nuptiarvm, et pactis in matrimonio conuentis. Barcionone, Déu & Simon, 1617. 370 l.

1762

Monner, Basil. Tractatus duo. Prior de matrimonio: posterior de clandestinis conjugiis. Secunda editione. Ienae, Bienstial, 1603. 348 p.

1763

Montserrat Meliá, Vicente. Derecho matrimonial canónico; comentario de los cánones 1012–1143, jurisprudencia seleccionado de los tribunales de Roma hasta el año 1960. Barcelona, Editorial Litúrgica Española [ᶜ1961] 599 p.
Bibliography: p. [577]–584.

1764

Morr, Johann, and Nikolaus Markar-Markaroff.

Die Verwaltung des hl. Ehesakramentes, für die Praxis zusammengestellt. Wien, Herder, 1946. 276 p.
"Literaturverzeichnis": p. 261.

1765

Mosiek, Ulrich. Kirchliches Eherecht. Unter Berücksichtigung der nachkonziliaren Techslage. Freiburg (i. Br.) Rombach (1968) 291 p. (Rombach Hochschul Paperback)
Bibliography at the end of each chapter.

1766

Mosiek, Ulrich. Kirchliches Eherecht. Unter Berücksichtigung der nachkonziliaren Rechtslage. [2., verb. und erw. Aufl.] Freiburg, Rombach [1972] 319 p. (Rombach Hochschul Paperback, Bd. 5)
Includes bibliographies.

1767

Mosiek, Ulrich. Kirchliches Eherecht: nachkonziliare Rechtslage u. konzipierte Neufassung. 3., neubearb. u. erw. Aufl. Freiburg im Breisgau, Rombach, 1976. 365 p. (Rombach Hochschul Paperback, Bd. 5)
Includes bibliographies and index.

1768

Moy de Sons, Kraft K. E., freiherr von. Das eherecht der christen in der morgenlandischen und abendlandischen kirch bis zur zeit Karls des Grossen nach den quellen dargestellt von dr. E. v. Moy. [l. th.] Regensburg, Pustet, 1833. 398 p.

1769

Moy de Sons, Kraft K. E., freiherr von. Das Eherecht der Christen in der morgenländischen und abendländischen Kirche bis zue Zeit Karls des Grossen. Nach d. Quellen dargestellt. 1. (einziger) Teil: Geschichte des christlichen Eherechts. Neudr. d. Ausg. Regensburg, (Pustet,) 1833. Aalen, Scientia-Verl., 1970. 398 p.
Includes bibliographical references.

1770

Muscettule, Franciscus M. De sponsalibus & matrimoniiis quae a fillisfam. Contrahuntur, parentibus inseiis vel juste invitis, cum V. Cl. Alexii Symmachi Mazochii adnotationibus atque additamentis, et responsum proveritate V. Cl. P. Virginii Valsechii. Juxta exemplar Romae impressum anno 1766. Bruxellis, Flon, 1771. 448 p.

1771

Müssener, Hermann. Das katholische eherecht in der seelsorgepraxis. 2. neubearb. und verm. aufl. Mit den eherechtlichen sonderbestimmungen aller diözesen der Fuldaer bischofskonferenz. Düsseldorf, Schwann [1933] 385 p.

1772

Müssener, Hermann. Das katholische Eherecht in der Seelsorgepraxis. 3. neubearb. und verm. Aufl., mit den eherechtlichen Sonderbestimmungen der deutschen Diözesen. Düsseldorf, Parmos-Verlag [1950] 446 p.

1773

Nace, Arthur J. The right to accuse a marriage of invalidity. Washington, D.C., The Catholic University of America Press, 1961. 289 p. (The Catholic University of America. Canon law studies, no. 413)
Bibliography: p. 269–278.

1774

Nediani, Cesare. Il vincolo matrimoniale come impedimento dirimente, secondo il diritto canonico. Bologna, Zanichelli, 1938. 126 p.

1775

Neumann, Johannes. Mischehe und Kirchenrecht. Das kanonische Eherecht: Trennende Kluft oder Anlass zur Besinnung? Würzburg, Echter-Verlat (1967) 58 p. (Katholische Akademie in Bayern. Akademie-vorträge, Heft 10)
Bibliographical footnotes.

1776

Neves, João da S. C., Bp. Guia prático do processo preliminar civil do casamento canónico concordatário (para uso de clero) Lisboa, União Gráfica [1949] 397 p.

1777

Noonan, John T. Power to dissolve; lawyers and marriages in the courts of the Roman Curia. Cambridge, Belknap Press of Harvard University Press, 1972. 498 p.
Includes bibliographical references.

According to Noonan, the book "centers on the functioning of the courts and committees of the Roman Curia in the dissolution of marriage." Using a historical method he tries to understand the impact of the application of rules by the competent authorities on actual persons. The book presents cases to illuminate the decisional process—competent authorities making critical choices about the structure of marriage—and the theory of marriage. It analyzes how canon law can incorporate the principles of love stated in the Gospels, or how the responsible officials can betray those principles by thinking of the human being in the process as abstract reality. It offers a deep study on the role of the Roman Curia throughout the centuries in matrimonial cases.

1778

Nyiri, István. A házassági kötelék (ligamen) mint bontó akadály az új kánonjogi kódeksz szerint. Székesfehéhérvár, Debredzenyi I., 1923. 59 p.
Bibliography: p. [57]

1779

O'Brien, Joseph P. The right of the state to make disease an impediment to marriage. Washington, D.C., The Catholic University of America Press, 1952 [i.e., 1953] 150 p. (The Catholic University of America. Canon law studies, no. 73)
Bibliography: p. 137–144.

1780

O'Connell, William, Father. De intima natura assistentiae matrimonialis ad normam Can. 1094. Romae, Catholic Book Agency, 1940. 89 p.
"Bibliographia": p. 5–6.

1781

O'Dea, John C. The matrimonial impediment of nonage, an historical synopsis and commentary. Washington, D.C., The Catholic University of America Press, 1944. 126 p. (The Catholic University of America. Canon law studies, no. 205)
Bibliography: p. 107–112.

1782

O'Donnell, Cletus F. The marriage of minors, an historical synopsis and commentary. Washington, D.C., The Catholic University of America Press, 1945. 268 p. (The Catholic University of America. Canon law studies, no. 221)
Bibliography: p. 240–251.

1783

Oesterle, Gerard. Consultationes de jure matrimoniali. Romae, Officium libri catholici, 1942. 376 p.
Bibliographical footnotes.

1784
O'Keefe, Gerald M. Matrimonial dispensations, powers of bishops, priests, and confessors. Washington, D.C., The Catholic University of America Press, 1927. 232 p. (The Catholic University of America. Canon law studies, no. 45)

1785
Olszewski, Franciszek. Gloszenie zapowiedzi małżeńskich w prawie kanonicznem. Lublin, Tow. Naukowe Katolickiego Uniwersytetu Lubelskiego, 1936. 136 p. (Katolicki Uniwersytet Lubelski. Rozprawy doktorskie, magisterskie i seminaryjne. 2. Wydział Prawa Kanonicznego. Rozprawy doktorskie, t. 6)
Bibliography: p. [127]–136.

1786
O'Mara, William A. Canonical causes for matrimonial dispensations; an historical synopsis and commentary. Washington, D.C., The Catholic University of America Press, 1935. 155 p. (The Catholic University of America. Canon law studies, no. 96)
Bibliography: p. 141–144.

1787
Pandini, Romualdo. Le cause matrimoniali nel diritto canonico. Come ottenere la nullità e lo scioglimento del matrimonio. Il Motu proprio di Paolo VI, sveltimento dell procedure, riduzione dei costi, estensione della competenza, costituzione dei tribunali, appelli, casi speciali ed eccezionali, comparazione con la legislazione italiana, giurisprudenza ecclesiastica e civile. Roma, DETS, 1973. 335 p. (Collana giuridica)

1788
Pansini, Giovanni. Note al matrimonio. Bari, Macrì, [1942] 66 p.
Includes bibliographical references.

1789
Petrovits, Joseph J. C. The new church law on matrimony. Philadelphia, McVey, 1919. 465 p. (Universitas catholica Americae, Washington, D.C. S. facultas theologica, 1918–1919, no. 6)
Bibliography: p. 453–458.

1790
Pile, (L'Abbé). Dissertation sur l'indissolubilité absolue du lien conjugal ou l'on prouve que tout mariage légitimement contracté . . . est indissoluble de sa nature. Paris, Le Clerc, 1788. 2 v.

1791
Plöchl, Willibald M. Das eherecht des magisters Gratianus. Leipzig und Wien, Deuticke, 1935. 113 p. (Wiener staats- und rechtswissenschaftliche studien, bd. 24)
"Verzeichnis der hauptsächlich verwendeten literatur": p. [7]–[10]

1792
Pospishil, Victor J. Motu proprio "Crebrae allatae" . . . [in Russian] . . . 1951. 23 p.
Includes bibliography.

1793
Die Rechtliche Ordnung der Mischehen. Die Bestimmungen vom Codex iuris canonici (1917) bis Matrimonia mixta (1970). Lateinisch-deutsch. Von d. dt. Bischöfen approb. Übers. Geschichtl. Aufriss u. Kommentar v. Johannes Günter Gerhartz. Trier, Paulinus-Verl., 1971. 157 p. (Nachkonziliare Dokumentation, Bd. 28)
Bibliography: p. 66–73.

1794
Reed, John J. Presumptions in theory and matrimonial practice. Woodstock, Md., Woodstock College, 1949. 58 p.
Bibliography: p. 55–58.

1795
Regatillo, Eduardo F. Derecho matrimonial eclesiástico. Santander, Sal Terrae, 1962. 459 p. (Biblioteca Comillensis)
Bibliography: p. [9]–10.

1796
Reina, Víctor de. Error y dolo en el matrimonio canónico. Pamplona, Universidad de Navarra, 1967. 307 p. (Colección canonica de la Universidad de Navarra)

1797
Reiner, János. Az egyházi házasságkötési jog tanának kifejlődése. Budapest, Stephaneum Nyomda, 1908. 204 p.
"Székfoglaló értekezésként olvasta a Szent-István-Társulat Tudományos-, és Irodalmi Osztályának 1907. deczember 12-én tartott ülésében."

1798

Rice, Patrick W. Proof of death in pre-nuptial investigation. Washington, D.C., The Catholic University Press, 1940. (The Catholic University of America. Canon law studies, no. 123)

1799

Rimlinger, Herbert T. Error invalidating matrimonial consent; an historical synopsis and commentary. Washington, D.C., The Catholic University of America Press, 1932. 84 p. (The Catholic University of America. Canon law studies, no. 82)
Bibliography: p. 67–71.

1800

Risk, James E. Marriage-contract and sacrament; a manual of the laws of the Catholic Church on marriage for the use of American lawyers. Chicago, Callaghan [1957] 187 p.

1801

Roberts, James B. The banns of marriage; an historical synopsis and commentary. Washington, D.C., The Catholic University of America Press, 1931. 140 p. (The Catholic University of America. Canon law studies, no. 64)
Bibliography: p. 124–128.

1802

Roberts, Rufus P. Matrimonial legislation in Latin and Oriental canon law: a comparative study. Westminster, Md., Newman Press, 1961. 110 p.
Bibliographical references included in "Notes" (p. 99–110).

1803

Rocca, Fernando della. Derecho matrimonial canónico: cuadros sinópticos. 1. ed. Madrid, Ediciones y Publicaciones Españolas, 1967 [c1966] 468 p. (Colección Sinopsis)
Includes bibliographical references.

1804

Rokahr, Ernst-Günter. Ehe ohne Treue?: die ehel. Treupflicht in d. Rechtsprechung d. Röm. Rota. München, Tuduv Verlagsgesellschaft, 1976. 134 p.
Bibliography: p. iv–x.

1805

Rosambert, André. La veuve en droit canonique jusqu'au XIVᵉ siècle. Paris, Dalloz, 1923. 249 p.
"Bibliographie": xviii p.

1806

Rüegg, Johann. Das Bestreitungsrecht der Ehe im kanonischen Recht. St. Gallen, 1948. 152 p.
Bibliography: p. [ix]–xiv.

1807

Sánchez, Tomás. Dispvtationvm de sancto matrimonii sacramento, tomi tres. Editio haec postrema superiorum auctoritate correcta; in qua, praeter vitam auctoris, locorum, quò faciliùs inueniantur, citationes charactere distinctae sunt. Antverpiae, Hasrey, 1614. 3 v. in 2.

1808

Sánchez, Tomás. Dispvtationvm de s. to matrimonii sacramento. Libri decem in tres tomos distribvti. Cvm triplici indice dispvtationvm: iure pontificio, & caesareo: & rerum omnium refertissimo. Venetiis, Guerilium, 1619. 551 p.

1809

Sánchez, Tomás. Disputationum de Sto. matrimonii Sacramento. Libri decem in tres tomos distributi. Cum triplici indice disputationum. Brixiae, Turlinum, 1624. 3 v.

1810

Sangmeister, Joseph V. Force and fear as precluding matrimonial consent; an historical synopsis and commentary. Washington, D.C., The Catholic University of America, 1932. 214 p. (The Catholic University of America. Canon law studies, no. 80)
Bibliography: p. 197–201.

1811

Šaruga, Matthias. De notione et de dissolutione necnon de fine matrimonii in ecclesia Orientali Serbica. Torino, Società editrice internazionale, 1939. 138 p.
Bibliography: p. [1]–13.

1812

Scharnagl, Anton. Katholisches eherecht, mit berücksichtigung des in Deutschland, Oesterreich und der Schweiz geltenden staatlichen eherechts. München, Kösel & Pustet [1935] 239 p.
"Quellen und literatur des katholischen eherechts": p. [11]–15.

1813

Schenk, Francis J. The matrimonial impediments

of mixed religion and disparity of cult. Washington, D.C., The Catholic University of America, 1929. 318 p. (The Catholic University of America. Canon law studies, no. 51)

Bibliography: p. [292]–306.

1814
Scheurl, Adolf, freiherr von. Die entwicklung des kirchlichen eheschliessungsrechts. Erlangen, Deichert, 1877. 177 p.

1815
Schiappoli, Domenico. Il matrimonio secondo il diritto canonico e la legislazione concordataria italiana. Napoli, Alvano, 1932. 323, [1] p.

1816
Schmalzgrueber, Franz. Sponsalia et matrimonium, seu Decretalium Gregorij IX. pont. max. liber IV. Ingolstadii, de la Haye, bibliopolae Academici; typis Grass, 1715. 930 p.

1817
Schnitzer, Joseph. Katholisches Eherecht; mit Berücksichtigung der im Deutschen Reich, in Oesterreich, der Schweiz und im Gebiete des Code civil geltenden staatlichen Bestimmungen. 5., vollständig neu bearb. Aufl. des Werkes: J. Weber, Die canonischen Ehehindernisse. Freiburg im Breisgau, Herder, 1898. 681 p.

Bibliographical footnotes.

1818
Schuh, Karlheinz. Neuordnung des Mischehen. Die kirchl. Regelungen u. Beitr. z. Praxis. Essen-Werden, Fredebneul u. Koenen, 1970. 98 p.

1819
Schwarz, Hans, Referendar. Ehebruch und Bigamie nach kanonischem Recht bis zum Erlass des Codex. [Zindorf, Bollmann, 1928] 72 p.

Bibliography: p. 4–5.

1820
Scott, Leonard G. A comparative study of the ecclesiastical tribunals of the United States and the Sacred Roman Rota in recent years (matrimonial cases). Rome, Pontificia Università lateranense, 1968. 245 p.

Bibliography: p. [233]–239.

1821
Sdralek, Maximilian. Hinkmars von Rheims kanonistisches Gutachten über die Ehescheidung des Königs Lothar II; ein Beitrag zur Kirchen-, Staats- und Rechts-Geschichte des IX. Jahrhunderts. Freiburg im Breisgau, Herder, 1881. 199 p.

1822
Sehling, Emil. Die unterscheidung der verlöbnisse im kanonischen recht. Leipzig, Veit & comp., 1887. 184 p.

1823
Semana de Derecho Canónico. Las causas matrimoniales; trabajos de la cuarta Semana de Derecho Canónico celebrada en el Monasterio de N.ª S.ª de Montserrat. Salamanca, 1953. 570 p.

1824
Semana de Derecho Canónico. El consentimiento matrimonial, hoy: trabajos de la XV Semana de Derecho Canónico. Barcelona, Banchs, 1976. 352 p.

Includes bibliographical references.

1825
Serrier, G. De quelques recherches concernant le mariage contrat-sacrement et plus particulièrement de la doctrine augustinienne des biens du mariage. Paris, de Boccard, 1928. 256 p.

1826
Sheed, Francis J. Nullity of marriage. New ed., rev. and enl. New York, Sheed and Ward [1959] 132 p.

1827
Siegle, Bernard A. Marriage today; a commentary of the Code of canon law. Staten Island, N. Y., Alba House [1966] 294 p.

Bibliography: p. [287]–290.

1828
Siegle, Bernard A. Marriage today; a commentary on the Code of canon law in the light of Vatican II and the ecumenical age. 2d. ed. Staten Island, N. Y., Alba House [1973] 347 p.

Bibliography: p. [339]–342.

1829
Sierra Nava, Luis. La reacción del episcopado

español ante los decretos de matrimonios del ministro urquijo de 1799 a 1813. Prólogo del Excmo. Sr. D. José F. de Lequerica. Bilbao, Ediciones Estudios de Deusto, 1964. 297 p.

1830

Silvino da Nadro, Father. De impedimento cognationis legalis. Milano, Centro Studi Cappuccini Lombardi, 1957. 128 p. (Centro studi cappuccini lombardi. [Pubblicazioni] 2)
   Bibliography: p. 7–13.

1831

La Simulazione nel matrimonio. Roma, Bulzoni, 1977. 63 p. (Quaderni romani di diritto canonico, anno 1)

1832

Singer, Mario. Die gemischten ehen, nach dem rechte der katholischen kirche. Aarau, Sauerländer & Co., 1927. 111, [1] p.
   "Angabe der häufiger zitierten literatur": p. [110]–111.

1833

Sipos, István. A katolikus házasságjog rendszere a Codex juris canonici szerint. 3. bőv. kiad. Pées, Haladás Nyomdarészvénytársaság, 1940. 422 p.

1834

Smet, Aloïs de. Les fiançailles et le mariage; traité canonique et théologique avec aperçus historiques et juridico-civils. Traduction française faite sur la 2. éd. latine, rev. et cor. Bruges, Beyaert, 1912. 712 p.
   "Bibliographie": p. [xix]–xxxi.

1835

Smet, Aloïs de. De sponsalibus & matrimonio; tractatus canonicus & theologicus. Brugis, Beyaert, 1909. 563 p.
   "Index bibliographicus": p. [xix]–xxvii.

1836

Smith, Charles E. Papal enforcement of some medieval marriage laws. University, La., Louisiana State University Press, 1940. 230 p.

1837

Soarez, Rodrigo, Juan López, and Diego Segura.

Tractatvs de bonis constante matrimonio acqvisitis, trivm clarissimorvm ivrisconsvltorvm hispanorvm. Adiecimus eiusdem D. Segurae Repetitiones tres, (quas versa indicat pagina) eandem materiam luculenter complectentes. Accesserunt . . . summaria & index copiosus. Coloniae Agrippinae, apud Ioannem Gymnicum, sub monocerote, 1590. 1000 p.

1838

Spada, Pietro. Casi matrimoniali. Milano, Istituto La Casa, 1973. 145 p. (Collana del ginepro)

1839

Staffa, Dino. De conditione contra matrimonii substantiam. Romae, Apud custodiam librariam Pont. Instituti Utriusque Iuris, 1952. 49 p.
   Bibliographical footnotes.

1840

Stalder, Johann. ABC des kirchlichen Eherechtes. Luzern, Rex-Verlag [1951] 31 p.

1841

Stapf, Franz. Vollständiger Pastoralunterricht über die Ehe; oder, über das gesetzund pflichtmässige Verhalten des Pfarrers vor—bei und nach der ehelichen Trauung nach den Grundsätzen des katholischen Kirchenrechts mit steter Rücksicht auf Civilgesetze. Neu hrsg. und bedeutund verm. von Carl Egger. Mit gnädisgster Genehmigung des Hochwürdigsten Generalvikariats des Bisthums. 6. verm. Aufl. Frankfurt am Main, Verlag der Wesché'schen Verlags-Buchhandlung, 1838. 439 p.

1842

Stolze, Ignatius. Quaenam fuit ratio cur ecclesia matrimonium quod ingennuus homo cum ancilla (vice versa) liberam eam putans contraxerat, nullum esse dixerit? Dissertatio inauguralis. Bonnae, König [1859] 32 p.

1843

Stutz, Ulrich. Zum neusten Stand des katholischen Mischehenrechts im Deutschen Reiche. Stuttgart, Enke, 1918. 20 p.

1844

Sullivan, Bernard O. Legislation and requirements for permissible cohabitation in invalid marriages; an historical synopsis and a commentary. Wash-

ington, D.C., The Catholic University of America Press, 1954. 186 p. (The Catholic University of America. Canon law studies, no. 356)
Bibliography: p. 174–179.

1845

Timlin, Batholomew T. Conditional matrimonial consent, an historical synopsis and commentary. Washington, D.C., The Catholic University of America Press, 1934. 381 p. (The Catholic University of America. Canon law studies, no. 89)
Bibliography: p. 361–367.

1846

Tobin, William J. Homosexuality and marriage; a canonical evaluation of the relationship of homosexuality to the validity of marriage in the light of recent Rotal jurisprudence. Rome, Catholic Book Agency [1964] 378 p.
Bibliography: p. [309]–330.

1847

Torre, Joannes, ed. Processus matrimonialis. Neapoli, M. d'Auria, 1947. 374 p.
"Bibliographia": verso of 4th leaf.
[Catholic Church. Congregatio de Disciplina Sacramentorum. Instructio Servanda a Tribunalibus Dioecesanis in Pertractandis Causis de Nullitate Matrimoniorum.]

1848

Torre, Joannes, ed. Processus matrimonialis. Editio 3. revisa et aucta recentissima jurisprudentia Rotali. Neapoli, M. d'Auria, 1956. 755 p.
Includes bibliography.
[Catholic Church. Congregatio de Disciplina Sacramentorum. Instructio Servanda a Tribunalibus Dioecesanis in Pertractandis Causis de Nullitate Matrimoniorum.]

1849

Torrubiano Ripoll, Jaime. Jurisprudencia matrimonial. Madrid [Imp. Castilla] 1932. 1 v.
"Todos los casos, los centenares de casos auténticos de matrimonios declarados nulos por la Sede apostólica."

1850

Triebs, Franz. Praktisches Handbuch des geltenden kanonischen Eherechts in Vergleichung mit dem deutschen staatlichen Eherecht für Theologen und Juristen. Breslau, Ostdeutsche Verlagsanstalt, 1927. v.
"Quellen- und Literatur-Nachweis" at end of v. 1–3.

1851

Triebs, Franz. Praktisches handbuch des geltenden kanonischen eherechts in vergleichung mit dem deutschen staatlichen eherecht für theologen und juristen. t. I–IV in einem band (gesamtausgabe) Breslau, Ostdeutsche verlagsanstalt, 1933. 769, [5] p.
Contains bibliographies.

1852

Ursaya, Dominicus. De matrimonii mullitate ex defectu consensus contrahentis, & moralis praesentiae parochi. Dissertatio theologico-legalis. Romae, Buagni & Monaldi, 1696. 143, 39 p.

1853

Van Ommeren, William M. Mental illness affecting matrimonial consent. Washington, D.C., The Catholic University of America Press, 1961 [i.e., 1962] 243 p. (The Catholic University of America. Canon law studies, no. 415)
Bibliography: p. 227–237.

1854

Van Vliet, A. H., and C. G. Breed. Marriage and canon law; a concise and complete account. London, Burns & Oates [1964] 308 p.
Bibliographical footnotes.

1855

Villar, Andrés. La prueba documental pública en las causas matrimoniales. Pamplona, Ediciones Universidad de Navarra, 1977. 249 p. (Colección canónica)
Bibliography: p. 245–249.

1856

Vincenti, Angelo. Impotenza e sterilità in rapporto alla validità del matrimonio nel diritto canonico & civile. Firenze, Cya, 1953. 116 p.
Bibliographical footnotes.

1857

Vlaming. T. M. Praelectiones iuris matrimonii ad normam Codicis iuris canonici quas ter edidit T.

M. Vlaming quarto edidit L. Bender. Bussum, Brand, 1950. 574 p.

Bibliographical footnotes.

1858

Wahl, Francis X. The matrimonial impediments of consanguinity and affinity; an historical synopsis and commentary. Washington, D.C., The Catholic University of America Press, 1934. 125 p. (The Catholic University of America. Canon law studies, no. 90)

Bibliography: p. [107]–113.

1859

Waltermann, Reinhold. Mischehe; Handreichungen zur Praxis. Dokumente, Dispensen, Formulare. Essen, Ludgerus Verlag [ᶜ1970] 127 p.

1860

Wanenmacher, Francis. Canonical evidence in marriage cases, being a revised and augmented writing of what was originally a dissertation entitled The evidence in ecclesiastical procedure affecting the marriage bond. [Philadelphia, 1935] 412 p. (The Catholic University of America. Canon law studies, no. 9)

Bibliography included in introduction.

1861

Weber, J. Die kanonischen Ehehindernisse nach dem geltenden gemeinen Kirchenrechte. Für en Kuratklerus praktische dargestellt. Freiburg im Breisgau, Herder, 1872. 459 p.

1862

Weber, J. Die kanonischn Ehehindernisse nach dem geltenden gemeinen Kirchenrechte. Für den Kuratklerus praktisch dargestellt. 2., mit der Ehescheidungslehre verm. Ausg. Freiburg im Breisgau, Herder, 1875. 460 p.

1863

Weber, J. Die kanonischen ehehindernisse sammt ehescheidung und eheprozess, mit berücksichtigung der staatlichen ehehindernisse in Deutschland, Oesterreich und der Schweiz. Ein vollständiges praktisches eherecht für den kuratklerus in Deutschland, Oesterreich und der Schweiz. 4., verb. und verm. aufl. Freiburg im Breisgau, Herder, 1886. 733 p.

Contains bibliographies.

1864

Weber, J. Katechismus des katholischen Eherechts. Zunächst für Studierende der Theologie und des Rechts. 3. verb. Aufl. Augsburg, Schmid, 1887. 240 p.

1865

Welie, Frans A. M. van. Canoniek huwelijksrecht. Nijmegen, Dekker & Van de Vegt, 1954. 448 p.

Bibliographical footnotes.

1866

Wenner, Joseph. Kirchliche Eheprozessordnung; Instruktionen nebst einschlägigen Vorshriften über das Verfahren in Ehenichtigkeits- und Inkonsummationssachen sowie bei Todesnachweis, Ehetrennung und Ehezulaussung. Mit Verweisungen und Sachverzeichnis. 2., verm. Aufl. Paderborn, Schöningh, 1950 [ᶜ1939] 288 p.

1867

Wenner, Joseph. Kirchliche Eheprozessordnung; Instrucktionen nebst einschlägigen Vorschriften über das Verfahren in Ehenichtigkeits- und Inkonsummationssachen sowie bei Todesnachweis, Ehetrennung und Ehezulassung. Mit Verweisungen und Sachverzeichnis. 3. erweiterte Aufl. Paderborn, Schöningh, 1956. 312 p.

1868

West, Morris L., and Robert Francis. Scandal in the assembly: a bill of complaints and proposal for reform in the matrimonial laws and tribunals of the Roman Catholic Church. New York, Morrow, 1970. 182 p.

1869

Whalen, Donald. The value of testimonial evidence in matrimonial procedure; an historical synopsis and commentary. Washington, D.C., The Catholic University of America Press, 1935. 297 p. (The Catholic University of America. Canon law studies, no. 99)

Bibliography: p. 269–279.

1870

White, Robert J. Canonical ante-nuptial promises and the civil law; an historical synopsis and commentary. Washington, D.C., The Catholic University of America, 1934. 152 p. (The Catholic University of America. Canon law studies, no. 91)

Bibliography: p. 141–144.

1871

Woeber, Edward M. The interpellations. Washington, D.C., The Catholic University of America Press, 1942. 161 p. (The Catholic University of America. Canon law studies, no. 172)
Bibliography: p. 143–147.

1872

Wrzaszczak, Chester F. The betrothal contract in the Code of canon law (canon 1017) Washington, D.C., The Catholic University of America Press, 1954. 253 p. (The Catholic University of America. Canon law studies, no. 326)
Bibliography: p. 237–245.

1873

Zapp, Hartmut. Die Geisteskrankheit in der Ehekonsenslehre Thomas Sanchez'. Köln, Böhlau Verlag, 1971. 157 p. (Forschungen zur kirchlichen Rechtsgeschichte und zum Kirchenrecht, Bd. 11)
Bibliography: p. [142]–151.

1874

Zeidler, Melchior. Tractatus de polygamia. Helmestadi, Hamm, 1690. 216, [12] p.

1875

Zetta, Celestino. Il matrimonio contratto naturale, sacramentale, giuridico secondo il nuovo Codice di diritto canonico. Trattatello teorico-pratico ad uso del giovane clero e del sacerdoti in cura d'anime. Torino, Marietti, 1920. 226 p.

1876

Zhishman, Joseph, ritter von. Das eherecht der Orientalischen kirch. Wien, Braumüller, 1864. 826 p.

DIVORCE

1877

Abate, Antonino. Lo scioglimento del vincolo coniugale nella giurisprudenza ecclesiastica. 2. ed. Roma, Desclée, 1965. 182 p.
Bibliography: p. 173–178.

1878

Abate, Antonino. Lo scioglimento del vincolo coniugale nella giurisprudenza ecclesiastica. 3. ed. Napoli, d'Auria, 1970. 173 p.
Bibliography: p. 165–171.

1879

Abate, Antonino. Lo scioglimento del vincolo coniugale nella giurisprudenza ecclesiastica. 4. ed. Napoli, d'Auria, 1972. 248 p.
Bibliography: p. 239–246.

1880

Angelis, Carlo N. de. La natura del vincolo matrimoniale e il privilegio paolino, con note processuali; dissertazione canonica. Napoli, Jovene, 1941. 131 p.
"Bibliografia": p. [xi]–xii.

1881

Beaudoin, Lucien. La dissolution du lien matrimonial en droit canonique et en droit civil canadien. Ottawa, 1948 [i.e., 1949] 359 p. (Universitas Catholica Ottaviensis. Series canonica, 15)
Bibliography: p. [319]–331.

1882

Bézae V., Théodore. Tractatio de repudiis et divortiis: in qua pleraeque de causis matrimonialibus. Genevae, Crispinum, 1569. 376 p.

1883

Bressan, Luigi. Il canone tridentino sul divorzio per adulterio e l'interpretazione degli autori. Roma, Università Gregoriana, 1973. 366 p. (Analecta Gregoriana, v. 194. Series Facultatis Iuris Canonici, Sectio B., n. 33)
Bibliography: p. [xiii]–xxvii.

The argument surrounding divorce has stirred the interest of the public. Religious books and magazines discuss the issue from pastoral, human, and theological perspectives. Despite this fervor of research, exploration, and new outlook, it is apparent that Catholics themselves are not very sure about the traditional position. This colloquy can bear fruit, however, if it adheres to the revealed truth, to explore and represent it to today's world. It is in the spirit of such research that the author studies the extensive problem of divorce, i.e., the doctrinal meaning and interpretation of canon seven of the twenty-fourth session of the Ecumenical Council of Trent, from 1563 to the present. It is not his intention to present a practical method to solve the ecumenical problem of a divorced person, but rather to offer elements of thought about the issue.

1884

Civisca, Luigi M. The dissolution of the marriage bond. Naples, d'Auria, Publisher to the Apostolic See, 1965. 158 p.

Bibliography: p. [8]–13.

1885

Delpini, Francesco. Divorzio e separazione dei coniugi nel diritto romano e nella dottrina della Chiesa fino al secolo V. Torino, Marietti, 1956. 138 p. (Scrinium theologicum; contributi di scienze religiose, 5)

Bibliography: p. 13–16.

This short but very interesting study takes a historical look at divorce and separation of the spouses in Roman Law and the teaching of the Church until the end of the fifth century. It presents the concept of marriage, the structure of the family in pagan society, and a collection of texts of the councils and the Fathers concerning the indissolubility of marriage. It is the intention of the author to determine if there was a discrepancy between practice and doctrine concerning divorce in the first few centuries of the Church's life in the pagan world. The final section focuses on the influence of ecclesiastical legislation on Roman Law.

1886

Dominici, Gildo. La dissoluzione del matrimonio di due non battezzati: studio storico-dottrinale sulla base di alcuni documenti inediti del secolo XVI. Roma, Pontificia Università Lateranense, 1971. 227 p.

Bibliography: p. 16–23.

1887

Dordett, Alexander. Kirchliche Ehegerichte in der Krise. Wien, Wiener Dom-Verl., 1971. 153 p. (WDV Report)

Includes bibliographical references.

1888

Flatten, Heinrich. Das Ärgernis der kirchlichen Eheprozesse. (Antrittsvorlesung) Paderborn, Schöningh, 1965. 35 p.

Bibliographical footnotes.

1889

Gregory, Donald J. The Pauline privilege; an historical synopsis and commentary. Washington, D.C., The Catholic University of America Press, 1931. 165 p. (The Catholic University of America. Canon law studies, no. 68)

Bibliography: p. 141–150.

The author studies the doctrine according to which a legitimate marriage between two nonbaptized parties (infidels), although consummate, can be dissolved in favor of faith by the Pauline privilege. The work starts with the general premise of the indissolubility of the matrimonial bond after the law of Moses, the marriage of Christians (or marriage as sacrament), and that of infidels. There are questions of whether the Church can dissolve a true marriage when one member of the infidel union converts to the Christian religion, and can this party enter a new marriage. Gregory analyzes the foundation of the Pauline privilege in the Holy Scriptures, presents a historical resumé of the subject and the legislation in the Code, and concludes with a practical appendix.

1890

Hopfenbeck, Albert. Privilegium Petrinum: e. rechtssprachl u. rechtsbergriffl. Unters. St. Ottilien, EOS Verlag, 1976. 205 p. (Münchener theologische Studien: 3, Kanonistische Abteilung; Bd. 35) (Münchener Universitäts-Schriften. Fachbereich Katholische Theologie)

Bibliography: p. xi–xxvi.

1891

Isaza Serna, Rodrigo. Efectos de la separación eclesiástica con relación a la patria potestad. Bogotá, Prensa Católica, 1969. 92 p.

Bibliography: p. 91–92.

1892

Kearney, Francis P. The principles of canon 1127. Washington, D.C., The Catholic University of America, 1942. 162 p. (The Catholic University of America. Canon law studies, no. 163)

Bibliography: p. [139]–144.

1893

Oddone, Andrea. Discutiamo sul divorzio. Milano, Vita e pensiero, 1947. 179 p.

"Bibliografia": p. [173]–174.

1894

Pfab, Josef. Aufhebung der ehelichen Lebensgemeinschaft, nach göttlichem, kirchlichem und bürgerlichem Recht. Salzburg, Müller [1957] 235 p. (Reihe Wort und Antwort, Bd. 17)

1895

Ugarte Pagés, José M. Manual de formularios referentes a las distintas causas de divorcio de que trata el Codex juris canonici. Madrid, Reus, 1930. 434, [2] p. (Manuales Reus de derecho, v. L)

1896

Vinyolas y Torres, Pablo. El divorcio canónico por causa del adulterio, según el "Codex iuris canonici," la legislación eclesiástica anterior a este, los clásicos, y las decisiones o sentencias de la Rota romana. Barcelona, Bosch, 1930. 338 p.

1897

Werkmeister, Benedict M. L. von. Bemerkungen über herrn Jägers Untersuchung: Ob die ehescheidung nach lehre der Schrift und der kirche ältesten geschichte erlaubt sey oder nicht? Vom dem verfasser des Beweiser, dass die den protestanten übliche ehescheidungen vom band, auch nach katholischen grundsältzen gültig sind. Würzburg und Bamberg, Göbhardt, 1805. 85 p.

Parish

1898

Fitzgerald, William F. The parish census and the liber status animarum; a historical synopsis and a commentary. Washington, D.C., The Catholic University of America Press, 1954. 111 p. (The Catholic University of America. Canon law studies, no. 339)
   Bibliography: p. 98–104.

1899

Mundy, Thomas M. The union of parishes; an historical synopsis and commentary. Washington, D.C., The Catholic University of America Press, 1945. 164 p. (The Catholic University of America. Canon law studies, no. 204)
   Bibliography: p. 145–149.

1900

Nassalski, Marjan. Formularium legale practicum in parochorum, vicariorum foraneorum nec non

curiarum episcopalium usum compositum cui binae documentarum appendices accedunt. Ed. 2., aucta et emendata. Wladislaviae [Druk H. Neumana w Włoclawku] 1905. 560, 214 p.
   "Conspectus operum in hoc libro adhibitorum": verso of 4th prelim. leaf.

1901

O'Rourke, James J. Parish registers, an historical synopsis and commentary. Washington, D.C., The Catholic University of America, 1934. 109 p. (The Catholic University of America. Canon law studies, no. 88)
   Bibliography: p. 93–95.

Cemeteries, Burial Law

1902

Bernard, Antoine. La sépulture en droit canonique du décret de Gratien au Concile de Trente. Paris, Domat-Montchrestien, 1933. 219 p.
   "Bibliographie": p. [201]–215.

1903

Friedberg, Emil. Die juristische facultät der universität Leipzig verkündigt die feier des andenkens an Dr. Bernh. Friedr. Rud. Lauhn ... Das kirchliche bestattungsrecht und die reichsgewerbeordnung. Leipzig, Edelmann [1887] 41 p.

1904

Hale, Joseph F. The pastor of burial; a historical synopsis and a commentary. Washington, D.C., The Catholic University of America Press, 1949. 247 p. (The Catholic University of America. Canon law studies, no. 234.)
   Bibliography: p. 218–223.

1905

Marantonio Sguerzo, Elsa. Evoluzione storico-giuridica dell'istituto della sepoltura ecclesiastica. Milano, Giuffrè, 1976. 345 p. (Pubblicazione dell'Istituto di studi storico-politici, Facoltà di scienze politiche, Università de Genova; 4)
   Includes bibliographical references and index.

1906

Petit, Gédéon. La part paroissiale ou quarte

funéraire. Québec, Faculté de droit canonique, Université Laval, 1946. 218 p. (Les thèses canoniques de Laval. Thèse no. 5)

Bibliography: p. [xiv]–xx.

1907

Petrakakos, Dom. A. Die Toten im Recht nach der Lehre und den Normen des orthodoxen morgenländischen Kirchenrecht und der Gesetzgebung Griechenlands. Leipzig, Deichert (Böhme), 1905. 248 p.

1908

Power, Cornelius M. The blessing of cemeteries; an historical synopsis and commentary. Washington, D.C., The Catholic University of America Press, 1943. 231 p. (The Catholic University of America. Canon law studies, no. 185)

Bibliography: p. 203–210.

PROCEDURAL LAW

1909

Adams, Donald E. The truth required in the preces for rescripts; a historical synopsis and a commentary. Washington, D.C., The Catholic University of America Press, 1960. 275 p. (p. 275 advertisement) (The Catholic University of America. Canon law studies, no. 392)

Bibliography: p. 245–250.

1910

Alberti da Pesaro, Innocentio. Ragionamenti intorno alla giustitia di N. S. Papa Sisto Qvinto. Vrbino, Ragusi, 1587. 83 p.

1911

Alciati, Andrea. Le lettere di Andrea Alciato, giureconsulto [a cura di] Gian Luigi Barni. Firenze, Le Monnier, 1953. 310 p.

Bibliographical footnotes. Bibliography: p. [297]–298.

1912

Angelus de Clavasio. Tractatio de restitutionibus venerabilis servi Dei Beati Angeli Carletti a Clavasio Pedemontani. Nunc primo in lucem edita, congruisque notis illustrata studio et labore . . . Honorii Marentini. Romae, Junchi, 1771–72. 2 v.

1913

Antonelli, Giovanni C. Tractatus posthumus de juribus, & oneribus clericorum in duos libros distributus in quibus utriusque juris controversiae difficiliores, & in foro frequentiores singulariter tractantur. Opus judicibus tàm ecclesiasticis, quàm saecularibus advocatis . . . maximè necessarium: Cui accedunt quamplurima recentissima decreta Sacrae congregationis concilii bullae regnantis s. d. n. Innocentii XII ac Decisiones Sacrae rotae romanae nullibi adhuc impressae. Cum duplici indice scilicet. Tractatus, & decisionum locupletissimo. Romae, Aloysii & Comitibus, 1699. 203, 165 p.

1914

Apollonius, Willem. Jus maiestratis circa sacra, sive Tractatus theologicus, de jure magistratus circa res ecclesiasticas, oppositus cl. d. professoris Nicolai Vedelii tractatui, De episcopatu Constantini Magni, ex authoritate, & jussu classis vvalachrianae adornatus. Medioburgi Zelandorum, Fierensium, 1642–43. 2 v. in 1.

1915

Aradillas Agudo, Antonio. Proceso a los tribunales eclesiásticos. 2. ed. Madrid, Sedmay, 1975. 265 p.

The author wanted this book to be an echo of pain and frustration: the pain of the spouses who failed in their quest for happiness; the pain of their families who became participants in the drama; and the pain of the children who will suffer interminably because of the inability of their parents to live together and by the inconsiderate attitude of the Church which has at hand the possible solution to the problem. The book is an accusation of the Church, but presented with love and respect. It offers theologico-canonico-philosophical grounds for an urgent restructuring of the administration of justice in the Church. It also contains lists of cases showing the failure of ecclesiastical justice; a brief explanation of the operation, composition, structure, and persons that constitute the courts; and an example of a court reform or *Reforma Tarancón*.

1916

Arcenegui y Carmona, Isidro de. Aportaciones del derecho canónico a la ciencia jurídica; conferencia pronunciada en la Facultad de Derecho y Ciencias Sociales de la Universidad de Buenos Aires, en agosto de 1949. Madrid, 1950. 44 p.

1917

Arias Gómez, Juan. El consensus communitatis en la eficacia normativa de la costumbre. Pamplona, Universidad de Navarra, 1966. 153 p. (Colección canónica de la Universidad de Navarra)
Bibliography: p. 151–153.

1918

Ayrer, Jacob, fl. Historischer Processus juris. In welchem sich Lucifer vber Jesum darumb dass er die Hellen zerstöhret eingenommen die Gefangene daraus erlöst vnd hingegen ihn Lucifern gefangen vnd gebunden habe, auff das allerhefftigste beklaget ... Sampt einem angeheckten Teutschen vnd Lateinischen vollkommenen Register. Franckfurt am Mayn, durch Wolffgang Richtern, in Verlegung M. Leonhardi Burcken, 1618. 742, [68] p.

1919

Ballerini, Pietro. De potestate ecclesiastica summorum pontificum et conciliorum generalium liber una cum vindiciis auctoritatis pontificiae contra opus Justini Febronii auctore Petro Ballerinio. Accedit appendix de infallibilitate eorumdem pontificum in definitionibus fidei. Veronae, Moroni, 1768. 306 p.

1920

Beaumont, Christophe de, Abp. of Paris. Instrucción pastoràl ... sobre los atentados hechos à la authoridad de la Iglesia por los decretos de los tribunales seculares en la causa de los Jesuitas. [1764?] 1 v. (unpaged)

1921

Bene, Tommaso del. De officio s. inqvisitionis circa haeresim. Cum bullis, tam veteribus, quàm recentioribus, ad eandem materiam, seu ad idem officium spectantibus. Pars prior [- posterior] Synopsi materiarvm, et indice rervm notabilium in hoc vulumine contentarum illustrata. Nvnc primvm in Ivcem prodit. Lvgdvni, Hvgvetam, 1666. 2 v.

1922

Bene, Tommaso del. De immvnitate et ivrisdictione

ecclesiastica, opvs absolvtissimvm, in dvas partes distribvtvm. Editio tertia prioribvs longe castigatior. Cvi accessere bvllae pontificiae, declarationes, & decreta. Summo studio, parique fide, partim à p. Fr. Angelo Lantvsca, partim ab eruditissimo viro d. Iacobo Pignatello ad annum vsque 1673. cum eorum indice collecta, recognita & in meliorem formam digesta. Lvgdvni, Arnavd & Borda, 1674. 2 v.

1923

Bernardis, Lazzaro M. de. Il processo; corso di diritto canonico tenuto all'Università di Genova, nell'anno accademico 1954–1955. [n. p.] Libreria Athena [1955?] 173 p.

1924

Bernini, Domenico. Il Tribunale Della S. Rota Romana Descritta Da Domenico Bernino, E dal medesimo dedicato Alla Santtita Din. S. Clemente XI. Roma, Bernabo, 1717. 18, 331, 17 p.

1925

Bissi, Bernardo. Decas ad moralem scientiam miscellaneos tractatus continens sivè selecta pro conscientiae casibus in sacro poenitentiali foro passim occurrentibus. Cum duplici indice. Genvae, Franchelli, 1693. 640 p.

1926

Bondini, Giuseppe. Del tribunale della sagra Rota romana, memorie storiche colle rispettive bolle de'pontefici, ridotte in compendio col metodo del guerra e volgarizzate. Roma, Fratelli Pallotta, 1854. 178 p.

1927

Bottoms, Archibald M. The discretionary authority of the ecclesiastical judge in matrimonial trials of the first instance. Washington, D.C., The Catholic University of America Press, 1955. 266 p. (The Catholic University of America. Canon law studies, no. 349)
Bibliography: p. 228–234.

1928

Böcken, Placidus. Tractatus de judiciis et processu judiciario ad Librum II. Decretalium Gregorii IX. Salisburgi, Mayr, 1726. 271 p.

1929

Böcken, Placidus, and Edmundo Reindl. Tractatus

de judiciis et processu judiciario ad librum II. Decretalium Gregorii IX. In alma archi-episcopali Universitate salisburgensi. Salisburgi, Mayr, 1723. 271, [19] p.

1930

Brand, Morton F., and Verner M. Ingram. The pastor's legal adviser. New York, Nashville, Abingdon-Cokesbury Press [1942] 237 p.

1931

Brandileone, Francesco. I lasciti per l'anima e la loro transformazione; saggio di ricerche storico-giuridiche. Venezia, Ferrari, 1911. 83 p.

1932

Braschi, Matteo. De pleno arbitrio humanae voluntatis in ultimis dispositionibus bonorum temporalium condendis, mutandis, & retractandis. Ubi dè testamentis, & haeredibus . . . plenè agitur, & accuratè disseritur. Accedit ad finem velitatio theologico-legalis Dè pace in scriptis danda offensori ab offenso: An & in quibus terminis obliget. Nùnc primùm editus, auctus, & in meliorem formam dispositus per illvstrissimvm, et reverendissimvm dominum D. Ioannem Baptistam Braschivm. Romae, Corbelletti, 1722. 490 p.

"Decisiones Sacrae rotae romanae, selectae, ac recentissimae": p. 299–452.

1933

Brunet, Jean Louis. Le parfait notaire apostolique et procureur des officialités, contenant les regles et les formules de toute sorte d'actes ecclésiastiques. 2. ed. revue, corrigée, & considérablement augm. Lyon, Duplain, 1775. 2 v.

1934

Bruno, Giuseppe A. Introduzione alla giurisprudenza canonica. [Torino] Nella Stamperia Reale di Torino, 1769. 314 p.

1935

Burke, Thomas J. Competence in ecclesiastical tribunals. [Washington, D.C.] 1922. 117 p.

Bibliography: p. 104–109.

1936

Calabuig Revert, J. José. Procedimientos judiciales eclesiásticos según las normas generales del Codex juris canonici y las particulares de algunos tribunales especiales. Madrid, Suarez, 1923. 2 v.

1937

Calcagnini, Carlos L., cardinal. De variatione ultimae voluntatis, Trebellianica, variisque, etiam ad feudalem materiam observationibus. Opus in tres tomos distributum, cum argumentis, summariis, & locupletissimo indice ad calcem cujusque voluminis. Romae, Mainardi, 1745–47. 3 v.

1938

Calderinus, Joannes. Tractatvs novvs avrevs et solemnis de haereticis. In qvo omnia qvae ad officivm inquisitorum contra haereticam prauitatem spectant ita ordinate, svbtiliter, et magistraliter in quadragintauno capitibus tractantur. Cvi adiecta est nova forma procedendi contra de haeresi inquisitos, praxim totam exactissime complectens. Cum summarijs, & indicibus. Venetiis, ad candentis salamandrae insigns, 1571.

1939

Calhoun, John C. The restraint of the exercise of one's rights. Washington, D.C., The Catholic University of America Press, 1965. 146 p. (The Catholic University of America. Canon law studies, no. 432)

Bibliography: p. 135–142.

1940

Carriere, Jos. Praelectiones theologicae majores in seminario sanctisulpitii habitae. De justitia et jure opera et studio. Parisiis, Méquignon Junior, 1839. 3 v.

1941

Carriere, Jos. Praelectiones theologicae majores in seminario sancti-sulpitii habitae. De contractibus opera et studio. Parisiis, Méquignon Junior and Leroux, 1844–1847. 3 v.

1942

Caspers, Paul. Der Güte- und Schiedsgedanke im kirchlichen Zivilgerichts-verfahren; eine kirchenrechtliche Untersuchung über das Wesen der episcopalis audientia. Düsseldorf, Triltsch-Verlag, 1954. 71 p.

Bibliography: p. v–x.

1943

Cassadorus, Gulielmus. Decisiones avreae . . . collectae, quotidianas materias tum maximè beneficiales, & praxim, ac stilum Curiae romanae concernentes. Non deest alphabeticus index, studiosis non minus necessarius, quàm vtilis. Parisiis, vaenalis est à Ponceto le Preux, 1545.

1944

Castracane, Francesco. Tractatvs de societatibvs, qvae fivnt svper officiis Romanae Cvriae. Nunc denuo in lucem editus per Iacobum Mascardum. Romae, Mascardi, 1609. 209, [46] p.

1945

Casus conscientiae. Curante P. Palazzini. Romae, Officium Libri Catholici, Catholic Book Agency, 1956. 5 v.

1946

Catholic Church. Codex juris canonici Orientalis. De judiciis. Code oriental de procédure ecclésiastique. Traduction annotée par F. Galtier. Lettre-préf. de Joseph Beltrami. Beyrouth, 1951. 581 p. (Université St. Joseph de Beyrouth. Faculté de théologie. Droit canonique oriental, 2)

Bibliography: p. [xxi]

1947

Cavazzana, Giuseppe. La giurisdizione straordinaria nel Codice di diritto canonico. [Milano, Gualdoni, 1942] 139, [1] p.

1948

Cerasi, Francesco. Album biografico di Roma. Avvocati della romana curia. Biografia dell'avvocato Cerasi Francesco. Roma, Pallotta, 1876. v. 1–6, 10–12.

1949

Clementi, Johannes. Le presunzioni come mezzo di prova secondo la pratica della S. R. Rota. Locarno, 1955. 88 p.

"Bibliografia e fonti": p. [7]–[8].

1950

Comes, José. Viridarium artis notariatus, sive Tabellionum viretum ... a Josepho Comes in duos divisum tomos. Gervndae, Oliva, 1704–06. 2 v.

1951

Connolly, Thomas A. Appeals, an historical synopsis and commentary. Washington, D.C., The Catholic University of America Press, 1932. 212 p. (The Catholic University of America. Canon law studies, no. 79)

"A theoretical and practical survey of the general legislation on appeals as contained in the Code of canon law."

Bibliography: p. 195–199.

1952

Connors, Charles P. Extra-judicial procurators in the Code of canon law. Washington, D.C., The Catholic University of America Press, 1944. 94 p. (The Catholic University of America. Canon law studies, no. 192)

Bibliography: p. 76–81.

1953

Cornopaeus, Nicolaus. Tractatus de norma iudicii in dirimendis controversiis religionis. VVittebergae, Lehman, 1603. 64 1.

1954

Corrado, Pirro. Praxis beneficiariae recentioribvs constitutionibus apostolicis, rotalibus decisionibus. Dubiorum quoque in dies occurrentium resolutionibus fimatae, Cancellariae apostolicae notabilibus perornatae, formulisque beneficialibus, pro ipsius praxis germana, tutaque intellegentia, locupletatae; recentiorique stylo datariae in resignationibus beneficiorum, necnon annuarum pensionum, ac fructuum reservatione, quinto libro, iuxta mentem auctoris morte praeuenti superaddito, nec aliàs impresso, vtillimè illustatae, accuratè veteri indici, nouo inserto, iuxtà ordinem materiarum. Venetiis, Balleonium, 1671. 400 p.

1955

Corradus, Pyrrhus. Praxis dispensationum apostolicarum, ex solidissimo romanae Curiae stylo, inconoussè servato, excerpta ... Tertia editio ab ipsomet auctore additionibus, partim suis in locis, partim in fine operis, adiectis, locupletata. Venetiis. Milochum, 1669. 448 p.

1956

Coyle, Paul R. Judicial exceptions; canonical commentary with historical synopsis and notes. Washington, D.C., The Catholic University of America Press, 1944, 142 p. (The Catholic University of America. Canon law studies, no. 193)

Bibliography: p. 119–123.

1957

Davis, John D. The moral obligations of Catholic

civil judges. Washington, D.C., The Catholic University of America Press, 1953. 237 p. (The Catholic University of America. Studies in sacred theology, 2d. ser., no. 78)

Bibliography: p. 205–216.

1958

Delbene, Thomas. Tractatvs de ivramento in qvo de eivs et voti relaxationibvs, irritationibus, commutationibus & dispensationibus necnon de mendacio, periourio, adiuratione, caterisque ad ipsa pertinentibus eruditissime tractatur. Cvi decisiones Sacrae Rotae Romanae ad hanc materiam spectantes accedunt. Lvgdvni, Hvgvetan & Barbier, 1669. 682 p.

1959

Diego Lora, Carmelo de. Estudios de derecho procesal canónico. [Pamplona, EUNSA, 1973] 2 v. (Colección canónica de la Universidad de Navarra)

Includes bibliographical references.

The author studies themes related to the exercise of the *potestas judicialis* and to matrimonial cases. The two-volume work starts with an analysis of the extent of civil and ecclesiastical jurisdictions in the Spanish Concordat of 1953; jurisdiction and its *extra-territorium* exercise; procedural nullity; and judicial control of the Church's central government, with emphasis on the teaching of the Second Vatican Council, and the subsequent responsibility of the Church. Part two of the study is devoted to the evaluation of documentary evidence and judicial confession in the proceedings of matrimonial nullity; reform of canonical matrimonial procedure, which studies the competence of the courts of the first instance, the new constitution of tribunals, and the firmness and enforceability of the declarative judgment of nullity of marriage. The work concludes with a very useful section devoted to pastoral function and the separation of spouses.

1960

Diego Lora, Carmelo de. Poder jurisdiccional y función de justicia en la Iglesia. Pamplona, Universidad de Navarra, 1976. 184 p. (Colección canónica de la Universidad de Navarra)

Includes bibliographical references and index.

The author searches for the specific judicial function of the Church's main offices within the broad jurisdictional power of the institution. After studying the unity and diversity of the legal powers, the book discusses the problem of administrative justice, and the system of administrative justice compatible with the unity of power in the Church; the peculiarity of administrative justice in the face of administrative activity; and the confrontation of interested parties, a permanent characteristic of the exercise of the judicial function.

1961

Donato, Michelangelo. De asylia sev De immvnitate locali resolvtiones forenses in quibus dubia omnia, quae per ciuilistas, canonistas, summistas, & theologios hac de re, nedum fuse, verùm etiam incidenter mota, aut controuersa sunt; iuxta Sacrae congregationis oracula, Rotae romanae decisiones, practicorumque obseruatam sententiam, facili methodo explanantur, resoluuntur. Cum trimplici, indice materiarum, argumentorum, ac rerum omnium notabilium. Romae, Manelphij, 1652. 251 p.

1962

Downs, John E. The concept of clerical immunity. Washington, D.C., The Catholic University of America Press, 1941. 163 p. (The Catholic University of America. Canon law studies, no. 126)

Bibliography: p. [133]–140.

1963

Droste, Franz. Canonical procedure in disciplinary and criminal cases of clerics. A systematic commentary on the "Instructio S. c. epp. et reg., 1880." Ed. by the Rev. Sebastian G. Messmer. New York, Cincinnati, Benzinger, 1887. 268 p.

1964

Ducasse, François. La pratique de la juridiction ecclesiastique, volontaire, gratieuse et contentieuse, fondée sur la droit commun. Nouvelle edition. Toulouse, Boude, 1705. 292, 260 p.

1965

Du Moulin, Charles. Tractatus de evictionibus Casparis Caballini. Secunda editio. Venetiis, Ziletti, 1573. 344 p.

1966

Dunnivan, John P. Prejudicial attempts in pending litigation; a historical synopsis and a commentary. Washington, D.C., The Catholic University of

America Press, 1960. 169 p. (The Catholic University of America. Canon law studies, no. 379)
Bibliography: p. 155–160.

1967

Eichmann, Eduard. El derecho procesal según el Código de derecho canónico; versión al castellano con adiciones complementarias de derecho español por Nicolás S. de Otto . . . y Ambrosio Sanz Lavilla. Barcelona, Bosch, 1931. 380 p.
"Literatura canónica procesal (fuentes bibliográficas)": p. 12–17.

1968

Eisenhofer, Heinrich. Die kirchlichen Gesetzgeber, Technik und Form ihrer Gesetzgebung. München, Zink, 1954. 111 p.
"Quellen [und] Literatur": p. vi–viii.

1969

Endemann, Wilhelm, Civilprozessverfahren nach der kanonistischen Lehre. Berlin, Heymann, 1890. 150 p.
"Sonderabdruck aus der Zeitschrift für deutschen civilprozess."

1970

Farinacci, Prospero. Repertorivm de vltimis volvntatibvs, cvm fragmentis. Prodit nvnc primvm ex manuscripto Bibliothecae clericorum regularium s. Sylvestri. Opera Zachariae Pasqvaligi. Adiectae svnt plvres recentissimae decisiones Rotae romanae, quae ad materiam concernunt. Lvgdvni, Boissat & Anisson, 1644. 164, [26] p., 29, [2] p., 312, [59] p.
"Decisiones Rotae romanae": 312, [51] p., at end.

1971

Feeney, Thomas J. Restitutio in integrum, an historical synopsis and commentary. Washington, D.C., The Catholic University of America Press, 1941. 169 p. (The Catholic University of America. Canon law studies, no. 129)
Bibliography: p. [149]–156.

1972

Fernández, Hugo. De confessionis judicialis momento in jure civili et in jure canonico, deque illius vi in causis nullitatem matrimonii spectantibus. Romae, 1955. 56 p.

1973

Finkelthaus, Sigismund. Tractatus de jure patronatus ecclesiastico, in quo materia juris patronatus ecclesiastici methodicè & succinctè declaratur . . . ut hodiè ecclesiarum Angustanae confessionis usui, & praxi in foro Electoratus Saxioniae commodè inservire possit. Lipsiae, Schürer & Götzii, 1639. 366, [68] p.

1974

Frichignono, Niccolo di Quaregna. Della politica, e regolata podesta giuridizionale della Chiesa. Torino, Nella Reale Stamparia, 1783. 2 v.

1975

Giacchi, Orio. Formazione e sviluppo della dottrina della interpretazione autentica in diritto canonico. Milano, "Vita e pensiero", 1935. 72 p. (Pubblicazioni della Università cattolica del Sacro cuore. Ser. 2: Scienze giuridiche, v. 44)

1976

Gismondi, Pietro. La prescrizione estintiva nel diritto canonico. Roma, Edizioni universitarie, 1940. 173 p. (Monografie dell'Istituto di diritto pubblico della Facoltà di giurisprudenza dell'Università di Roma, 2)
Bibliographical footnotes.

1977

Glynn, John C. The promotor of justice his rights and duties. Washington, D.C., The Catholic University of America Press, 1936. 337 p.

1978

Gómez, Bayo. Praxis ecclesiastica, et secvlaris. Valliscleti, Murillo, 1640. 578, [57] p.

1979

Guazzini, Sebastiano. Sebastiani Gvazzini Tractatvs ad defensam inqvisitorvm, carceratorvm, reorvm & condemnatorum super quocumque crimine. [Liber primvs] tomo dvo. Ed. novissima. Lvgdvni, Apud Valançol, typographum, 1672. 2 v. in 1.
No more published.

1980

Guilfoyle, Merlin J. Custom, an historical synopsis and commentary. Washington, D.C., The Catholic University of America Press, 1937. 151 p. (The

Catholic University of America. Canon law studies, no. 105)

Bibliography: p. 139–141.

1981

Hackett, John H. The concept of public order. Washington, D.C., The Catholic University of America Press, 1959. 101 p. (The Catholic University of America. Canon law studies, no. 399)

Bibliography: p. 92–96.

1982

Hageneder, Othmar. Die geistliche Gerichsbarkeit in Ober- und Niederösterreich; von den Anfängen bis zum Beginn des 15. Jahrhunderts. Graz, Wien, Köln, Böhlau in Komm, 1967. 344 p. (Forschungen zur Geschichte Oberösterreichs, 10)

Bibliography: p. [302]–304.

1983

Hannan, Jerome D. The canon law of wills; an historical synopsis and commentary. Washington, D.C. The Catholic University of America, 1934. 517 p. (The Catholic University of America. Canon law studies, no. 86)

1984

Haring, Johann B. Der kirchliche strafprozess; eine praktische anleitung für kirchliche richter. Graz, Moser, 1931. 76 p.

"Literatur": p. viii.

1985

Heiner, Franz X. Der kirchliche zivilprozess, nach geltendem rechte praktisch dargestellt. Köln, Bachem, 1910. 144 p.

1986

Helle, Heinrich. Das kirchliche vermögen von der ältesten zeit bis auf Constantin den Grossen, Inaugural-dissertation, August, 1875. Paderborn, Schöningh, 1876. 58 p.

1987

Herrmann, Horst. Ecclesia supplet. Das Rechtsinstitut der kirchlichen Suppletion nach c. 209 CIC. Amsterdam, Grüner, 1968. 363 p. (Kanonistische Studien und Texte, Bd. 24)

Bibliography: p. xvii–xii.

1988

Hickey, James A. De judice synodali ac pro-synodali. Romae, Apud custodium librariam Pont. Instituto Utriusque Juris, 1951. 141 p. (Pontificium Institutum Utriusque Juris. Theses ad lauream, n. 78)

Bibliography: p. 135–141.

1989

Hofmann, Karl, Die freiwillige gerichsbarkeit (iurisdictio voluntaria) im kanonischen recht. Paderborn, Schönigh, 1929. 98 p. (Görres-gesellschaft zur pflege der wissenschaft im katholischen Deutschland. Veröffentlichungen der Sektion für rechts und staatswissenschaft, 53 hft.)

1990

Hollweck, Joseph. Das testament des geistlichen nach kirchlichem und bürgerlichem recht. Mainz, Kirchheim, 1901. 123 p.

1991

Hottinger, Johann Jacob. Ecclesiasricum in saecularem dissertationem. Lucernae, Wyssing, 1721. 294, [4] p.

1992

Huber, Ulricus. De foederibus testamentis. Dissertationes juridico theologicae VII, accedit, de Praetorio quod Paulus commemorat I Phil. 13. Franequerae, Amama & Taedama, 1688. 152, 110 p.

1993

Jullien de Pommerol, André. Juges et avocats des tribunaux de l'Église. Rome, Officium libri catholici, 1970. 567 p. (Studia et documenta juris canonici, l)

Includes bibliographical references.

Intended as an introduction to legal canonical practice, with special reference to the responsibility and formation of judges and attorneys, this book comprises many addresses by the author, dean of the Rota, to young people who participate in special exercises to become acquainted with legal practice. It deals with legal procedure in the Church; the responsibilities in legal matters of the bishop, ecclesiastical judge, and attorney; the priestly condition required to become a judge in an ecclesiastical court; spiritual formation and its influence on the priest-judge; and the canonical formation required for the exercise of the judicial functions. A third part is devoted to useful advice.

1994

Kaps, Johannes. Das Testamentsrecht der Weltgeistlichen und Ordenspersonen in Rechtsgeschichte, Kirchenrecht und bürgerlichem Recht Deutschlands, Österrichs und der Schweiz. Buchenhain vor München, Verlag Christ Unterwegs, 1958. 304 p.
Includes bibliography.

1995

Kérészy, Zoltán. A ius exclusivae (vétójog) a pápaválasztásnál. Budapest, Politzer, Zs., 1904. 119 p.

1996

Khoury, Joseph. La jurisprudence de la Sacrée rote romaine dans les causes des églises orientales. Romae, Officium libri catholici, 1972. 2 v.
Bibliography: v. 1, p. [199]–207.

1997

Kiene, Johann. Die haftung des erben aus den delikten des erblassers nach kanonischem recht. Inaugural-dissertation. Friedrichshafen, Lincke, [1878] 1 p. 1., 33 p., 8°.

1998

Kirchliches Prozessrecht: Sammlung neuer Erlasse; lat.-dt., eingel. von Heribert Schmitz. Trier, Paulinus-Verlag, 1976. 143 p. (Nachkonziliare Dokumentation; Bd. 39)

1999

Krtiszka, Joseph. Dissertatio inauguralis juris publici ecclesiastici de origins juris appellandi ad Sedem Romanam. Pragae, Hraba, 1776. 100, 10 p.

2000

Kubic, Stanislaus J. Invalidity of dispensations according to canon 84, § 1; a historical synopsis and a commentary. Washington, D.C., The Catholic University of America Press, 1953 [i.e., 1954] 108 p. (The Catholic University of America. Canon law studies, no. 340)
Bibliography: p. 97–101.

2001

Lazzarato, Damiano. Iurisprudeentia pontificia. [Romae] Typis Polyglottis Vaticanis [1956]–63. 2 v. in 4.

2002

Lefebvre, Charles. Les pouvoirs du juge en droit canonique; contribution historique et doctrinale à l'étude du canon 20 sur la méthode et les sources en droit positif. Paris, Librairie du Recueil Sirey, 1938. 339 p.
"Bibliographie": p. [309]–322.

2003

Lega, Michele, Cardinal. Praelectiones in textum iuris canonici de iudiciis ecclesiasticis in scholis Pont. Sem. Rom. habitae. Romae, Typis Vaticanis, 1896–1901. 4 v.

2004

Lemieux, Delisle A. The sentence in ecclesiastical procedure, an historical synopsis and commentary. Washington, D.C., The Catholic University of America Press, 1934. 131 p. (The Catholic University of America. Canon law studies, no. 87)
Bibliography: p. 115–118

2005

Leo, Friedrich J. Erklärung des cap. 12 in VI^{to} de appellationibus 2.15 Ein beitrag zur entwickelungsgeschichte des canonischen civilprocesses. Königsber i. Pr., Hartungsche, 1899. 61 p.

2006

Leone, Giovanni, F., Bp. Thesavrvs fori ecclesiastici. Episcopis, ac eorvm vicariis omnibusq₃; iudicibus ecclesiaticis etiam in foro poenitentiali versantibus perutitilis, & necessarius. Multis nuper additionibus, opera Octauij Leonis, ipsius auctoris ex fratre nepotis locupletatus. Cum singularum materiarum indice locupletissimo. Romae, Ruffinelli & Facciotti, 1616. 488, [75] p.

2007

Lickleder, Helmut. Der Streitgegenstand im kanonischen Zivilprozessrecht. [Erlangen, 1961?] 111, [5] p.
Bibliography: p. [116]

2008
Linenberger, Herbert. The false denunciation of an innocent confessor; a commentary with historical notes on the manner of making judicial denunciations. Washington, D.C., The Catholic University of America Press, 1949. 205 p. (The Catholic University of America. Canon law studies, no. 236)
Bibliography: p. 182–189

2009
Llano Cifuentes, Rafael. Naturaleza jurídica de la "fictio iuris." Madrid, Ediciones Rialp, 1963. 196, [3] p. (Colección canónica del Estudio General de Navarra, 5)
Bibliographical footnotes.

2010
Lo Castro, Gaetano. La qualificazione giuridica delle deliberazioni conciliari nelle fonti del diritto canonico. Milano, Giuffrè, 1970. 306 p. (Seminario giuridico della Università di Bologna. [Pubblicazioni] 54)
Includes bibliographical references.

2011
Lohmuller, Martin N. The promulgation of law. Washington, D.C., The Catholic University of America Press, 1947. 139 p. (The Catholic University of America. Canon law studies, no. 241)
Bibliography: p. 117–122.

2012
Lombardo, Luigi. Il concetto di buona fede nel diritto canonico (contributo storico dogmatico) [Roma] Libreria dell'Università di Roma, 1944. 335 p. (R. Università di Roma. Monografie dell'Istituto di diritto pubblico della Facoltà di giurisprudenza, 1)

2013
Lombardo, Luigi S. Il principio nullum crimen sine proevia lege poenali nel diritto penale canonico e la norma del can. 2222, sec. 1 del C. I. C. Estratto dagli Annali del Seminario Giuridico dell'Università di Catania, I (1947). Napoli, Jovene, 1947. 40 p.

2014
López, Fratre Ludovico. Tractatus de contractibus et negotiationibus duobus contenti libris. Brixiae, apud societatem Brixienfem, 1596. 2 v. in 1.

2015
Luca, Giovanni B. de, cardinal. Theatrvm veritatis, et ivstitiae, sive Decisivi discvrsvs, ad veritatem editi in forensibus controuersijs canonicis, & ciuilibvs, in quibus, in Vrbe aduacatus, pro vna partium scripsit, vel consultus repondit Io. Baptista de Lvca. Romae, Corbelletti, 1669–78. 16 v. in 19.

This treatise contains different topics discussed in ecclesistical and civil courts by the author in his capacity as attorney and consultant. The work covers eighteen books dealing with feoffment, obligations towards the princes or the republic; jurisdiction and competent forum; usufruct and leasing of land; usury and interest with dowry; donations, sale and acquisitions, contracts; loans; and wills and heirs. It also discusses trusts, successions; ecclesiastical benefices, in general and specifically as they affect canons, dignitaries, pastors and parishes; and patronage and ecclesiastical pensions. Book fourteen is divided into five parts and studies the condition and situation of monks and religious persons; marriage, betrothal and divorce; alms and contributions; ecclesiastical immunity; and practical annotations on the Council of Trent, in matters related to reformation and forensics: Book fifteen is devoted to trials, the role of the Roman Curia in legal matters, and to legal propositions which seem to be in conflict with reason. Book sixteen offers a general index of the *Theatrum*. The last two books deal with documents related to the College of the Apostolic Secretaries, and commentaries on a constitution by Innocence XI.

2016
Luca, Giovanni B. de, cardinal. Commentaria ad Constitutionem sanctae mem. Innocentii XI. de statutariis successionibus; cum particulis statutorum, & legum excludentium foeminas propter masculos, tam intra statum ecclesiasticum quàm extra illum. Accedit De pensionibus ecclesiasticis ad ornatum constitutionis ejusdem pontificis, de illis ultra medietatem non transferendis; cum variis indultis transferendi ac retinendi ecclesiasticas pensiones. Venetiis, Balleoniana, 1726. 223 p.

2017
Luca, Giovanni B. de, cardinal. Estilo legal. Obra escrita en italiano por el eminentísimo cardenal Juan Bautista de Luca. Traducida al castellano por el licenciado en sagrados canones, y opositor a las

cathedras de la Universidad de Huesa, Diego Perez Mozún. Madrid, Martinez Abad, 1784–91. 4 v.

2018

Lupi, Ignazio. De casibvs et censvris reservatis ... tractatus absolutissimus. In hac 3. editione, iuxta constitutiones apostolic recenter emanatas, mvltis alijs additionibvs svpra secundam ... locupletatus a Martino Antonio Gverrino. Bergomi, Ruberorum, 1725. 296 (i.e., 696) p.

2019

Lynch, Timothy. Contracts between bishops and religious congregations; a historical synopsis and a commentary. Washington, D.C., The Catholic University of America Press, 1946 [i.e., 1947] 232 p. (The Catholic University of America. Canon law studies, no. 239)
  Bibliography: p. 203–212.

2020

Maffei, Francesco, marchese. Dell'impiego del danaro. 2. ed. accresciuta d'una lettera enciclica di Sua Santità e d'altura lettera dell'autore alla medesima Santità Sua. Roma, Bernabò & Lazzarini, 1746. 3 v. in 1.

2021

Mainz (Archdiocese). Laws, statutes, etc. Untergerichts ordnung des ertzstiffts Meyntz inn welcher gantz fleissig angezeygt wie vnd welcher gestalt an allen vnd jeden obgemelts ertzstiffts auch andern vndergerichten in recht gehandelt vnd procedirt werden soll vnd mag schultheyssen schöffen richtern vnd andern so an gerichten zühandeln haben vast dienlich vnnd behülfflich jetzt newlich gemeynem nutz zü güt gemacht geordent vnnd auffgericht. [Meyntz] 1535. 27 1.

2022

Mancini, Vincent. Di ivramento eiusque vi, & effectu, tractatvs amplissimvs, in quo sanè omnia quae ad contractus, & iudicia, tàm in foro contentioso, quàm conscientiae occurrere solent, quam exactissimè discutiuntur. Cum duplici indice. Venetiis, Zenari, 1601. 548 p.

2023

Mantica, Francesco, cardinal. Tractatvs de coniectvris vltimarvm volvntatvm in libros dvodecim distinctvs. Postrema editio, infinitis quibus passim scatebat, mendis repurgata. Cum indice rerum & materiarum insignium locupletissimo. Lugduni, Tinghi, Beraud, et Michaël, 1585.

2024

Mantica, Francesco. Vaticanae lucubrationes de tacitis et ambiguis conventionibus. In libros XXVII dispertitae, Editio postrema, magno studio a mendis. Benevae, Cramer, Perachon et Cramer Filii, 1723. 2 v.

2025

Marchetti, Aemilius. De regimine solutionum debitorum mutato valore pecuniae. Romae, Pontificium Athenaeum Antonianum, 1958. 144 p. (Studia Antoniana, 11)

2026

Marchius, Ewaldus, fl. Nucleus tractatus practici de ivre et ivstitia theologis omnibvs, canonistis, ivrisperitis, animarum curam gerentibus, negotia forensia tractantiibus, omnibusque tam ecclesiasticis, quam saecularibus, pro conscientiae suae regimine utilissimus, totam materiam circa obligationem restitutionis, quoad forum internum & externum, brevitate ac delucide continens, ex cortice ervtvs. Coloniae Agrippinae, Friessem, 1658.

2027

Mariani, Goffredo. La legislazione ecclesiastica in materia d'arte sacra. Roma, Ferrari [1945] 269 p. (Pontificia comissione centrale per l'arte sacra. [Pubblicazioni] 8)
  "Bibliografia": p. [261]–265.

2028

Martin, Thomas O. Adverse possession, prescription and limitation of actions. The Canonical "Praescriptio". A commentary on Canon 1508. Washington, D.C., 1944. 208 p. (The Catholic University of America. Canon law studies, no. 202)

2029

Martino da Fano, fl. Trattati "De positionibus" attribuiti a Martino da Fano, in un codice sconosciuto dell'Archiginasio di Bologna (B2794, 2795) a cura di Ugo Nicolini. Milano, "Vita e pensiero", 1935. 3–86 p. (Orbis romanus, biblioteca di testi medievali a cura dell'Università cattolica del Sacro cuore, v [i.e., iv])

2030

Massa, Antonio. Tractatus ad formulam cameralis obligationis. Genae, Lippold, 1608. 457 p.

2031

Mazzacane, Elio. La litis contestatio nel processo civile canonico. Napoli, Jovene, 1954. 262 p. (Pubblicazioni dell Facoltà giuridica dell'Università di Napoli, 15)

2032

McManus, Martin J. Presentation of evidence in canon law and American trials; a comparative study, excerpt. Rome, Catholic Book Agency, 1965. 70 p.
  Bibliography: p. [67]–68.

2033

Medina López, Gabriel. Sistema probatorio canónico y notas concordantes con el derecho positivo colombiano. Bogotá, Iris, 1968. 174 p.
  Bibliography: p. 163–166.

2034

Melichar, Erwin. Gerichtsbarkeit und Verwaltung im staatlichen und kanonischen Recht. Wien, Manz, 1948. 134 p.
  "Literaturverseichnis": p. [131]–134.

2035

Mier Vélez, Angel de. La bueno fe en la prescripción y en la costumbre hasta el siglo XV. [Pamplona, Universidad de Navarra, 1968] 234 p. (Colección canónica de la Universidad de Navarra. Cuadernos, 10)
  Bibliography: p. 231–234.

2036

Molano, Eduardo. La autonomía privada en el ordenamiento canónico; criterios para su delimitación material y formal. Pamplona [Universidad de Navarra] 1974. 316 p. (Colección canónica)
  Bibliography: p. [299]–316.

2037

Moreno Hernández, Miguel. Derecho procesal canónico. Prólogo de Eloy Montero. Madrid, Aguilar, 1956. 591 p.
  Includes bibliographies.

2038

Moreno Hernández, Miguel. Derecho procesal canónico. 2. ed. actualizada. Barcelona, Bosch, c1975. 3 v.
  Includes bibliographies and indexes.

By nature, the Church is a legally perfect society, and therefore endowed with judicial power to enact laws and adopt provisions. This statement is supported by the practice of the Church since its beginnings, i.e., complainants, witnesses, judges, subpoenas, verdicts, and trials in the court of law (*fuero externo*), completely different from the acts of confession (*fuero penitencial*). Through time, the jurisdiction of the ecclesiastical court was greatly reduced; despite this, the Church did establish a magnificent procedural law, formed with elements of German and Roman laws, special statutes of the Church, and traditional and customary provisions. In 1306, Clement V introduced summary procedure for some specific causes. The Council of Trent brought essential transformation into canonical procedure. The Roman Rota gained much prestige based upon its jurisprudence in the eighteenth century; Próspero Lambertini, a great canonist and pope (Benedict XIV), introduced important innovations in canonical procedure concerning marriage and religious profession. Pius X profoundly reformed the Roman Curia; and the code followed in 1917; since then some procedural laws have been published. The author studies, in three volumes (devoted to proceedings, appendixes to proceedings, and jurisprudence), the institutions of canonical procedural law, and analyzes the works by canonists and experts in civil procedure. He also studies the legal nature of canonical procedure and its external form. It can be said, in brief, that this is a complete and vauluable treatise on canonical procedure. Each chapter is preceded by a summary and abundant bibliography. The work ends with excellent indexes of authors, subjects, and legislations.

2039

Moriarty, Eugene J. Oaths in ecclesiastical courts, an historical synopsis and commentary. Washington, D.C., The Catholic University of America Press, 1937. 115 p. (The Catholic University of America. Canon law studies, no. 110)
  Bibliography: p. 101–103.

2040

Mostazo, Franciscus a. Tractatus de causis piis in genere et in specie. Lugduni, Anisson, 1717. 2 v. in 1.

2041

Motivum juris, de jure asyli, ejusque judice competente summarium. n. p., 1700, 98 p.

2042

Motzenbächer, Rudolf. Die Rechtsvermutung im kanonischen Recht. München, Kommissionsverlag K. Zink, 1958. 507 p. (Münchener theologische Studien. 3. Kanonistische Abt., 10 Bd.)
Bibliography: p. xxii–[xxxiv]

2043

Navarro Viola, Miguel. Patronato, recursos de fuerza y escomuniones su historia y derecho estudiados en la causa sobre destitución del benemérito cura rector de San Cristóbal, Don Juan de Dios Arenas. Buenos Aires, Biedma, 1887, 306 p.

2044

Noone, John J. Nullity in judicial acts; a historical conspectus and a commentary. Washington, D.C., The Catholic University of America Press, 1950. 147 p. (The Catholic University of America. Canon law studies, no. 297)
Bibliography: p. 123–138.

2045

Oldrado da Ponte. Consilia, seu Responsa, & quaestiones aureac, in qvibvs ea qvae ad qvotidianvm vsvm in forensibvs negotijs, & controversiis spectant, subtilissimè & exactissimè perstringuntur. Cum expunctionibus, castigationibus et nouis aditionibus acutissimi iureconsulti Domini Rainaldi Corsi, Cum summarijs, & indice. Venetiis, Zilettum, 1571. 167 1.

2046

Oliva e Sousa, Feliciano de. Tractatus de foro ecclesiae, principaliter materiam utriusque potestatis spiritualis, scilicet & temporalis respiciens. In quo utriusque fori ecclesiastici & secularis, plures quaestiones, quae quotidie incidunt in praxim, disputantur ac resolutionem accipiunt. Cum indicibus quaestionum, summariorum & materiarum locupletissimis. Coloniae Allobrogum, Chouet, Tournes, Cramer, Perachon, Ritter, & Tournes, 1705. 3 v. in 1.

2047

Opipari, Caesar. La capacità processuale delle persone morali. Roma, Pontificia Università Lateranense, 1973. 49 p.
Bibliography: p. xiii–xix.

2048

Paolucci, Marco A. Dissertationes legales complectentes materias utriusque juris in foro judicatas ad normam recentissimarum S. R. R. decisionum, liber primus [-secundus] recollectus per Thomam Torellum. Cum indicibus locupletissimis. Venetiis, Pezzana, 1626. 2 v.

2049

Pastor, Ludwig, Freiherr von. Allgemeine Dekrete der römischen Inquisition aus den Jahren 1555–1597. Nach dem Notariatsprotokoll des S. Ufficio zum ersten Male veröffentlicht von Ludwig von Pastor. Freibur im Breisgau, St. Louis, Mo., 1912. 71 p.

2050

Pavloff, George C. Papal judge delegates at the time of the Corpus iuris canonici. Washington, D.C., The Catholic University of America Press, 1963. 59 p. (The Catholic University of America. Canon law studies, no. 426)
Bibliography: p. 54–56.

2051

Pawluk, Tadeusz. Kanoniczna praktyka procesowa w sprawach małżeńskich. Warszawa, Akademia Teologii Katolickiej, 1975. 219 p.

2052

Pellegrini, Carlo, bp. Praxis vicariorvm, et omnium in vtroque foro iusdicentium qvatvor partibvs comprehensa: in prima continentur omnia, quae ad vicariorum quorumcumque potestatem, atque officium pertinent. In secunda traditur praxis procedendi in causis ciuilibus. In tertia methodus in gradu appellationis. In quarta vero habetur exactissima practica criminalis. Cum obseruationibus vtriusque iuris; imo & municipalis neapolitani necnon formulis singulorum actorum iudicialium. Omnia fere conplectens, quae per pontificias, ac caesareas leges, conciliorum decreta, sacrarum congregationum declarationes, ac Sacre Rotae decisiones ad haec sancita fuerunt. Cum triplici indice copiosissimo. Venetijs, Groppum, 1969. 474 p.

2053

Pellegrini, Carlo, Bp. Praxis vicariorvm, et omnium in vtroque foro iusdicentium qvatvor partibvs comprehensa . . . Cum obseruationibus vtriusque iuris; imō et municipalis Regni neapolitani; necnon formulis singulorum actorum indicialium. Omnia fere complectens, quae per pontificias, ac caesareas leges, conciliorum decreta, sacrarum congregationum declarationes, ac Sacra rotae decisiones ad hac sancita fureunt. Venetiis, Tiuani, 1681. 474, [32] p.

2054

Pellegrini, Carlo, Bp. Praxis vicariorm et omnium in vtroque foro iusdicentium qvatvor partibvs comprehensa. Omnia fere complectens, quae per pontifivias, ac caesareas leges, consiliorum decreta, sacrarum congregationum declarationes, ac Sacrae rotae decisiones ad haec sancita fuerunt. Cum triplici indice copiosissimo. Venetiis, Feltrini, 1706. 474, [32] p.

2055

Pellegrino, Piero. I provvedimenti interlocutori nella teoria canonistica delle impugnazioni. Padova, CEDAM, 1969. 238 p. (Pubblicazioni dell' Istituto di diritto publico della Facoltà di giurisprudenza, Università degli studi di Roma, ser. 3, v. 16)
Includes bibliographical references.

2056

Peregrini, Alessandro. Tractatus de duello. Venetiis, Dusinello, 1614. 232 p.

2057

Pernicone, Joseph M. The ecclesiastical prohibition of books. Washington, D.C., The Catholic University of America Press, 1932. 267 p. (The Catholic University of America. Studies in canon law, no. 72)
Bibliography: p. [249]–257.

2058

Petrani, Aleksy. De relatione iuridica inter diversos ritus in ecclesia catholica. Taurini, Marietti, 1930. 107 p.
Bibliography: p. [vii]–ix.

2059

Philippot, Robert. De dubio in jure praesertim canonico seu in canonem decimum quintum Codicis juris canonici. Notae historicae, doctrinales et exegeticae, excerptae e dissertatione ad lauream in Facultate Juris Canonici Pontificiae Universitatis Gregorianiae. Brugis, Beyaert, 1947. 212 p.
Bibliography: p. x–xiv.

2060

Pici, Dominico. De contractibus sine certa solemnitate non valitaris Ad cap. CLI libri primis statutorum urbis commentaria. Romae, Phaeum, 1641. 416 p.

2061

Pickard, William M. Judicial experts: a source of evidence in ecclesiastical trials; a historical synopsis and a commentary. Washington, D.C., The Catholic University of America Press, 1958. 226 p. (The Catholic University of America. Canon law studies, no. 389)
Bibliography: p. 212–217.

2062

Pieronek, Tadeusz. Normy ogólne kanonicznego procesu sądowego. Warszawa, Akademia Teologii Katolickiej, 1970. v. 1 (Zarys prawa kanonicznego, t. 4. Prawo procesowe, zesz. 1)

2063

Pinna, Giovanni M. Praxis iudicialis canonica; cum praefatione Francisco Roberti. Romae, Officium Libri Catholici, 1952. 267 p.
Bibliographical footnotes.

2064

Pinto, Pio V. La giustizia amministrativa della Chiesa. Milano, Giuffrè, 1977. 377 p.
Bibliography: p. [353]–361.

2065

Pitonius, Franciscus, bp. De controversiis patronorum nec non ab eis praesentatorum. Venetiis, Ex typographia Balleoniana, 1746. 2 v.

2066

Pitonius, Franciscus M. De controversiis patronorum, nec non ab eis praesentatorum ad beneficia & cappellanias quascumque, & alia relicta pia. Venetiis, Ex typographia Balleoniana, 1763. 2 v. in 1.

2067

Pitonius, Franciscus M. Disceptationum ecclesiasticarum, in quibus frequentiora ecclesiastici fori litigia unà cum decretis tam datariae apostolicae, quàm sacrarum congregationum particularium, & generalium, necnon decisionibus Sacrae Rotae Romanae continentur. Venettis, Ex typographia Balleoniana, 1763. 4 v. in 2.

2068

Pius XII, pope. La personalità e la territorialità delle leggi specialmente nel diritto canonico; studio storico-giuridico. Roma, Tipografia Poliglotta Vaticana, 1912. 33 p.

2069

Pius XII, pope. La personnalité et le territorialité des lois, particulièrement dans le droit canon; étude historique-juridique. Rome, Scientia catholica, 1945. 30 p.

2070

Pius XII, pope. Da personlidade e da territorialidade das leis especialmente no direito canônico; estudio histórico-jurídico. Tradução portuguêsa no Seminário de Direito Internacional Privado da Faculdade de Direito, dirigido pelo professor Haroldo Valladão. Rio de Janeiro, 1953. 42 p.
Bibliographical footnotes.

2071

Pizarro, Néstor A. Acción de despojo: sus fuentes en derecho canónico. Córdoba, República Argentina, Impr. de la Universidad, 1943. 53 p. (*His* Cuadernos de derecho civil, 2)
Bibliographical footnotes.

2072

Politi, Alessandro. De patria in testamentis condendis potestate, libri quatuor. Florentiae, typis regiae celsitudinis, apud Jacobum de Guiduccis, & Sanctem Franchi, 1712. 272 p.

2073

Pontas, Jean, Dictionarium casuum conscientiae, seu Praecipuarum difficultatum circa moralem, ac disciplinam ecclesiasticam decisiones. Accedunt menda Pontasiana, sive observationes quaedam circa opus gallicum Pontasii. Item fr. Danielis Concina, praefatio ad lectorem, & animadversiones critico-morales in praefata menda Pontasiana, cum actuario duorum casuum, qui in hoc dictionario desiderabantur. Venetiis, Bortoli, 1744. 3 v.

2074

Postio, Lodovico. De svbhastatione tractatus non superfluus, sed necessarius, & ad praxim aptatus, & ordinatus. Iunctis ad materiam Decisionibus Rotae romanae vltra centum alibi non impressis. Maceratae, ex officina Carboniana, 1644. [600] p.

2075

Powers, Francis J. Religious liberty and the police power of the state; a study of the jurisprudential concepts underlying the problem of religious freedom and its relationship to the police power in the United States, with special reference to recent decisions of the United States Supreme Court on the subject. Washington, D.C., The Catholic University of America Press, 1948. 184 p.
Bibliography: p. 164–182.

2076

Processus judiciarius. Processus judiciarius Ioannis Andree. Et Juris defensoriū, vna cū pcurato₄ manuali. [Impressum oppido Nürmbergeñ, per Weyssenburger, 1510. [4], [4] 1

2077

Puza, Richard. Res iudicata. Rechtskraft u. fehlerhaftes Urteil in den Decisionen d. Römischen Rota. Graz, Leykam, 1973. 147 p. (Grazer rechts- und staatwissenschaftliche Studien, Bd. 29)
"Quellen-, Literatur- und Abkürzingsverzeichnis": p. 11–16.

2078

Riera Rius, Jaime. Procedimientos eclesiásticos de conformidad con el derecho canónico y las disposiciones de la Ven. jerarquía católica de Colombia; con referencias al Código civil colombiano. 2. ed., aumentada. [Medellín, Granamérica, 1962] 268 p.
Bibliography: p. [7]–[8].

2079

Rivet, L. Quaestiones iuris ecclesiastici publici, tractatae in Universitate gregoriana. Romae, 1912. 243 p.

2080

Roberti, Francesco. De processibus; opus ad Codicis schemata exactum, SS. Congregationum instructionibus normisque S. R. Rotae conlatis, jurisprudentia Tribunalium Apostolicorum inspecta et cum iure canonico orientali comparatum. 4. ed. In Civitate Vaticana, Apud custodiam librariam Pontificii Instituti Utriusque Iuris, 1956. v.

Includes bibliography.

2081

Rocca, Fernando della. Canonical procedure; philosophical-juridic study of book IV of the Code of canon law. Translated by John D. Fitzgerald. Milwaukee, Bruce, [1961] 384 p.

Includes bibliography.

2082

Rodrigues, Manuel. Qvaestiones regvlares et canonicae envcleatae, sive resolutiones quaestionum regularium ad compendium ita redactae, vt verum nucleaum contineant. Accesserunt plerisque resolutionibus notata, quibus seorsim, partim quaedam auctori omissa supplentur, partim aliorum idem cum illo, vel diuersum sentientium rationes pari breuitate excerptae expenduntur₃ vnaque bullarij indulta intertexta recensentur. Salmanticae, Ramirez, 1628.

2083

Roelker, Edward G. Invalidating laws. Paterson, N. J., St. Anthony Guild Press, 1955. 197 p.

Includes bibliography.

2084

Roelker, Edward G. Precepts. Paterson, N. J., St. Anthony Guild Press, 1955. 251 p.

2085

Ronke, Maximilian K. Die rechtliche bedeutung des irrtums in Codex juris canonici. Neisse, F. Bärr's buchdruckerei g.m.b.h., 1931. 132 p.

2086

Rosignoli, Gregorio. Novissima praxis theologico-legalis in vniversas . . . de contractibvs controversias. Mediolani, Vigoni, 1678. 555 p.

2087

Rosignoli, Gregorio. Novissima praxis theologico-legalis in vniversas de dote controuersias. Opus omnibus sacrae, & moralis theologiae, & iuris vtriusque professoribus valde vtile. Cum duplici indice, altero titulorum, altero rerum locupletissimo. Milan, Malatesta, 1691. 2 v.

2088

Rosignoli, Gregorio. Novissima praxis theologico-legalis in vniversased tutoribus & curatoribus controuersias. Mediolani, Malatesta, 1695–1699. 2 v.

2089

Romser, Paul. Libellus de jure et justitia, ac potissimùm de contractibus. Olim ad disputandum propositus, nunc recusus cum indice materiarum in primâ editione desiderato. Salisbvrgi, Mayr, 1669. 490, [26] p.

2090

Roussier, Jules. Le fondement de l'obligation contractuelle dans le driot classique de l'église. Paris, Domat-Montchrestien, 1933. 250 p.

"Bibliographie": p. [241]–248.

2091

Roye, François de. Ad titulum de ivre patronatvs libro tertio decretalium. Eivsdem De ivribvs honorificis in ecclesiâ libri duo. Andegavi, Avril, 1667. 247, 103 p.

2092

Rugiero, Agnellus S. de. De testamento canonico, sive Commentaria ad cap. Cum esses, de testamentis . . . ac Tractatus theorico-practicus, in quo de origine, & progressu tribunalis rev. Fabricae S. Petri de urbe, adpellati . . . et aliae quaestiones, ejusdem argumenti peculiares . . . pertractantur. Duplici adiecto indice. Neap., Valiero, 1711. 303 p.

2093

Schiara, Antonio. Theologia bellica omnes ferè difficultates ad militiam tum terrestrem, tum maritimam pertinentes complectens . . . in octo libros distributa . . . cum triplici indice. Romae, de Buagnis, 1702. 2 v.

2094

Schirmer, Dietrich. Rechtsgeschichtliche Untersuchungen zum Johannes-Evangelium. [Erlangen, 1962] 280 p.

Bibliography: p. 269–280.

2095

Schmitz, Heribert. Appellatio extraiudicialis. Entwicklungslinien einer kirchlichen Gerichtsbarkeit über die Verwaltung im Zeitalter der klassischen

Kanonistik (1140–1348). München, Hueber, 1970. 161 p. (Münchener theologische Studien. 3; Kanonistische Abt., 29. Bd.)
Bibliography: p. xi–xviii.

2096

Sesto, Gennaro J. Guardians of the mentally ill in ecclesiastical trials; a canonical commentary with historical notes. Washington, D.C., The Catholic University of America Press, 1956. 179 p. (The Catholic University of America. Canon law studies, no. 358)
Bibliography: p. 163–172.

2097

Simoncelli, Ottavio. Tractatvs de decretis caeterisqve solemnitatibvs in contractibus minorum aliorum'ue his similium adhibendis. Per auctorem hac houa ed. additionibus quamplurimis exornatus & ab erroribus diligenter expurgatus. Venetiis, de Fraciscis, 1583. 167 p.

2098

Simoncelli, Ottavio. Tractatvs de decretis, caeterisqve solemnitatibvs in contractibus minorum, aliorumque his similium, adhibendis. Hac noua editione ab erroribus expurgatus, necnon ab ipso auctore additionibus quamplurimis exornatus. Venetiis, Zenarij, 1619. 152 p.

2099

Smith, Sebastian B. The new procedure in criminal and disciplinary causes of ecclesiastics in the United States: or, a clear and full explanation of the instruction "Cum magnopere," issued by the S. Congr. de Prop. Fide, in 1884, for the United States. 3d rev. ed. New York, Pustet, 1898, c1887. p. 8–304.

2100

Socha, Hubert. Die Analogie zwischen der Hirtengewalt und der Dominativgewalt der klösterlichen Laienoberen. München, Hueber, 1967. 268 p. (Münchener theologische Studien. 3. Kanonistische Abteilung, 27. Bd.)
Bibliography: p. xix–xl.

2101

Socueba, Fernandez G. de. Instrucción manual para la más breve expedición de los casos practicos,

y disputas de immunidad local, Noticia histórica de su origen, progressos, y estado. A la inteligencia de las más modernas constituciones pontificias. Sevilla, Castilla [1776] 335 p.

2102

Sonntag, Nathaniel L. Censorship of special classes of books, Canons 1387–1391; a history and commentary. Washington, D.C., The Catholic University of America Press, 1947 [i.e., 1948] 147 p. (The Catholic University of America. Canon law studies, no. 262)
Bibliography: p. 118–126.

2103

Stephan, Christoph. Das disziplinarrecht der katholischen kirche nach dem Codex iuris canonici (Can. 2142–Can. 2194), insbesondere das amotionsverfahren gegen unabsetzbare pfarrer. Köln, Orthen, 1937. 52 p.
"Literaturverzeichnis": p. 5–8.

2104

Stryk, Johann S. Dissertatio ivridica de ivre liciti sed non honesti, svb praesidio Io. Samuelis Strykii in avditorio maiori d. III. Februar. anno 1702 placido eruditorum examini submittit. [Halle] typis Orphanotrophii Glauch [1702?] 146, [4] p.

2105

Stryk, Samuel. Examen juris feudalis, ex novissimis ejus interpretibus in gratiam auditorum collectum, ac methodo institutionum dispositum. Ed. 2, auctior & correctior. VVitebergae, Schrey & Henckel, 1679. 436 p.
"Appendix de solennibus investiturarum et taxa dignitatum Imperii. Subjectis qvisbusdam juramentorum formulis."

2106

Suárez, Francisco. Tractatvs de legibvs ac deo legislatore in decem libros distributus. Conimbricae, de Loureyro, 1612. 1266, [29] p.

2107

Suárez de Paz, Gonzalo. Praxis ecclesiastica, et saecularis, in quo acta processuum omnium utriusque fori causarum cum actionum forumlis sermone hispano composita, & ad hodiernum stylum accommodata traduntur, & ordinantur. Editio novissima caeteris, quae hucusque prodiere, longè emendatior, & auctior: cui accesserunt S. Rotae romanae Decisiones novissimae, et selectissimae, auctoris Praxim laudantes, & confirmantes, & synopsis operis idaeam prae oculis exhibens; cum indicibus novis etiam, et locupletissimis. Matriti, Marin, 1790. 323, 84, 140, 108 p.

2108

Sylvestre, Lucien. Le cathédratique; histoire, commentaire canonique et législation canadienne. Québec, Faculté de droit canonique, Université Laval, 1946 [colophon 1947] 175 p. (Les Thèses canoniques de Laval, thèse no. 6)
"Bibliographie": p. [xv–xxvii]

2109

Teichmann, Albert F. R. De litis contestationis juris canonici indole. Dissertatio inauguralis. Berolini, typis expressit Schade, 1867. 94 p.

2110

Thierney, William J. Authorized ecclesiastical acts. Washington, D.C., The Catholic University of America Press, 1961. 228 p. (Catholic University of America. Canon law studies, no. 414)
Bibliography: p. 217–224.

2111

Thomas, Alphonsus J. The juridical effect of doubtful cessation of law, according to the Code of canon law. Québec, Faculté de droit canonique, Université Laval [1950] 110 p. (Les Thèses canoniques de Laval. Thèse no. 9)
Bibliography: p. [xi]–xviii.

2112

Trombetta, Aloisio. Praxeos regulae circa contractus rerum ecclesiasticarum rite ineundos, sacrae congregationis episcoporum et regularium subsecretario. Iuxta principia juris expriaitas. Roma, Salviucci, 1865. 245, 10 p.

2113

Vaughan, William E. Constitutions for Diocesan Courts, a historical synopsis and commentary. Washington, D.C., 1944. 210 p. (The Catholic University of America. Canon law studies, no. 210)

2114

Vismara, Giulio. Episcopalis audientia, l'attività,

giurisdizionale del vescovo per la risoluzione delle controversie private tra laici nel diritto romano e nella storia del diritto italiano fino al secolo nono. Milano, "Vita e pensiero", 1937. 184 p. (Pubblicazioni della Università cattolica del Sacro cuore. Ser. 2: Scienze giuridice. vol. 54)
Bibliographical footnotes.

2115

Vulpe, Marcellus. Praxis ivdicialis fori ecclesiastici. Trani, Typis Valerij, 1636. 606 p.

2116

Wirth, Paul. Der Zeugenbeweis im kanonischen Recht, unter besonderer Berücksichtigung der Rechtsprechung der Römischen Rota. Paderborn, Schöningh, 1961. 287 p.
Bibliography: p. [13]–18.

2117

Wissenbach, Johannis J. Disputationes iuris civilis. Cum indice disputationum et respondentium. Ad calcem adjectae sunt contradictiones juris canonici. Heilbronnae, Franci, 1665. 687, 27, 43 p.

2118

Woywod, Stanislaus. Canonical decisions of the Holy See. New York, Wagner; London, Herder [c1933] 309 p.

2119

Wriedt, Klaus. Die kanonischen Prozesse um die Ansprüche Mecklenburgs und Pommerns auf das rügische Erbe, 1326–1348. Köln, Böhlau, 1963. 223 p. (Veröffentlichungen der Historischen Kommission für Pommern. Reihe 5: Forschungen zur prommerschen Geschichte, Heft 4)
Bibliography: p. 217–223.

2120

Wypler, Carolus. Consensus legislatoris pro consuetudine in Ecclesia: doctrina Medii Aevi ac doctoris Fr. Suarez. Roma, [s. n.], 1974. 46 p.
Bibliography: p. [7]–10.

2121

Zaccaria. Natura giuridica del rapporto di offerta e accettazione di "stipendium missae." Padova, CEDAM, Milani, 1942. 238 p.

CRIMES AND PENALTIES

2122

Alvarez Arias, Constantino. La monición canónica y pastoral; líneas históricas, funciones y sistema en la legislación de la Iglesia. Salamanca, 1965. 259 p.
  Bibliography: p. [xxvii]–xxxi.

2123

Amicus, Petrus. Brevis modvs examinandi in cavsis criminalibvs. Summa curiositate in publicam vtilitatem nouiter redactus. Romae, Facciottum, 1631. 24 p.

2124

Aradillas Agudo, Antonio. Proceso a los tribunales eclesiasticos. Madrid, Sedmay, 1974, 1975 printing. 265 p.

The author wanted this book to be an echo of pain and frustration: the pain of the spouses who failed in their quest for happiness; the pain of their families who became participants in the drama; and the pain of the children who will suffer interminably because of the inability of their parents to live together and by the inconsiderate attitude of the Church which has at hand the possible solution to the problem. The book is an accusation of the Church, but presented with love and respect. It offers theologo-canonico-philosophical grounds for an urgent restructuring of the administration of justice in the Church. It also contains lists of cases showing the failure of ecclesiastical justice; a brief explanation of the operation, composition, structure, and persons that constitute the courts; and an example of a court reform or *Reforma Tarancón.*

2125

Ayrinhac, Henry A. Penal legislation in the new code of canon law (liber V), revised by Rev. P. J. Lydon. New York, Cincinnati, Benziger, 1936. 340 p.

2126

Böcken, Placidus. Tractatus de delictis, ad lib. V Decretalium Gregorii IX. In alma, & archi-episcopali Universitate salisburgensi unacum parergis ex universo jure ... disputationi academicae subjectus & defensus à praenobili ac doctissimo domino Michaele Antonio de Nicolleti. Salisburgi, Mayr, 1725. 258, [14] p.

2127

Bourque, John R. The judicial power of the church, canon 1553, §1. Washington, D.C., The Catholic University of America Press, 1953. 149 p. (The Catholic University of America. Canon law studies, no. 337)
  Bibliography: p. 137–141.

2128

Bouscaren, Timothy L. Reserved cases; pocket outlines for confessors. Milwaukee, Bruce, [1956] 15 p.

2129

Braun, Carl. De suspensione ex informata conscientia ob occulta solum crimina inferenda. Dissertatio inauguralis. Wirceburgi, Thien, 1868. 35 p.

2130

Bruno, Cayetano. La lectura y los libros prohibidos; legislación eclesiástica. Rosario, "Apis", 1954. 59 p. (Cuadernos didácticos Didascalia, no. 4)
  Bibliography: p. 59.

2131

Cabassut, Jean. Juris canonici theoria et praxis, ad forum tam sacramentale quàm contentiosum, tum ecclesiasticum, tum seculare. Opus exactum non solum ad normam juris communis & romani, sed etiam juris francici. Editio postrema ab ipso authore recognita & aucta. Lugduni, Borde & Arnaud, 1698. 600, [70] p.

2132

Cadena y Eleta, José. Tratado teórico-práctico de procedimientos eclesiásticos en materia civil y criminal. 2. ed. Madrid, del Amo, 1894. 1 v.

2133

Caglioti, Bruno. La discrezionalità del giudice nel diritto penale canonico. Palermo, 1969. 109 p.
  Bibliography: p. 101–105.

2134

Cappello, Felice M. De poenitentia. Ed. 7. accurate emendata et aucta. [Torino] Marietti, [1963] 729 p. (*His* Tractatus canonico-moralis de sacramentis, v. 2)

Includes bibliographical references and index.

2135

Cappello, Felice M. Tractatus canonico-moralis de censuris, iuxta Codicem iuris canonici. Ed. 3. recognita et emendata. Taurinorum Augustae, Marietti, 1933. 515 p.

2136

Casey, James V. A study of canon 2222, §1; a historical synopsis and a commentary. Washington, D.C., The Catholic University of America Press, 1949. 127 p. (The Catholic University of America. Canon law studies, no. 290)

Bibliography: p. 103–107.

2137

Chelodi, Giovanni. Ius poenale et ordo procedendi in indiciis criminalibus iuxta Codicem iuris canonici. Ed. 3, aucta et emendata. Tridenti, Ardesi, 1933. 182 p.

2138

Chelodi, Giovanni. Ius poenale et ordo procedendi in iudiciis criminalibus iuxta Codicem iuris canonici. Editio 4., recognita et aucta a Vigilio Dalpiaz. Tridenti, Ardesi, 1935. 191 p.

2139

Chiericato, Giovanni. Discordiae forenses civilies et criminales in duos tomos distributae. Ed. tertia. Venetiis, Balleoniana, 1766. 2 v. in 1.

2140

Christ, Joseph J. Dispensation from vindictive penalties; an historical conspectus and commentary. Washington, D.C., The Catholic University of America Press, 1943. 285 p. (The Catholic University of America. Canon law studies, no. 174)

Bibliography: p. 255–265.

2141

Ciolli, Alessandro. Commentario practico delle censure latae sententiae oggidi in vigore nella Chiesa. 7. ed. accresciuta. Siena, Bernardino, 1895. 232 p.

2142

Ciprotti, Pio. De consummatione delictorum attento eorum elemento obiectivo in iure canonico. Romae, Pont. Instituti Utriusque Iuris, 1936. v.

Bibliography: v. 1, p. [7]–10; [95]–97.

2143

Ciprotti, Pio. De iniuria ac diffamatione in iure poenali canonico. Roma, Pont. Instituti Utriusque Iuris, 1937. 143 p.

"Bibliographia": p. [7]–9.

2144

Cloran, Owen M. Previews and practical cases: Code of canon law, book five, Delicts and penalties, canons 2195–2414. Milwaukee, Bruce [1951] 350 p.

Bibliography: p. 323–335.

2145

Colonnensis, Bonaventura. Tractatvs de prohibitione dvelli. In qvo qvicqvid a Clem. VIII pontifice max. de duello sancitum est, breuiter explicatur. Florentiae, Sermartelliana, 1625. 50 p.

2146

Conran, Edward J. The interdict. Washington, D.C., The Catholic University of America Press, 1930. 163 p. (The Catholic University of America. Canon law studies, no. 56)

Bibliography: p. 154–157.

2147

Couvreur, Gilles. Les pauvres ont-ils des droits? recherches sur le vol en cas d'extrême nécessité, depuis la Concordia de Gratien (1140) jusqu'à Guillaume d'Auxerre (†1231) Roma, Università Gregoriana, 1961. 346 p. (Analecta Gregoriana, v. 111. Series Facultatis Theologicae: sectio B, n. 34)

Bibliography: p. [xv]–xxxix.

2148

Desprez, Edouard. De l'abolition de l'emprisonnement. Paris, Dentu, 1868. 202 p.

2149

Diaz, Bernard. Ioannis Bernardi Diaz de Luco, decretorum, doctoris. Practica criminalis canonica. Venetiis, de Nicholius, 1560. 275 p.

2150

Diaz de Luco, Juan B., bp. Practica criminalis canonica. Nouissimè recognita, duodecim capitibus aucta, amplissimis scholijs locupletata, quibus vtrà iuris communis sanctiones, propè infinita decreta anti-quissimorum conciliorum catholicae ecclesiae & sacrosancti Tridentini, nec non nouissimorum romanorum pontificum constitutiones (quas motus proprios appellant) simulque diuersarum prouinciarum & diaecesum statuta municipalia interpretantur. A doctore Ignatio Lopez de Salsedo. Accesserunt etiam huic editioni, egregia responsa cardinalium, qui Concilij Tridentini interpretationi praesunt, quae mirè ad hanc canonicam practicam desiderabantur, aptissimè constituto. Opus profectò omnibus iuris pontificij, & caesarei professoribus . . . necessarium. Antverpiae, Keerbergium, 1593. 626 (i.e., 625), [40] p.

2151

Diaz de Luco, Juan B., bp. Practica criminalis canonica. Venetiis, Guerilius, 1614. 638 p.

2152

Dicastillo, Juan de. Tractatvs dvo de ivramento, perivrio et adivratione, nec non de censvris et poenis ecclesiasticis. Antverpiae, Mevrsio, 1662 190, 516 p.

2153

Dordett, Alexander. Der geistliche Charakter der kirchlichen Gerichtsbarkeit; eine rechtshistorische Studie über die Bestrebungen der Antikurialisten zur Beschränkung der "iurisdictio coactiva." Wien, 1954. 223 p.

"Quellen- und Literaturverzeichnis": p. 209–215.

2154

Eichmann, Eduard. Das Strafrecht des Codex iuris canonici. Paderborn, Schöningh, 1920. 248 p.

2155

Eltz, Louis A. Cooperation in crime, an historical conspectus and commentary. Washington, D.C., The Catholic University of America, 1942. 298 p. (The Catholic University of America. Canon law studies, no. 156)

Bibliography p. [185]–193.

2156

Farinacci, Prospero. Consilia sive responsa atque decisiones cavsarvm criminalivm. Coloniae, excudebat Philippvs gamonetvs, 1649. 1 v.

2157

Finzi, Marcello. La legislación canónica y los delitos de falsedad. Buenos Aires, Universidad de Córdoba, 1945. 62 p.

Published also as Córdoba, Argentine republic Universidad nacional.

Instituto de derecho comparado. Publicaciones. Ser. B, no. 21.

Bibliographical footnotes.

2158

Floronus, Lucas. Tractatvs de prohibitione dvelli. Nunc primum in lucem editus. Venetiis, Scott, 1610. 132 p.

2159

Follerio, Pietro. Canonica criminalis praxis, in vnum congesta; in qua de ordine procedendi in vrbe, alliisue ecclesiasticis curiis, pertractatur; qualiterue iudices ecclesiastici, ethice, economicè, & politicè, se habere debeant, Marcellina nvncvpata. Cum summarijs, & repertorio editis, per . . . Aloysium Antonium cognomento de Maria . . . necnon additionibus aliquibus factis per Franciscum Antonium. Venetiis, Rubini, 1583.

2160

Gasparro, Francesco M. Institutiones criminales tribus partibus distributae. Additis indicibus necessariis. Opus posthumum. Venetiis, Pezzana, 1771. 108 p.

2161

Goodricke, H. Tentamina jurisprudentiae rationalis de jure puniendi divino et humano in quibus rationes, fines, jura et natura peonarum divinarum et humanarum explicantur multaequae utilissimae quaestiones philosophicae et theologicae, justituiam divinam et dei regimen morale praecipus spectantes enodantur & illustrantur. Groningae, Bolt, 1766. 276 p.

2162

Gulczynski, John T. The desecration and violation of churches; an historical synopsis and commentary. Washington, D.C., The Catholic University of America Press, 1942. 126 p. (The Catholic University of America. Canon law studies, no. 159)

2163
Heiner, Franz X. Der kirchliche strafprozess, praktisch dargestellt. Köln, Bachem, 1912. 232 p.

2164
Hohenlohe-Schillingsfürst, Constantin, Father. Beiträge zum Einflusse des kanonischen Rechts auf Strafrecht und Prozessrecht. Innsbruck, Verlagsanstalt Tyrolia, 1918. 71 p.

2165
Hollweck, Joseph. Die kirchlichen Strafgesetze, zusammengestellt und commentirt. Mainz, Kirchheim, 1899. 384 p.

2166
Hughes, James A. Witnesses in criminal trials of clerics, an historical synopsis and commentary. Washington, D.C., The Catholic University of America Press, 1937. 140 p. (The Catholic University of America. Canon law studies, no. 106)
Bibliography: p. 123–128.

2167
Katz, Edwin. Ein grundriss des kanonischen strafrechts. Berlin und Leipzig, Guttentag, 1881. 211, [1] p.
"Poenitentiale remense": p. [161]–202.

2168
Krehbiel, Edward B. The interdict: its history and its operation, with special attention to the time of Pope Innocent III, 1198–1216. Merrick, N. Y., Richwood, [1977]. 184 p.
Bibliography: p. 164–173.

2169
Król, John J. The defendant in contentious trials, exclusive of vincular cases; an historical synopsis and commentary. Washington, D.C., The Catholic University of America Press, 1942. 207 p. (The Catholic University of America. Canon law studies, no. 146)
Bibliography: p. 185–191.

2170
Lega, Michele, Cardinal. Commentarius in iudicia ecclesiastica iuxta Codicem iuris canonici. Curante Victorio Bartoccetti. Romae, Anonima Libraria Cattolica Italiana, 1950. 3 v.
Bibliographical footnotes.

2171
Liuzzi, Ferruccio A. De delictis contra auctoritates ecclesiasticas (cann. 2331–2340). Romae, Officium libri catholici, 1942. 164 p.
"Bibliographia": p. [xiii]–xvi.

2172
Love, Paul L. The penal remedies of the Code of Canon Law. Washington, D.C., The Catholic University of America Press, 1960. 179 p. (The Catholic University of America Press. Canon law studies, no. 404)
Bibliography: p. 169–173.

The author analyzes penal remedies, both crime-preventive and crime-repressive, of canonical legislation. It is his intention "to present the general concept and characteristics of these remedies in so far at they constitute a legal unit or institute in the present legislation of the Church," and to study their concrete application in the section of the code. The author concludes that the foundation for penal remedies under the study is found at least implicitly in the Council of Trent, and explicitly in the instructions *Sacra Haec,* issued by the Sacred Congregation for Bishops and Regulars in 1880, and *Cum Magnopere* issued by the Sacred Congregation for the Propagation of the Faith, and which aims to handle disciplinary and criminal cases of clerics in the United States of America. The book also offers an interesting study on canonical remedies in pre-Code legislation.

2173
Lünenborg, Heinrich. Der versuch im strafrecht des Codex juris canonici. Mainz, Kirchheim, 1931. 39, [1] p.
"Benutzte literatur": p. [5]–[7]

2174
Mantuano, Ginesio. La riserva di legge nell'ordinamento penale della Chiesa. Padova, CEDAM, 1975. v. (Pubblicazioni dell'Istituto di diritto pubblico della Facoltà di giurisprudenza, Università degli studi di Roma; ser. 3, v. 27)

2175
Martini, Nicolaus. Praxis criminalis ad theoricam accomadata. Romae, typis Petri Ferri, 1728. 224 p.

2176
McCoy, Alan E. Force and fear in relation to delictual imputability and penal responsibility; an historical synopsis and commentary. Washington, D.C., The Catholic University of America Press, 1944. 160 p. (The Catholic University of America. Canon law studies, no. 200)
Bibliography: p. 137–143.

2177
Megalius, Marcellus. Praxis criminalis canonica pro foro eclesiastico regulari, ac seculari. Mutinae, Cafriono [1638] 522, [46] p.

2178
Meier, Carl A. Penal administrative procedure against negligent pastors, an historical synopsis and commentary. Washington, D.C., The Catholic University of America Press, 1941. 247 p. (The Catholic University of America. Canon law studies, no. 140)
Bibliography: p. 227–235.

2179
Meile, Joseph. Die beweislehre des kanonischen prozesses in ihren grundzügen unter berücksichtigung der modernen prozessrechtswissenschaft. Bazenheid, Kalberer, 1925. 156 p.
"Quellen und literature": p. ii–iv.

2180
Milan (Diocese) Forum Archiepiscopale. Decisiones criminales. Avthore Ivlivo Chartario. Olim a Carolo Chartario typis commissae, iterum in lucem prodeunt. Romae, Ex typographia Vaticana, et Camerali, 1676. 538 p.

2181
Millan de Quiñones, Diego. Gregorianae collectionis de iudiciis, ac de sent. & re iud. titvlorvm interpretatio breuem iudiciorum, ecclesiasticae & secularis iurisdictionis, ac rerum iudicatarum tractatus continens. Ticini, Bartolo, 1617. 182, [10] p.

2182
Miranda, Ludovicus de. Ordinis ivdiciarii, Et de modo procedendi in Causis criminalibus tàm in Foro Ecclesiastico, quàm saeculari quaestiones XXX. Venetiis, Fontana, 1629. [2 v. in 1]

2183
Morgante, Marcello. De casu fortuito in iure poenali canonico; studium historico-iuridicum. Romae, Apud Custodiam Librariam Pont. Instituti Utriusque Iuris, 1950. 87 p.
"Bibliographia": p. vii–xii.

2184
Myrcha, Marian A. Dowod ze świadków w procesie kanonicanym. Lublin, Tow. Naukowe Katolickiego Uniwersytetu Lubelskiego, 1936. 163 p. (Katolicki Uniwersytet Lubelski. Rozprawydoktorskie, magisterskie i seminaryjne. 2. Wydział Prawa Kanonicznego. Rozprawy doktorskie, t. 3)
Bibliography: p. [159]–163.

2185
Der Ordo "invocato Christi nomine". Mit unterstützunder Forschungsgemeinschaft der deustchen wissenschaft und des Ministeruims für schulwesen und volkskultur in der Tschechoslovakischen republik. Heidelberg, Winter, 1931. 165 p. (Quellen zur geschichte des römisch-kanonischen processes im mittelalter, hrsg. von dr. Ludwig Wahrmund. v. bd. hft.1)
"Literatur": p. [xvii]–xix.

2186
Palazzini, Giuseppe. Ius fetus ad vitam eiusque tutela in fontibus ac doctrina canonica usque ad saeculum XVI. Urbaniae, "Bramantes", 1943. 3–219 p.
Bibliographical footnotes.

2187
Parres, Cecil L. The concept of the division of crimes into public, notorius and occult according to the code of canon law. Romae, Catholic Book Agency, 1967. 104 p.
Bibliography: p. [99]–102.

2188
Pawluk, Tadeusz. Kanoniczne procesy szczególne. Warszawa, Akademia Teologii Katolickiej, 1971. 366 p. (Zarys prawa kanonicznego. Prawo procesowe, t. 4., zesz. 3)
Includes bibliographical references.

2189
Pellegrini, Germanus J. Jus ecclesiae poenale. v. 1,

"De delictis." Napoli, d'Auria, Pontificius Editor, 1962. 3 v.

Bibliography: v. 1, p. [189]–190.

2190

Perathoner, Anton. Kirchliches Gerichtswesen und kirchliches Strafrecht nach dem neuen Codex juris canonici. Brixen, Weger, 1919. 151 p.

A paraphrase, with comments, of the 4th and 5th books (c. 1552–2414) of the Codex juris canonici.

A continuation of, and bound with, the author's Kurze Einführung in das neue kirchliche Fesetzbuck. Brixen, 1919.

2191

Péries, George. La procédure canonique moderne dans les causes disciplinaires et criminelles; notions pratiques sur les tribunaux ecclésiastiques et le fonctionnement des officialités. Paris, Roger & Chernoviz, 1898. 387 p.

"Bibliographie": p. [xiii]–xvi.

2192

Pitigiani, Francesco, d'Arezzo. Practica criminalis canonica. In his secunda editione cum aliquibus additionibus praedicti authoris cura, & delegentia Hilarionis Sacchetti. Venetiis, Ciotto, 1607. 507, [4] p.

2193

Politi, Vincenzo. Il conatus delicti nell'ordinamento penale della Chiesa. Palermo, 1968. 160 p.

Bibliographical footnotes.

2194

Quinn, Hugh G. The particular penal precept. Washington, D.C., The Catholic University of America Press, 1953. 108 p. (Catholic University of America. Canon law studies, no. 303)

Bibliography: p. [83]–88.

2195

Quintana Reynés, Lorenzo. La prueba en el procedimiento canónico, con un apéndice al liro "Las causas de nulidad de matrimonio y su tramitación," prólogo del dr. d. Joaquín Dualde Gómez. Barcelona, Bosch, [1943] 290 p.

"Bibliografia": p. [5]–6.

2196

Quintela, Antonio. El atentado en el proceso canónico. [Pamplona] Eunsa [1972] 211 p. (Colección canónica de la Universidad de Navarra)

Bibliography: p. [205]–211.

2197

Riccio Pepoli, Rosario. Practica ecclesiastica civile, criminale ed appeliazione con la practica delli SS. sacramenti per li Parochi, Confessori, e vicarj foranei; con le formole all'uso moderno; e con l'avvertenze dove conviene e dove differisce la prattica ecclesiastica, e laicale. Napoli, Nicolo & Rispoli. 1730. 4, 208, 24 p.

2198

Rocca, Fernando della. Instituciones de derecho procesal canónico. [Versión castellana de Pacífico de Iragui] Buenos Aires, Desclée, De Brouwer [1950] 466 p.

Bibliography: p. 413–415.

2199

Rocca, Fernando della. Istituzioni di diritto penale canonico. Torino, Unione tipografico-editrice torinese, 1961. 236 p.

Includes bibliographical references and index.

2200

Santoro da Melfi, Father. Practica criminalis ad sancte administrandam iustitiam in Ordine fratrum minorum S. Francisci Regul. obseru. iuxta praescriptum statutorum generalium, ex sacris canonibus, & probatis auctoribus compendiosè collecta; generali capitvlo romano, ann. MDCXXXIX probante, & mandante. Nunc, quia & exteris vtilis apparuit, per eiusdem authorem. Secondo reuisa, & correcta. Romae, Moneta, 1645. 200 p.

2201

Scaccia, Sigismvndus. Tractatvs de ivdiciis cavsarvm civilivm, criminalivm, et haereticalivm. Liber Primvs [Liber Secvndcs] Venetiis, Bertanos, 1648. 2 v. in 1. 426, 688 p.

2202

Schmalzgrueber, Franz. Crimen fori ecclesiastici, seu Decretalium Gregorij IX. pont. max. liber V. Ingolstadii, de la Haye; Grass, 1717–18. 2 v. 1226 p.

Issued in 1727 as v. 6–7 of the author's Jus ecclesiasticum universum . . . in quinque libros Decretalium Gregorii IX. . . . Editio secunda.

2203

Simon, Dieter. Der Deliktsversuch nach kanonischem Recht. Basel, Helbing & Lichtenhahn, 1965. 160 p. (Basler Studien zur Rechtswissenschaft, Heft 75)

Bibliography: p. ix–xxiv.

2204

Sinistrari, Luigi M. Practica criminalis illvstrata; hoc ẹst, Commentarii perpetvi et absolvti in practicam criminalem Fratrvm Minorvm; in qvibvs textvs accuratissima explicatione dilucidatur in obscuris, necessarijs additionibus suppletur in defectiuis, & discussis quaestionibus maximè practicabilibus, totius materiae criminalis completè traditur theoria et praxis. Opvs novvm. Indicibus saecularibus commodum, regularibus vtile, praelatis verò prouincialibus, ac localibus minorum, obseruantiae regularis, ac strictioris omninò necessarium. Editio 2. ab avctore recognita. Mediolani, de Clericis, 1702–03. 2 v. in 1.

2205

Smith, Mariner T. The penal law for religious. Washington, D.C., The Catholic University of America Press, 1935. 3–169 p. (The Catholic University of America. Canon law studies, no. 98)

Bibliography: p. 155–158.

2206

Smith, Sebastian Bach. The new procedure in criminal and disciplinary causes of ecclesiastics in the United States. Or a clear and full explanation of the instruction "Cum magnopere", issued by the S. Congr. de Prop. fide, in 1884, for the United States. New York and Cincinnati, 1887. [7]–298 p.

2207

Sole, Giacomo. De delictis et poenis; praelectiones in lib. V Codicis iuris canonici quas in Pontif. Romae, Neo-Eboraci, Pustet, 1920. 452 p.

Bibliographical footnotes.

2208

Strigl, Richard A. Das Funktionsverhältnis zwischen kirchlicher Strafgewalt und Öffentlichkeit. Grundlagen, Wandlungen, Aufgaben. München, Hueber, 1965. 240 p. (Münchener theologische Studien. 3. Kanonistische Abteilung, 21 Bd.)

Bibliography: p. xi–xxv.

2209

Szmyd, Wojciech. Kary kościelne. Kraków [Wydawn. księży jezuitów] 1929. 190, ii p. (Rozpraw z zakresu prawa kościelnego t. 2)

"Wykaz dzieł, na które się w tekście powołuję": p. [7]

2210

Vermiglioli, Giovanni M. Consilia criminalia ad defensam in Romana cvria edita. Romae, sumptibus Blasij Deuersin, 1658. 628, [91] p.

2211

Zambelli, Leone, di Piacenza. Ivris criminvm regvlae generales iudicio regularium maximopere vtiles, ac necessariae, vt iudices religiosi, religiose muneri proprio, a principio ad finem vsque, in qualibet causa, satisfacere possint. Bononiae, Ferronio. 1635. 325, [46] p.

2212

Zauli, Domenico. Observationes canonicae, civiles, criminales, & mixtae non solùm statutis civitatis Faventiae, sed juri communi accomodatae. Editio secunda ab ipso auctore novis ovservationibus locupletata, & in duos tomos divisa cum duplici opioso indice materiarum. Accedit in fine . . . primi voluminis dissertatio illm̃i & rmi. p. Francisci Mariae Muscẹtulae . . . De matrimoniis filiorumfam. insciis vel rationabiliter invitis parentibus contractis. Romae, Mainardi, 1723–24. 2 v.

MISCELLANEOUS TOPICS

SYNODS

2213

Ancona, March of. Rota. Decisiones Rotae provinciae Marchiae, authore Stephano Gratiano, cum additionibus eiusdem authoris: in qvibvs mvlta definivntvr iuxta receptas doctorum sententias, & veram praxim, praecipuè sacrae Rotae romanae. Omnia nvnc postremo diligentivs edita, cum duplici indice, tam argumentorum, quàm rerum quae in decisionibus, & additionibus continentur. Genevae, sumptibus Samuelis Chouët, 1664. 384, [46] p.

2214

Andrieu, Pierre. Quelques textes normands des décrétals de Grégoire IX. Rouen, Lestringant, 1934. 15 p.

2215

Arnold, Franz. Das diözesanrecht nach den schriften Hinkmars von Rheims; eine untersuchung über den ursprung und die entstehungszeit des diözesanrechtes. Wien, Kommissionsverlag Mayer, 1935. 218 p.
"Quellen und literatur": p. [202]–208.

2216

Artonne, André, Louis Guizard and Odette Pontal. Répertoire des statuts synodaux des diocèses de l'ancienne France, du XIIIᵉ à la fin du XVIIIᵉ siècle. Préf, par Gabriel Le Bras. Paris, Centre national de la recherche scientifique, 1963 [i.e. 1964] 516 p. (Institut de recherche et d'histoire des textes. Documents, études et répertoires, 8)
Bibliography: p. [15]–16.

2217

Artonne, André, Louis Guizard, and Odette Pontal. Répertoire des statuts synodaux des diocèses de l'ancienne France du XIIIᵉ à la fin du XVIIIᵉ siècle. Préf. par Gabriel Le Bras. 2. éd. rev. et augm. Paris, Éditions du Centre national de la recherche scientifique, 1969. 550 p. (Documents, études, et répertoires, 8)
Includes bibliographies.

2218

Ayacucho, Peru (Diocese). Synodo, 1st, 1629. Constituciones synodales del Obispado de Guamanga (Perú) 1629, [ordenadas por] Francisco Verdugo. Cuernavaca, México: Centro Intercultural de Documentación, 1970. 6, 116, 24 p. (Sínodos diocesanos) (CIDOC fuentes; no. 8: Serie segunda)

2219

Aymans, Winfried. Kollegium und kollegialer Akt im kanonischen Recht; eine rechtsbegriffliche Untersuchung insbesondere aufgrund des Codex iuris canonici. München, Hueber, 1969. 206 p. (Münchener theologische Studien. 3. Kanonistische Abteilung, Bd. 28)
Bibliography: p. xiii–xx.

2220

Azpilcueta, Martín de. Praelectiones in cap. Si quando & cap. Cum contingat. de rescript. in causa propria cantoriae conimbricensis axiomata quae versa pagella docet discutientes, cum copiosi indice. Conimbricae, ex officina Iohannis Barrerii & Iohãnis Aluari, 1543. 188 p.

2221

Barquisimeto, Venezuela (Diocese). Sínodo Diocesano, 1st, 1951. Constituciones sinodales de la diócesis de Barquisimeto, Venezuela, 1951. Cuernavaca, México, Centro Intercultural de Documentación, 1971. 194 p. (Sínodos diocesanos) (CIDOC fuentes; no. 19: Serie segunda)

2222

Bologna (Archdiocese) Synod, 1788. Synodus diocessana bononiensis ab . . . Andrea Joannetto S. R. E. cardinali et bononiensis ecclesiae archiepiscopo celebrata diebus II, III, et IV, septembris anno MDCCLXXXVIII. Bononiae, apud Longhi et a Volpe impressores archiepiscopales, 1788. 324, 200.

2223

The Bishops' synod. (the first synod of St. Patrick): a symposium with text, translation, and commentary, edited by M. J. Faris. Liverpool, Francis Cairns, 1976. 63, [11] p.
Bibliography: p. 61–63.

2224

Bouix, Dominique. Tractatus de concilio provinciali. Editio 2. ab ipsomet auctore recognita. Parisiis, Ruffet, 1862. 592 p.

2225

Briacca, Giuseppe. Gli statuti sinodali novaresi di Papiniano Della Rovere. (a. 1298). Milano, Vita e pensiero, 1971. 306 p. (Pubblicazioni dell' Università cattolica del S. Cuore. Saggi e ricerche. Serie 3: Scienze storiche, 5)
Bibliography: p. [1]–10.

2226

Catholic Church. Diocese of Arequipa, Peru. Synodo Diocesana, 1684. Constituciones synodales del Obispado de Arequipa, 1684, [hechas y ordenadas por] Antonio de León. Cuernavaca, México, Centro Intercultural de Documentación, 1971. 208, 37 p. (Sínodos diocesanos) (CIDOC fuentes, no. 12: Serie segunda)

2227

Catholic Church. Archdiocese of Semarang, Indonesia. Statuta pro diocesibus provinciae ecclesiasticae de Semarang. [Semarang?] 1962. 71 p.

2228

Catholic Church. Archdiocese of Tegucigalpa. Sínodo Diocesano, 2d, 1930. Estatutos sinodales, Tegucigalpa, Honduras, 1930, [celebrados por] Agustín Hombach. Cuernavaca, México, Centro Intercultural de Documentación, 1971. 103 p. (Sínodos diocesanos) (CIDOC fuentes, no. 14: Serie segunda)

2229

Catholic Church. Diocese of Vich, Spain. Synodus. Constitutiones synodales Dioec. Vicen. in unum collectae, renovatae, & auctae sub Emmanuele a Muñoz et Giul. Vici, Ex officinâ Morera, 1748. 132 p.

2230

Catholic church in Mexico. Provincial council. Concilio III, Provincial Mexicano, publicado con las licencias necessarias por Mariano Galvan Rivera. Mexico, 1859.

2231

Concilia Pragensia. Prager Synodal-Beschlüsse. Zum ersten Male zsgest. u. mit einer Einl. vershen v. C. Höfler. (Nachdr. d. Ausg. Prag 1862) Wien, Geyer, 1972. 116 p.
Includes bibliographical references.

2232

Constance (Diocese) Synod. Constitvtiones et decreta synodi diocesanae constantiensis, edita ac promvlgata diezo, octobris, anno MDCIX praesidente, Iacobo, episcopo Constant Constantiae, ex Typographaeo Nicolai Kalt, 1609 [i.e., 1610] 346, [1] p.

2233

Constitutiones synodales ecclesiae zagrebiensis pro clero diocesano recusae et extractu nombiliorum pro jure ecclesiastico novissimo conciliorum ecclesiae hungaricae e collectione eterffiena adductao juseu et authoritata. Domini Romini Maximiliani Verhovaca. Zagrebiae, Typis Novoszelianis, 1805.

2234

Daubuz, Charles. De impvtatione primi peccati

Adae epistola et carmen propemticum. Ad Antonivm Garissolivm. Montalbani, Typis P. Braconerii, 1648. 47 p.

2235

Didier, Noël. Les églises de Sisteron et de Forcalquier du XIe siècle à la Révolution; le problème de la "concathédralité." Paris, Libr. Dalloz, 1954. 240 p. (Essais et travaux; collection publiée par la Faculté de droit . . . de l'Université de Grenoble, 4)
Bibliography: p. [vii]–xviii.

2236

Dittrich, Paul. Die Meissener Diözese unter der Kirchenpolitik der Landesherren des 16. und 17. Jahrhunderts. Leipzig, St. Benno-Verlag [1961]. 87 p. (Studien zur katholischen Bistums- und Klostergeschichte, Bd. 1)
Bibliography: p. 9–10.

2237

Domenico Quesada da Napoli. Decreta . . . Dominici a Neapoli sac. monasterii Montis Casinen, abbatis . . . Edita in dioecesana synodo sacrarum congregationum rescriptis vallata. Anno Domini MDCLII Innocentio X pont. max. Editio altera, Beneventi, ex typografia Nicolai Pignatelo, 1736. 264 p.

2238

Donnelly, Francis B. The diocesan synod; an historical conspectus and commentary. Washington, D.C., The Catholic University of America, 1932. 142 p. (The Catholic University of America. Canon law studies, no. 74)
Bibliography: p. 125–129.

2239

Dumont, Karl T. Sammlung kirchlicher Erlasse, Verordnungen und Bekanntmachungen für die Erzdiocese Köln. Nach dem inhalte geordnet und hrsg. Amtliche Ausg. Köln, Bachem, 1874. 532 p.

2240

Florence (Diocese) Council. Statuta concilii Florentini. Florence, Philipp Junta, May 23, 1518.

2241

Frascati (Diocese) Synod, 1763. Constitutiones synodales ecclesiae tusculanse seu Synodus tusculansa a celsitudine regia eminentissima Henrici episcopi inequlani . . . in cathedrali tusculano templo apostolorum principia a. Petri calutrata diabua VIII, IX, X, et XI septembris A. D. MDCCLXIII. Romae, excudebat Jo: Canerusus Salomoni, 1764. 947, [1] p.

2242
Garissoles, Antoine. Decreti synodici Carentoniensis de impvtatione primi peceati Adae explicatio et defensio. Montalbani, Braconerios, 1648. 821 p.

2243
Greensburg, Pa. (Diocese) Synod. First synod of the Diocese of Greensburg, convoked Dec. 11, 1961, Blessed Sacrament Cathedral, Greensburg; synodal statutes. William G. Connare, Bishop of Greensburg. [Greensburg, 1963] 166 p.

2244
Hess, Hamilton. The Canons of the Council of Sardica, A.D. 343; a landmark in the early development of Canon law. Oxford, Clarendon Press, 1958. 170 p. (Oxford theological monographs, v. 1)
Bibliography: p. 159–163.

2245
La Paz, Bolivia (Diocese). Sínodo Diocesana, 2d, 1638. Constituciones sinodales del Obispado de Nuestra Señora de La Paz del Perú. Cuernavaca, México, Centro Intercultural de Documentación, 1970. 6, 77, 14 p. (Sínodos diocesanos) (CIDOC fuentes; no. 9: Serie segunda)

2246
La Paz, Bolivia (Diocese). Sínodo Diocesano, 3d, 1738. Constituciones synodales del Obispado de La Paz, Bolivia, 1738. Cuernavaca, México, Centro Intercultural de Documentación, 1970. 37, 220, 57 p. (Sínodos diocesanos) (CIDOC fuentes; no. 10: Serie segunda)

2247
La Paz, Bolivia (Diocese). Sínodo Diocesano, 4th, 1883. Constituciones sinodales, La Paz, Bolivia, 1883. Cuernavaca, México, Centro Intercultural de Documentación, 1970. 23, 154 p. (Sínodos diocesanos) (CIDOC fuentes; no. 6: Serie segunda)

2248
Lima (Archdiocese). Sínodo Diocesano, 1613. Constituciones synodales del Arzobispado de los Reyes en el Piru, 1613. Cuernavaca, México, Centro Intercultural de Documentación, 1970. 4, 200, 21 p. (Sínodos diocesanos) (CIDOC fuentes; no. 11: Serie segunda)

2249
Lima (Archbishopric). Constituciones synodales del arçobispado de Los Reyes en el Perv. [Lima] Reimpression por Morel, 1754. 2 v. in 1.

2250
Lima (Archdiocese). Sínodo Diocesano, 13th, 1926. Constituciones sinodales, Lima, Peru, 1926. Cuernavaca, México, Centro Intercultural de Documentación, 1972. 41 p. (Sínodos diocesanos) (CIDOC fuentes; no. 18: Serie segunda)

2251
Louis, William F. Diocesan archives; a historical synopsis and commentary. Washington, D.C., The Catholic University of America Press, 1941. 101 p. (The Catholic University of America. Canon law studies, no. 137)
Bibliography: p. 89–91.

2252
Mainz (Archdiocese). Laws, statutes, etc. Undergerichts ordnung des ertzstiffts Meyntz, inn welcher gantz fleissig angerzeygt, wie und welcher gestalt an allen. (Meyntz), 1535. 27 1.

2253
Marchetti, Giovanni. Del Concilio di Sardica e de'suoi canoni sù la forma de'giudizj ecclesiastici; dissertazione polemico-canonica pel dritto delle appellazioni romane. Roma, L. Perego Salvioni, 1783. 211 (i.e., 212) p.

2254
Murphy, Francis J. Legislative powers of the provincial council; a historical synopsis and a commentary. Washington, D.C., Catholic University of America Press, 1947. 158 p. (The Catholic University of America. Canon law studies, no. 257).
Bibliography: p. 131–138.

2255
Naples (Archdiocese) Curia. Decisiones cvriae archiepiscopalis neapolitanae, in qvibus praxis rervm civilivmm criminalium, & ecclesiasticarum in

eadem curia tractatarum dilucide continetur. Pars prima [-tertia] . . . Nunc secundo in lucem editum . . . Avthore Io. Aloysio Riccio. Accessere dvo indices. Neapoli, ex typographia Dominici de Ferdinando Naccarani, 1622. 3 v. in 1.

2256
Neumann, Johannes. Synodales Prinzip; der grössere Spielraum im Kirchenrecht. Freiburg, Herder, 1973. 117 p. (Kirche im Gespräch)
Includes bibliographical references.

2257
Pole, Reginald, *Cardinal*. De concilio liber. Romae, Apud P. Manutium, 1562. 64 1.

2258
Ravenna (Archdiocese) Synod. Synodus diocesana quam sub faustissimis auspiciis sanctissimi in Christo patris Pii papae secti celebravit Antonius Codronchi archiepiscopus Ravennas in ecclesia metropolitana xiii. xii. xi. kal. sect. anno MDCCXC. Ravennae, ex Typographia Archiepiscopali, 1791. 459 p.

2259
Riccio, Giovanni L. Praxis rerum quotidianorum fori ecclesiastici et in Curia Archiepiscopali Neapolitana discussarum. Neapoli, Sauus, 1650. 505 p.

2260
San José, Costa Rica (Archdiocese). Sínodo Diocesano, 4th. 1944. Statuta synodalia Archidioecesis Sancti Iosephi in Costa Rica. 1944. Cuernavaca, México, Centro Intercultural de Documentación, 1971. 263 p. (Sínodos diocesanos) (CIDOC fuentes; no. 16: Serie segunda)

2261
Somerville, Sir Robert. The councils of Urban II. Amsterdam, Hakkert, 1972. v. (Annuarium historiae conciliorum. Supplementum, v. 1)
Bibliography: v. 1, p. xiii–xxi.

2262
Sucre, Bolivia (Archdiocese). Sínodo, Diocesano, 1773. Constituciones sinodales del Arzobispado de La Plata (Bolivia) 1773. Cuernavaca, México, Centro Intercultural de Documentación, 1971. 2 v. (Sínodos diocesanos) (CIDOC fuentes; no. 5: Serie segunda)

2263
Tarvisio (Diocese). Constitutiones . . . Augusti archiepiscopi Zacco Dei & Apostolicae Sedis gratis episcopi Tarvisini promulgatae in synodo dioecesana diebus 2. 3. 4. mensis Septembris 1727. Tarvisii, Planta, 1728. 222 p.

2264
Toulouse (Archdiocese). Decisiones capelle sedis archiepiscopalis Tholose vna cum additionibus additis per egregium virum dominŭ Stephanum Auffrerij . . . ac per eum correpte vigili cura: incipiŭt feliciter. Postremoq$_3$ iterum diligenter limate ac nouis additionib[9] decorate nouiter additis. Lugduni, venundantur ab Stephano Gueynard [1508] [56] p.

2265
Treviso (Diocese). Synod, 1911. Synodus Dioecesana Tervisina habita in Folesia Cathedrali disbus XXIV, XXV, XXVI Aprilis MCMXI. Tervisii, ex Typographia Coop. Tarvisino, 1911. 275 p.

2266
Venice (Archdiocese) Synod, 1592. Synodvs Veneta ab illustriss, et reuerendiss. d.d. Lavrentio Priolo patriarcha Venetiarvm, Dalmatiaeque primate, secundo anno sui patriarchatus celebrata. Diebus 9. 10. et 11. settembris, 1592. sanctiss. d. n. Clemente Octavo pontifice maximo sedente. Venetiis, ex Typographia Pinelliana, 1668. 211, [5] p.

2267
Venice (Archdiocese) Synod, 1594. Synodvs Veneta secvnda ab illustriss. et reuerendiss. d. d. Lavrentio Priolo patriarcha Venetiarvm, Dalmatiaeque primate, quarto anno sui patriarchatvs celebrata. Diebus 15. 16. 17. nouembris 1594. sanctiss. d. n. Clemente Octavo pontifice maximo sedente. Venetiis, ex Typographia Pinelliana, 1668. 78, [2] p.

2268
Venice (Archdiocese) Synod, 1667. Synodvs diaecesana Veneta secvnda, ab illustriss. et reuerendiss. in Christo patre, et d. d. Io: Francisco Mavroceno miseratione diuina patriarcha Venetiarum. Dalmatiaeq; primate, &c celebrata diebus 18. 19. et 20. mensis aprilis 1667. Accesservnt constitutio Pij papae V. de Medicis, et series opinionum damnatarum à Sacra suprema congregatione sanctissimae inquisitionis almae vrbis, sub diebus 24. septembris

1665, et 18. martj 1666. Venetiis, ex Typographia Pinelliana, 1668. 67 p.

2269

Venice (Archdiocese) Synod, 1653. Synodvs diaecesana Veneta ab illustriss. et reuerendiss. in Christo patre, et d. d. Io: Francisco Mavroceno miseratione diuina patriarcha Venetiarum, Dalmatiaeq; primate, &c celebrata diebus 17. 18. et 19. mensis iunij 1653. Accesservnt decreta generalia visitationis eius patriarchalis, cum alijs decretis, et instructionibus pro visitatoribus concionatoribus, et missae coeremonijs. Venetiis, ex Typographia Pinelliana, 1668. 72 p.

2270

Venice (Archdiocese). Constitvtiones. et privilegia patriarchatvs, et cleri venetiarvm. Illustrissimi, ac reuerendissimi d. d. Ioannes Trivisani ivris vtrivsqve doct. patriarchae Venetiarum, Dalmatiaeque primatis, etc. ivssv edita. Venetiis, ex Typographia Pinelliana, 1668. 118, [14] p.

2271

Venice (Archdiocese) Synod, 1741. Acta, et decreta synodi Venetae habita, et promulgata ab illustrissimo, et reverendissimo in Christo patre, et d. d. fr. Francisco Antonio Corriario ordinis capuccionorum miseratione divina patriarcha Venetiarum Dalmatiaeque primate &c diebus 18. 19. et 20. mensis aprilis 1741. Venetiis, ex Typographia Ducali, & Patriarchali Pinelliana, 1741. 7, 91 p.

CONGREGATIONS OF ROMAN CHURCH

2272

Catholic Church. *Cancellaria Apostolica.* Bvlla S. N. D. Pauli diuina providentia papae IIII. super erectione officiii S. R. E. Camerae Apostolicae regentis. Romae, apud Antonium Bladum Imps. Cameralem, [1559] [9] 1.
Side notes.

2273

Catholic Church. *Congregatio de propaganda fide.* Regulae et constitutiones collegiorum pontificiorum avenionensium a sacra Congregatione de propaganda fide anno millesimo septingentisimo decimo octavo confirmatae. Accedunt instructiones

eusdem s. Cong. pro archiepiscopis, & episcopis habentibus loca in collegiis avenionensibus. Romae, ex typographia sac. Cong. de prop. fide, 1780. 29 p.

2274

Catholic Church. *Pope* Elenchvs congregationum, tribunalium, & collegiorum almae Vrbis, alphabetico ordine digestus. Accedit catalogus . . . cardinalium. Necnon eorumdem, qui de praesanti sunt ordinum regularium protectores. As syllabus . . . signaturae gratiae & iustitiae votantium, ac referendariorum. Cum indice in fine. Romae, typis reu. Cam. apost., 1714. 77 p.

2275

Catholic Church. Pope, 1503–1513 (Julius II). Regule expectatiuaru$_3$ & prerogatiurū ta$_3$ familiariū q̃$_3$ aliorū nuper apposite cū earum commento. [Ancone, Impressum expensis Hieronymi Soncini, 1516] [61] p.

2276

Catholic Church. Pope, 1523–1534 (Clemens VII). Regvle ordinationes & constitutiones Cancellarie. s. dñi nostri dñi Clementis diuina prouidentia papa. VII: lecte & publicate in Cancellaria Apostolica nouiter impresse [Rome, Cancelleria apostolica, 1526]

2277

Della punizione degli eretici e del Tribunale della Santa Inquisizione; lettere apologetiche, 1789. 2 v.

2278

Dziob, Michael W. The Sacred congregation for the Oriental church. Washington, D.C., The Catholic University of America Press, 1945. 181 p. (The Catholic University of America. Canon law studies, no. 214)
Bibliography: p. 160–167.

2279

Fuller, Richard. Letters concerning the Roman chancery. Baltimore and Charleston, 1840? 276 p.

2280

García, Pablo. Orden que comunmente se guarda en el Santo Oficio de la Inquisición, acerca del procesar en las causas que en él se tratan; conforme a lo que está proveído por las instructiones antiguas y nuevas. Recopilado por . . . Secretario del Consejo de la Santa General Inquisición . . . En Valencia, En la oficina de Antonio Bordazar de Artazu, Impressor del Santo Officio, 1736. 78 p.

2281
Honorante, Romualdo. Praxis Secretariae Tribunalis Cardinalis Urbis Vicarii. Secunda editio novis additionibus aucta et illustrata. Romae, Excudebant B. Franzesi et C. Paperi, 1762. 342 p.

2282
Leo, Marco P. Praxis ad litteras maiores poenitentiarii, et officij sacrae poenitentiariae apostolicae in qvatvor partes distribvta. In quibus declarantur singularum formularum clausulae, & traditur modus praefatas litteras exequendi. Romae, ex typographia Ludouici Grignani, 1644. 640 p.

2283
Loemel, Hermann. Defensi decreti sacrae congregationis . . . S. R. E. cardinalium a . . . Urbano VIII . . . ad indicem librorum. Coloniae, Typ. Camerae, 1634. 198 p.

2284
Luca, Giovanni. Liber 15. Part I De indiciis, et de Praxi Curvae Romanae, Par. II. Relatio Romanae Curvae Forensis, eiusque Tribunalium, Et Congregationum. Romae, Typis Haerredum, Corbelletti, 1673.

2285
Mantica, Francesco, cardinal. Vaticanae lvcvbrationes de tacitis et ambigvis conuentionibus, in libros XXVII dispertitae. Editio postrema magno studio a mendis repurgata & allegationibus characterum diuersitate distinctis ornatius edita; cum indice uberrimo. Genevae, sumptibus Iacobi Chouët, 1645. 2 v. in 1.

2286
Masini, Eliseo, brother. Sacro Arsenale Overo Prattica Dell' Officio Della Santa Inquisitione. Nuouamente correto, & ampliato. Bologna, Ad instanza del Baglioni, 1665. 432, [64], 32 p.

2287
McManus, Frederick R. The Congregation of Sacred Rites. Washington, D.C., The Catholic University of America Press, 1954. 180 p. (The Catholic University of America. Canon law studies, no. 352) Bibliography: p. 160–170.

2288
Navar, Tiburce. Manvdvctio ad praxim executionis litterarum sacrae Poenitentiariae. Opera r. p. Tibvrtii Navar . . . Quoad absolutiones, dispensationes, rehabilitationes votorum commutationes, &c. impertiendas. Addito etiam in fine modo scribendi, & recurrendi ad sacram Poenitentiariam in casibus sanctae Sedi reseruatis praesertim occultis. Romae, typis reuer. Camerae apost., 1588. 276 p.

2289
Petra, Vicenzo. De sacra poenitentiaria apostolica pars prima. Romae, ex typografia Josephi Nicolai de Martiis, 1712. 394 p.

2290
Pittono, Johannes B. Constitutiones pontificiae et romanarum congregationum decisiones ad consursum parochialium, et beneficiorum collationem spectantes. Venetiis, 1731. 480 p.

2291
Plettenberg, Hunold. Notitia congregationum et tribunalim Curiae romanae. Hildesii, typis Joan. Leonardi Schlegelii episc. & summi capituli typogr., 1693. 790 p.

2292
Sheehy, Robert F. The Sacred Congregation of the Sacraments; its competence in the Roman Curia. Washington, D.C., The Catholic University of America Press, 1954. 141 p. (The Catholic University of America. Canon law studies, no. 333) Bibliography: p. 130–134.

Church and State

2293
Arbeloa, Victor M. Separación de Iglesia-Estado en España. Madrid, Mañana, 1977. 76, [1] p. (Colección Aperos del cristianismo, 13)
Includes bibliographical references.

2294
Badii, Cesare. Ius canonicum comparatum cum edictis legum civilium de re ecclesiastica. Taurini, prostat apud Marietti, 1925. 584 p.

2295

Barrett, John D. M. A comparative study of the councils of Baltimore and the Code of canon law. Washington, D.C., The Catholic University of America Press, 1932. 223 p. (The Catholic University of America. Canon law studies, no. 83)
Bibliography: p. 209–212.

2296

Bartlett, Chester J. The tenure of parochial property in the United States of America. Washington, D.C., 1926. 108 p. (Universitas catholica Americae. Facultas juris canonici. Canon law studies, no. 31)
Bibliography: p. 102–103.

2297

Calvo, Juan. Concordato y acuerdos parciales: política y derecho. Pamplona, Ediciones Universidad de Navarra, 1977. 205 p. (Colección canónica)
Includes bibliographical references.

2298

Catholic Church. Pope. Ragioni della Sede Apostolica nelle presenti controversie colla Corte di Torino. [Rome] 1732.

2299

Catholic Church. Pope. Scritture ed atti trasmessi d'ordine di nostro signore al sacro collegio concernenti le ragioni della Sede appostolica nelle presenti controversie colla corte di Torino. [Roma] 1731. 312 p.

2300

Catholic Church. Treaties, etc., 1800–1823 (Pius VII). Concordato fra Sua Santità Pio VII, sommo pontefice, e Sua Maestà Ferdinando I, re del Regno delle Due Sicilie, con l'allocuzione pronunziata nel Concistoro de' 16 marzo 1818, con le lettere e gl'indulti apostolici, co' documenti citati nel Concordato e co' decreti e le sovrane disposizioni finora publicate. Napoli, Stamperia della Società filomatica, 1818. v.

2301

Catholic Church. Treaties, etc. I concordati di Pio XII (1939–1958): (Belgio, Germania, Portagallo, Spagna, Argentina, Bolivia, Colombia, Rep. Domicana, Haiti), a cura di Pio Ciprotti ed Anna Talamanca. Milano, Giuffrè, 1976. 130 p. (Testi per escreitazioni, Università degli studi di Camerino, Facoltà di giurisprudenza; sezione 15, no. 7)

2302

Catholic Church. Treaties, etc. I concordati di Giovanni XXIII et dei primi anni di Paulo VI, 1958–1974: Austria, Germania, Jugoslavia, Spagna, Svizzera, Argentina, Bolivia, Colombia, Paraguay, El Salvador, Tunisia, Venezuela, a cura di Pio Ciprotti ed Elisa Zampetti. Milano, Giuffrè, 1976. 152 p. (Testi per escreitazioni, Università degli studi di Camerino, Facoltà di giurisprudenza sezione 15, no. 8)

2303

Catholic Church. Treaties, etc., 1922–1939 (Pius XI). La soluzione della questione romana nelle convenzioni lateranensi, sottoscritte il giorno 11 febbraio 1929. Roma, Tip. Poliglotta vaticana, 1929. 98 p.

2304

Eichmann, Eduard. Kirche und staat. Paderborn, Schöningh, 1912–14. 2 v. (Quellensammlung zur kirchlichen rechtsgeschichte und zum kirchenrecht. Hrsg. von Eduard Eichmann, 1)

2305

Escobedo G. A., José. Las relaciones entre la Iglesia y el Estado en la historia, la doctrina y los cánones. Madrid, Librería General Suárez, 1927. 130 p.
Includes bibliographical references.

2306

Fresneau, Armand. De la constitution politique des états de l'église. Paris, Auguste Vaton, 1860. 232 p.

2307

Friedberg, Emil. Die mittelalterlichen lehren über das verhältniss von staat und kirche (erster theil). Leipzig, Edelmann, 1874. 29 p.

2308

Gentrup, Theodore. Die kirchliche Rechtslage der deutschen Miderheiten katholischer Konfession in Europa, eine Materiliensammlung. Berlin, Deutsche Ruchschau, 1928. 472 p. (Handbücher des Ausschusses für Minderheitenrecht)
Includes bibliography.

2309

Girón y Arcas, Joaquín. La situación jurídica de la iglesia católica en los diversos estados de Europa y de América; notas para su estudio. Madrid, Suárez, 1905. 379 p. (Biblioteca de derecho y de ciencias sociales [XXIV])

2310

Heston, Edward L. The alienation of church property in the United States. An historical synopsis and commentary. Washington, D.C., The Catholic University of America Press, 1941. 222 p. (The Catholic University of America. Canon law studies, no. 132)

2311

Hinschius, Paul. De jure patronatus regio. Berolini, typis Gustavi Schade [1855] 79, [1] p.

2312

Iung, Nicolas. El derecho público de la Iglesia en sus relaciones con los estados. Pref. de P. Andrieu-Guitrancourt. Traducción y referencias al Concordato español de 1953 por Isidoro Martín. Madrid [Instituto de Estudios Políticos] 1957. 385 p. (Biblioteca de cuestiones actuales)
Bibliography: p. 330–334.

2313

Iung, Nicolas. Le droit public de l'Église dans ses relations avec les états; pref. de M. l'abbé Andrieu-Guitrancourt. Paris, Procure générale du clergé, 1948. 341 p.
"Bibliographie": p. [329]–332.

2314

Jannaccone, Costantino. I fondamenti del diritto ecclesiastico internazionale. Milano, Giuffrè, 1936. 230 p.
Bibliographical footnotes.

2315

Kaiser, Joseph H. Die Politische Klausel der Konkordate. Berlin, Muncher, Duncrer & Humblot, 1949.

2316

Kremer, Michael N. Church support in the United States. Washington, D.C., Catholic University of America Press, 1930. (Catholic University of America. Canon law studies, no. 61)

2317

Lackits, Jorge S. Derecho público eclesiástico, donde se trata de la iglesia cristiana y de la concordia de la potestad sagrada con la civil: traducida en Castellano por D. Jacobo Gallegos-Fajardo. Valencia, Librería de Mallen y Sobrinos, 1842. 416 p.

2318

Lat, Leontius L. De subordinatione status Catholici ad Ecclesiam. Romae, Ferrari, 1955. 109 p.

2319

Llano Cifuentes, Rafael. Curso de direito canônico: a Igreja e o Estado à luz do Vaticano II. São Paulo, Edição Saraiva, 1971. 274 p.
Includes bibliographical references.

2320

Monroy Cabra, Marco G. Régimen concordatario colombiano. Bogotá, Editorial Temis, 1975. 290 p.
Bibliography: p. [273]–275.

2321

Nessel, William. First amendment freedoms, papal pronouncements, and concordat practice; a comparative study in American law and public ecclesiastical law. Washington, D.C., The Catholic University of America Press, 1961. 268 p. (Catholic University of America. Canon law studies, no. 412)
Bibliography: p. 251–258.

2322

Olalia, Alexander A. A comparative study of the Christian constitution of states and the constitution of the Philippine commonwealth. Washington, D.C., The Catholic University of America Press, 1944. 136 p. (The Catholic University of America. Canon law studies, no. 206)
Bibliography: p. 118–122.

2323

Peignot, Gabriel. Prècis historique et analytique; des pragmatiques, concordats, déclaration, constitution, convention et autres actes relatifs a la discipline de l'eglise, en France, depuis Saint Louis jusqu'a Louis XVIII. Paris A. Renouard, 1817. 156 p.

2324

Pérez Mier, Laureano. Iglesia y estado nuevo; los concordatos ante el moderno derecho público.

Prólogo de E. F. Regatillo, S. I. Madrid, Ediciones Fax, 1940. 730 p.
"Nota bibliográfica": p. [709]–715.

2325

Semana de Derecho Canónico, 13th, Saragossa, 1971. La institución concordatoria en la actualidad. Trabajos de la 13. Semana de Derecho Canónico. Salamanca, 1971. 576 p.
Includes bibliographical references.

2326

Stiglich Gazzani, Fernando. Relaciones Estado-Iglesia en el Perú; separación y colaboración entre la Iglesia y el Estado en el Peru. Ponencia sustentada en el Congreso Nacional Extraordinario de Colegios de Abogados del Peru. Callao, 1969. 96 p.
Bibliography: p. 81–82.

ADMINISTRATION

2327

Adami, Franco E. Ecclesia minoribus aequiparatur. Valore della massima e connessi problemi di qualificazione giuridica dei controlli canonici sull'amministrazione degli enti ecclesiastici. Padova, CEDAM, 1970. 317 p. (Pubblicazioni della Facoltà di giurisprudenza dell'Università di Padova, 58)

2328

Berardi, Carlo S. Idea del governo ecclesiastico. A cura di Arnaldo Bertola e Luigi Firpo: introd. di Arnaldo Bertola, testo critico e note di Luigi Firpo. Torino, Giappichelli [1963] 269 p. (Istituto giuridico dell'Università di Torino. Testi inediti o rari, 6)
Bibliographical footnotes.

2329

Bouix, Dominique. Tractatus de Curia Romana, seu de cardinalibus, Romanis congregationibus, legatis, nuntiis, vicariis et protonotariis apostolicis. Parisiis, Bourguet-Calas, 1880. 711 p. (*His* institutiones juris canonici in varios tractatus divisae)

2330

Catholic Church. Cancellaria Apostolica. Taxe Cācellarie Apostolice & taxe Sacre Penitētiarie itidē aplice. Parisiis, Venundantur per Tossanū Denis, 1520. 42 1.

2331

Catholic Church. Congregatio sacrorum rituum. Nuova tassa, e riforma delle spese per le cause delle beatificazioni, e canonizzazioni, e dell'altre spese per la solennità dell medisime beatificazioni, e canonizzazioni, fatta e pubblicata per ordine di . . . papa Benedetto XIV. In Roma, nella Stamperia della Reverenda Camera Apostolica, 1741. 28 p.

2332

Comyns, Joseph J. Papal and Episcopal administration of church property. Washington, D.C., The Catholic University of America Press, 1942. 155 p. (The Catholic University of America. Canon law studies, no. 147).

2333

Delgado, Gregorio. La Curia Romana, el gobierno central de la Iglesia. Pamplona, Ediciones Universidad de Navarra, 1973. 531 p. (Colección canónica de la Universidad de Navarra)
"Algunos de los textos más significativos en relación con la reforma de la Curia Romana": p. [485]–531.
Bibliography: p. 451–482.

In the decree, *Christus Dominus*, n. 9, of Vatican II, the bishops recommended the reform of the Roman Curia. On August 15, 1967, Paul VI responded to that recommendation by promulgating the constitution, *Regimini Ecclesiae Universae*, embodying that reform. It can be said that the current transformation of the Curia was prompted by the bishops' new awareness of their collegiality and diocesan pastoral function in and after Vatican II. Since then many writers have studied the subject, including Delgado who offers an extensive and in depth analysis of the central government of the Church. Sections are devoted to the central administrative departments, supreme council of government, mixed commissions, and State Secretariat; and to the departments of Public Affairs of the Church, the Doctrine of Faith, Oriental Churches, the Bishops, the Discipline of the Sacraments, the Divine Cult, the Clergy, the Religious, Catholic Teaching, the Laymen, and Economic Affairs of the Holy See. An appendix lists the most pertinent documents used in the study.

2334

Jaeger, Leo A. The administration of vacant and quasi-vacant diocese in the United States; historical synopsis of general legislation and commentary. Washington, D.C., The Catholic University of America Press, 1932. 236 p. (The Catholic University of America. Canon law studies, no. 81)

Bibliography: p. 222–227.

2335

Luca, Giovanni B. de, Cardinal. Tractatus de officiis venalibus vacabilibus Romanae curiae; cum juribus, seu documentis, informationibus, responsis, & decisionibus super suppressione Collegii secretariorum apostolicorum. Accedit alter tractatvs De locis montium non vacabilium urbis. Cvm nonnvllis svmmorvm pontificvm constitutionibus; nec non Sacrae Rotae romanae decisionibus ad materiam facientibus, suis locis optimè adjectis. Venetiis, ex typographia Balleoniana, 1735. 308 p.

2336

Pujo, Maurice. De la législation civile, criminelle et administrative des états pontificaux. Paris, Cotillon, 1862. 211 p.

2337

Semana de Derecho Canónico. 9th, El Escorial, 1962. Aspectos del derecho administrativo canónico; trabajos de la IX Semana de Derecho Canónico. Salamanca, 1964. 270 p.

Bibliographical footnotes.

2338

Vuillefroy, A. Traité de l'administration du culte catholique. Principes et règles d'administration. Extraits des lois des décrets et ordinannances royales. Paris, Joubert, Libraire de la cour de cassation, 1842. 528 p.

DICTIONARIES

2339

André, Michel. Cours alphabétique et méthodique de droit canon dans ses rapports avec le droit civil ecclésiastique, contenant tout ce qui regarde les concordats de France et des autres nations, les canons de discipline, les usages du Saint-Siège, la pratique et les règles de la Chancellerie romaine, la hiérarchie ecclésiastique, avec droits et devoirs des membres de chaque degré, en un mot, tout ce qui regarde les personnes, les choses et les jugements. Nouv. éd., entièrement refondue et con-

sidérablement augm. Paris, Boullotte, 1852–53. 5 v.

2340

André, Michel. Diccionario de derecho canónico traducido del que ha escrito en francés el abate Andrés . . . arreglado á la jurisprudencia eclesiastica española antigua y moderna. Contiene todo lo que puede dar un conocimiento exacto, completo y actual de los cánones, de la disciplina, de los concordatos. Y particularmente todo lo comprendido en el derecho canónico, bajo los nombres de personas, cosas y juicios eclesiásticos. Aumentado con numerosas adiciones y articulos nuevos, algunos importantisimos del derecho canónico que tienen relación con la medicina legal é hijiene pública, tales como aborto, infanticidio . . . etc., etc. Por D. Isidro de la Pastora y Nieto . . . Bajo la dirección del Excmo. é Illmo. Sr. D. Judas José Romo. Madrid, de la Peña, 1847–48. 4 v. in 2.

2341

Carthagena, Bartholomeus á. Enchiridon juris utriusque: seu definitiones distinctiones et questiones clare et breviter definitae juris canonici et civilis. Madrid, 1715.

2342

Cartagena, Bartolomé. Enchiridion iuris utriusque: seu, Definitiones, distinctiones, et quaestiones clare et breviter definitae iuris canonici et civilis. Synopsi bifaria, & in priore quidem omnes Decretalium; in posteriore verò omnes Institutionum imperialium. Authore B. S. [i.e. Stephan Dobner] Libros ac titulos breviter ac perspicuè explanantes ac enucleantes. Francofurti ad Moenum, Fleischer, 1761. 275 p.

2343

Carthagena, Bartholomeus á. Enchiridon juris utriusque, seu definitiones distinctiones & questiones clare & breviter definitae juris canonici et civilis. Madrid, Ibarra, 1770. 315 p.

2344

Duprat, Pardoux. Lexicon ivris civilis et canonici: sive potivs, Commentarivs de verborvm quae ad vtrumque ius pertinent significatione, antiquitatum romanarum elementis, & legum pop. rom. copiosissimo indice, adauctus: abhinc septem annis Pardulphi Prateij diligentia delineatus: nunc verò ita constructus, & supra omnes omnium editiones, tot tamque praeclaris & graecis & latinis dictionibus illustratus, vt parum ad eius eximium splendorem desiderari possit. Quid praeterea in hac secunda editione praestitū sit, epistola ad lectorem docebit. Lvgdvni, apvd Gulielmvm Rovillivm, 1574. 638 p.

2345

Indelicato, Salvatore. Dizionario canonico concordatario. Edito da Armando Fattinnanzi. Roma [Casa editr. Enciclop. del cristianesimo, 1953] 451 p.
  Bibliography: p. [449]–451.

2346

Köstler, Rudolf. Wörterbuch zum Codex juris canonici. München, Kösel & Pustet [1927–29] 379 p.

2347

Lydon, Patrick J. Ready answers in canon law; a practical summary of the Code for the parish clergy. New York, Cincinnati [etc.] Benziger Brothers, 1934. 533 p.

2348

Petra, Vincentius. Commentaris ad constitutiones apostolicas, seu bullas singulas summorum pontificium in Bullario Romano contentas secundum collectionem Cherabini. Romae, Typis Josephi Nicolai de Martiis, 1705–1706. 2 v.

2349

Pontas, Jean. Dictionarium casuum conscientiae, seu Praecipuarum difficultatum circa moralem, ac disciplinam ecclesiasticam decisiones. Accedunt menda Pontasiana, sive observationes quaedam circa opus gallicum Pontasii. Item fr. Danielis Concina . . . praefatio ad lectorem, & animadversiones critico-morales in praefata menda Pontasiana, cum actuario duorum casuum, qui in hoc dictionario desiderabantur. Venetiis, apud Antonium Bortoli, 1744. 3 v.

2350

Practica omnivm terminorvm Rotae, et aliorvm tribvnalivm Romanae Curiae omnibus curialibus necessaria & vtilissima. Vna cum festa Palatij. A Flaminio Parisio examinata & approbata; atque anno 1585 in lucem edita. Romae, Apud G. Facciottum, 1631. 56 p.

CONGRESSI

2351

Congrès de droit canonique, Institut catholique, Paris, 1947. Actes; cinquantenaire de la Faculté de droit canonique, Paris, 22–26 avril 1947. Paris, Letouzey & Ané [1950] 414 p. (Bibliothèque de la Faculté de droit canonique de Paris)
  Includes bibliographies.

2352

Congresso internazionale di diritto canonico, 2d, Milan, 1973. Persona e ordinamento nella Chiesa: Atti del II Congresso internazionale di diritto canonico: Milano, 10–16 settembre 1973, Autori vari. Milano, Vita e pensiero, 1975. 594 p.

2353

Congressus Iuridicus Internationalis, Rome, 1934. Acta Congressus Iuridici Internationalis VII saeculo a decretalibus Gregorii IX et XIV a codice Iustiniano promulgatis Romae, 12–17 Novembris 1934. Romae, Apud Custodiam Librariam Pont. Instituti Utriusque Iuris, 1935–37. 5 v.

2354

Conventus Canonistarum Hispani-Germanus, Salamanca, 1972. De lege Ecclesiae fundamentali condenda. Salmanticae, Consejo Superior de Investigaciones Científicas, Instituto San Raimundo de Peñafort, 1974. 195 p. (Monorafías Canónicas Peñafort, 17)
  Includes bibliographical references.

2355

International Congress of Medieval Canon Law, 4th, Toronto, Ont., 1972. Proceedings of the fourth International Congress of Medieval Canon Law, Toronto, 21–25, August, 1972, edited by Stephan Kuttner. Città del Vaticano, Biblioteca Apostolica Vaticana, 1976. 541 p.
  Includes bibliographical references and index.

2356

Semana de Derecho Canónico. 12th, Santiago de Compostela, 1968. Dinámica jurídica postconciliar. Salamanca, 1969. 335 p.

2357

Semana de Derecho Canónico, 14th, Braga, Portugal, 1972. El Concilio de Braga y la función de

la legislación particular en la Iglesia: trabajos de la XIV Semana Internacional de Derecho Canónico, celebrada en Braga bajo el patrocinio del señor Arzobispo Primado. Salamanca, Consejo Superior de Investigaciones Científicas, Instituto San Raimundo de Peñafort, 1975. 475 p.
Includes bibliographical references.

OTHER SUBJECTS

2358
Alfau Durán, Vetilio. El derecho de patronato en la República Dominicana. Santo Domingo, Editora Educativa Dominicana, 1975. 124 p. ([Publicaciones] Academia Dominicana de la Historia; v. 38)
Bibliography: p. [121]–124.

2359
Alonso, Joaquín M. Derechos de la conciencia erronea y otros derechos; diálogo para nuestro tiempo. Prólogo del Emmo. P. Arcadio María, Cardenal Larraona. Madrid, Editorial Coculsa, 196? v.
Bibliographical footnotes.

2360
Amort, Eusebius. De origine, progressu, valore, ac fructu indulgentiarum, nec non de dispositionibus ad eas lucrandas requisitis, accurata notitia historica, dogmatica, polemica, critica ... Accedunt quaestiones practicae, & responsa Sacrae congregationis indulgeniarum recentissima. Venice, Recurti, 1738. 508 p.

2361
Apostolic constitutions. French. La version syriaque de l'Octateuque de Clément, traduite par François Nau; rééditée par Pio Ciprotti. Milano, Giuffrè, 1967. 106 p. (Università degli studi di camerine. Istituto giuridico. Testi per esercitazioni, sezione 7, n. 4)
Bibliographical footnotes.

2362
Bastnagel, Clement V. The appointment of parochial adjutants and assistants. Washington, D.C., The Catholic University of America Press, 1930. (Catholic University of America. Canon law studies, no. 58)

2363
Bauduin, Gulielmus. De consuetudine in jure canonico. Dissertatio canonica. Lovanii, Excudebant Vanlinthout Fratres [1888] 230 p.

2364
Bauer, Joachim. Die Schrift "de pressuris ecclesiasticis" des Bischofs Atto von Vercelli: Untersuchung und Edition. Heidelberg, Schmidt, 1975. 197, xxx, 168 p.
Bibliography: p. 183–197, first part.

2365
Bleynianus, Antonius F. In theoriam et praxim beneficiorum ecclesiasticorum methodica et familiaris introductis. Turoni, Hishael, 1616. 498 p.

2366
Bušek, Vratislav. Poznámky k vývoji přísahy rozhodovací a doplňovací v právu kanoniském; současně odpověď na Dr. Turečka "Glosy o povaze některých přísah v kanonickém právu," 1930. V Bratislavě, Nákl. Právnické faculty University Komenského; v komisi F. Řivnáče v Praze, 1931. 124 p. (Knihovna Právnické fakulty University Komenského v Bratislavě, sv. 34)

2367
Carreri, Alessandro. De potestate Romani pontificis adversus impios politicos. Padua, Bolseta, 1599. 86 1.

2368
Catholic Church. Congregatio pro Doctrina Fidei. Dekret "Die Aufsicht der Hirten der Kirche über Bücher," Kongregation für die Glaubenslehre. Ausführungsbestimmungen zu Artikel 4 Abs. 1 und 2 des Dekretes. Geschäftsordnung für die Zulassung neuer Lehrbücher für den schulischen Religionsunterricht. Kriterienkatalog für Zulassungsverfahren zur kirchlichen Beurteilung von Unterrichtsmaterialien, Deutsche Bischofskonferenz, [Gesamtwerk] eingel. und kommentiert von Heribert Heinemann. Trier, Paulinus-Verlag, 1976. 56 p. (Nachkonziliare Dokumentation; Bd. 52)

2369
Catholic Church. Liturgy and Ritual, Ceremonial. Caeremoniale Episcoporum Ivssv Clementis VIII Pontificis Maximi nouissimi reformatum. Venice, Misserini, 1600.

2370

Catholic Church. Pontificius Coetus Studiosorum Iustitia et Pax. La Iglesia y los derechos del hombre, Comisión Pontificia Justitia et Paz. 1st ed. [Santiago de Chile?] Instituto Chileno de Estudios Humanísticos, [1976] 85 p.
Includes bibliographical references.

2371

Cenci, Luigi. Additiones ad eius Tractatum de censibus, vna cum CXLII. Sacrae Rotae Romanae decisionibvs ad materiam spectantibvs hactenus non impressis. Cum duplici indice copiosissimo, capitum, & materiarum. Venetiis, Apud C. Thomasinum, 1629. 243 p.

2372

Cenci, Luigi. De censibvs tractatvs, editio novissima. In qva non modo additiones, et S. R. romanae decisiones iam separatim impressae, sed & aliae pleraeque ab ipso authore manuscriptae suis locis repositae sunt, nec non Io. Baptistae Leonelij, & Ludouici Molinae commentaria ad bullam Pij v. De censibus ... Opus nunc absolutissimum ... Avgvstae Tavrinorvm, Tarini, 1638. 868, [20] p.

2373

Cenci, Luigi. De censibvs tractatvs, editio novissima. In qva non modo additiones, et S. R. romanae decisiones iam separatim impressae, sed & aliae pleraeque ab ipso authore manuscriptae suis locis repositae sunt, nec non Io. Baptistae Leonelij, & Ludouici Molinae commentaria ad bullam Pij V. De censibus ... Opus nunc absolutissimum ... Venetiis, apud Paulum Balleonium, 1651. 826 p.

2374

Cenci, Luigi. De censibvs, totam materiam ... theoricè, & practicè explicatam continens: Cvi accesservnt non modo additiones, & Sacrae Rotae romanae decisiones iam separatim impressae, sed & aliae pleraeque ab ipso athore manuscriptae suis locis repositae sunt; necnon Ioannis Baptistae Leonelij, & Ludouici Molinae commentaria ad bullam Pij V. De censibus ... Opus nunc absolutissimum ... Editio postrema. Lvgdvni, sumptibus Lavrentii Arnavd, Petri Borde, Ioan. & Petri Arnavd, 1676. 2 v. in 1.

2375

Condorelli, Mario. Destinazione di patrimoni e soggettività giuridica nel diritto canonico; contributo allo studio degli enti non personificati. Milano, Giuffrè, 1964. 192 p. (Pubblicazioni della Facoltà di giurisprudenza, Università di Catania, 51)
Includes bibliographical references and indexes.

2376

Costello, John M. Domicile and quasi-domicile. Washington, D.C., The Catholic University of America Press, 1930. (The Catholic University of America. Canon law studies, no. 60)

2377

Dee, Dacian. The manifestation of conscience. Washington, D.C., The Catholic University of America Press, 1960. 102 p. (The Catholic University of America. Canon law studies, no. 410)
Bibliography: p. 94–98.

2378

Díaz Díaz, Alfonso. Derecho fundamental de asociación en la Iglesia. [Pamplona] EUNSA [1972] 275 p. (Colección canónica de la Universidad de Navarra. Cuadernos, 18)
Bibliography: p. [265]–272.

2379

Dieck, Ignaz R. F. Die vermögensrechtliche Stellung der Mendikanten-Verbandsformen. [Köln, 1966] 128, 2 p.
Bibliography: p. iv–xiii.

2380

Dooley, Eugene A. Church law on sacred relics. Washington, D.C., The Catholic University of America Press, 1931. 143 p. (The Catholic University of America. Canon law studies, no. 70)
Bibliography: p. 127–131.

2381

Dubé, Arthur J. The general principles for the reckoning of time in canon law; an historical synopsis and commentary. Washington, D.C., The Catholic University of America Press, 1941. 299 p. (The Catholic University of America. Canon law studies, no. 144)
Bibliography: p. [273]–281.

2382

Ernst, Albert C. Free admission to the church for sacred rites. Washington, D.C., The Catholic Uni-

versity of America Press, 1964. 136 p. (The Catholic University of America. Canon law studies, no. 380)
Bibliography: p. 105–131.

2383
Farinacci, Prospero. Tractatus de haeresi. Jn quo per quaestiones, regulas, ampliationes, limitationes, quidquid iure civili & canonico: quidquid sacris conciliis, summorúmque pontificum constitutionibus sancitum, & communiter in ea materia receptum; quidquid denique in praxi seruandum, breui methodo illustratur. Cum argumentis, summariis, & indice locupletissimo. Editio novissima. Lvgdvni, sumptibus Laurentij Anisson, & soc., 1650. 346, [129] p.

2384
Finnegan, John T. Selected questions on the computation of time in canon law. Rome, Officium Libri Catholici—Catholic Book Agency, 1965. 82 p.
Bibliography: p. [xvii]–xxiii.

2385
Fransen, Gérard. Le dol dans la conclusion des actes juridiques, évolution des doctrines et système du Code canonique. Gembloux (Belgique) Duculot, 1946. 431, [1] p. (Universitas catholica lovaniensis: Dissertationes ad gradum magistri in Facultate theologica vel in Facultate iuris canonici consequendum conscriptae. Ser. II, t. 37)
"Index bibliographique": p. [xiii]–xxxii.

2386
Frison, Basil M. The retroactivity of law, an historical synopsis and commentary. Washington, D.C., The Catholic University of America Press, 1946. 221 p. (The Catholic University of America. Canon law studies, no. 231)
Bibliography: p. 194–202.

2387
Gagnon, Edouard. La censure des livres. Montréal, Grand séminaire, 1945 [i.e., 1946] 223 p. (Theologica montis regii, 5)

2388
Gerhardt, Bernard C. Interpretation of rescripts; a commentary with historical notes. Washington, D.C., The Catholic University of America Press,

1959. 154 p. (The Catholic University of America. Canon law studies, no. 398)
Bibliography: p. 147–150.

2389
Gismondi, Pietro. Saggio su "la prescrizione estintiva" in alcuni decretalisti. Firenze, S. editoriale G. U. F., 1937. 73, [4] p.
"Bibliografia": p. [71]–73.

2390
Giudice, Vincenzo del. Del diritto d'autore e del divieto di reimpressione e traduzione riguardo al Codex iuris canonici. Roma, Athenaeum, 1921. 46 p.
Bibliographical footnotes.

2391
Godefroy, Jacques. De interdicta Christianorvm cum gentilibus communione epistola, deqve pontificatv maximo, nvm Christiani imperatores cum aliquando geserint. Genevae, Supt. I. A. & S. de Tournes, 1654. 40 p.

2392
Goecke, Feodor. De exceptione spolii. Berolini, Schade [1858] 107, [1] p.

2393
Gongora, Joannes de. Disceptatio perpolita, et singvlaris, licêt imprameditate apud Salmanticense theatrum in ore magistrorum habita. Ad Salvivm Ivlianvm, lib. 3. Ad Vrseium Ferocem in 1. quidam 19. D. De manumissis testamento. Pro obtinenda caesarea vesperorum cathedra, & eisdem verbis, quibus tunc auditoribus dicta, nunc typographo dictata. Salmanticae, apud Didacum â Cossio [1636?] 28 p., 1 1.

2394
Gorino-Causa, Mario. Il "favor piae causae" nelle disposizioni "pro anima" secondo il diritto canonico e il diritto ecclesiastico dello stato. Torino, Giappichelli, 1937. 57 p.

2395
Gutiérrez Martín, Luis. La dispensa de la ley del celibato eclesiástico. Roma, Pontificia Universidad Lateranense, 1974. 122 p.

2396

Hering, Carl J. Aequitas und Toleranz; gesammelte Schriften. Hrsg. von Erich Fechner, Ernst von Hippel und Herbert Frost. Bonn, Bouvier Verlag, Grundmann, 1971. 240 p.
Includes bibliographical references.

2397

Hove, Alphonse van. De consuetudine. De temporis supputatione. Mechliniae, H. Dessain, 1933. 288 p. (Commentarium Lovaniense in Codicem iuris canonici, v. 1, t. 3)
Includes bibliographies.

2398

Hove, Alphonse van. De rescriptis. Mechliniae, Dessain, 1936. 286 p. (Commentarium Lovaniense in Codicem iuris canonici, v. 1, t. 4)
Bibliography: p. [1]–2.

2399

Imbert, Jean. Les hôpitaux in droit canonique (du décret de Gratien à la sécularisation de l'administration de l'Hôtel-Dieu de Paris en 1505) Paris, Vrin, 1947. 334 p.
"Bibliographie": p. [311]–329.

2400

Kapsanēs, Geōrgios. Hē poimantikē diakonia kata tour hierous kanonas . . . [in Greek] 1976. 201 p.
Bibliography: p. [193]–196.

2401

Kekumano, Charles A. The secret archives of the diocesan curia; a historical synopsis and a commentary. Washington, D.C., The Catholic University of America Press 1954. 98 p. (The Catholic University of America. Canon law studies, no. 350)
Bibliography: p. 90–94.

2402

Kohls, Eugene C. An interpretation of canon 1500: the division of property and debts in the division of a territorial moral person. Rome, Pontifical Lateran University, 1966. 115 p.
Bibliography: p. [xii]–xvi.

2403

Korth, Francis N. Canon law for hospitals. St. Louis, Catholic Hospital Association of the United States and Canada [1962] 40 p.

2404

Lackmann, Heinrich. Die kirchliche Bücherzensur nach geltendem kanonischem Recht, unter Berücksichtigung ihrer geschichtlichen Entwicklung und der heutigen Reformgedanken. Köln, Greven Verlag, 1962. 101 p. (Arbeiten aus dem Bibliothekar-Lehrinstitut des Landes Nordrhein-Westfalen, Heft 20)
Bibliography; p. 97–101.

2405

Landau, Peter. Entstehung des kanonischen Infamiebegriffs von Gratian bis zur Glossa ordinaria. Köln, Graz, Böhlau, 1966. 176 p. (Forschungen zur kirchlichen Rechtsgeschichte und zum Kirchenrecht. Bd. 5)
Bibliography: p. [164]–167.

2406

Landau, Peter. Jus patronatus: Studien zur Entwicklung des Patronats im Dekretalenrecht und der Kanonistik des 12. und 13. Jahrhunderts. Köln, Böhlau, 1975. 230 p. (Forschungen zur kirchlichen Rechtsgeschichte und zum Kirchenrecht, Bd. 12)
Bibliography: p. 216–221.

2407

Landolt, Adolf. Das Naturrecht im Codex iuris canonici. Basel, 1951. 88 p.
Bibliography; p. v–x.

2408

Lessius, Leonardus. De ivstitia et ivre ceterisque virtutibus cardinalibus, libri qvatvor. Editio vltima, avcta et emendata. Parisiis, 1628. 866, [24 +] p.

2409

Lessius, Leonardus. De ivstitia et ivre ceterisq$_3$ virtuibus cardinalibus libri qvatvor, ad 22. D. Thomae à quaest. 47. vsque ad q. 171. Ed. 7 auctior et castigatior; cum Appendice de monte pietatis. Antverpiae, ex officina Planitiniana Balthasaris Moreti, 1632. 825, [69] p.

2410

Löbmann, Benno. Der kanonische Infamiebegriff in seiner geschichtlichen Entwicklung; unter besonderer Berücksichtigung der Infamielehre des Franz Suarez. Leipzig, St. Benno-Verlag, 1956. 141 p. (Erfurter theologische Studien, Bd. 1)
Bibliography: p. 8.

2411

Luca, Carlo A. de. De confidentiali haeredis institvtione, et svstitvtione, tractatvs coesarevs ... Cum argumentis capitum, indice sententiarum & verborum, & in fine catalogus operum legalium ab authore editorum. Neapoli, typis F. Mollo, svmptibvs C. Troysii, 1697. 344 p.

2412

Luca, Giovanni B. de, cardinal. Commentaria ad Constitvtionem ss. d. n. D. Innocentii XI de statvtariis svccessionibvs cum particulis statutorum, & legum excludentium foeminas propter masculos, tàm intrà Statum ecclesiasticum, quàm extrà illum. Et De pensionibvs ecclesiasticis ad ornatum alterius constitutionis eiusdem sanctissimi domini nostri de illis vltrà medietatem non transferendis. Accedunt infine indulta varia transferendi & retinendi pensiones ecclesiasticas. Opus posthumum. Romae, apud I. B. Bvssottvm, 1684. 2 v. in 1.

2413

Luca, Giovanni B. de, cardinal. Commentaria ad Constitutionem sanctae mem. Innocentii XI. de statutariis successionibus; cum Particulis statutorum, & legum excludentium foeminas propter masculos, tam intra statum ecclesiasticum, quàm extra illum. Accedit De pensionibus ecclesiasticis ad ornatum constitutionis ejusdem pontificis, de illis ultra medietatem non transferendis; cvm variis indvltis transferendi, ac retinendi ecclesiasticas pensiones. Venetiis, apud Paulum Balleonium, 1716. 174, [2], 59 p.

2414

Luca, Giovanni B. de, cardinal. Commentaria ad Constitutionem sanctae mem. Innocentii XI. De statutariis successionibus; cum particulis statutorum, & legum excludentium foeminas propter masculos, tam intra statum ecclesiasticum, quàm extra illum. Accedit De pensionibus ecclesiasticis ad ornatum Constitutionis ejusdem pontificis, de illis ultra medietatem non transferendis; cvm variis indvltis transferendi, ac retinendi ecclesiasticas pensiones. Venetiis, ex typographia Balleoniana, 1735. 223 p.

2415

Luca, Giovanni B. de, cardinal. Commentaria ad Constitutionem sanctae mem. Innocentii XI. de statutariis successionibus; cum particulis statuto-

rum, & legum excludentium foeminas propter masculos, tam intra statum ecclesiasticum, quam extra illum. Accedit De pensionibus ecclesiasticis ad ornatum Constitutionis ejusdem pontificis, de illis ultra medietatem non transferendis; cum variis indultis transferendi ac retinendi ecclesiasticas pensiones. Neapoli, ex typographia L. Laurentii, 1758. 223 p.

2416

MacKenzie, Eric F. The delict of heresy in its commission, penalization, absolution. Washington, D.C., The Catholic University of America Press, 1932. 126 p. (The Catholic University of America. Canon law studies, no. 77)

Bibliography: p. vii–xi.

2417

Martín-Retortillo, Lorenzo. Libertad religiosa y orden pública (un estudio de jurisprudencia). Madrid, Editorial Tecnos [1970] 94 p.

2418

Mastrofini, M. Le usure, libri tre; discussione. Milano, G. Silvestri, 1832. 478 p. (Biblioteca scelta di opere italiane antiche e moderne, v. 294)

2419

Mudryĭ, Sofron S. De transitu ad alium ritum (a Byzantino-Ucraino ad Latinum) dissertatio historico-juridica. Romae, PP. Basiliani, 1973. 182 p.

Bibliography: p. [xiii]–xxiii.

2420

Mühlebach, Albert. Die infamie in der decretalen gesetzgebung. Eine kirchenrechtlich-historische untèrsuchung. Paderborn, Schöningh, 1923. 106 p.

"Verzeichnis der quellen und literatur": p. [v]–xv.

2421

Oliveira, Oscar de. Os dízimos eclesiásticos do Brasil nos períodos da Colônia e do Império. Belo Horizonte, Universidade de Minas Gerais, 1964. 218 p. (Coleção Estudos, 3) (Universidade de Minas Gerais. Publicação no. 320)

Bibliography: p. 215–218.

2422

Olivero, Giuseppe. Dissimulatio e tolerantia

nell'ordinamento canonico. Milano, Giuffrè, 1953. 208 p. (Università di Catania. Pubblicazioni della Facoltà di giurisprudenza, 18)

Bibliographical footnotes.

2423

Ontalba y Arce, Pedro de. Manifiesto canónico legal del absoluto, y libre derecho del Rey Nuestro Señor a la percepción de las vacantes mayores, y menores de las Iglesias de Indias, y su conversión en qualesquiera usos convenientes al estado. Madrid, de Peralta, 1737. 89 l.

2424

Pellegrini, Germanus J. De affinitate in jure canónico. Roma, Marietti, 1960. 233 p.

Bibliography: p. [7]–13.

2425

Piekoszewski, Jan, La légitimation des enfants naturels simples par le mariage subséquent (étude de droit canonique). Paris, Peyronnet [1952] 104 p.

Bibliography: p. [9]–13.

2426

Prusak, Bernard P. The canonical concept of particular church before and after Vatican II. Rome, Pontifícia Università Lateranense, 1967. 174 p.

Bibliography: p. [157]–171.

2427

Ragazzini, Severino M. La potestà nella Chiesa: quadro storico-giuridico del diritto costituzionale canonico, presentazione dell'Eminentissimo Cardinale Arcadio Larraona. Roma, Pontificia Università Lateranense, 1963. 376 p.

Bibliography: p. [xxiii]–xxx.

2428

Regan, Michael J. Canon 16; a historical synopsis and a commentary. Washington, D.C., The Catholic University of America Press, 1959. 149 p. (The Catholic University of America. Canon law studies, no. 307)

Bibliography: p. 132–139.

2429

Reissner, Edward A. Canonical employer-employee relationship: canon 1524. Washington,

D.C., The Catholic University of America Press, 1964. 113 p. (The Caholic University of America. Canon law studies, no. 427)

Bibliography: p. 105–110.

2430

Richstatter, Thomas. Liturgical law today: new style, new spirit. Chicago, Franciscan Herald Press, [c1977]. 234 p.

Bibliography: p. 181–225.

2431

Richter, Wilhelm. De origine et evolutione interdicti usque ad aetatem Ivonis Carnotensis et Paschalis II. Varia documenta collegit notisque illustravit Willelmus Richter. Romae, apud aedes Universitatis Gregoriannae, 1934. 2 v. (Pontificia Universitas Gregoriana. Textus et documenta, Series theologica, 12–13)

"Tituli abbreviati" (bibliography): v. 1, p. [8]–10.

2432

Riesner, Albert J. Apostates and fugitives from religious institutes; an historical conspectus and commentary. Washington, D.C., The Catholic University of America Press, 1942, 168 p. (The Catholic University of America. Canon law studies, no. 168)

Bibliography: p. 144–151.

2433

Rocca, Fernando della. La contumacia nel diritto canonico; appunti di esegesi critica sulle fonti. Roma, Edizioni universitarie, 1943. 101, [1] p. (Monografie dell'Istituto di diritto pubblico della Facoltà di giurisprudenza nell'Università di Roma, 11)

2434

Rodimer, Frank J. The canonical effects of infamy of fact; a historical synopsis and a commentary. Washington, D.C., The Catholic University of America Press, 1954. 161 p. (The Catholic University of America. Canon law studies, no. 353).

Bibliography: p. 144–153.

2435

Rosignoli, Gregorio. Novissima praxis theologico-legalis in vniversas de cambiis, et permvtationibvs controversias. Ed. 2. Ex pvrgata, et adavcta cvm doplici indici, altero tivlorvm, altero rerum locupletissimo. Mediolani, Malatesta, 1697. 649 p.

2436

Rosignoli, Gregorio. Novissima praxis theologico-legalis ad titvlvm de patria potestate et ad quartum decalogi praeceptum. Milan, Malatesta, 1709. 492 p.

2437

Russo, Andreas. De damnatione ad expensas in iure canonico speciali relatione habita ad ius civile italicum. Romae, Officium libri catholici, 1941. 77, [3] p.
"Index bibliographicus": p. [9]–11.

2438

Sullivan, John G. The relevance of three common-law jurists for a theory of interpretation of canon law. Roma, Pontificia Università Lateranense, 1966. 186 p.
Bibliography: p. [181]–186.

2439

Tatarczuk, Vincent A. Infamy of law; a historical synopsis and commentary. Washington, D.C., The Catholic University of America Press, 1954. 119 p. (The Catholic University of America. Canon law studies, no. 357)
Bibliography: p. 110–114.

2440

Tazzioli, Vittorino. Aspetti giuridici della insemi-nazione artificale umana nel diritto canonico. Modena, Immacolata Concezione, 1966. 74 p.
Bibliography: p. 71–74.

2441

Thompson, William. Quasi-domicile, an historical study. St. Meinrad, Ind., Abbey Press, 1956. 110 p.
Bibliography: p. 101–106.

2442

Torre, Joannes. De pactis fvtvrae svccessionis tractatus tripartitus. Additis supra ducentas sacrae Rotae romanae recentissimis, ac grauioribus decisionibus nusquam impressis, quorumuis capitum materias punctualiter tangentibus. Vna cvm locvpletissimis tam totivs operis, quàm singularum decisionum indicubus, seruato ordine ad lectoris commoditatem. Venetiis, apud Nicoluam Pezzana, 1694. 383 p., 10 l., 244, 168 p.

2443

Wolter, Udo. Ius canonicum in iure civili: Studien qur Rechtsquellenlehre in d. neueren Privatrechtsgeschichte. Köln, Wien, Böhlau, 1975. 225 p. (Forschungen zur neueren Privatrechtsgeschichte, Bd. 23)
Bibliography: p. [201]–218.

2444

Zubka, Jan, Proces beatyfikacyjny i kanonizacyjny. Warszawa, Akademia Teologii Katolickiej, 1969. 466 p. (Zarys prawa kanonicznego, t. 4. Prawo procesowe, zesz. 2)

APPENDIX

1

Barbosa, Agostinho, bishop. Collectanea bullarii aliarumque summorum pontificum constitutionum, necnon praecipuarum decisionum. Lugduni, Durand, 1637. 690 p.

2

Barbosa, Agostinho. Collectanea doctorum, qui suis in operibus Concilii Tridentini loca referentes. Venetiis, Apud Baleonium, 1643. 435 p.

3

Barbosa, Agostinho. Collectanea doctorum, qui in suis operibus Concilii Tridentini loca referentes. Lugduni, Borde, 1651. 492 p.

4

Barbosa, Agostinho. Collectanea doctorum, qui in suis operibus Concilii Tridentini loca referentes. Lugduni, Borde, 1686. 492 p.

5

Barbosa, Agostinho. Collectanea doctorum, qui in suis operibus Concilii Tridentini loca referentes, illorum materiam indicenter tractarunt. & varias quaestiones, in foro ecclesiastico versantibus maxime utiles, deciderunt ... Hac ultima editione ab ipso auctore recognita, & quamplurimorum additamentorum accessione sesquiampluis aucta. Cum summariis, et quinque indicibus copiosis. Lugduni, sumptibus Borde, et Arnaud, 1704. 492 p.

This work presents the material discussed in twenty-five sessions of the Ecumenical Council which met in Trent, Italy, from 1545 to 1563, with an impressive reference to the most authoritative writings of experts on the subject. The book is enhanced by the indexes of the decrees of the council, the chapters, apostolic bulls and constitutions, decisions of the Roman Rota, decisions of the Congregation of Cardinals, and by a comprehensive subject index.

6

Barbosa, Agostinho. Collectanea doctorum tam veterum quam Recentiorum in ius pontificum universum. Lugduni, sumptibus L. Durand, 1636, 1716. 6 v. [v. 6, Lugduni, Sumpt. Anisson et Posuel, 1716]

7

Barbosa, Agostinho. Collectanea doctorum tam verterum quam recentiorum, in ius pontificium universum, tomus tertius [tomus quartus]. Lugduni, Sumpt. L. Durand, 1637.

8

Barbosa, Agostinho. Collectaneorvm in ivs Pontificvm Tomi Sex. I. Liber primus, & secundus. II. Liber tertius, & quartus. III. Liber quintus. IV. Sextus decretalium, vna cum Clementinis, & Extranagantibus. V. Decretum Gratiani. VI. Selectae interpretationes universi Iuris Pontificj. Lugduni, 1747.

9

Barbosa, Agostinho. Juris canonici interpretationes selectae ... Tomus sextus. Lugduni, Sumpt. P. Borde, 1688.

10

Barbosa, Agostinho. Juris ecclesiastici universi. Lugduni, Sumpt. L. Durant, 1634. 1,008 p.

11

Barbosa, Agostinho. Juris ecclesiastici vniversi libri tres: in qvorvm I. De personis, II. De locis, III. De rebus ecclesiasticis plenissime agitur. Ed. nouissimia, ab auctore recognita &, erroribus ablatis, vtiliter locupletata. Lvgdvni, Sumpt. haer. P. Prost, P. Borde, & L. Arnavd, 1645. 2 v. in 1.

12

Barbosa, Agostinho. Juris ecclesiastici universi libri tres. Lugduni, Anisson & Posuel, 1718. 2 v.

13

Barbosa, Agostinho. Pastoralis solicitvdinis, sive De officio, et potestate episcopi tripartita descriptio. Hac postrema ed. ab ipsomet auctore multis in locis varijs resolutionibus illustrata, integris titulis, & allegationibus locupletata; alijsque insignibus accessionibus cumulata. Venetiis, F. Baba, 1630. 934 p.

Includes also the author's Formvlarivm episcopale, and Apostolicae constitvtiones, et decreta aliquot (66 p. at end)

14

Barbosa, Agostinho. Pastoralis solicitudnis, sive de officio et potestate parochi, tripartita descriptio. Lugduni, Durand, 1634. 536 p.

15

Barbosa, Agostinho. Pastoralis solicitudinis de officio et potestate parochi. Venetiis, Milochus, 1662. 495 p. [Bound with: Catholic Church. Pope, 1665–1667 (Alexander VI) Index librorum prohibitorum Alexandri VII. pontificis maximi jussu editus. Romae, Typ. Apostolicae, 1664. 410 p.]

16

Barbosa, Agostinho. Pastoralis solicitudinis sive de officio, et potestate episcopi, tripartita descriptio. Lugduni, Sumpt. Ph. Borde, 1665. 478 p.

17

Barbosa, Agostinho. Pastorlais solicitvdinis, sive de officio, et potestate episcopi tripartita descriptio. Hac postrema ed. ab ipsomet auctore multis in locis varijs resolutionibus illustrata, integris titulis, & allegationibus locupletata; alijsque insignibus accessionibus cumulata. Lugduni, Arnaud, 1678. 934 p.

Includes also the author's Formvlarivm episcopale, and Apostolicae constitvtiones, et decreta aliquot (66 p. at end)

18

Barbosa, Agostinho. Pastoralis solicitudinis. Lugduni, Arnaud, 1679. 456 p.

19

Barbosa, Agostinho. Praxis exigendi pensiones contra calvmniantes, & differentes illas soluere. Lvgdvni, Sumpt. L. Dvrand, 1636.

20

Barbosa, Agostinho. Praxis exigendi pensiones contra colomniantes et differentes illas soluere. Cui accesserunt vota aliquot decisiva canonica. Vltima editio. Lugduni, Sumpt. L. Durand, 1636.

21

Barbosa, Agostinho. Praxis methodica exigendi

pensiones, adversus alumniantes, et differentes eas solvere. Cui accesserunt Vota plurima decisiva, et consultiva canonica. Ultima edition prioribus emendatior. Lugduni, sumpt. R. Borde, et Arnaud, 1702. 101, 374, 356 p.

22

Barbosa, Agostinho. Repertorium juris civilis et canonici. Lugduni, Goy, 1675. 250 p.

23

Barbosa, Agostinho. Repertorium juris civilis et canonici, in quo alphabetico ordine principaliores et practicae utriusque juris conclusiones collectae indicantur, & magna doctorum copia exornantur. Opvs posthvmvm studio & industria d. Simonis Vaz Barbosae digestum. Editio novissima, a mendis expurgata. Lvgdvni, sumpt. P. Borde, J. & P. Arnaud, 1689. 250 p.

24

Barbosa, Agostinho. Repertorium juris civilis et canonici, in quo alphabetico ordine principaliores, & practicae utriusque juris conclusiones collectae indicantur, & magnâ doctorum copiâ exornantur. Opus postumum . . . studio & industriâ d. Simonis Vaz Barbosae, J. U. D. . . . apprimè digestum. Editio novissima, à mendis quae prioribus irrepserant, expurgata. Lugduni, apud Boudet, Declaustre, De Ville, & De la Roche, 1712. 250 p.

25

Barbosa, Agostinho. Sacrosanctum, oecumenicum Concilium tridentinum, additis declarationibus cardinalium ejusdem Concilii interpretum, ex ultima recognitione Joannis Gallemart; nec non remissionibus Augustini Barbosae, & annotationibus practicis cardinalis de Luca, cum variis Rotae romanae decisionibus. Editio novissima exactiore correctione (quam umquam alias) castigata; & mendis . . . expurgata . . . Matriti, ex typographia regia, vulgo, de la Gazeta. 1769. 677 p.

26

Barbosa, Agostinho. Sacrosanctum, oecumenicum Concilium tridentinum, additis declarationibus cardinalium ejusdem Concilii interpretum, ex ultima recognitione Joannis Gallemart, nec non remissionibus Augustini Barbosae, et annotationibus practicis cardinalis de Luca, cum variis Rotae romanae decisionibus. Editio novissima exactiore correctione (quam umquam alias) castigata; & mendis . . . diligentissimè expurgata . . . Matriti, apud M. Escribano, 1779. 677 p.

27

Barbosa, Agostinho. Summa Apostolicarum Decisionum. Excudegat J. de Tournesi, 1650.

28

Barbosa, Agostinho. Summa Apostolicarum Decisionum, extra jus commune vagantium. Lugduni, Arnaud, 1680. 506 p.

29

Barbosa, Agostinho. Thesaurus locorum communium jurisprudentiae, ex Axiomatibvs Augustini Barbosae, et analectis Joh. Ottonis Taboris aliorumque concinnatus. 2. ed., emendatior reddita curâ Tobiae-Ottonis Taboris, u. j. d. Cum privilegio s. Caes, maj. &c. Noribergae & Francofvrti, sumpt. M. & J. F. Endterorum; typis B. Ch. Wustii, 1670. 888 p.

30

Barbosa, Agostinho. Thesaurus locorum communium jurisprudentiae, ex aciomatibus Augustini Barbosae et analectis Joh. Ottonis Taboris aliorumqve concinnatus. Editio post Tobiae Ottonis Taboris secundam tertis, novis axiomatibus Samuelis Strykii aucta. Lipsiae, Sumptu J. F. Gleditsch, 1691. 528, 436 p.

31

Barbosa, Agostinho. Thesavrvs locorvm commvnivm jvrisprvdentiae, ex Axiomatibvs Avgvstini Barbosae, et Analectis Ioh. Ottonis Taboris aliorvmqve concinnatvs. Ed. 4 novis aciomatibus ex recentioribus autoribus magna ex parte auctior facta ab A. Ch. Rösenero. Lipsiae, T. Fritsch, 1707. 662, 421 p.

32

Barbosa, Agostinho. Thesaurus locorum communium iurisprudentiae. Lipsiae, Apud T. Fritsch. 1719.

33

Barbosa, Agostinho. Tractatus de canonicis et dignitatibus. Lugduni, Prost, 1648. 2 v. in 1.

This book contains two treatises which were published in 1648 and 1655 (*Pastoralis solicitudo sive de officio et potestate parochi*). The first deals with all aspects of the life of the canon (i.e., a clergyman belonging to the chapter of a cathedral or collegiate church) and his duties in the choir and in the chapter. The second treatise, divided into three parts, covers the appointment and obligations of the parish priest, the administration of sacraments as one of the great responsibilities of the pastor, and the rights of the parish priest. Both expositions conclude with comprehensive indexes of terms and subjects.

34

Barbosa, Agostinho. Tractatus de canonicis et dignitatibus. Lugduni, Arnaud, 1679. 2 v. in 1.

35

Barbosa, Agostinho. Tractatvs varii: qvorvm I. De axiomatibus iuris vsufrequentioribus. II. De appellatiua vertorum vtriusque iuris significatione. III. De locis communibus argumentorum iuris. IV. De clausulis vsufregentioribus. V. De dictionibus vsufrequentioribus. Circa iudiciorum, contractuum, vltimarum voluntatum, & delictorum cognitionem. Nunc recens recogniti, & praeter illa, quae passim obiter intertexta, multis cascrae Rotae decisionibus, & quamplurium doctorum . . . resolutionibus illustrati . . . Accesserunt svmma rerum, & indices. Lvgdvni, sumpt. Ph. Borde, L. Arnavd, & C. Rigavd, 1660. 818 p.

Barbosa examines several meaningful topics: the most used axioms in law; the appellative significations of terms in both civil and canon law; *de locis communibus,* or the common places of arguments of law; the most used clauses; and dictions. The knowlege of these subjects, according to the author, is useful and necessary when studying and debating matters related to trials, contracts, wills, and crimes. The work ends with a comprehensive index of the most important terms and subjects quoted.

36

Barbosa, Agostinho. Tractatus varii. Lugduni, Arnaud, 1678. 684 p.

37

Barbosa, Agostinho. Tractatus varii: quorum I. De axiomativus juris usufrequentioribus. II. De appelativa verborum utriusque juris significatione. III. De locis communibus argumentorum juris. IV. De clausulis usufrequentioribus. V. De dictionibus

usufrequentioribus. Circa judiciorum, contractuum, ultimarum voluntatus, & delictorum cognitionem, in disputando, & consulendo valde utiles,
& necessarij. Nunc recens recogniti, & praeter illa,
quae passim obiter intertexta, multis sacraé Rotae
decisionibus, & quam recentiorum resolutionibus
illustrati. Accesserunt summae rerum & indices.
Lugduni, sumpt. P. Borde, J. & P. Arnaud, 1699.
684 p.

38

Barbosa, Agostinho. Tractatvs varii: qvorvm I. De
axiomatibus iuris vsu frequentioribus. II. De ap-
pelatiua verborum vtriusque iuris significatione.
III. De locis communibus argumentorum iuris. IV.
De clausulis vsu frequentioribus. V. De dictionibus
vsu frequentioribus. Circa iuriciorum, contractuum, vltimarum voluntatum, & delictorum cognitionem, in disputando, & consulendo valde vtiles,
& necessarij. Nunc recens recogniti, & praeter illa,
quae passim obiter intertexta, multis Sacrae Rotae
decisionibus & quamplurium doctorem [!] tam
veterum, quam recentiorum resolutionibus illustrati. Accesserunt svmmae rerum, & indices.
Lvgdvni, sumptibus Ph. Borde, L. Arnavd, & C.
Rigavd, 1718. 818 p.

39

Bonnet, Piero. L'essenza del matrimonio canonico:
contributo allo studio dell'amore coniugale. Padova, CEDAM, 1976. (Pubblicazioni dell'Istituto di
diritto pubblico della Facoltà di giurisprudenza,
Università degli studi di Roma; ser. 3, v. 30)
    Includes bibliographical references and indexes.

    The author affirms that the institution of mar-
riage has always attracted the interest of canonists.
After the Second Vatican Council (1962–1965) the
solicitude for the doctrine became even livelier,
and included harsh criticisms of certain essential
aspects of present canonical discipline. In many
instances the discussions attacked the essential
structure of marriage or the need for its legal
institutionalization. It seems, frequently enough,
that there is a gap between the reality sanctioned
by the laws and the human truth to be disciplined;
this reality becomes particularly intolerable in the
case of marriage, which engages the human being
deeply and totally, because canon law regulates
one of his most fundamental and inalienable personal rights.

40

Carrillo Aguilar, Alfonso. Disolución del vínculo
y potestad de la Iglesia: (¿puede la Iglesia disolver
el matrimonio sacramental consumado?) Córdoba,
A. Carrillo, 1976. 323 p.

    This work concerns the dissolution of the bond
of marriage and the jurisdiction of the Church.
The author's theme is that marriage, though a
mystery, becomes luminous when enlightened by
faith. The work is divided into four parts: juridico-
theological accuracy of concepts; divine-human
covenant (the author studies the foundation of the
indissolubility of marriage as well as the possibility
of dissolution in some instances); the question of
dissolving a consummated sacramental marriage
or finding a motive for the dissolution; and the
nature and dimension of the jurisdiction of the
Church concerning the dissolution of marriage.

41

Catholic Church. *Congregatio pro ecclesia orientali.*
Codificazione canonica orientale: fonti. [Roma]
Tipografia poliglotta vaticana, 1931–
    "Bibliographia": v. 11, p. [xiii]
    Acta Romanorum Pontificum a Clemente I ad
Coelestinum III (fontes) Series III, v. 1 and 2.

    These sources of Oriental canon law, which
contain the acts of the popes from approximately
A.D. 90 to A.D. 1198 (from Clement I to Celestin
III), assume great importance because of the authorities who issued them, and the subjects treated.
These writings by the Roman pontiffs, embracing
the first twelve centuries, serve to illustrate the
memory of the Church with its canon law, and to
illuminate part of the history of the European
kingdoms. It is worth noting the helpful role the
introduction plays in providing a historical synopsis
of the popes to familiarize the reader with the basic
facts of the period under consideration.

41a

Catholic Church. *Congregatio pro ecclesia orientali.*
Codificazione canonica orientale: fonti. [Roma]
Tipografia poliglotta vaticana, 1931–
    "Bibliographia": v. 11, p. [xiii]
    Testi vari di diritto nuovo (1550–1902) Fascic.
I, parts 1 and 2.

    In 1929, Pope Pius XI created a commission of
cardinals to study the preparation of a complete

and updated Oriental code, a task accomplished only partially in the previous centuries privately or by mandate of his papal predecessors. As a result of his action, two special committees were established: one to research and collect the sources of Oriental law; the other to study them for the preparation of the code. Among the innumerable documents they collected were those of ecumenical councils, constitutions and decisions of the pontiffs and Roman congregations, specific synods, canonical provisions of different origin, and customs. The oriental canonical codification reproduces here this very valuable and necessary legal material.

42

Fagnani, Prospero. Commentaria in quinque libres decretalium. Romae, Expensis I. Casoni, 1661. 4 v.

Index

43

Fagnani, Prospero. Commentaria in primam (quintam) parte Decretalium. Romae, Expensis I. Casoni, 1661. 5 v., 1 v. index.

44

Fagnani, Prospero. Commentaria in primum [inquintvm] librum decretalium. Venetiis, Apud Paulum Balleonium, 1697. 5 v. in 3. [v. 3, 1696]

The reader interested in the history of canon law will find a great deal of help in this truly comprehensive three-volume commentary on the five books of the Decretals. Volume one is devoted entirely to the first book, which is preceded by a helpful subject index, covering such theological matters as the Holy Trinity and the Catholic faith, ecclesiastical legislations, and secular occupations. Volume two analyzes books two and three of the Decretals related to trials, the sacraments, the status of the clergy and some irregularities, ecclesiastical property, etc. Volume three contains a short commentary on the fourth book, related to marriage and divorce; and a more extensive analysis of book five, concerning inquisition, heresy, apostasy, homicide, Jewish people, excommunication, privileges, etc. Every chapter throughout the treatise is preceded by a detailed summary of the issues studied. Volume three also offers an extensive and most helpful index of terminology and subjects.

45

Fagnani, Prospero. Jus canonicum sive commentaria absolutissima in V. libros decretales . . . Tomus primus complecteus primam partem primi libri decretalium [in secundam partem quintilibri decretali]. Coloniae Agrippinae, Apud I. W. Friessen juniorem, Anno 1676. 5 v. in 3.

46

Fagnani, Prospero. Jus canonicum: sive commentaria absolutissima in V. libros Decretales, cum indice. Coloniae Agrippinae, Haeredes I. Widenfelt, 1681. 2 v. in 1.

47

Fagnani, Prospero. Tractatus ex Commentariis Prosperi Fagneni Super Decretalibus Seorsum recusus. De opinione Probabili. Romae, Sumptibus J. Casoni, 1665.

48

Fornés, Juan. La noción de "status" en derecho canónico. Pamplona, Ediciones Universidad de Navarra, 1975. 349 p. (Colección canónica de la Universidad de Navarra)

Bibliography: p. 335–349.

The author starts by pointing out that in canonical literature *status* embraces a diversity of meanings: a general one (without legal significance in itself); and more specific ones, related to the legal condition of the person by reason of his situation in the community or of his personal circumstances. This work tries to find the limits of, and establish a system for, the nuances of the many concepts of *status* used in canon law, searching for the predominant significance, i.e., for that which has more influence in the way of conceiving the arrangement or social structure of the Church. It studies the provisions adopted in the constitution *Lumen Gentium* at Vatican II and the contribution of the subsequent canonical doctrine to establish the present meaning of *status*. The work reviews the doctrines which throughout history have treated the issue explicitly or indirectly. The author clarifies that this is not a historical monograph in the proper sense (as the historical references in the book could mislead someone), but a strictly legal work on the notion of *status* in canon law. Historical data are offered only to place the ideas of the authors in the proper context.

49

Kelly, William, S. J. Pope Gregory II on divorce and remarriage: a canonical-historical investigation of the letter Desiderabilem mihi, with special reference to the response Quod proposuisti. Roma, Università Gregoriana, 1976. 333 p. (Analecta Gregoriana; v. 203: Sectio Facultatis Iuris Canonici; Sectio B, no. 37)

Bibliography: p. [317]–326.

The subtitle explains the extent of this work: a canonical-historical investigation of the letter *Desiderabilem mihi,* with special reference to the response *Quod proposuisti.* In the letter written by Pope Gregory to St. Boniface in A.D. 726 a paragraph is found which is studied by Kelly. This paragraph became a source of confrontation and polemics for it apparently allows divorce and remarriage in a particular case. In part one research is focused on the eighth century: the letter, the paragraph, Pope Gregory II, and St. Boniface; part two is devoted to the interpretation of the text through the centuries, with special reference to Gratian; and part three proposes a critical evaluation.

50

Lex Ecclesiae: Estudios en honor del Dr. Marcelino Cabreros de Anta. Salamanca, Universidad Pontificia, 1972. 694 p. (Biblioteca Salmanticensis, 1. Studia, 1.)

Includes bibliographical references.

This book contains several studies on ecclesiastical legislation written by respected Spanish canonists. It opens with a general part covering real humanism and integral humanism; peculiar characteristics of certainty in the juridico-canonical regulation; and the right to initiatives. Another section is devoted to historical studies. The third part deals with constitutional law of the Church: sacramentality and legality; the origin of the Episcopal College (Is it an ecclesiastical institution or of divine origin?); and the new diocesan curia. The fourth part contains research on marriage law, especially as it relates to today's problems, and it is considered in ecumenical perspective. The following section is devoted to procedural law, such as Vatican II and the problems of ecclesiastical justice. Part six contains ecclesiastical public law: concordats; religious freedom and equality; and ecclesiastical patrimony in the legislation on con-

cordats by John XXIII and Paul VI. A section entitled "Varia" concludes the series of studies in the book.

51

Luca, Giovanni B. de. Il dottor volgare, overo Il compendio di tvtta la legge ciuile, canonica, feudale, e municipale . . . moralizato in lingua italiana per istruzione e comodità maggiore di questa prouincia. Roma, Stamperia di G. Corvo, 1673. 15 v. in 10.

52

Luca, Giovanni B. de. Il dottor volgare; ovvero, Il compendio di tutta la legge civile, canonica, feudale e municipale, nelle cose più ricevute in pratica del cardinale Giambatista de-Luca e dal medesimo moralizzato in lingua italiana. Firenze, Coi tipi di V. Batelli, 1839–43. 4 v.

53

Luca, Giovanni B. de. S. Rotae Romanae Decisiones Et Sum. Pontificum Constitutiones Recentissime Et Selectissime, Theatrum Veritatis Et Justitiae Eminentissime D. Cardinale De Luca Eivsqve Tractatus De Officiis Venal. Et Stat. Successionibus Amplectentes, confirmantes, laudantes, etc. Studio & opera Clariss. J. U. D. Argumentis, Summariis & Indicibus necessariis exornata & juxta Titulorum seriem & Discursum ordinem dispositae. Coloniae Allobrogorum. Sumptibus J. A. Cramer & P. Perachun, 1700. 9 v. in 1.

54

Luca, Giovanni, B. de. Sacrae Rotae romanae Decisiones, et cummorum pontificum constitutiones recentissimae, Theatrum veritatis & justitiae cardinalis de Luca, ejvsqve tractatvs De officiis venal. et stat. successionibus amplectentes, confirmantes, & laudantes. Argvmentis, svmmariis, et indicibvs necessariis exornatae, ac juxta titulorum seriem & discursuum ordinem dispositae. Venetiis, apud P. Balleonium, 1707–08. 4 v.

55

Luca, Giovanni B. de. Svmma sive compendivm Theatri veritatis, et ivstitiae. Romae, Typis B. Lupardi, 1679. 334 p.

56

Luca, Giovanni B. de. Treatrum Veritatis, et Justitiae sive Decisivi Discursus. Liber III. De Jurisdictione et Foro Competenti. Pars II De Praeminentiiis et Praecedentiis. Romae, Typis Haeredum Corbeletti, 1669.

57

Luca, Giovanni B. de. Theatrum veritatis & justitiae, sive Decisivi discursus per materias, seu titulos distincti, & ad veritatem editi in forensibus controversiis canonicis & civilibus, in quibus in urbe advocatus pro una partium scripsit, vel consultus respondit. Venetis, apud P. Balleonium, 1706. 15 v. in 6. ——— Repertorium, seu Index generalis rerum notabilitum . . . a Nicolao Falconio . . . elaboratum: Accedit in fine . . . Index decisionum, constitutionum, ac allegationum additarum in hac veneta impressione. Venetiis, apud Balleonium, 1706. 623 p.

58

Luca, Giovanni B. de. Theatrum veritatis & justitiae, sive Decisivi discursus per materias, seu titulos distincti, & ad veritatem editi in forensibus controversiis canonicis & civilibus, in quibus in urbe advocatus pro una partium scripsit, vel consultus respondit. Venetiis, apud P. Balleonium, 1716. 15 v. ——— Repertorium, seu index generalis rerum notabilium, quae continentur in Theatro veritatis & justitiae cardinalis de Luca, a Nicolao Falconio . . . ejusdem Theatri auctoris alumno elaboratum. Accedit in fine hvjvs volvminis index decisionum, constitutionum, ac allegationum additarum in hac veneta impressione. Venetiis, apud P. Balleonium, 1716. 613 p.

59

Luca, Giovanni B. de. Theatrum veritatis, et justitiae, sive decisivi discursus per materias, seu titulos distincti, & ad veritatem editi in forensibus controversiis canonicis & civilibus, in quibus in Urbe advocatus, pro una partium scripsit, vel consultus respondit. Venetiis, Ex Typographia Balleoniana, 1734. 15 v. 12. ——— Repertorium, seu index generalis rerum notabilium, quae continentur in Theatro veritatis & justitiae cardinalis de Luca, a Nicolao Falconio. Venetiis, Ex Typographia Balleoniana, 1734. 589 p.

60

Luca, Giovanni B. de. Theatrum veritatis, et justitiae, sive decisivi discursus per materias, sentitulos

distincti, et ad veritatem editi in forensubus controversis Canonicis et Civilibus, in quibus in Urbe Advocatus, pro una partium scripsit, vel consultus respondit. Tractatus de Officiis venalibus vacabilibus Romanae Curiae. Neapoli, Ex Typographia Laurentii, 1758. 18 v. in 13.

This treatise contains various topics discussed in ecclesiastical and civil courts by the author in his capacity as attorney and consultant. The work covers eighteen books dealing with feoffment, obligations towards the princes or the republic; jurisdiction and competent forum; usufruct and leasing of land; usury and interest with dowry; donations, sale and acquisitions, contracts; loans; and wills and heirs. It also discusses trusts, successions; ecclesiastical benefices, in general and specifically as they affect canons, dignitaries, pastors and parishes; and patronage and ecclesiastical pensions. Book fourteen is divided into five parts and studies the condition and situation of monks and religious persons; marriage, betrothal and divorce; alms and contributions; ecclesiastical immunity; and practical annotations on the Council of Trent, in matters related to reformation and forensics. Book fifteen is devoted to trials, the role of the Roman Curia in legal matters, and to legal propositions which seem to be in conflict with reason. Book sixteen offers a general index of the *Theatrum*. The last two books deal with documents related to the College of the Apostolic Secretaries, and commentaries on a constitution by Innocence XI.

61

Luca, Giovanni B. de. Theatrum veritatis, et justitiae, sive decisivi discursus per materias, seu titulas distincti, et ad veritatem editi in forensibus controversiis canonicis et civilbus, in quibus in Urbe Advocatus, pro una partium scripsit, vel consultus respondit. Venetiis, Ex Typographia Balleoniana, 1759. 12 v.

62

Luca, Giovanni B. de. Tractatus de officiis venalibus vacabilibus Romanae curiae; cum juribus seu documentis, informationibus, responsis, & decisionibus super suppressione Collegii secretariorum apostolicorum. Accedit alter Tractatvs de locis montium non vacabilium urbis. Cum nonnullis summorum pontificum constitutionibus; nec non sacrae Rotae romanae decisionibus ad materiam facientibus, suis locis optimè adjectis. Venetiis, ex typographia Balleoniana, 1726. 308 p.

63

Luca, Giovanni B. de. Tractatus de officiis venalibus vacabilibus Romanae Curiae; cum juribus, seu documentis, informationibus, responsis, & decisionibus super suppressione Collegii Secretariorum Apostolicorum. Accedit alter tractatus De locis montium non vacabilium urbis. Cum nonnullis summorum pontificum constitutionibus: necnon S. Rotae Rom. decisionibus ad materiam facientibus, suis locis optimè adjectis. Venetiis, Ex Typographia Balleoniana, 1759. 308 p.

NAME INDEX

(The numbers refer to entries, not pages or dates)

SUBJECT INDEX

(The numbers refer to entries, not pages or dates)

☆ U.S. GOVERNMENT PRINTING OFFICE : 1981 O - 330-292 : QL 3